I0762542

50 STATES
500 GARDENS

Experience the Beauty of America's Public Gardens

pil

Publications International, Ltd.

Contributing writer: Lisa Brooks

Images from Shutterstock.com and Wikimedia Commons

ISBN: 979-8-89746-061-8

Manufactured in China.

8 7 6 5 4 3 2 1

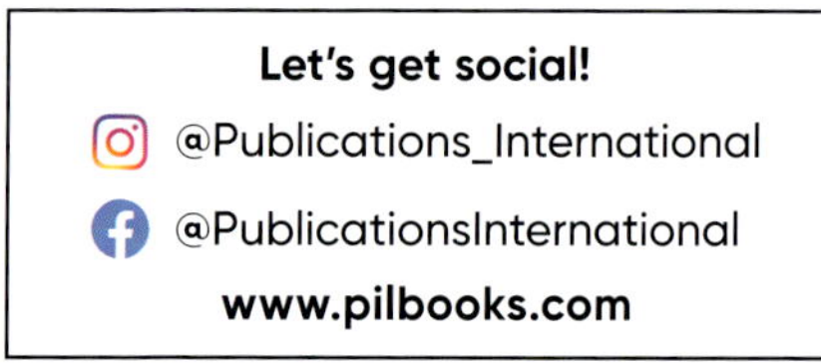

TABLE OF CONTENTS

INTRODUCTION

A day spent in a beautiful garden is never a day wasted. In this book, you'll discover the best gardens America has to offer, from well-known destinations like the District of Columbia's United States Botanic Garden and California's Conservatory of Flowers to lesser known gems like Pennsylvania's Longwood Gardens or Boston's Arnold Arboretum. Thanks to our country's various climates, cultural influences, and histories, the gardens revealed here present a rich aesthetic, environmental, and regional diversity. Herb gardens, rose gardens, Japanese gardens, desert gardens, aquatic gardens, and many more uniquely designed sites await discovery. Whether you're a fan of public gardens, curious about what's out there, or adding destinations to your vacation list, there are lots of gardens in these pages to impress and inspire you!

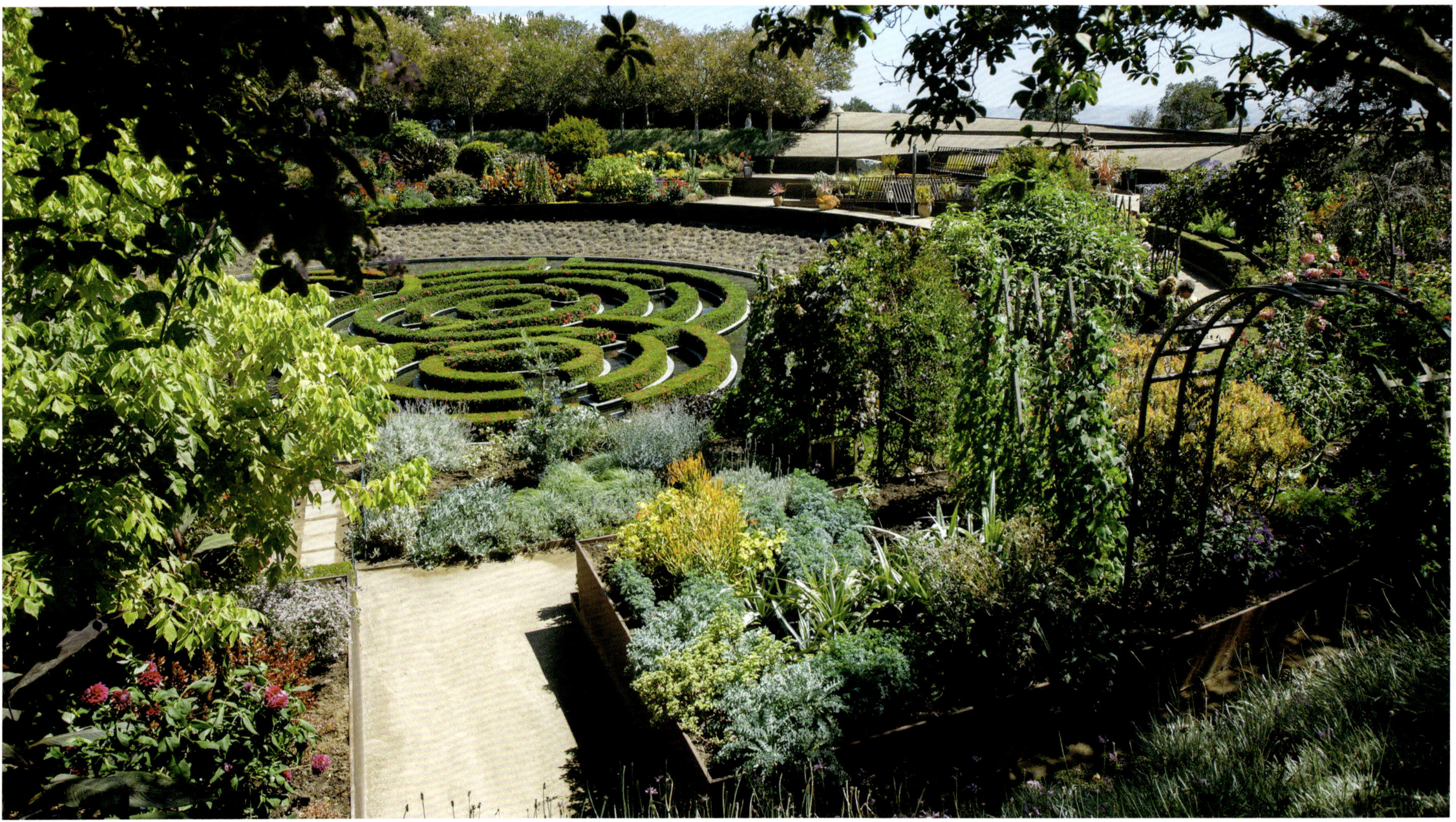

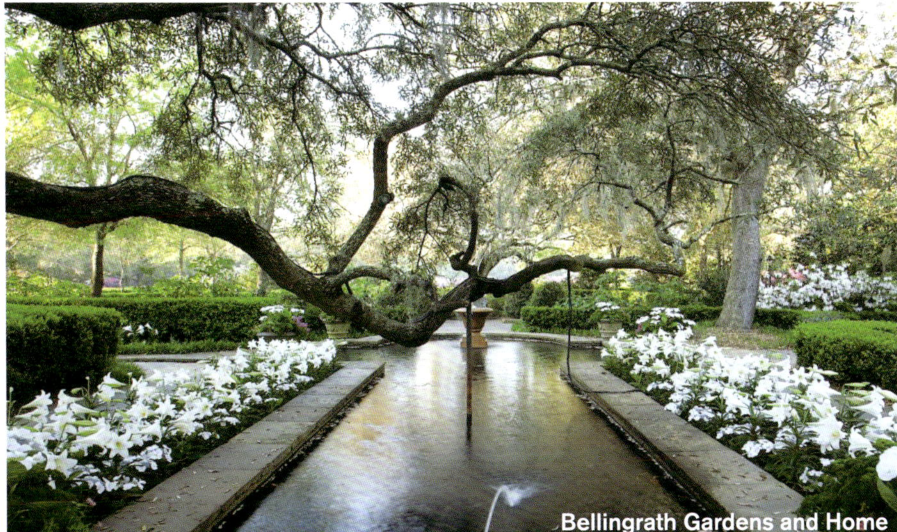

A decorative pool in the formal gardens. The grounds also include the Asian-American Garden, Bayou Observatory, Rose Garden, Gazebo Garden, Rockery, architectural attractions, and plenty of walking paths.

Aldridge Gardens
Hoover, Alabama

The property on which the 30-acre Aldridge Gardens now sits was purchased in 1977 by Eddie Aldridge. Along with his father, Loren, Aldridge cultivated and patented a double-flowering form of Oakleaf Hydrangea known as "Snowflake." Today, the garden is known for these beautiful hydrangeas, native plants and trees, and its five-acre lake.

Bellingrath Gardens and Home
Theodore, Alabama

In the spring of 1932, the original owners of Bellingrath Gardens and Home, Walter Bellingrath–one of the first Coca-Cola bottlers in the Southeast–and his wife, Bessie, invited the public to enjoy their extensive property. The beautiful 65-acre garden and its historic home (now a museum) have been open year-round since 1934.

Birmingham Botanical Gardens
Birmingham, Alabama

A 67-acre respite in the middle of the city of Birmingham, these gardens showcase the biodiversity that Alabama is known for. In addition to two dozen distinct garden spaces, this oasis features more than 30 original sculptures, miles of walking paths, a conservatory, and a public horticulture library and archive.

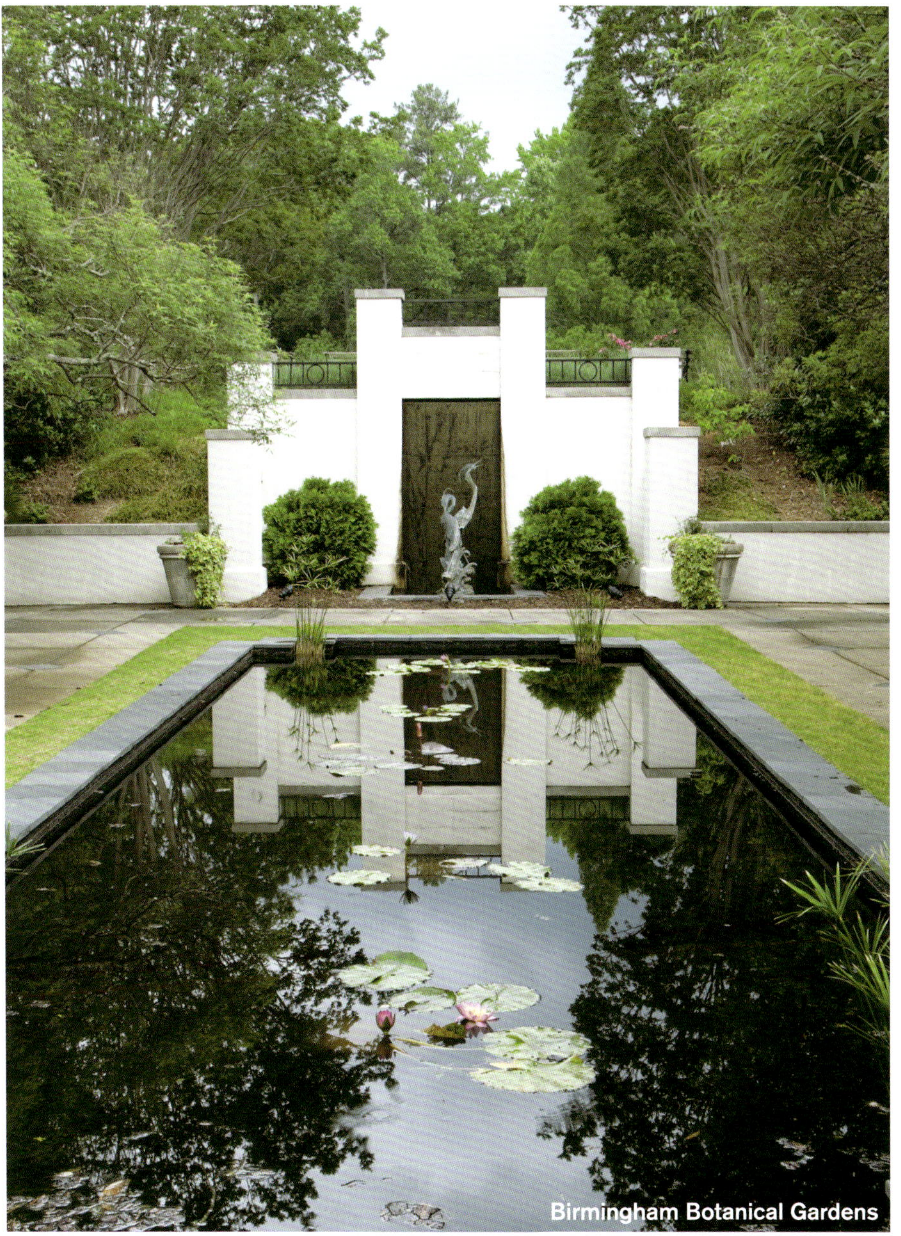

The gardens provide quiet walking paths, contemplative spaces, pools, and glades.

Dothan Area Botanical Gardens
Dothan, Alabama

Volunteers cultivated the first garden, the Rose Garden, on this 48-acre property in 1994. Today, this garden is best known for its extensive collection of camellias, which bloom from October to March, lending bright color to the drab winter months. Visitors can also peruse the Azalea Garden, the Pollinator Garden, and the Japanese Maple Grove.

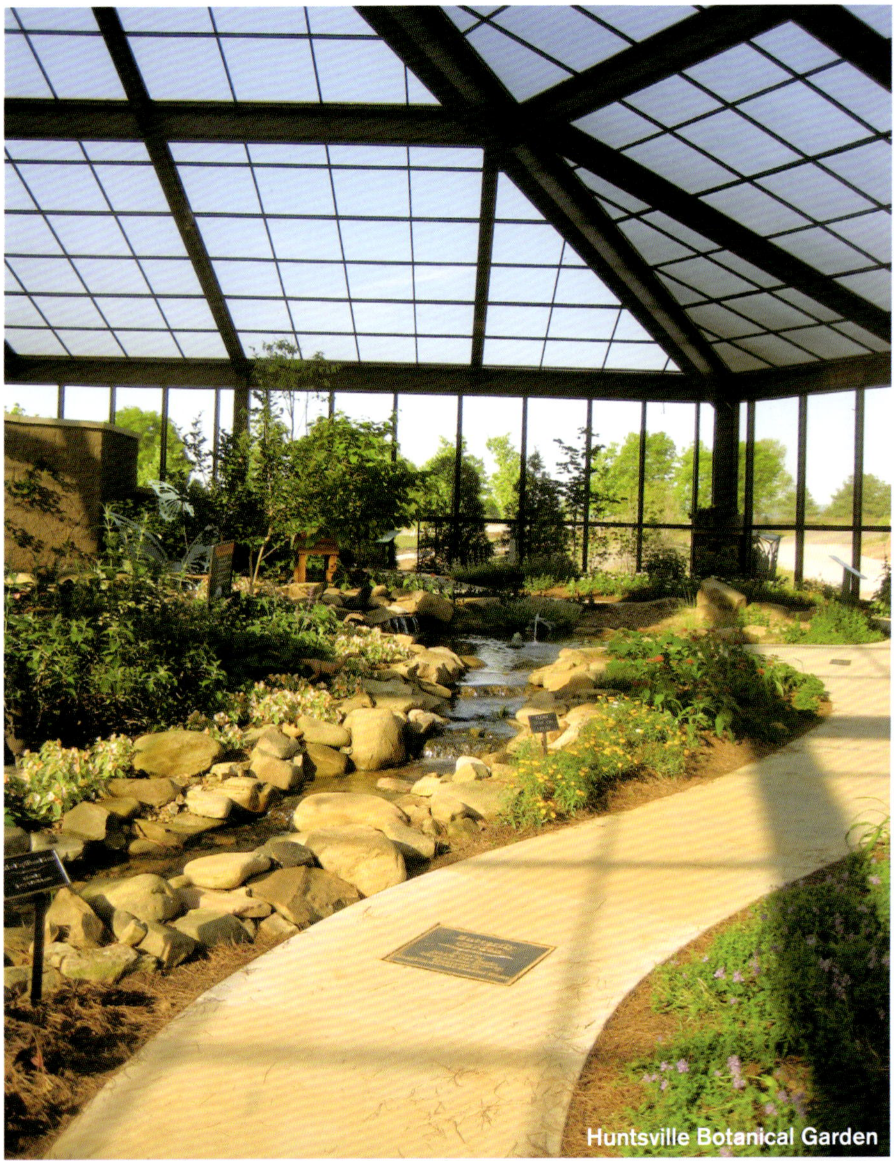

Huntsville Botanical Garden

The butterfly house allows visitors to stroll through a butterfly-friendly ecosystem, surrounded by these magical insects.

Huntsville Botanical Garden
Huntsville, Alabama

Visitors can admire a wide range of Alabama's native plants at this 118-acre garden, which features everything from grassy meadows and floral displays to aquatic environments and wooded groves. In addition to its many tranquil trails and stunning botanical displays–including a daylily garden with more than 700 cultivars–the garden is perhaps best known for its Purdy Butterfly House, believed to be the nation's largest open-air butterfly exhibit.

Mobile Botanical Gardens
Mobile, Alabama

In 1974, the City of Mobile, Alabama, leased 100 acres of land to the South Alabama Horticultural & Botanic Society to create the Mobile Botanical Gardens. Showcasing one of the most diverse plant collections on the Gulf Coast, some of the garden's popular attractions include a stunning display of azaleas, a man-made bog, a pollinator garden, and the largest collection of Japanese maples in the Southeast.

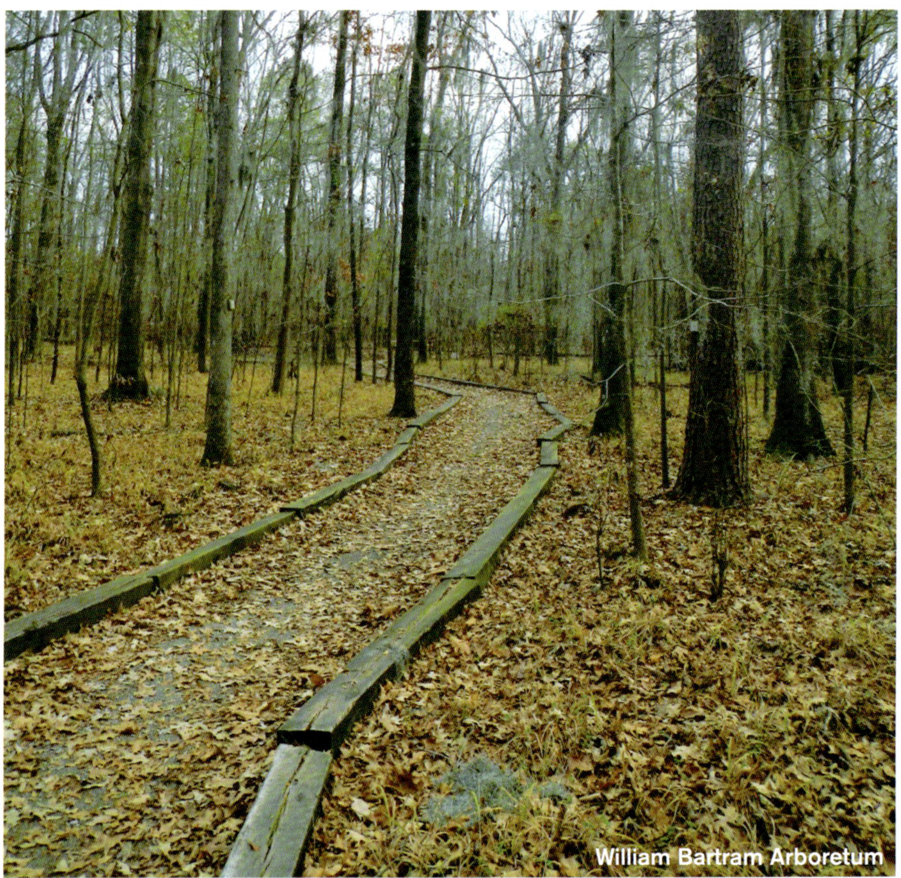

William Bartram Arboretum

The arboretum's boardwalk and paths meander through forests, bogs, and wildflower fields.

William Bartram Arboretum
Wetumpka, Alabama

This 30-acre arboretum in Wetumpka was named in honor of eighteenth-century naturalist William Bartram. The arboretum is part of the 165-acre Fort Toulouse-Jackson Park, and features a winding path that leads visitors past bogs, forests, and wildflowers, many of which Bartram sketched when he visited the area in 1776. The trail leads to the historic Fort Toulouse before ending near the Tallapoosa River.

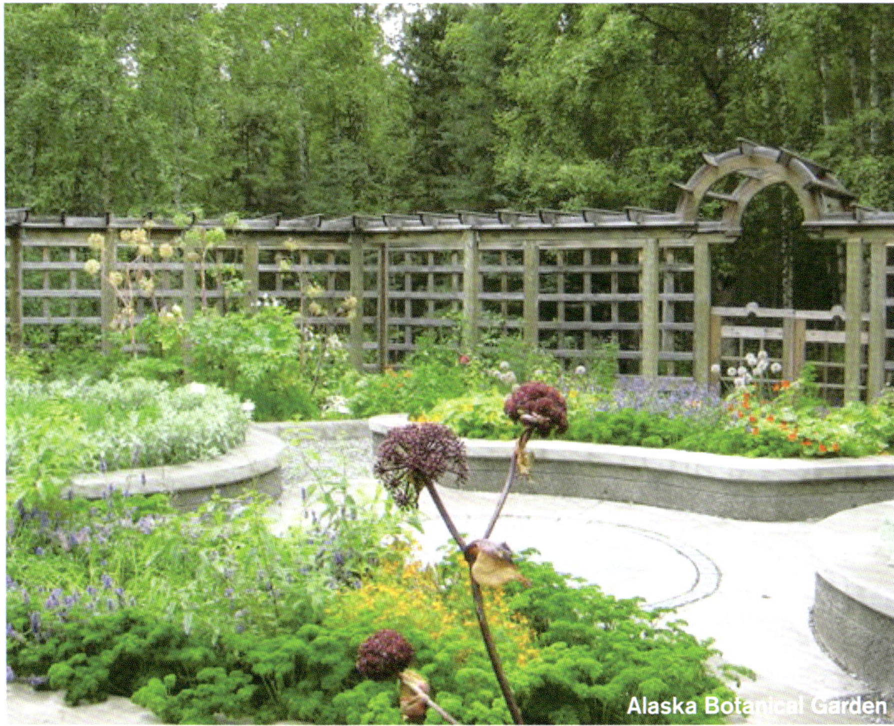

The Herb Garden was constructed in 1996 and features a variety of medicinal and culinary herbs.

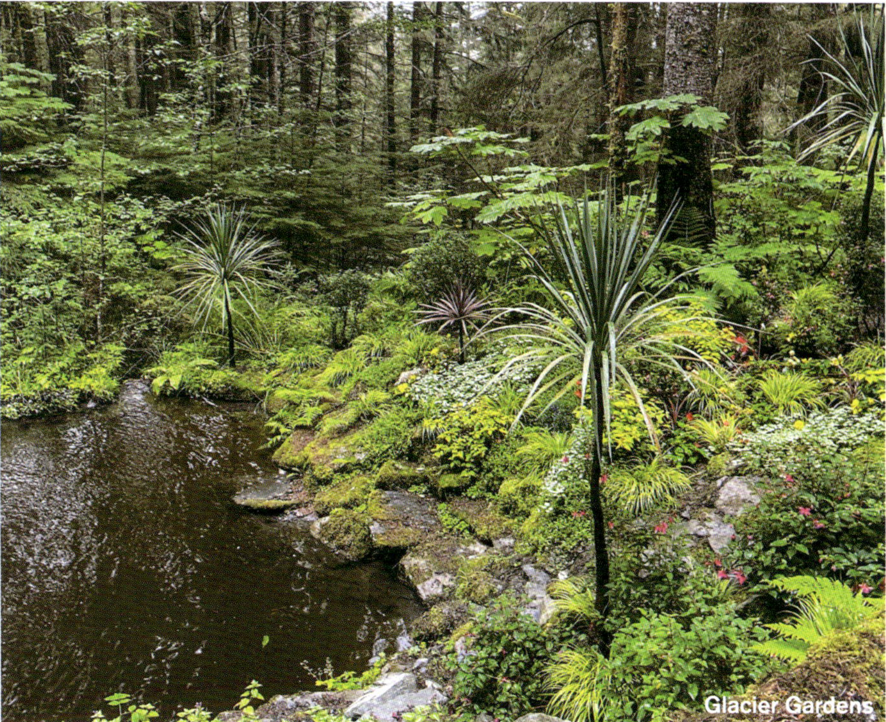

The landscaped terrain of Glacier Gardens is surprisingly lush.

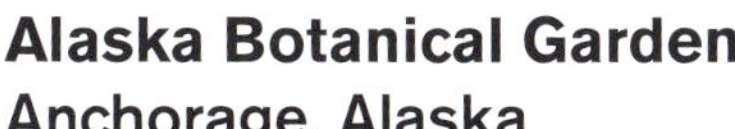

Alaska Botanical Garden
Anchorage, Alaska

Alaska may be known for snow and ice, but this 100-acre garden–which is open even during the coldest of winter months–puts its diverse greenery on stunning display. Natural spruce and birch forest surround the property, which features trails and a half-mile paved loop for visitors to explore. Hardy perennials, including poppies, irises, roses, and 80 different kinds of peonies, lend color, while more than 350 species of alpine plants thrive in their natural habitat.

Georgeson Botanical Garden
Fairbanks, Alaska

Situated on the campus of the University of Alaska Fairbanks, this garden of only five acres makes up for its small size by displaying the fruits of some big experiments in subarctic horticulture. Thanks to long hours of summer sunlight in this northern locale, the garden showcases plants and vegetables that grow to huge proportions! More than 3,000 of Alaska's native plants are on display, but the garden is perhaps best known for its collection of non-native peonies.

Glacier Gardens
Juneau, Alaska

Glacier Gardens is located within the Tongass National Forest. The garden is renowned for its floral displays and mesmerizing hanging gardens. Its one-of-a-kind Flower Towers consist of colorful foliage spilling from the roots of upturned trees. Guided tours escort visitors through amazing Alaskan temperate rainforest and offer scenic views of Juneau.

Worth Exploring in Alaska

Jensen-Olson Arboretum
Juneau, Alaska

- A Juneau gem, this site houses a nationally-accredited collection of primrose, some species of which are grown nowhere else in North America

Worth Exploring in Arizona

The Arboretum at Flagstaff
Flagstaff, Arizona

- 750 species of native Colorado plants on 200 acres
- At 7,150 feet of elevation, one of the highest-elevation public gardens in the U.S.

Destination Forever Ranch and Gardens
Near Yucca, Arizona

- Rural, 40-acre, off-grid property
- Cultivates and protects approximately 2,000 cacti, succulents, and trees

Tucson Botanical Gardens
Tucson, Arizona

- Features a collection of 20 gardens on 5.5 acres
- Highlights include the Cactus and Succulent Garden and the seasonal Cox Butterfly and Orchid Pavilion

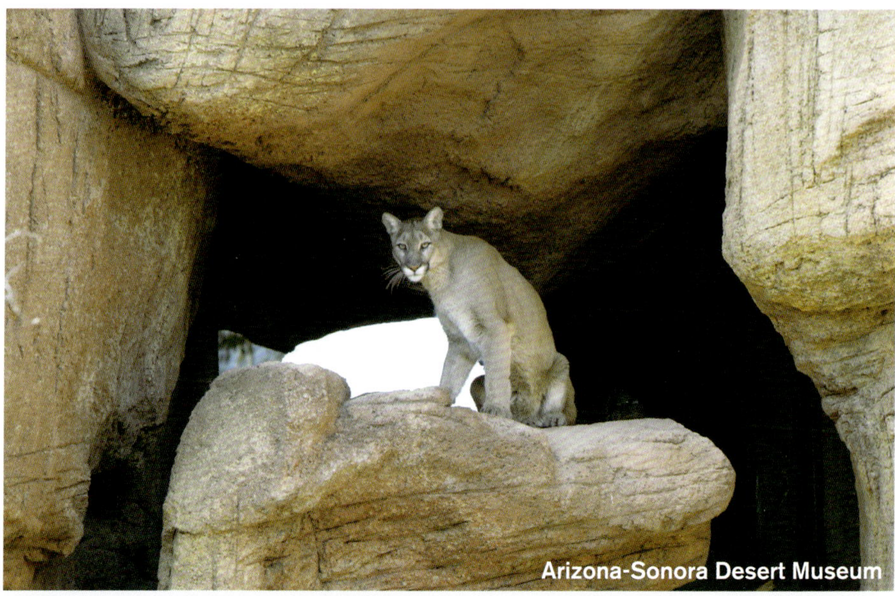

Arizona-Sonora Desert Museum

The museum's diverse collection of wildlife includes large mammals like cougars. Visitors can view the wildlife from several miles of walking paths.

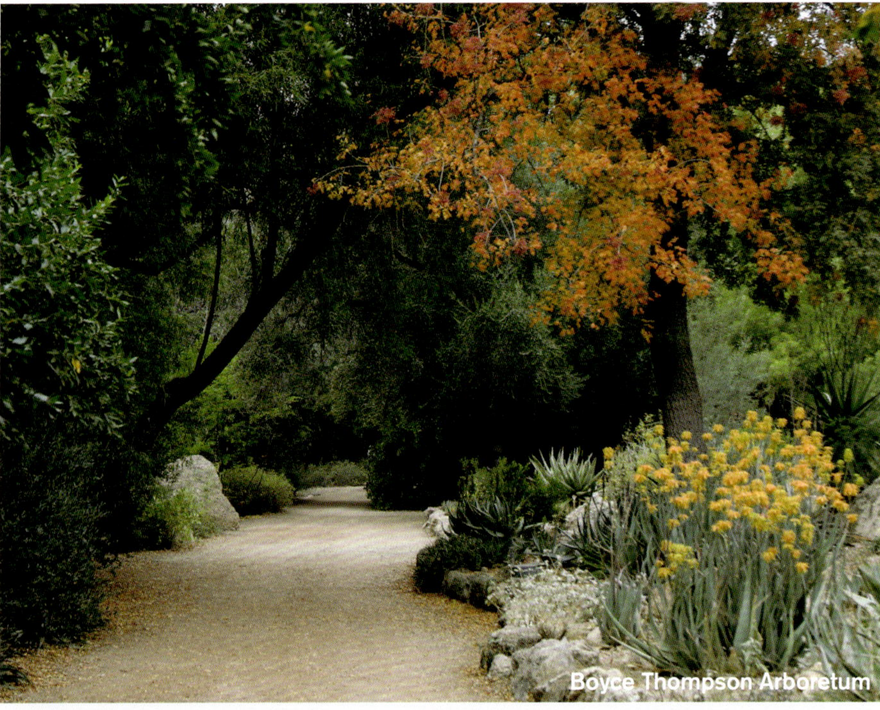

Boyce Thompson Arboretum

Walking trails go past wildflower gardens, cactus gardens, greenhouses, a butterfly garden, and other botanical displays.

Arizona-Sonora Desert Museum
Tucson, Arizona

This 98-acre property showcasing the flora and fauna of the Sonoran Desert is so much more than a simple "museum." Considered one of the top attractions in Tucson, the institution includes a zoo, botanical garden, aquarium, natural history museum, and an art gallery. More than 56,000 individual plant specimens, almost 250 animal species, and one of the most comprehensive regional mineral collections in the world are housed at the museum.

Boyce Thompson Arboretum
Pinal County, Arizona

Established in 1924 on 392 acres, this arboretum is both the oldest and largest botanical garden in the state of Arizona. Home to three nationally accredited collections, the property boasts five miles of trails winding through the beauty of the Arizona desert. Exhibits include a cactus garden, aloe garden, and palm and eucalyptus groves, as well as plants from Australia and South America. Bird-watchers may glimpse more than 250 species in the arboretum.

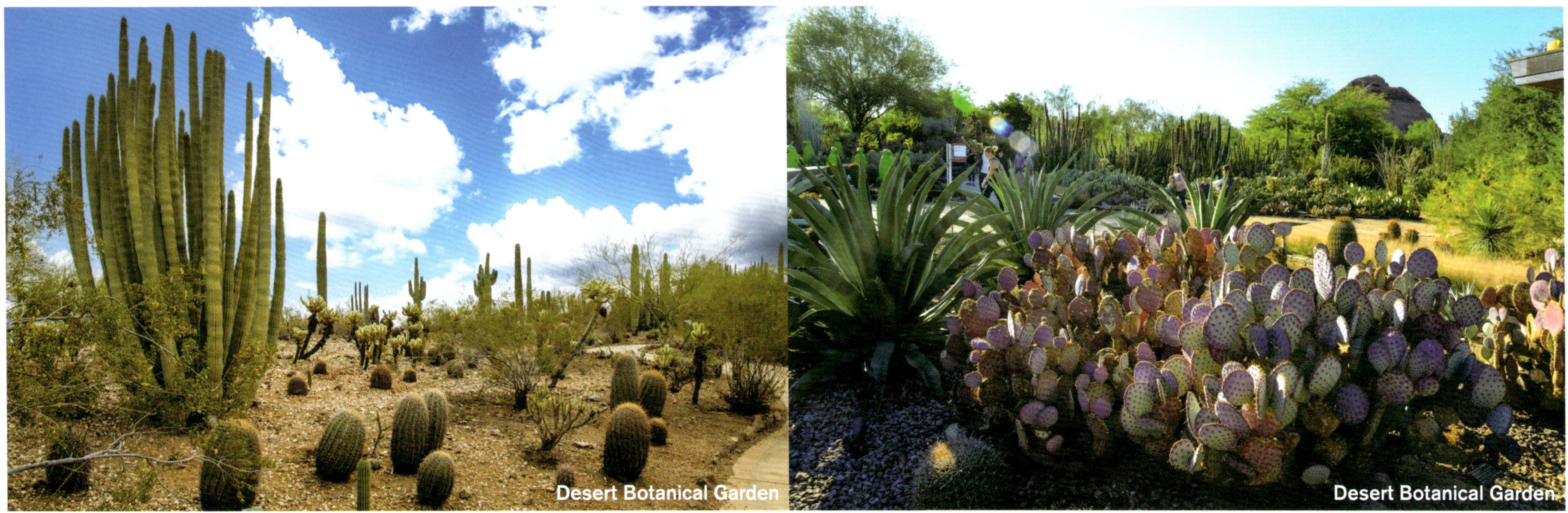

Desert plants are well represented on the grounds, including thousands of agave and cacti plants.

Desert Botanical Garden
Phoenix, Arizona

The beautiful Desert Botanical Garden was founded in 1937 by the Arizona Cactus and Native Flora Society in an effort to preserve the fragile desert ecosystem of this Sonoran Desert region. The property features several nature trails that guide visitors past the unique plants and wildlife found in one of the hottest and driest parts of the world. Trails include the popular Desert Discovery Trail, where a variety of cactus and succulents grow, and the Sonoran Desert Nature Trail, where curious nature lovers can learn about how the plants and animals who call the desert home are able to survive with little water.

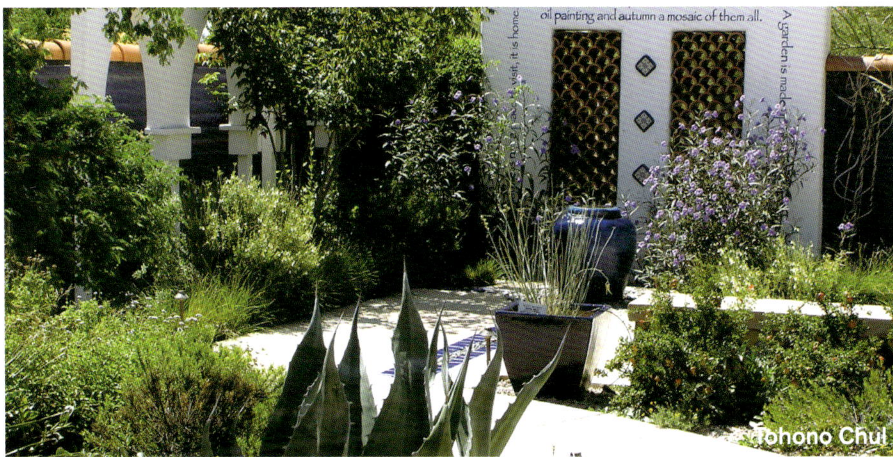

The Desert Living Courtyard features a variety of themed sections, including the Moorish Garden, seen here. Other sections include the Barrio Garden, Meditation Garden, Dry Shade Garden, Wildlife Garden, Xeriscape Garden, and Container Garden.

Tohono Chul
Tucson, Arizona

Part lush botanical garden, part vibrant art gallery, and part charming bistro, Tohono Chul is often termed one of Tucson's best-kept secrets. The 49-acre property features trails that wind through a variety of habitats, including riparian areas and desert palm canyons, with particular attention paid to cultivating plants that attract butterflies and hummingbirds. The art gallery focuses on regional artists and the culture of the Southwest, while the bistro whips up dishes made of locally sourced ingredients for public and private gatherings. Tohono Chul provides a diverse selection of tours and programs for visitors to learn about the surrounding desert and its unique ecology.

Arkansas Arboretum
Little Rock, Arkansas

Located within Pinnacle Mountain State Park, this 71-acre arboretum was cultivated to reflect the six geographical regions found in Arkansas, including the hills and plateaus of the Ozarks and the rock formations of the Ouachita Mountains. A 0.6-mile paved interpretive trail leads visitors through the tranquil property.

Botanical Garden of the Ozarks
Fayetteville, Arkansas

A Japanese garden, four-season garden, vegetable and herb garden, and children's garden are just a few of the 12 "themed" gardens that make up this eight-acre attraction. The property also features the only butterfly house in Arkansas, a collection of beehives, and the "Bat Tower"–a T-shaped roost designed to welcome Ozark big-eared bats.

Worth Exploring in Arkansas

Peel Museum and Botanical Gardens
Bentonville, Arkansas

- 1800s Italianate-styled mansion
- Gardens include a Rose Garden, Herb Garden, and an apple orchard

South Arkansas Arboretum
El Dorado, Arkansas

- More than 12 acres of native plants and exotic species
- Features paved walking trails and rentable pavilions and gazebos

Garvan Woodland Gardens

Among other attractions, the grounds feature the "Garden of the Pine Wind," a Japanese garden.

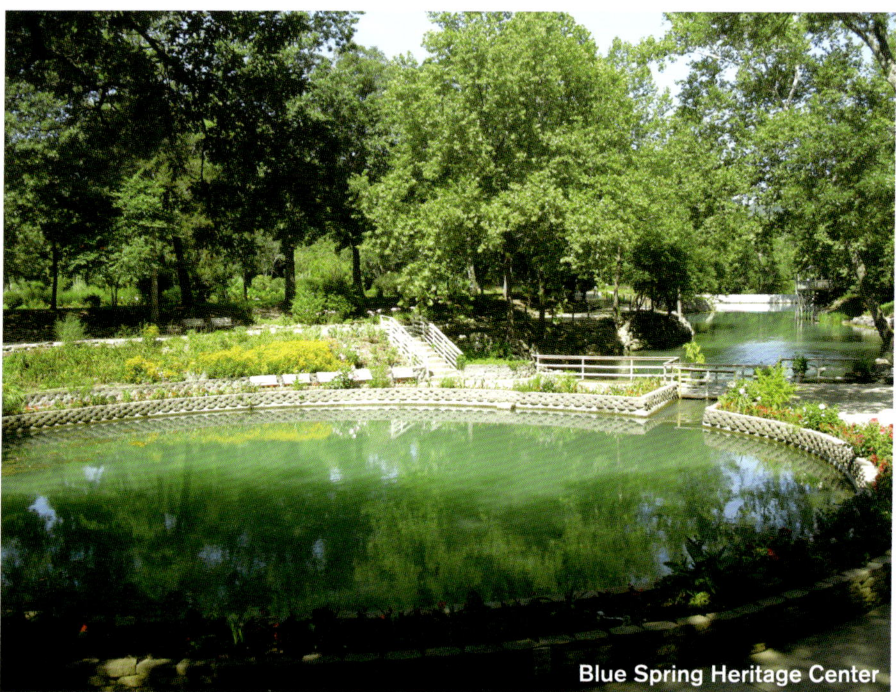
Blue Spring Heritage Center

The Blue Spring has been a tourist destination since 1948.

Garvan Woodland Gardens
Hot Springs, Arkansas

This 210-acre garden is named after local philanthropist Verna Cook Garvan, who, as a self-taught gardener, planted thousands of the plants and flowers now flourishing at the site. After her death in 1993, Garvan left the 210-acre property to the University of Arkansas. The university has added a beautiful flagstone and redwood pavilion in her honor.

Blue Spring Heritage Center
Eureka Springs, Arkansas

Centered around the beautiful Blue Spring, which pours 38 million gallons of clear water into a lagoon every day, this 33-acre property offers more than just colorful blooming gardens. Visitors can also explore sites that speak to the area's rich history, including a rock shelter dating back thousands of years and an 1840s flour mill.

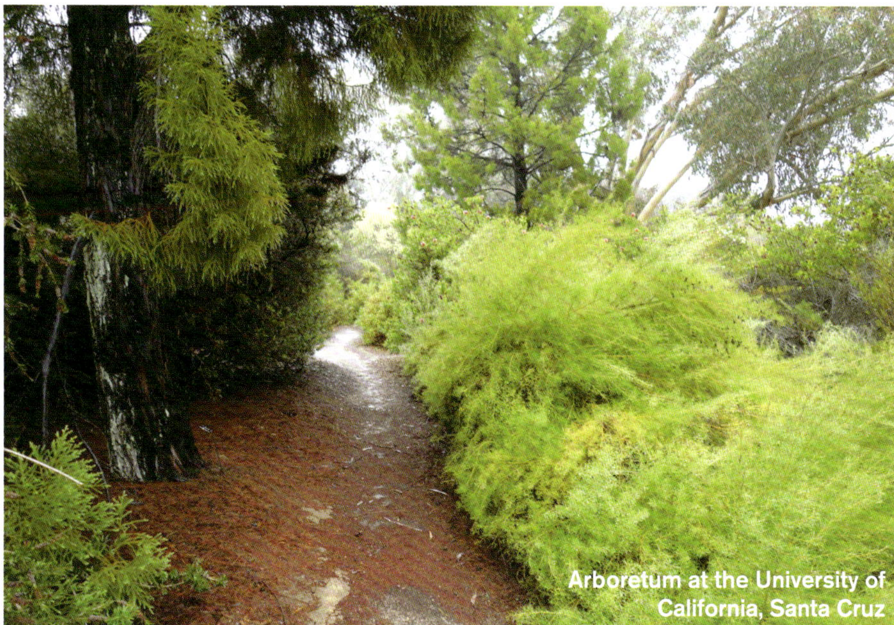

There are several miles of walking paths and benches on site.

Arboretum at the University of California, Santa Cruz
Santa Cruz, California

This garden, which sits on 115 acres within the University of California, Santa Cruz campus, features more than 300 rare plant species from Mediterranean climates. The garden is considered a "living laboratory," where both students and nature lovers can learn about the unique ecology on display. The arboretum also houses large collections of plants from Australia, New Zealand, and South Africa, as well as native California species, many of which are found nowhere else in the United States. Additional gardens include the fragrant Aroma and Succulent Gardens, the Butterfly Garden, and a collection of nearly every type of conifer from around the world.

Alta Vista Botanical Gardens
Vista, California

There are 17 unique garden zones spread out across this property, featuring plants and flowers from around the globe. Eucalyptus trees from Australia, Mediterranean olive and fig trees, tropical flowers, and rare fruits like South American cherimoya are just a few of the botanical beauties awaiting visitors. In addition to its lush vegetation, the garden prides itself on showcasing art created by local artisans. Imaginative sculptures, colorful mosaics, and unique garden benches are located throughout the property, lending it an air of whimsy. The garden is also home to thousands of milkweed plants, making it a welcome habitat for monarch butterflies.

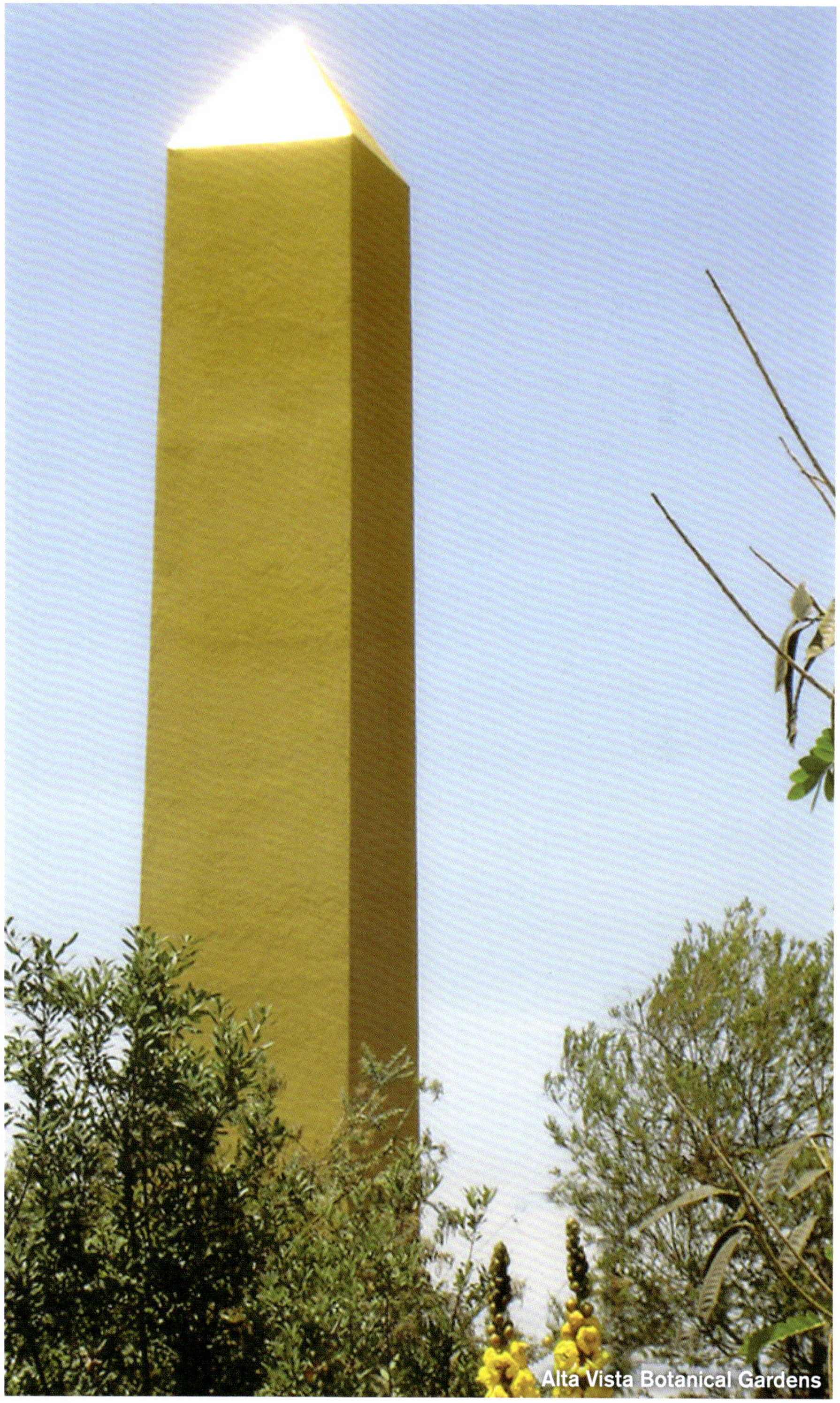

Alta Vista Botanical Gardens

The Welcome Garden Obelisk stands over 30 feet tall.

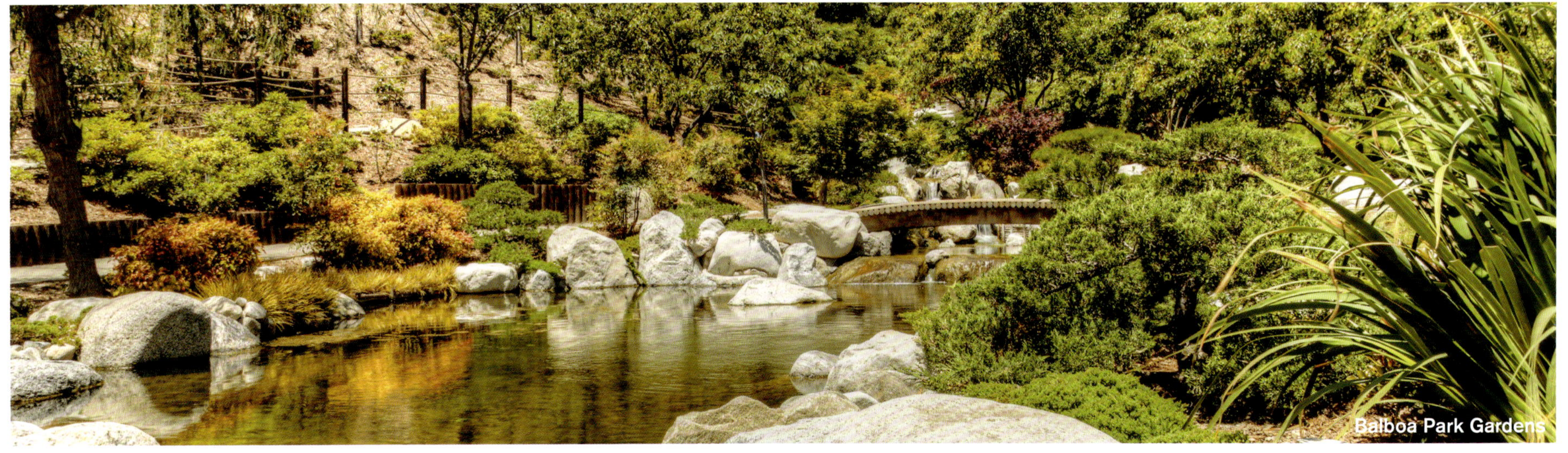

Balboa Park Gardens

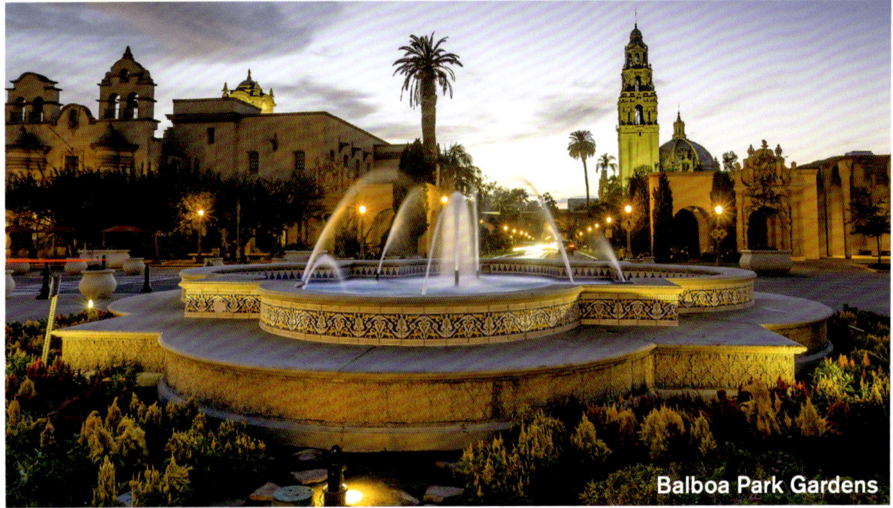

Balboa Park Gardens

Balboa Park Gardens
San Diego, California

Nestled within Balboa Park–one of the oldest urban parks in the United States–are a collection of individual gardens where city dwellers can find a tranquil botanical respite. Mild San Diego weather ensures a year-round display of more than a dozen landscapes, from meticulously manicured flower gardens to natural preserves. Visitor favorites include the Japanese Friendship Garden, created in honor of San Diego's sister city, Yokohama, Japan, and the lush Palm Canyon, a tropical oasis containing hundreds of palm trees. Another can't-miss exhibit is the Botanical Building and Lily Pond, created for the 1915 Panama-California Exposition, where thousands of ferns, orchids, and tropical plants grow in a historic lath structure. The park also contains an award-winning, world-renowned rose garden, in bloom from March through December.

Worth Exploring in California

Blake Garden
Kensington, California

- Designed by landscape architect Mabel Symmes
- Used as a teaching facility for UC Berkeley College of Environmental Design

California Botanic Garden
Claremont, California

- Contains 86 acres of native California plants
- Houses 70,000 plants representing 2,000 species

California State University Northridge Botanic Garden
Northridge, California

- A collection of more than 1,200 plant species on a mere 1.5 acres
- Features trees, wildflowers, cacti, and native food including berries and gourds

Chavez Ravine Arboretum
Los Angeles, California

- Contains trees from around the world
- Specimens include Brazilian coral trees and Canary Island pines

Clovis Botanical Garden
Clovis, California

- Features a Mediterranean garden, a sensory garden, and a cactus garden
- Emphasizes water conservation

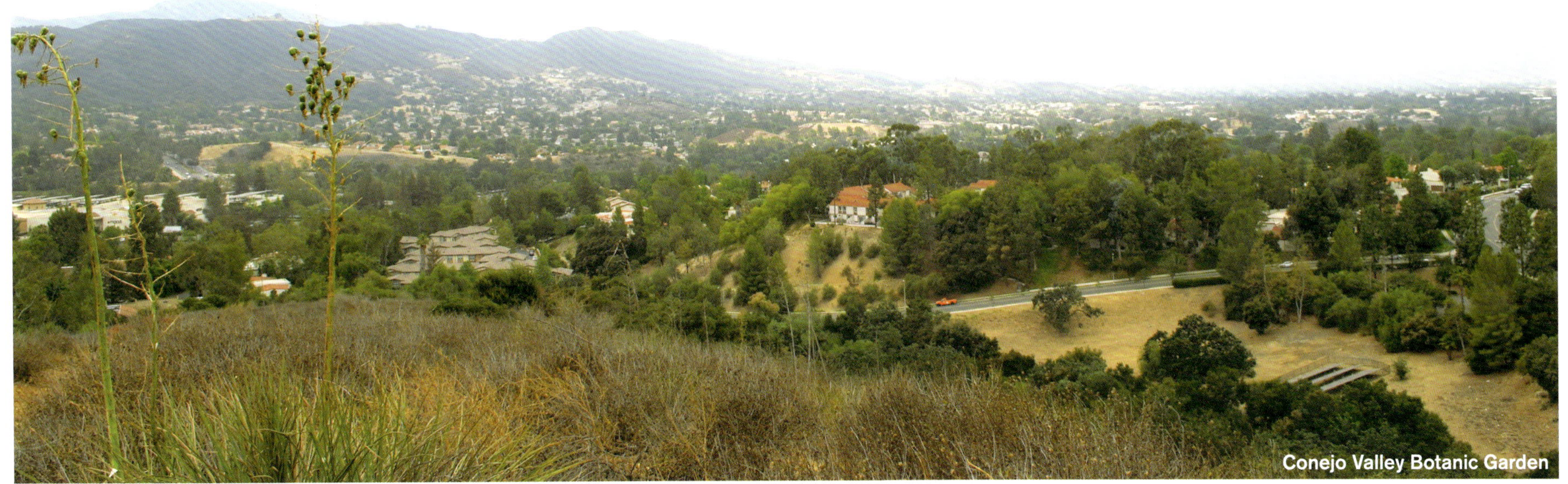

Conejo Valley Botanic Garden

The gardens sit atop a hill, providing a view of the surrounding landscape.

Conejo Valley Botanic Garden
Thousand Oaks, California

The city of Thousand Oaks surrounds this 33-acre property, which offers visitors 15 unique gardens to explore. From a bird habitat and butterfly garden to a rare fruit orchard and a kids' adventure garden, there's an outdoor attraction to appeal to everyone. Located high on a hill, the garden offers views of the Conejo Valley below, with overlooks located on meandering hiking trails on the property.

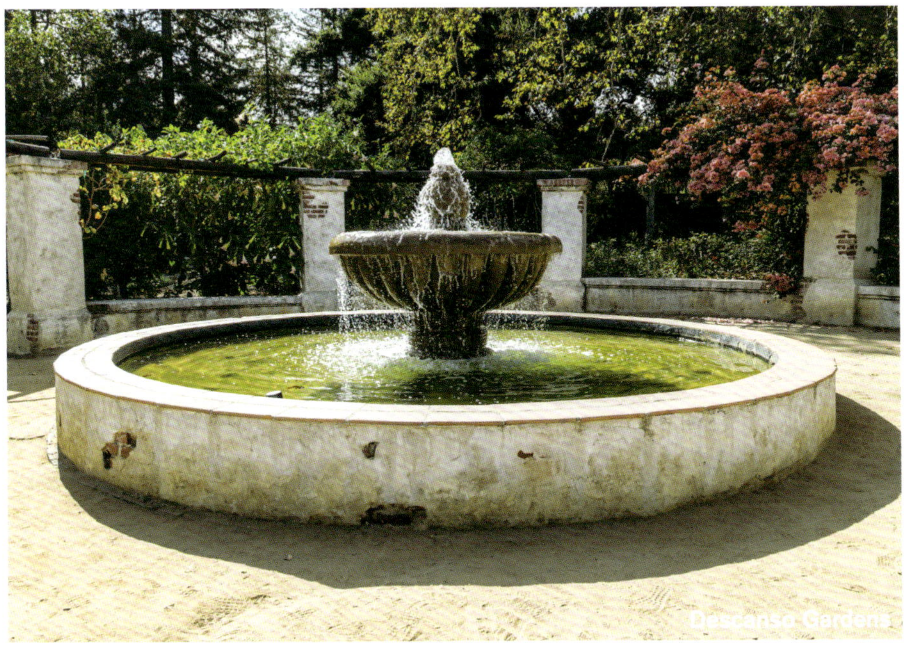

Descanso Gardens

Descanso Gardens
La Cañada Flintridge, California

Located just 20 minutes from downtown Los Angeles, this botanical garden provides a welcome oasis from city life. Highlights include the California Garden, which showcases trees, plants, and flowers native to the state, and the Ancient Forest, filled with plant species that have survived relatively unchanged for millions of years. The park is also known for its lilacs, which have been specially cultivated to thrive in California's climate.

Eddy Arboretum
Placerville, California

This arboretum, founded by James G. Eddy in 1925 and given to the people of the United States in 1934, is part of the Pacific Southwest Research Station of the U.S. Forest Service. It is best known for its well-studied and researched collection of more than 90 species of native and exotic pine and fir trees, said to be the best-documented conifers in the world.

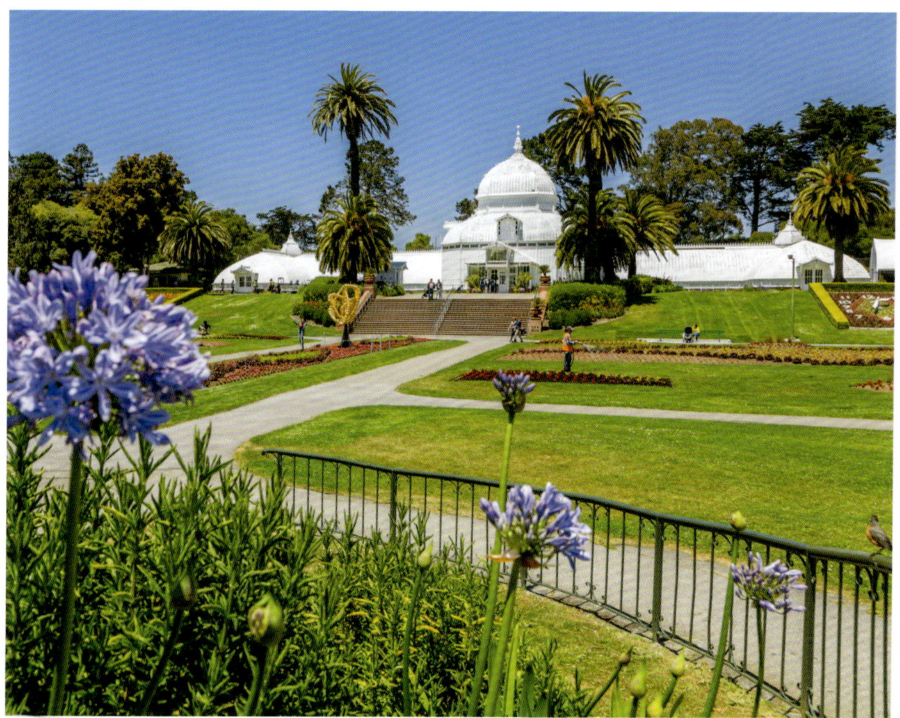

The elaborate Victorian conservatory features a 60-foot-high central dome and symmetrical, arch-shaped wings that span 240 feet in length.

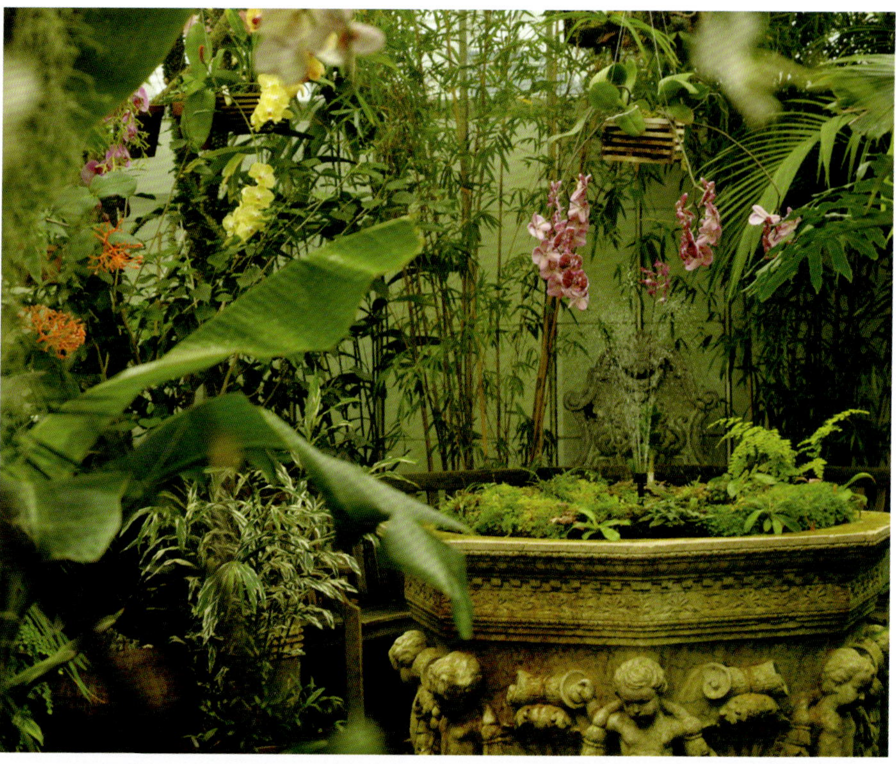

The conservatory is worth visiting for its large collection of orchids alone.

Conservatory of Flowers
San Francisco, California

Located in the famed Golden Gate Park, this greenhouse and botanical garden contains an impressive collection of rare and exotic plants and flowers. The historic greenhouse is considered the oldest wood and glass conservatory in North America, constructed in 1879.

Inside, visitors are greeted with a diverse selection of greenery. The Aquatic Plants Gallery contains orchids, hibiscus, and carnivorous pitcher plants, as well as a giant water lily. Highland and Lowland Tropics galleries recreate the humid climates of tropical mountaintops and forest floors, and showcase the unique plants that thrive in these areas. The Potted Plants Gallery features an assortment of flowering trees and shrubs in decorative urns from around the world. The Conservatory also houses a rare Corpse Flower in its West Gallery. Native to Indonesia, these huge flowers, which can grow as high as 15 feet tall, emit a foul scent when they bloom. But far from driving visitors away, the Conservatory's Corpse Flower is one of its biggest draws!

Thanks to its historic significance, the Conservatory of Flowers is listed on the National Register of Historic Places and is a California Historical Landmark.

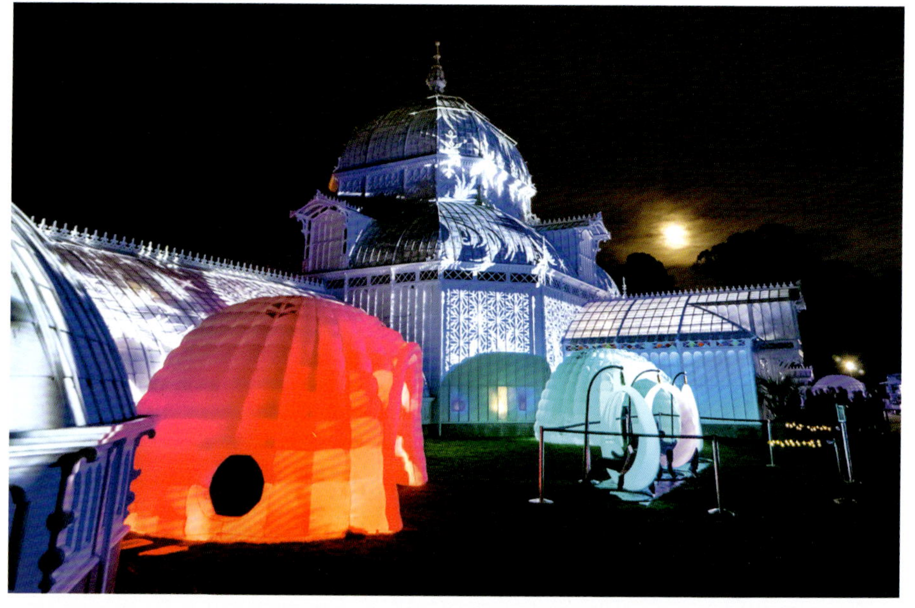

An evening attraction features the conservatory in multicolored splendor. Dazzling light projections are now a frequent occurrence.

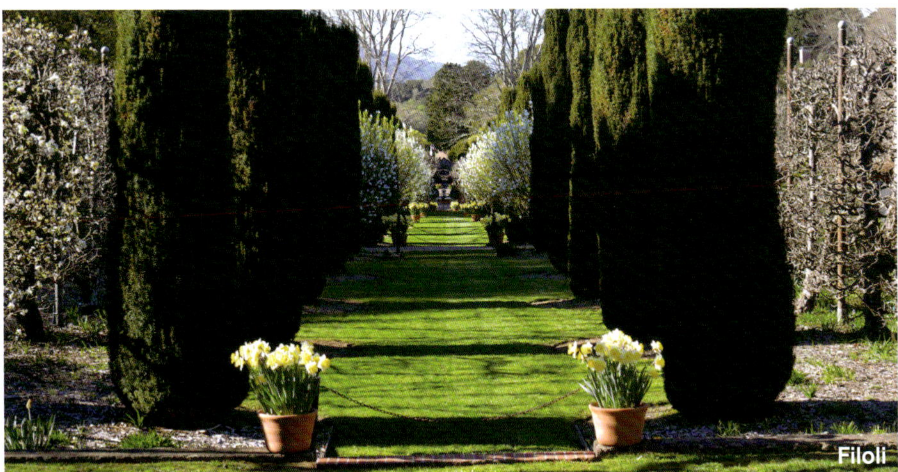
Filoli

Filoli
Woodside, California

Also known as the Bourn-Roth Estate, this historic country house was constructed in 1917 for entrepreneur William Bowers Bourn II. The home is surrounded by 16 acres of meticulously manicured gardens, which, in turn, are surrounded by 654 acres of natural land. Visitors to the property can tour the Georgian Revival-style manor, stroll through colorful flower gardens, or hike through shaded oak and redwood forest.

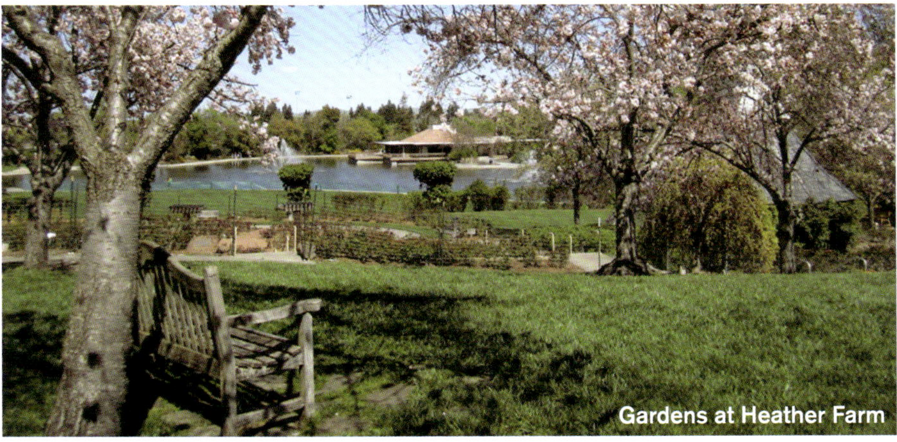
Gardens at Heather Farm

Gardens at Heather Farm
Walnut Creek, California

Created as a nonprofit volunteer organization in the 1970s, this six-acre property is open to the public 24 hours a day free of charge. Gardens include a butterfly garden with milkweed and passion vines, and the Mural Garden, which features African sumac trees and a variety of herbaceous shrubs. The farm is also renowned for its Cowden Rose Garden, considered by many to be the most beautiful rose garden in the Bay Area.

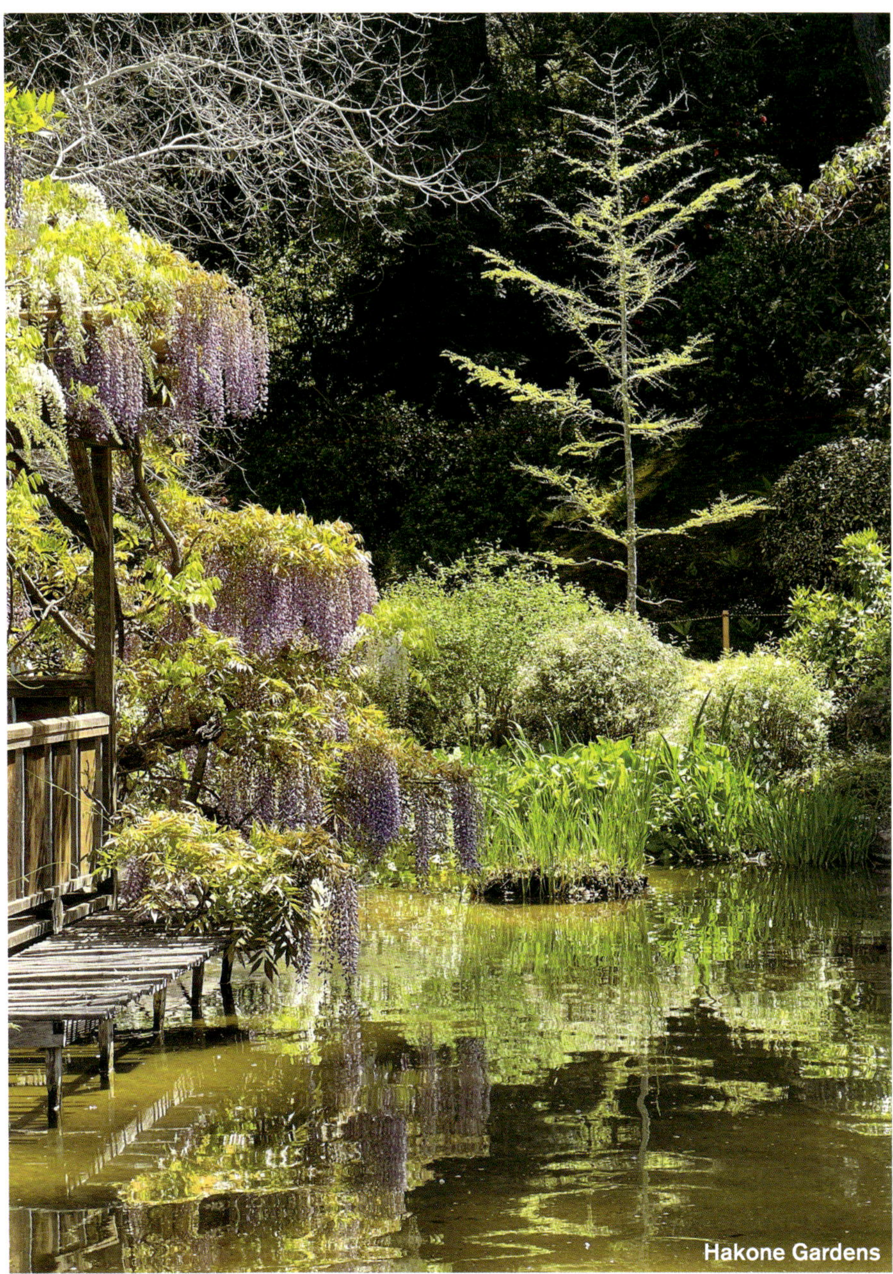
Hakone Gardens

Hakone Gardens
Saratoga, California

This 18-acre property is one of the oldest Japanese-style residential gardens in the Western Hemisphere. Conceived in 1916 by Isabel Stine after the San Francisco resident took a trip to Japan, the gardens are modeled upon and named after Fuji-Hakone-Izu National Park. The property features a Zen Garden, a Tea Garden, and a Bamboo Garden, as well as a tranquil koi pond and Japanese-style structures.

The Huntington
San Marino, California

Purchased as a working ranch by Henry E. Huntington in 1903, the citrus groves, alfalfa crops, and nut and fruit orchards that once made up this property have made way for 130 acres of diverse plant collections. Visitors can explore many different themed gardens that showcase plants from around the globe, which have been carefully cultivated to thrive in the California climate. Highlights include the Desert Garden, containing one of the world's largest and oldest collections of cacti, and the Japanese Garden, which features hundreds of bonsai trees and a fully furnished Japanese-style house. Also notable is the 12-acre Chinese Garden, the largest outside of China. It contains man-made lakes, waterfalls, a tea house, and pavilions connected by footbridges.

The Huntington also stands out for its collection of 80 different camellia species, and has been recognized by the International Camellia Society as a Camellia Garden of Excellence. Native to parts of East Asia, the first camellia in California is believed to have arrived on a Japanese steamer in 1888. Today, that same specimen is proudly on display in the institution's Camellia Garden.

Other gardens on this historic property include the Australia Garden, Palm Garden, Rose Garden, and the English-themed Shakespeare Garden.

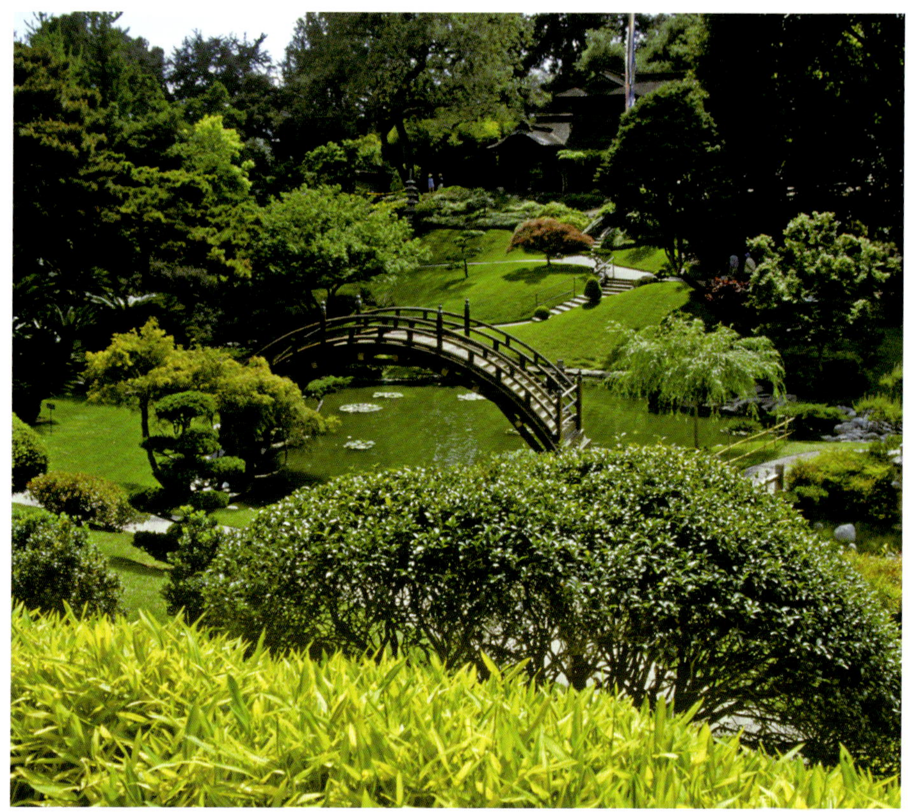

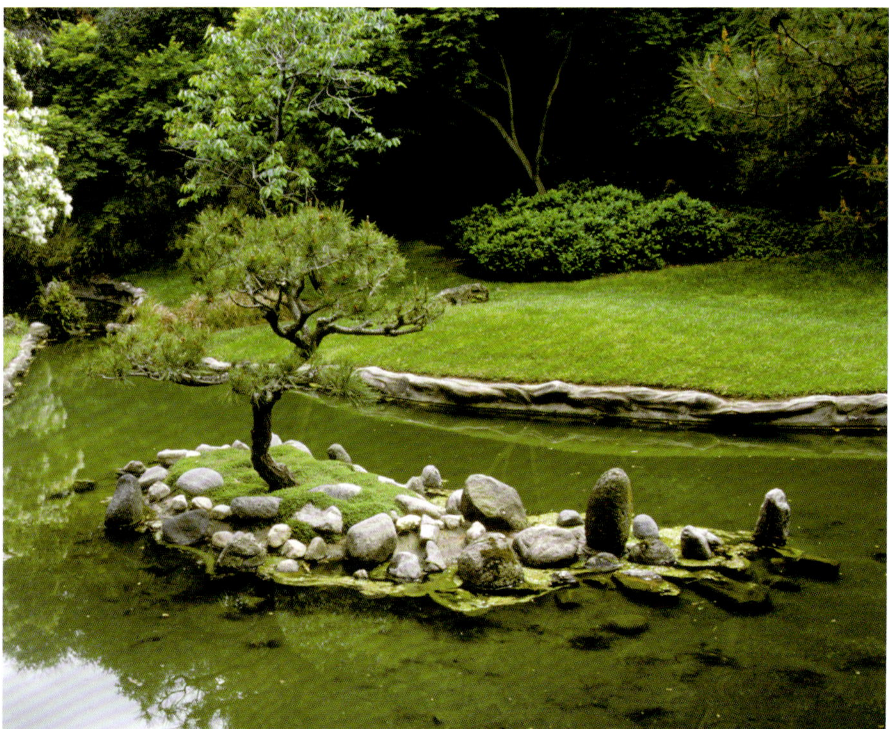

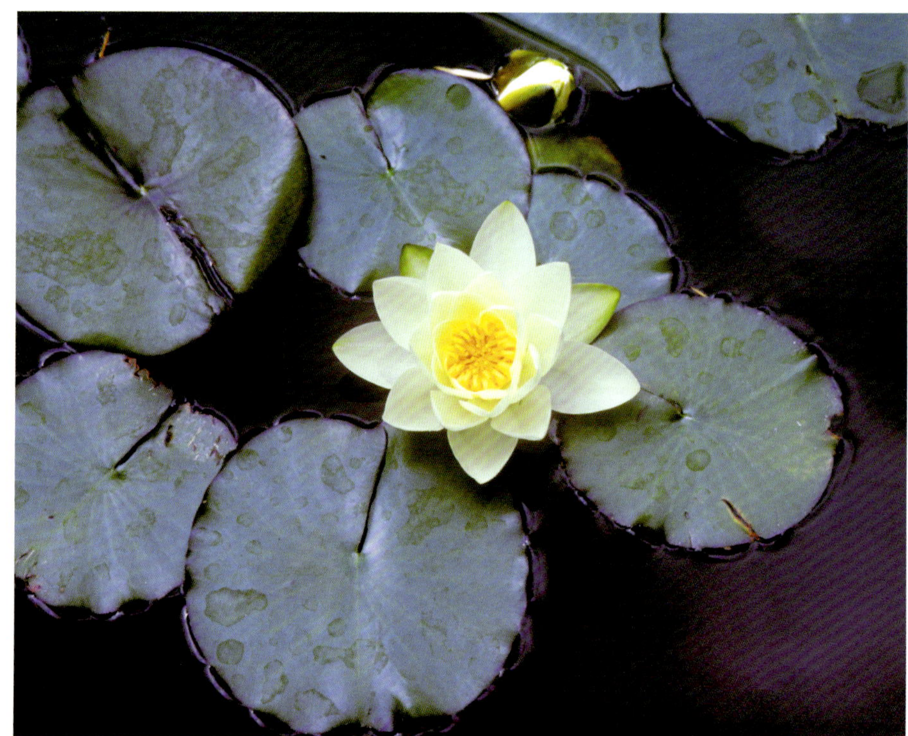

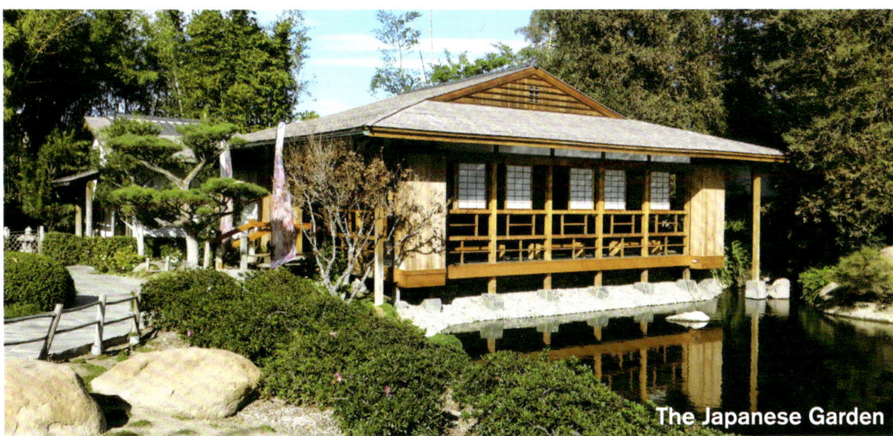

The garden grounds include a tea house and *Shoin* building (pictured).

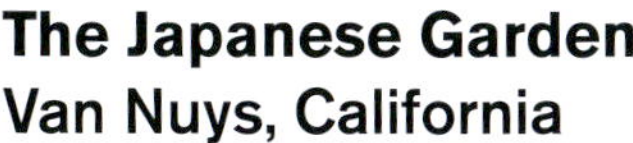

The Japanese Garden
Van Nuys, California

The Japanese name of this 6.5-acre garden in the Lake Balboa district of the San Fernando Valley is *SuhioEn*, meaning "garden of water and fragrance." Constructed next to a water reclamation plant, the ponds and irrigation on the grounds make use of the reclaimed water, demonstrating the worth of conservation. The property includes a Zen meditation garden, a "wet" garden with waterfalls and lakes, and an authentic tea house.

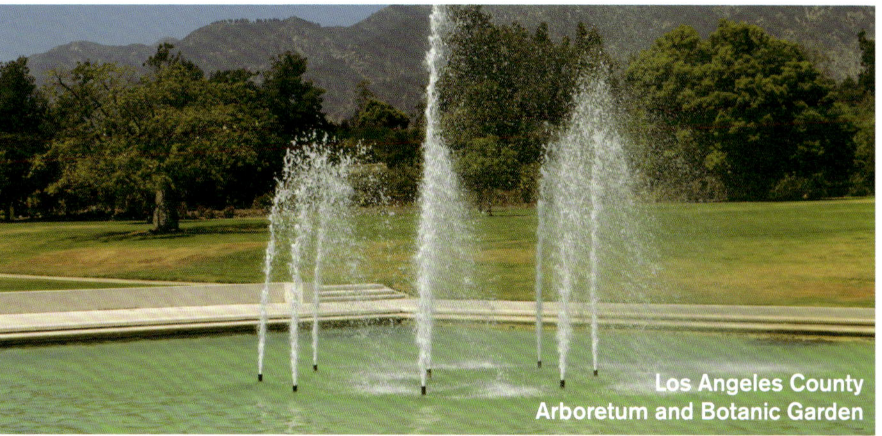

The grounds include waterfalls, ponds, and fountains.

Los Angeles County Arboretum and Botanic Garden
Arcadia, California

The plants in this 127-acre arboretum and botanical garden are grouped according to their geographical area of origin, with displays from South America, Australia, the Mediterranean, South Africa, Asia, and North America represented. Additional gardens include an herb garden, rose garden, and tropical greenhouse. The property is also home to a flock of colorful peafowl, descendants of a group of birds originally imported from India in 1879.

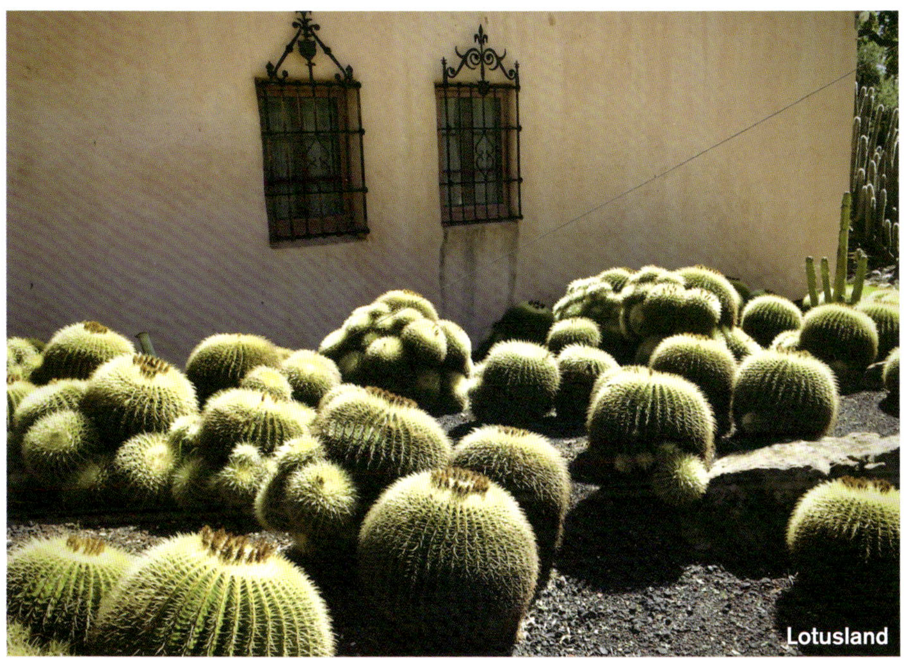

The grounds are full of delightful surprises, like this little group of golden barrel cacti.

Lotusland
Montecito, California

Ganna Walska, a Polish opera singer and garden enthusiast, started creating this botanical garden in the 1940s when she used the property as her private residence. She named it Lotusland, adding grottos, pools, and thousands of exotic plants, including, of course, many species of lotus. Today, Lotusland is prized for its Cactus Garden, the pollinator-attracting Insectary Garden, and its famous Aloe Garden, which contains more than 160 species.

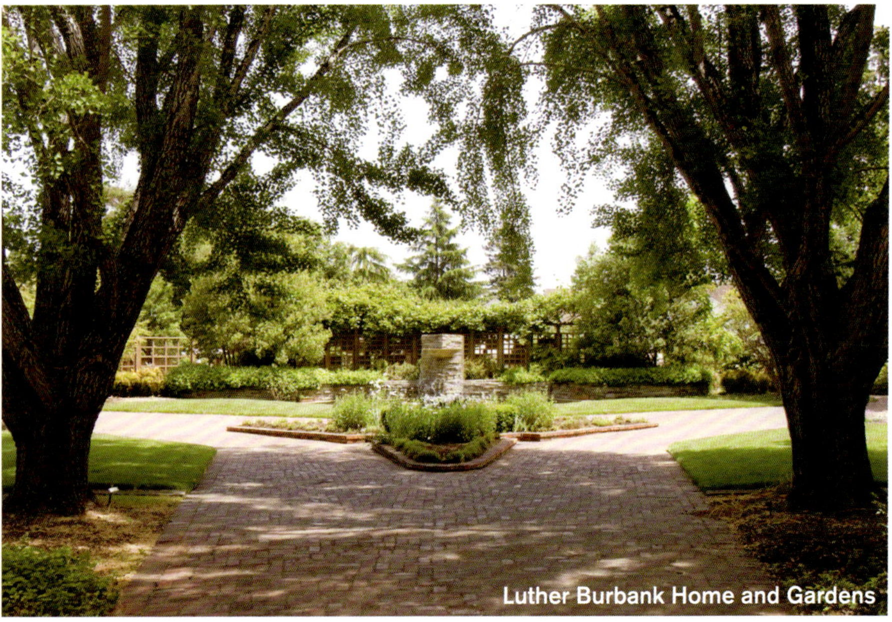

Luther Burbank Home and Gardens

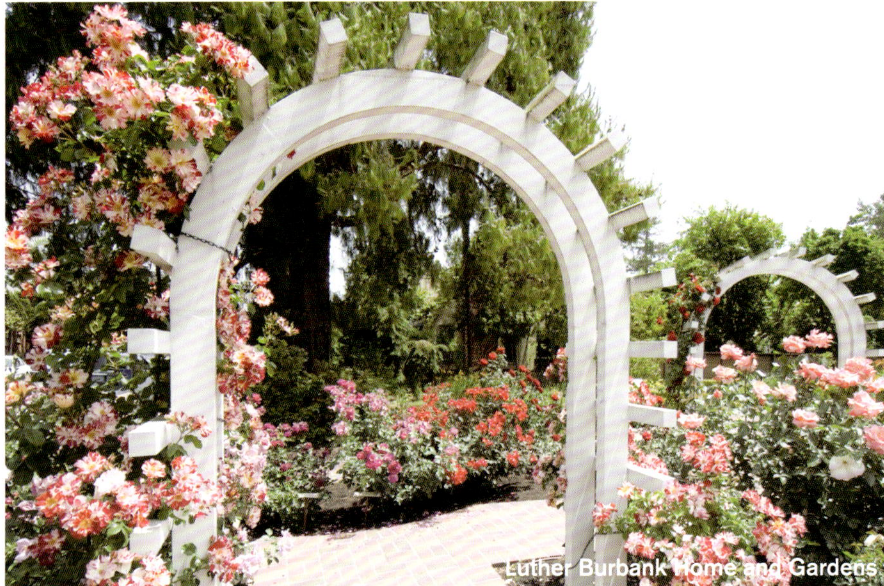

Luther Burbank Home and Gardens

Luther Burbank Home and Gardens
Santa Rosa, California

This property features the former home and garden of famed horticulturalist Luther Burbank, who welcomed visitors here–including Thomas Edison and Henry Ford–during the early 1900s. Visitors are still welcome to tour the property, which today is bursting with color and life. Gardens filled with carnations, daffodils, roses, poppies, and Shasta daisies ensure year-round blooms. The site also includes a garden with medicinal plants, an edible plant garden, and a wildlife habitat garden.

Other California Gardens

Labadie Arboretum
Oakland, California

- A botanical arboretum with a history museum vibe, featuring species from around the globe
- Located on the campus of Merritt College
- Named in honor of horticulture professor Emile Labadie

Mathias Botanical Garden
Los Angeles, California

- Contains more than 3,000 plants on 7.5 acres
- Named for botanist Mildred E. Mathias, who was known for her work in botany, horticulture, and conservation
- Highlights include native Hawaiian plants, a fern garden, and an herbarium with 150,000 dried and pressed specimens
- The only free public botanical garden in Los Angeles

San Luis Obispo Botanical Garden
San Luis Obispo, California

- Specializes in cultivating plants from Mediterranean environments
- Specimens featured are from the Mediterranean basin, California, Chile, Australia, and South Africa
- Highlights include a Children's Garden and a Fire Safe Garden, which demonstrates landscaping principles to protect property from wildfires

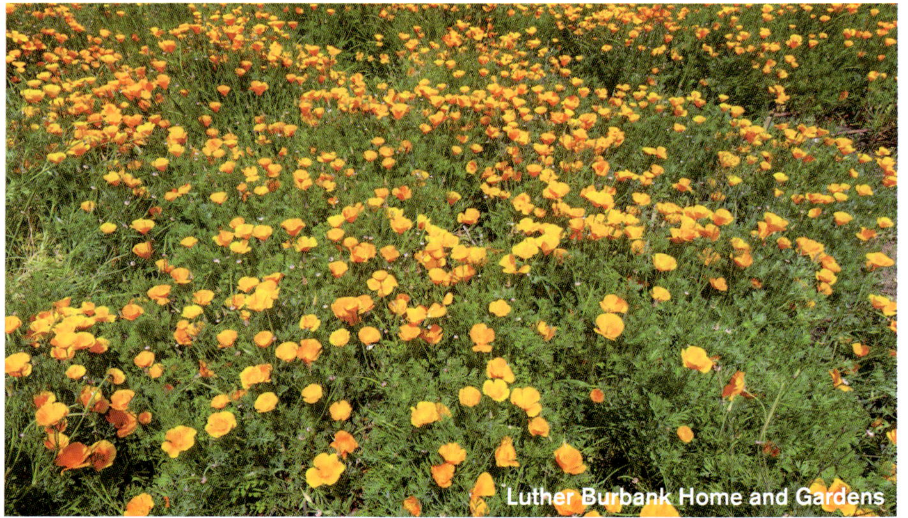

Luther Burbank Home and Gardens

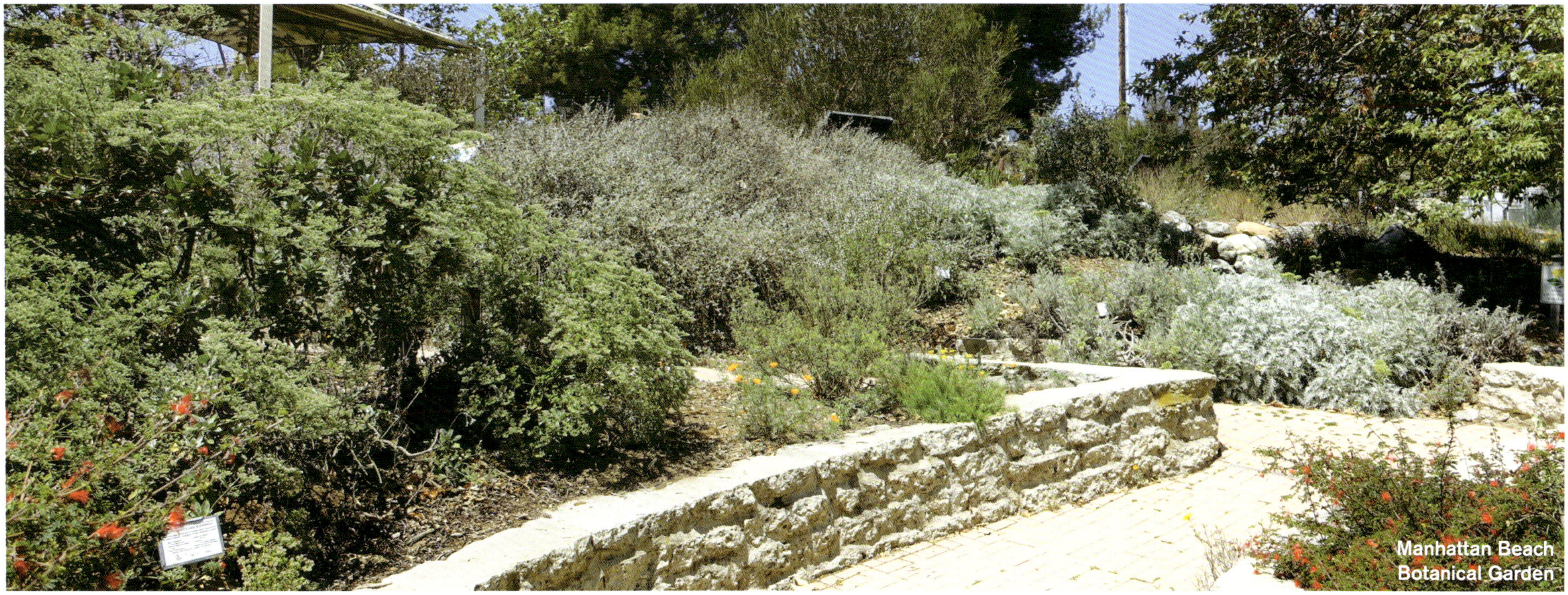

The grounds are small, but situated within stroll-friendly Polliwog Park.

Manhattan Beach Botanical Garden
Manhattan Beach, California

The grand opening of this small garden–which is free to the public and open all day, every day–was, fittingly, on Earth Day in 2001. When it was first established, the 0.66-acre garden was used to teach visitors how ecologically friendly gardening–cultivating the land without use of herbicides, pesticides, or fertilizers–could be beneficial to both the environment and humans. The same methods are in use today, carried out by the volunteers who care for the property. Visitors can explore the many California-native plants in the garden, including island snapdragon, purple sage, and the beach primrose, the official Manhattan Beach city flower.

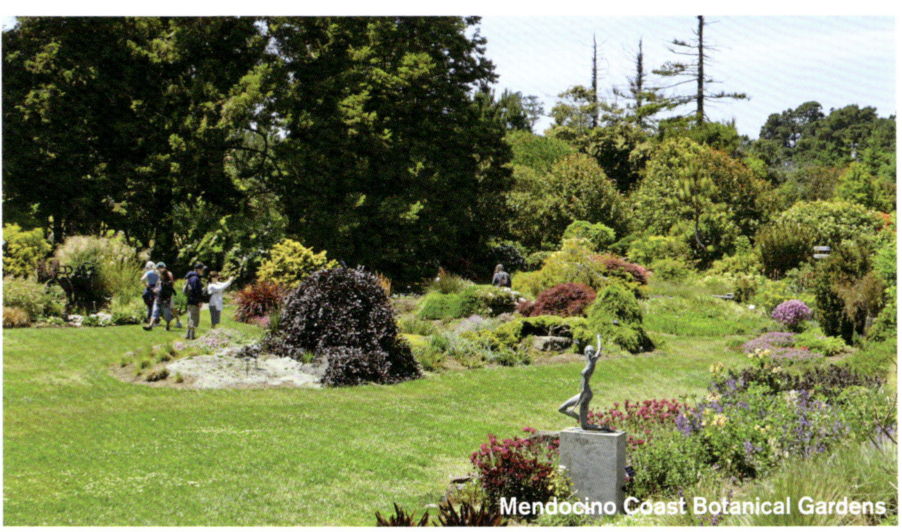

Mendocino Coast Botanical Gardens
Fort Bragg, California

Tucked between Highway One and the Pacific Ocean, this 47-acre garden was established in 1961 and features plants especially suited to the acidic, rocky soil and salt-laden winds of the California coastal climate. Plants on display include colorful flowers like roses, rhododendrons, magnolias, and begonias, as well as succulents, conifers, and heaths and heathers. The property's Dahlia Garden is one of the most sought-after locations for local photographers, who use the celebratory blooms as a dramatic backdrop in photos. There is also a vegetable garden and orchard on site, which supplies fresh produce to the property's popular garden café.

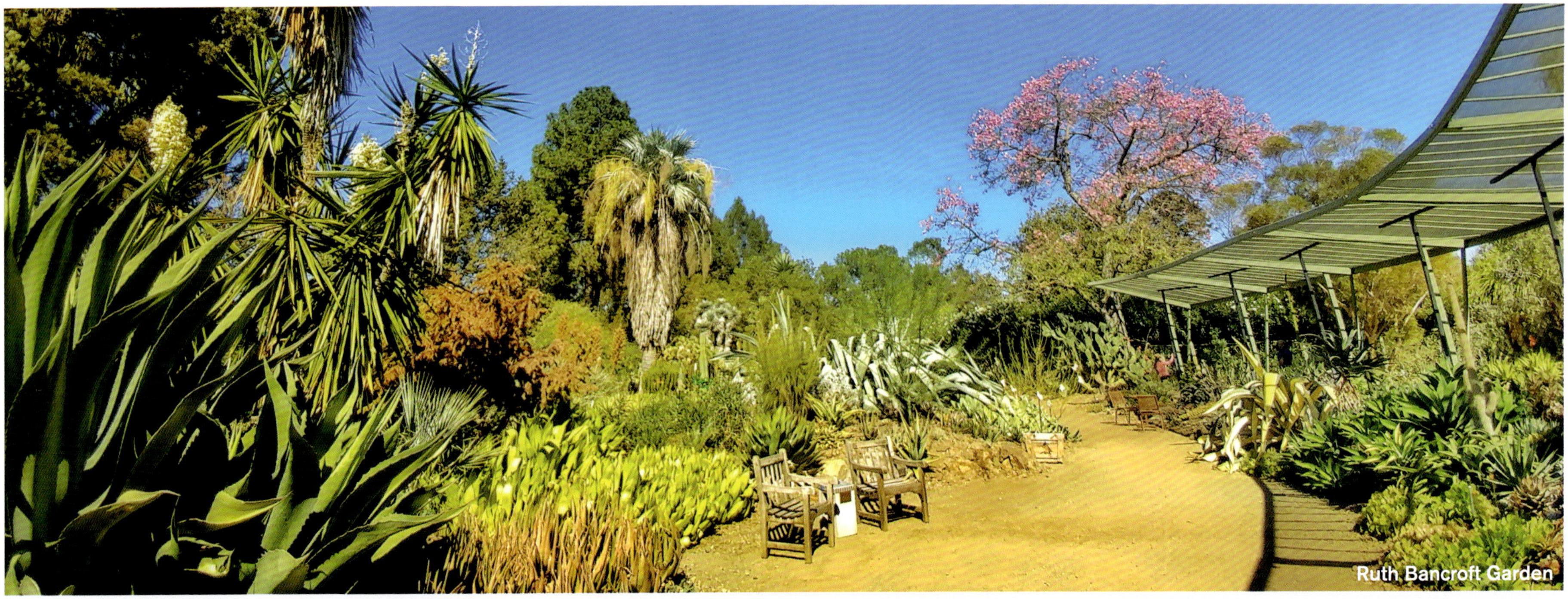

The garden contains drought-resistant plants native to California as well as Mexico, Chile, Australia, and South Africa.

Ruth Bancroft Garden
Walnut Creek, California

Ruth Bancroft was a California resident who was fascinated by nature, especially the wildflowers, succulents, and drought-resistant plants near her farm in Walnut Creek. Eventually, her love of "dry gardening"–gardening with a minimal amount of irrigation–led to the creation of this 3.5-acre property that contains more than 2,000 drought-resistant cacti, succulents, trees, and shrubs. With its agaves, aloes, yuccas, and so much more, the garden has been lauded by botanical organizations as an outstanding collection of xerophytes, or plants that can survive with little water, and is proof that greenery can thrive when local conditions are taken into consideration.

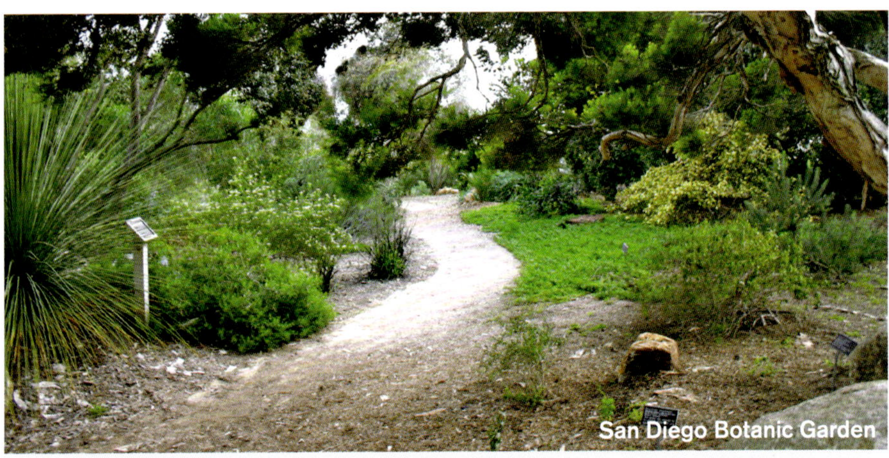

The site offers four miles of walking paths to explore.

San Diego Botanic Garden
Encinitas, California

This 37-acre property north of San Diego offers visitors a tranquil garden oasis and ocean views, with miles of trails and 29 themed gardens to explore. Several different microclimates are present within the region, providing the conditions for everything from lush tropical rainforest to dry desert. Highlights include the Native Plants and Native Peoples Trail, which features local plants and a replica of a Kumeyaay village, representing the earliest inhabitants of the area. The Subtropical Fruit Garden and Herb Garden showcase edible plants cultivated with water-conservation methods. And three Children's Gardens, including the largest on the West Coast, provide plenty of interactive fun for young guests.

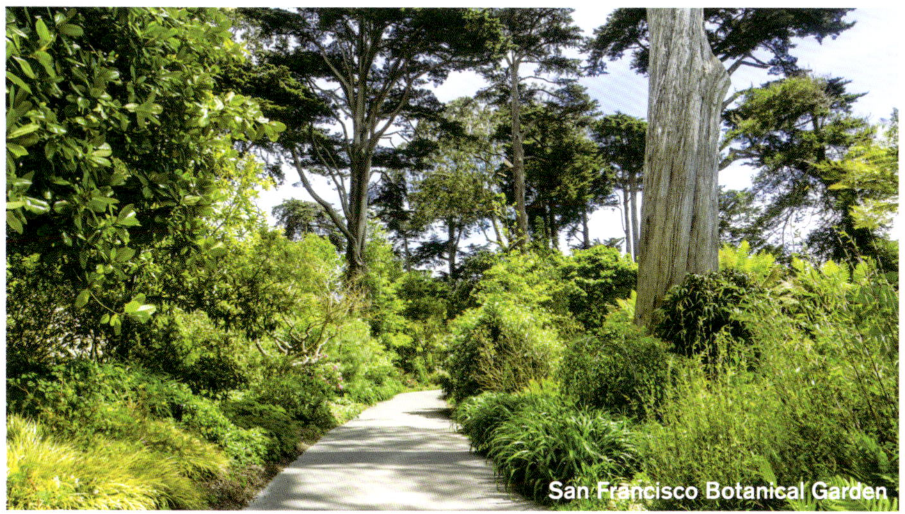

San Francisco Botanical Garden

San Francisco Botanical Garden
San Francisco, California

Part of the Gardens of Golden Gate Park, this arboretum covers 55 acres and features almost 9,000 plants from around the world, including Chile, Australia, and Asia. An Ancient Plant Garden displays "living fossils," while a Fragrance Garden delights the senses with vibrant color and scent. Conifers, succulents, and palm trees are scattered throughout the property.

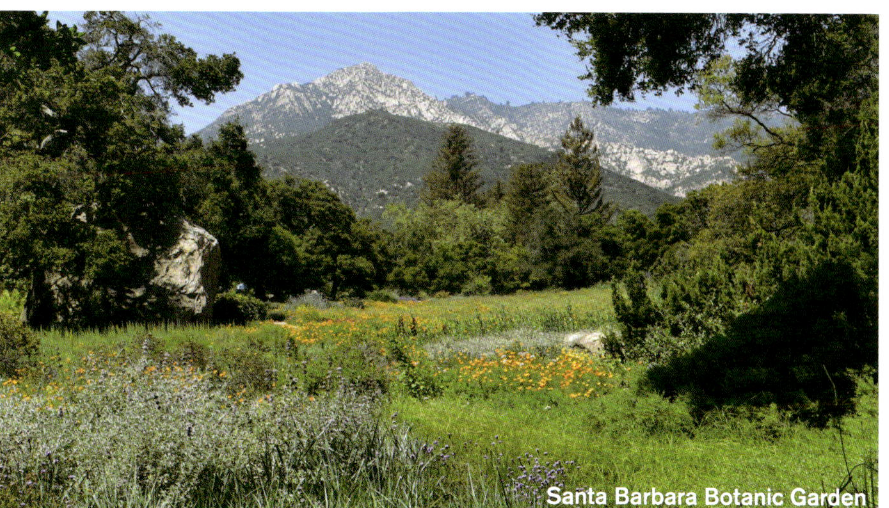

Santa Barbara Botanic Garden

Santa Barbara Botanic Garden
Santa Barbara, California

The goal of this 78-acre garden is to teach visitors about the importance of native plants and their connectivity to the well-being of our planet. Almost six miles of hiking trails lead guests through 11 ecosystems–including desert, meadow, and canyon–that display the diverse California flora found in each area.

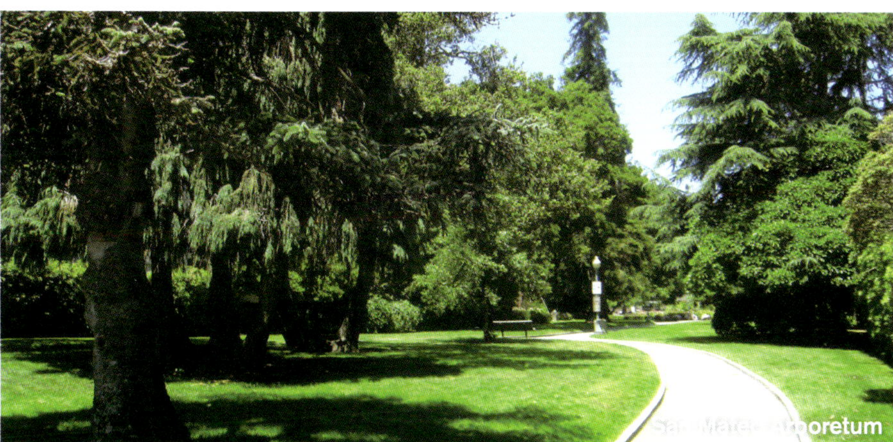

San Mateo Arboretum

San Mateo Arboretum
San Mateo, California

Located within San Mateo's Central Park, this natural botanical oasis features paths that wind through old stands of pine, oak, cedar, and redwood. The trees were planted more than 100 years ago by horticulturalist John Hays McLaren, who served as superintendent of San Francisco's Golden Gate Park for 53 years.

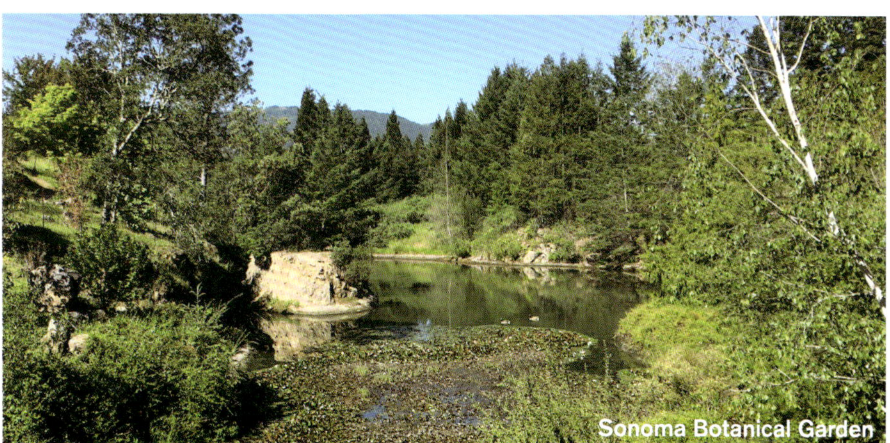

Sonoma Botanical Garden

Sonoma Botanical Garden
Glen Ellen, California

Showcasing both native California specimens and Asian plants, this botanical garden contains around 20,000 specimens representing close to 1,500 individual species. Collections include native and ancient conifers and a 13-acre legacy Cabernet Sauvignon vineyard, Sonoma's iconic wine grape. Also on display are Chinese maples and Asian roses, lilies, and magnolias.

South Coast Botanic Garden
Palos Verdes Estates, California

This 87-acre property has the unique distinction of being one of the world's first botanical gardens to be located over a sanitary landfill! Now, this beautiful garden, a living example of land reclamation, features 200,000 plants and trees from more than 2,500 different species. Some popular features include a Display Greenhouse containing tropical plants, Japanese and Mediterranean gardens, a native plant habitat, and a shady Banyan Grove.

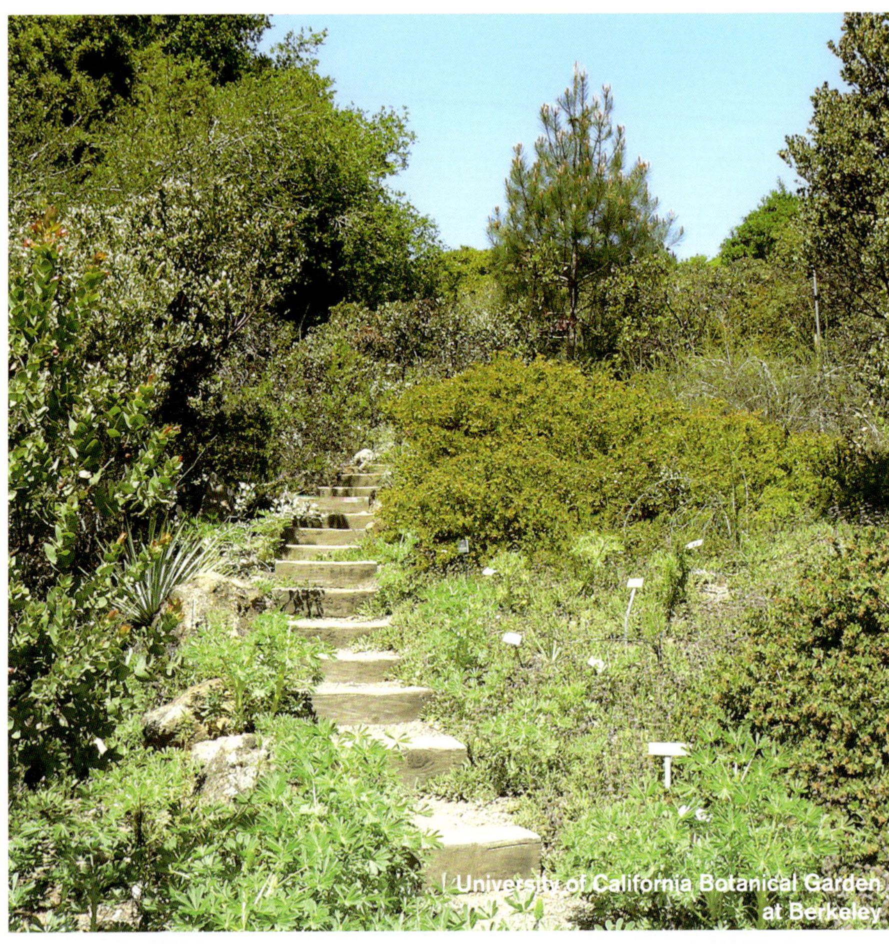
University of California Botanical Garden at Berkeley

The California chaparral section features dense thickets of shrubs and trees that have moisture-conserving thick leaves.

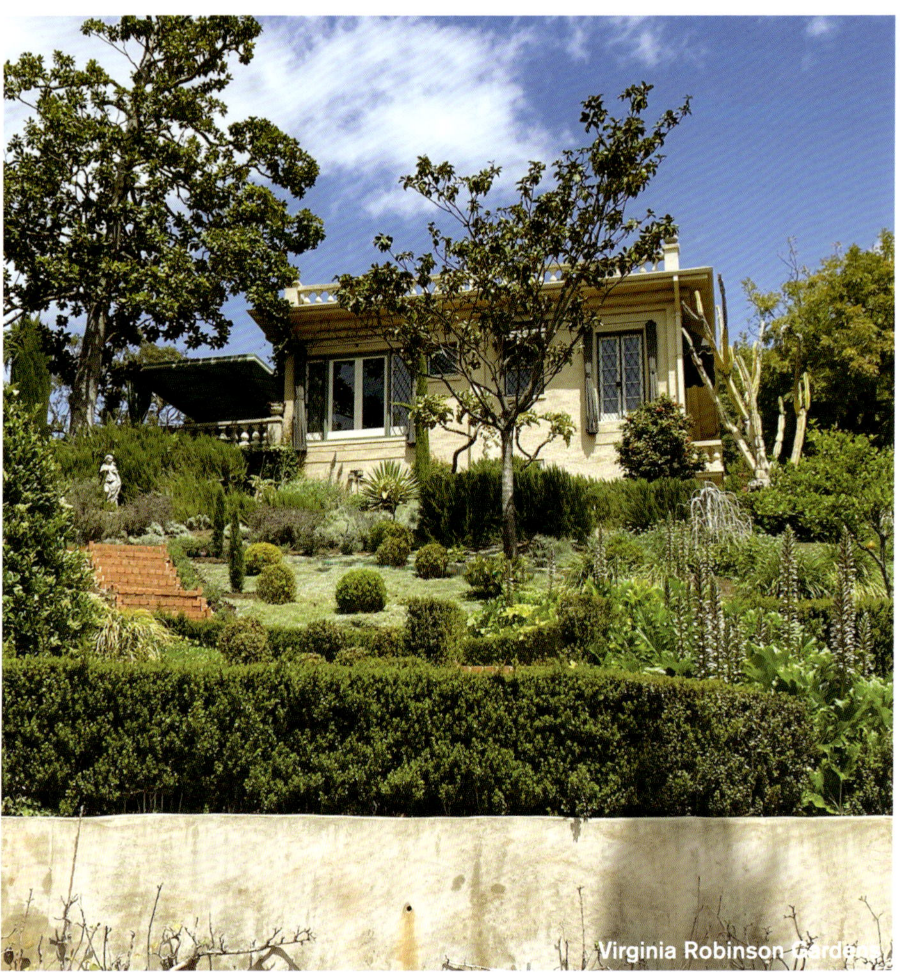
Virginia Robinson Gardens

The 6.2-acre grounds are filled with plants that were largely chosen by the Robinsons.

University of California Botanical Garden at Berkeley
Berkeley, California

Located within the University of California Berkeley campus, this 34-acre garden overlooking the San Francisco Bay is renowned for its diverse assortment of rare and endangered species. More than 10,000 plants from all over the world are on display, with four of the garden's collections–cycads, ferns, magnolias, and oaks–earning national recognition for horticultural practices by the North American Plant Collections Network.

Virginia Robinson Gardens
Beverley Hills, California

Once the private residence of Virginia Dryden Robinson and Harry Winchester Robinson, this historic mansion and botanical garden is considered the earliest estate in posh Beverley Hills. In addition to the 1911 Beaux Arts-style house, the gardens reflect vintage Hollywood glamour, with a Neoclassical Italianate terrace garden, a sprawling Great Lawn, and a rose garden featuring the Eiffel Tower rose, Virginia's favorite variety.

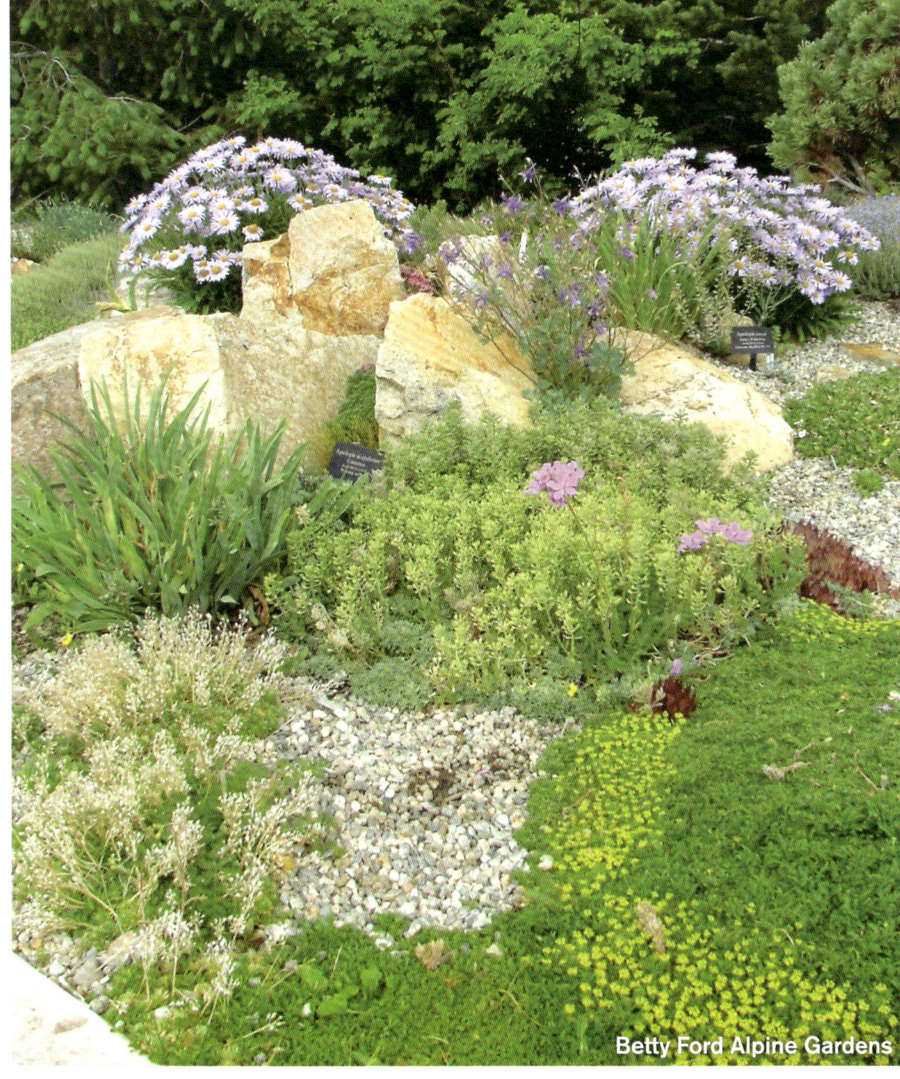

Over 500 varieties of wildflowers burst into bloom at various times in this alpine setting.

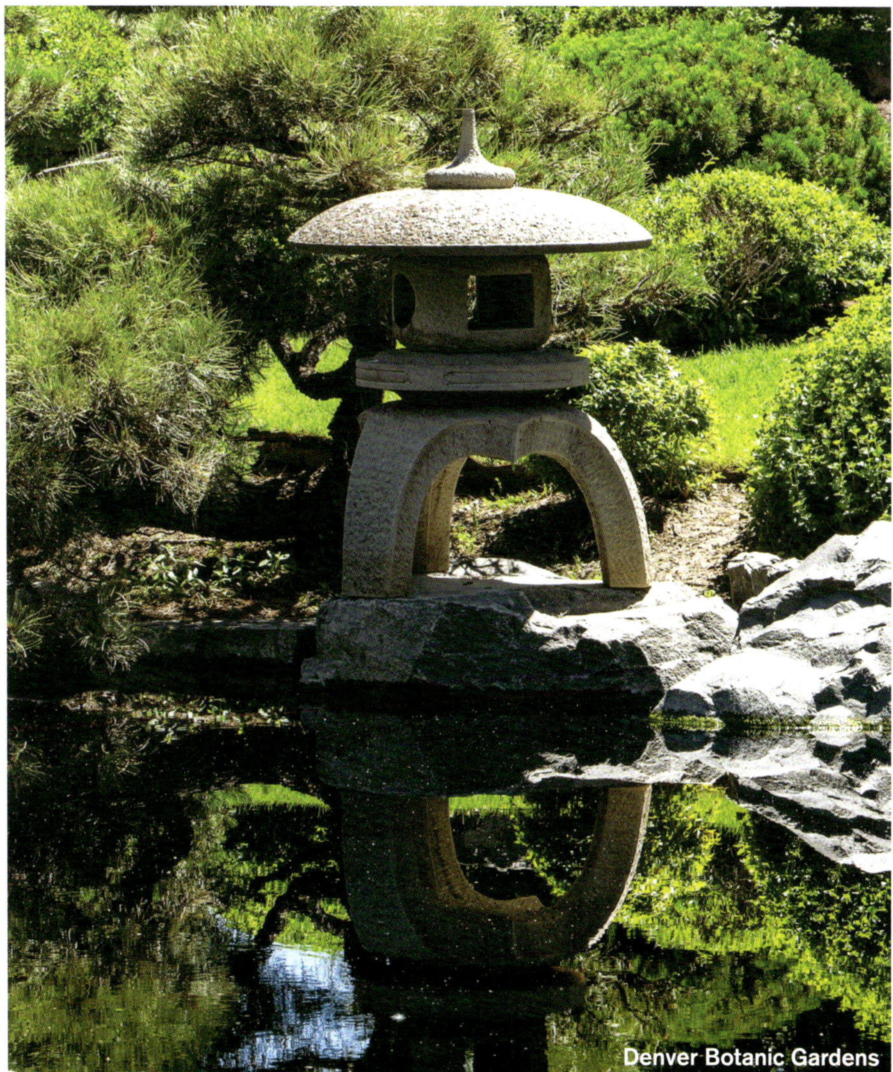

Ponds and other quiet, contemplative spots provide visitors with opportunities to stop and relax.

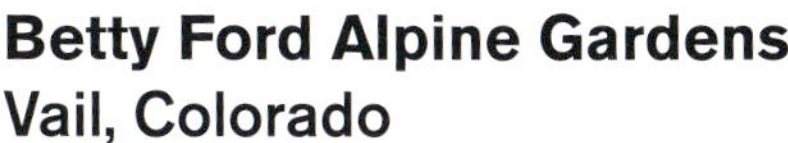

Betty Ford Alpine Gardens
Vail, Colorado

As the only botanical garden in North America to focus exclusively on the protection and conservation of alpine plant species, the Betty Ford Alpine Gardens is a unique destination for garden lovers. Located 8,200 feet above sea level in the Rocky Mountains, the stunning setting makes a perfect backdrop for the 2,000 varieties of plants on the property. Gardens include Colorado native plants such as larkspur, blue lupine, and white mariposa lilies, as well as species from alpine regions around the world, including the Drakensberg Mountains of South Africa and the Asian Himalayas. A visitor favorite is the Alpine Rock Garden, which features a 120-foot waterfall.

Denver Botanic Gardens
Denver, Colorado

The main location of this pair of botanic gardens sits on 24 acres just outside of downtown Denver and features a wide variety of plants from around the world. Some of the site's arid gardens showcase the natural beauty found in Colorado, while internationally inspired gardens house plants from Japan, China, and the tropics. The site also includes ornamental gardens bursting with color, cool shaded gardens, and water gardens with aquatic plants. A second location, near Littleton, is a 700-acre plant refuge and working farm. The site includes 2.5 miles of nature trails, numerous wildflower gardens, and historic buildings dating back to the 1800s.

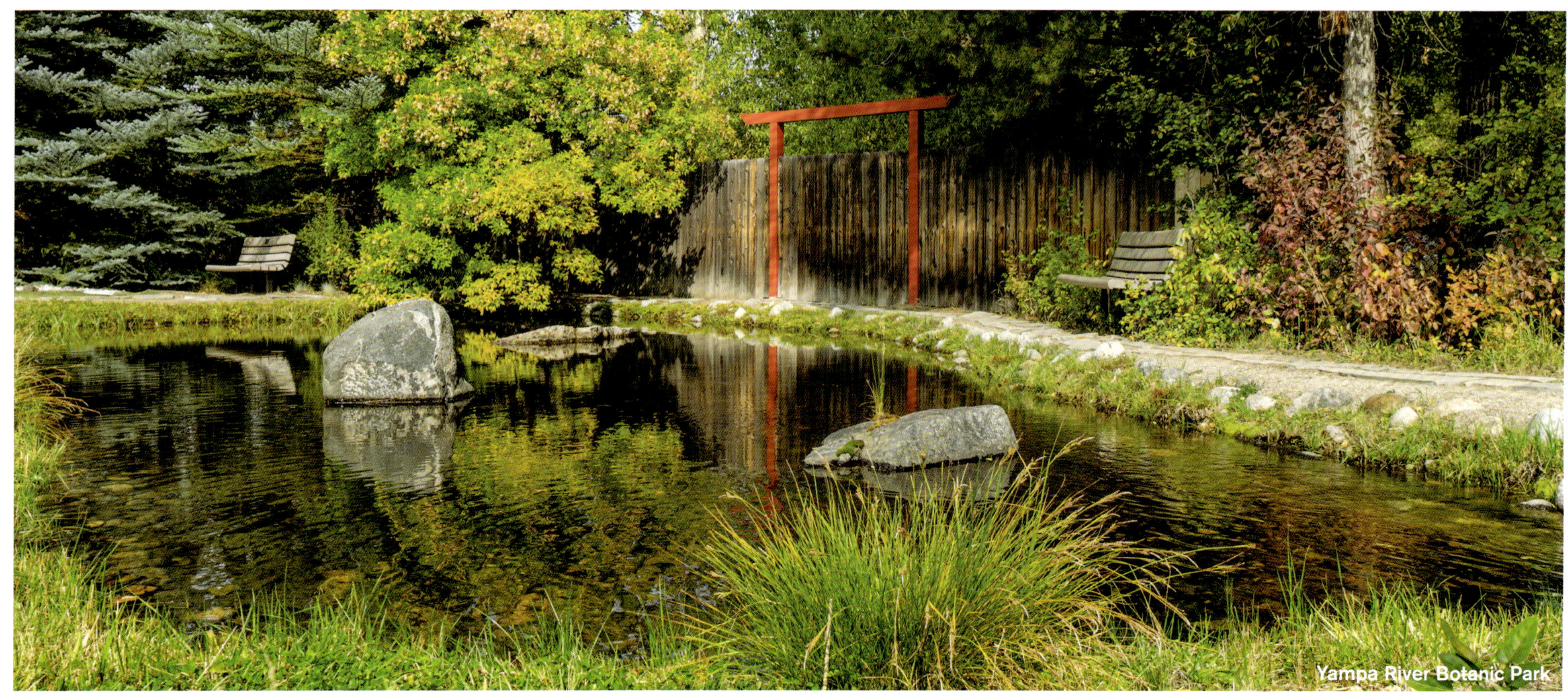
Yampa River Botanic Park

Yampa River Botanic Park
Steamboat Springs, Colorado

Established in 1995, the land on which this garden sits used to be a flat horse pasture. But over the decades, the six-acre property has transformed into a lush, green paradise housing 66 individual gardens. This is especially amazing considering that the park only gets about 60 days a year without a killing frost. Highlights include the Hummingbird and Butterfly Gardens, the Medicinal Garden, and Sascha's Rock Garden, which was the first garden to be created in the park and includes plants from Siberia, Japan, Mongolia, and Patagonia. There are both guided and unguided tours, with the Serenity Walk being one popular option. As a community hub, the park also features live music, free programs, and educational opportunities.

Worth Exploring in Colorado

The Gardens on Spring Creek
Fort Collins, Colorado

- This 12-acre site includes a Children's Garden and a half-acre lawn with event pavilion
- Famous for its tropical butterfly house

Montrose Botanic Gardens
Montrose, Colorado

- Features flora that thrives in the high desert
- The historic Homestead Garden recreates the landscape of early settlers

Western Colorado Botanical Gardens
Grand Junction, Colorado

- Gardens include a Cactus Garden, Japanese Garden, and Antique Rose Garden
- The Rainforest Garden houses tropical plants, koi fish, turtles, and butterflies

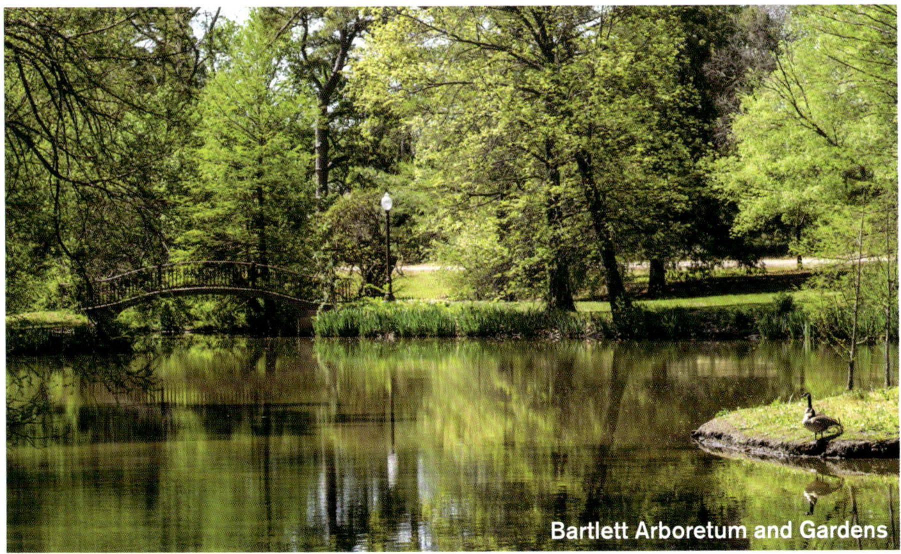
Bartlett Arboretum and Gardens

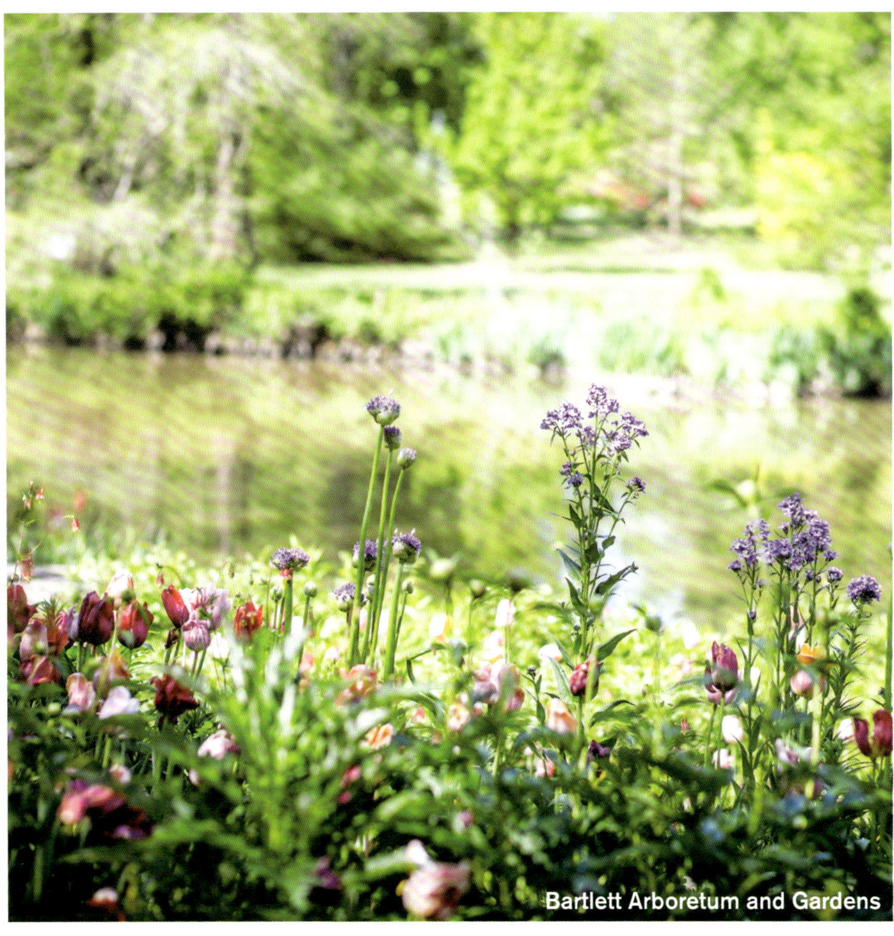
Bartlett Arboretum and Gardens

Bartlett Arboretum and Gardens
Stamford, Connecticut

Named after Francis A. Bartlett, founder of the F.A. Bartlett Tree Expert Company, this garden first opened to the public in 1966. As a notable dendrologist–an expert in the science and study of woody plants–Bartlett envisioned a garden where specimens were not only grown, but also studied and used for educational purposes. Today, 13 gardens span over 93 acres, showcasing the botanical gems Connecticut has to offer. Collections include a Conifer Garden, the Nut Tree Collection, a Fruit and Vegetable Garden, and an Herbarium with thousands of dried plants, seeds, flowers, and fruits from around the world.

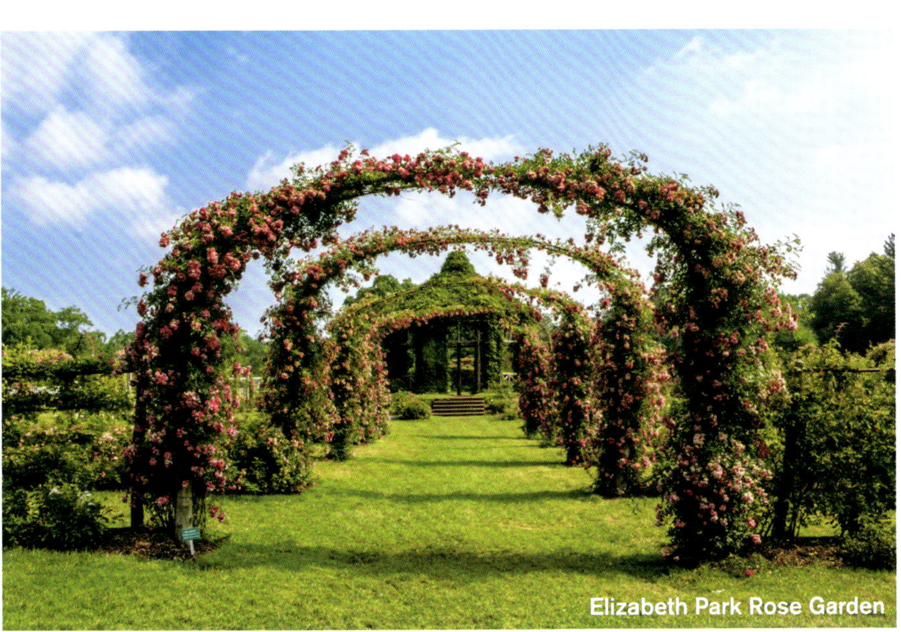
Elizabeth Park Rose Garden

Elizabeth Park Rose Garden
Hartford, Connecticut

Located within Hartford's Elizabeth Park are formal gardens, green spaces, walking trails, and historic greenhouses. The park itself spans 102 acres and is listed on the National Register of Historic Places. It is well-known locally for offering free concerts and events and being a fantastic recreational destination. But it is the property's Helen S Kaman Rose Garden, named for the park's first president, that makes this site world-famous. The garden was the first municipal rose garden in the United States, and is the third-largest rose garden in the country. The collection includes more than 15,000 rose bushes comprised of 800 varieties, which bloom throughout the summer.

Worth Exploring in Connecticut

Bellamy-Ferriday House and Garden
Bethlehem, Connecticut

- Property contains an eighteenth-century house surrounded by manicured gardens
- Roses, peonies, and 15 varieties of lilac bloom here

Butler-McCook House and Garden
Hartford, Connecticut

- The oldest house in Hartford, built in 1782
- A restored Victorian ornamental garden is located behind the house

Edgerton Park
New Haven, Connecticut

- A 20-acre park also known as the Frederick F. Brewster Estate
- Features sprawling gardens and original estate buildings, including greenhouses

Florence Griswold Museum Gardens
Old Lyme, Connecticut

- Historic gardens surrounding a house that contains an art gallery
- The 12-acre site contains flowers, herbs, vegetables, and other plants

Glebe House and Gertrude Jekyll Garden
Woodbury, Connecticut

- Dating back to about 1740, the house is one of the earliest historic house museums in the U.S.
- The garden is named for horticulturalist and writer Gertrude Jekyll

Harkness Memorial State Park
Waterford, Connecticut

- 304 acres featuring a Renaissance Revival mansion, formal gardens, and greenhouse
- Each of the six gardens has its own theme

Hollister House
Washington, Connecticut

- An English-style garden filled with colorful flowers, blooming from April to October
- The property's Georgian-style home was built in 1770

Marsh Botanical Garden
New Haven, Connecticut

- Located on the campus of Yale University
- Established in 1899 by Othniel Charles Marsh, an alumnus who bequeathed his estate and plants to Yale

Pardee Rose Garden
Hamden, Connecticut

- Contains annuals, perennials, herbs, and more than 50 varieties of roses
- A two-acre garden that was created in 1922

Wickham Park
Manchester, Connecticut

- Spans 280 acres of gardens, woodlands, ponds, and fields
- Highlights include an English Garden, a Lotus Garden, and a Sensory Garden

Glebe House and Gertrude Jekyll Garden

The Gertrude Jekyll Garden was commissioned to enhance the grounds around the Glebe House.

Mt. Cuba Center
Hockessin, Delaware

The plant collections found on the rolling hills of this property focus on native species of eastern North America. More than 500 acres of natural land surrounds the garden, which is well known for its stunning displays of wildflowers. Highlights include the colorful Formal Gardens and the meandering Dogwood Path.

Delaware Center for Horticulture
Wilmington, Delaware

With a mission focused on bringing green spaces and fresh produce to urban areas, the Delaware Center for Horticulture is a true oasis in the middle of the city of Wilmington. Along with creating the first urban farm in the city, the center supports community gardens and urban forests. In fact, the center has planted more than 18,500 trees in the area and maintains 22 public landscapes in Wilmington. Their urban farm donates fresh fruits and vegetables to those facing food insecurity, while the center's return-to-work program provides landscaping training to adults returning to employment after incarceration or substance use recovery.

Worth Exploring in Delaware

Delaware Botanic Gardens at Pepper Creek
Dagsboro, Delaware

- Gardens sit on a mix of plateau, woodlands, and 1,000 feet of tidal waterfront
- Spans 37 acres and features ADA compliant trails for accessibility

Marian Coffin Gardens
Wilmington, Delaware

- Features early twentieth-century gardens of landscape architect Marian Coffin
- Statues, paved walkways, marble stairs, and a reflecting pond have also been restored

Mill Pond Garden
Lewes, Delaware

- Filled with native plants that attract birds, pollinators, and wildlife
- A member of the National Wildlife Federation and a Certified Wildlife Habitat

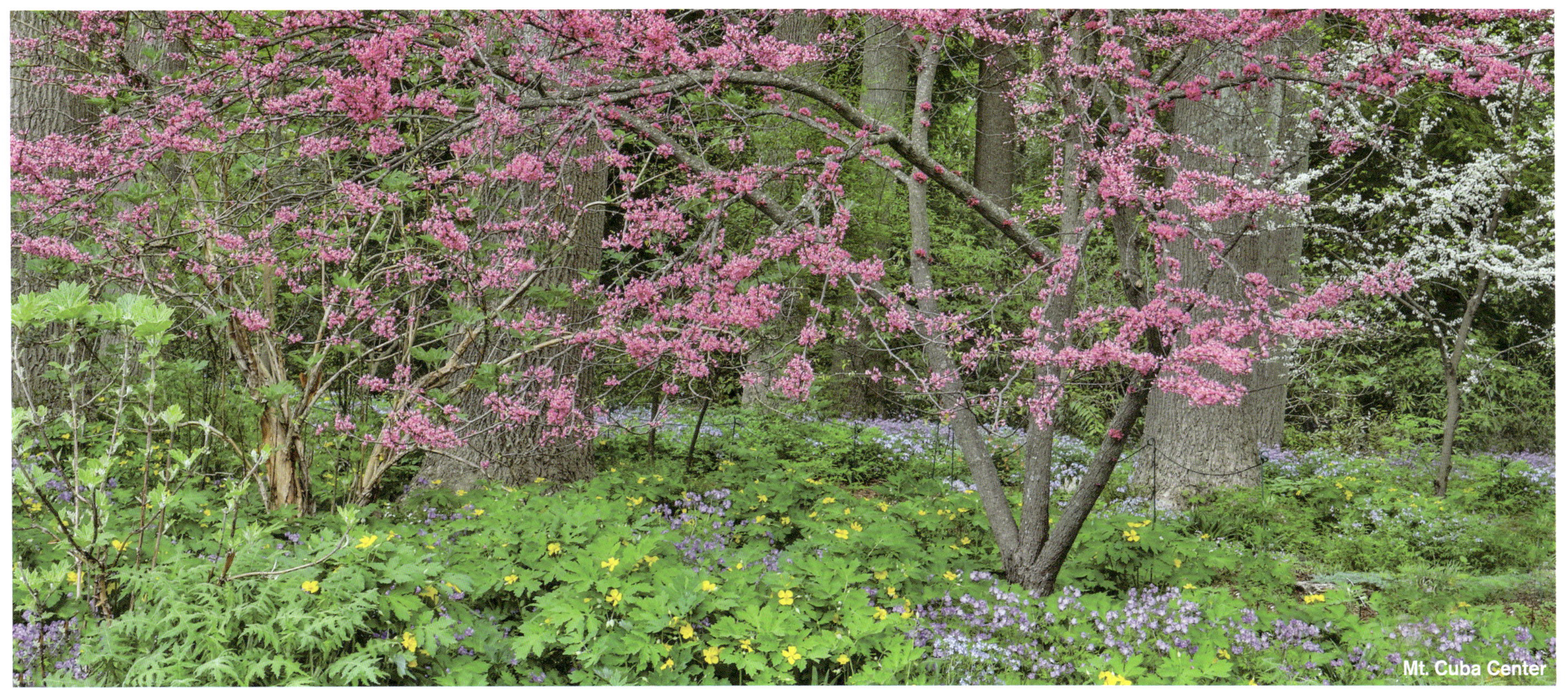
Mt. Cuba Center

Redbud trees bloom in the spring at Mt. Cuba Center.

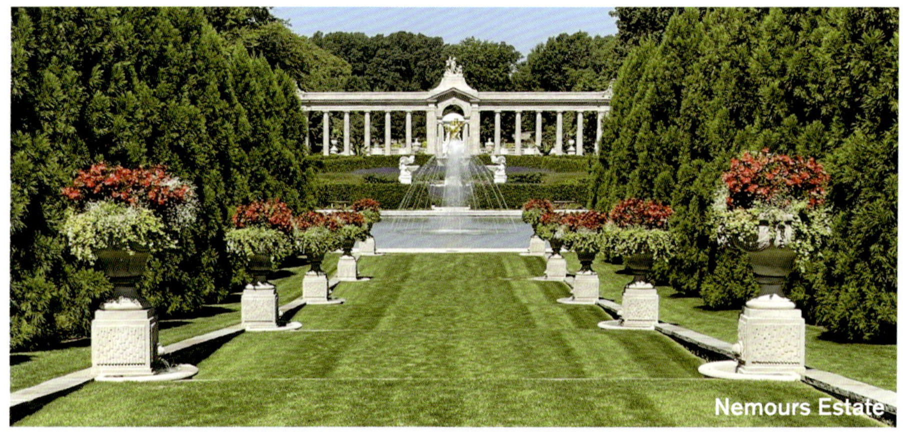

A perfectly manicured vista of lawn ends in a reflecting pool and colonnade.

University of Delaware Botanic Gardens
Newark, Delaware

These gardens are not just stunning to view–they're also used as a living laboratory for undergraduates and graduates studying horticulture, plant science, entomology, and landscape design. Collections include the Emily Clark Garden, featuring conifers and evergreens, and the Trial Garden, displaying award-winning annuals and tropical plants.

Zwaanendael Park and Herb Garden
Lewes, Delaware

This property, named after the first European settlement in Delaware, is known locally as "Z Park." It contains a museum, a central fountain, and a colorful garden, as well as the Fisher-Martin Herb Garden, an authentic eighteenth-century herb garden planted with herbs that would have been used by colonial housewives.

Nemours Estate
Wilmington, Delaware

Named after a town in France, this estate contains a French neoclassical mansion and French formal gardens on 200 sprawling acres. The *jardin à la française* is the largest such garden in North America, with a Boxwood Garden, Maze Garden, Sunken Gardens and more beautiful landscaping patterned after the gardens of Versailles.

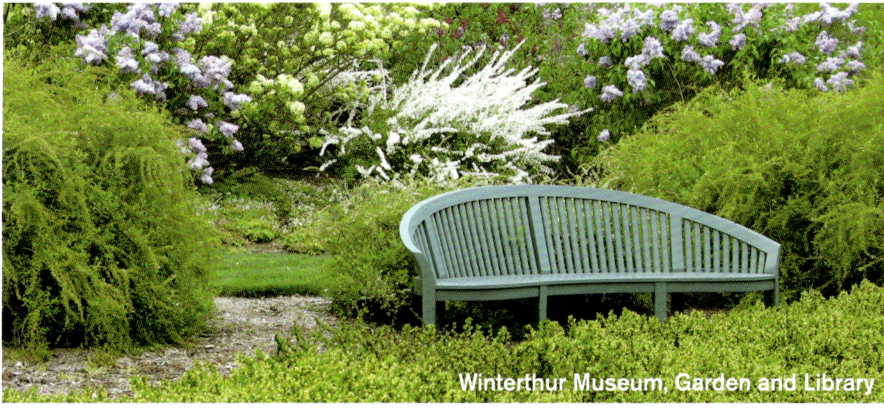

The curving paths of the garden provide quiet nooks and endless views. The original designer of the garden, Henry Francis du Pont, followed the contours of the landscape when planning its features.

Winterthur Museum, Garden and Library
Winterthur, Delaware

Americana is on proud display within the 175-room house on this property, which contains nearly 90,000 objects made or used in America, some dating back to 1640. A thousand acres of protected woodlands and meadows surround the house, and a 60-acre garden showcases plants, trees, and flowers that provide year-round color.

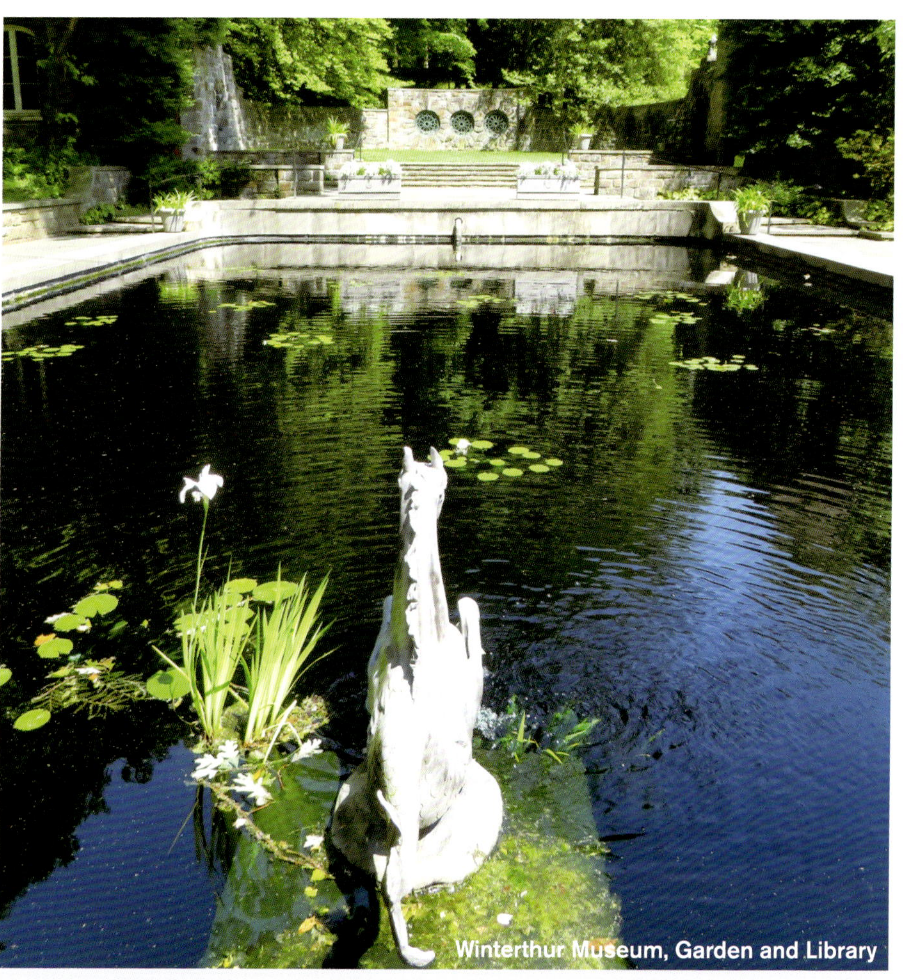

A seahorse statue stands guard over the reflection pool outside the museum.

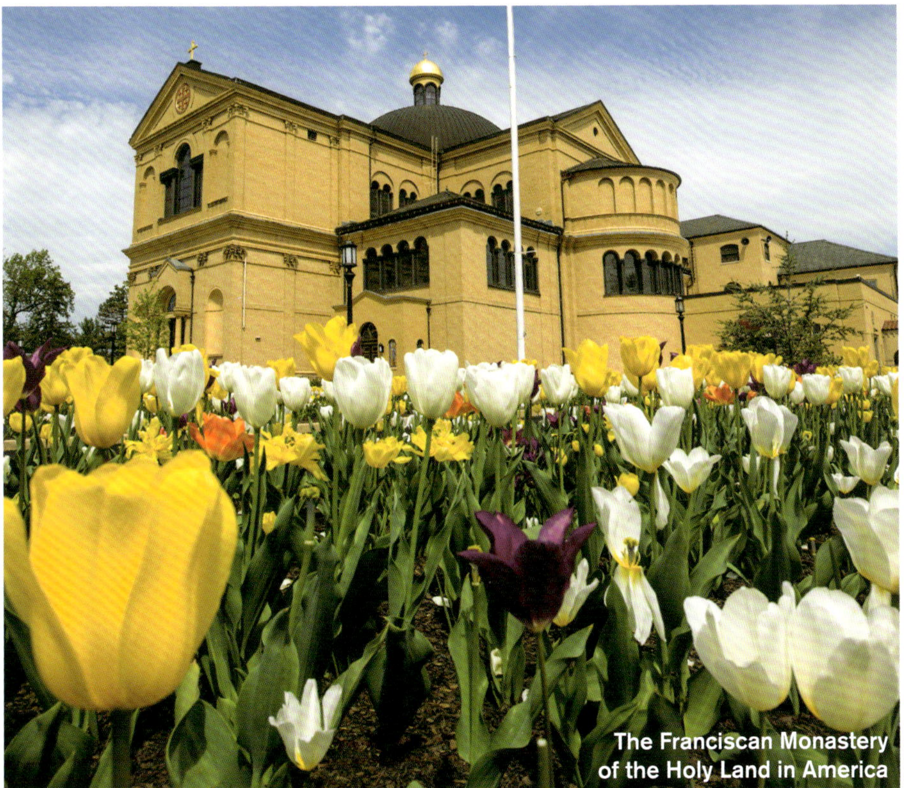

Tulips brighten the grounds of the monastery every spring.

Worth Exploring in D.C.

American University Arboretum and Gardens
Washington, D.C.

- Gardens prominently feature tulips and daffodils, as well as black-eyed Susans and coneflowers
- Tree species in the arboretum include Korean cherry, scarlet oak, and American papaw

Tudor Place
Washington, D.C.

- Housed six generations of Martha Washington's descendants, from 1805 to 1983
- Self-guided tours of the house and 5.5-acre garden are available on weekends

The Franciscan Monastery of the Holy Land in America
Washington, D.C.

An oasis of tranquility in the middle of the nation's bustling capital city, this Franciscan Monastery is often overlooked by tourists. But this 42-acre property, with its beautiful church and century-old garden, is worth a visit. The garden contains a path that winds past roses and native plants, and volunteers are welcome in the vegetable garden.

Hillwood Estate, Museum and Gardens
Washington, D.C.

Once the home of businesswoman and philanthropist Marjorie Merriweather Post, the museum at the Hillwood Estate contains more than 17,000 pieces of art and valuable objects, including two Fabergé eggs. The 25-acre garden was first designed in 1926. The grounds are maintained to ensure flowers, including an impressive collection of orchids, are always blooming, even in winter.

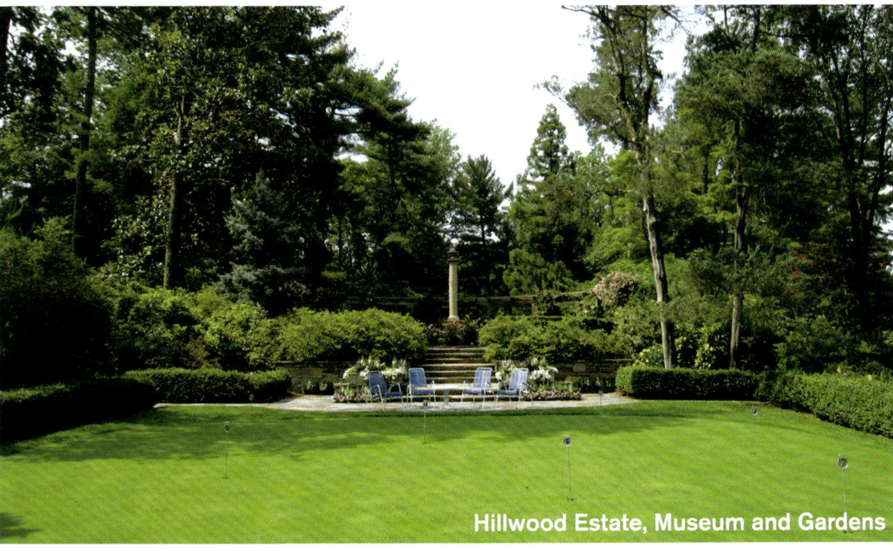

Along with features like a French parterre, rose garden, and Japanese garden, the grounds of Hillwood include a putting green (seen here).

United States National Arboretum
Washington, D.C.

Situated on 451 acres northeast of the Capitol building, the United States National Arboretum is used by the USDA for botanical research on trees, shrubs, grass turf, and ornamental plants. But it also welcomes more than 700,000 visitors every year who come to enjoy the arboretum's many display gardens and collections.

The property was first established in 1927, when President Calvin Coolidge signed the National Arboretum Act into law. It was merged into the USDA's Agriculture Research Service in 1953. Since then, researchers at the Arboretum have developed many new techniques and technologies for the floral and nursery industries, resulting in nine patents and several new biopesticides, which meet the EPA's ecological standards. The gardens have grown from those used merely for research to entire collections of plant groups.

Highlights include the National Bonsai and Penjing Museum, the world's first museum dedicated to the art of bonsai, and the National Herb Garden, which showcases herbs from around the world in themed gardens. Also popular is the arboretum's Azalea Collection, which blooms by the thousands every spring. But perhaps the most notable features on the property are the two weeping Japanese cherry trees, planted in the 1950s, that stand proudly just outside the Herb Garden.

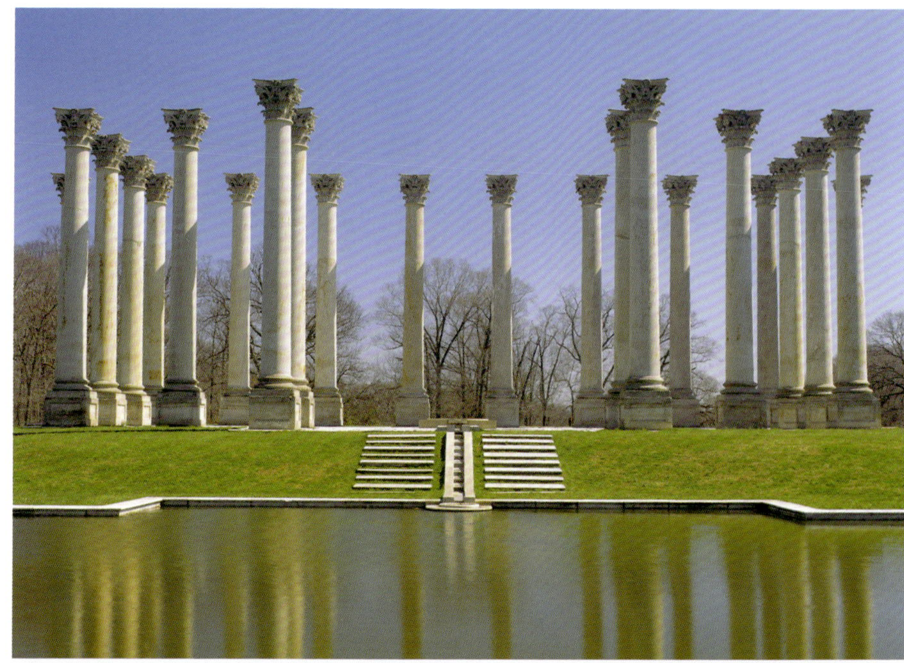

The National Capitol Columns consist of 22 Corinthian columns that were once part of the U.S. Capitol.

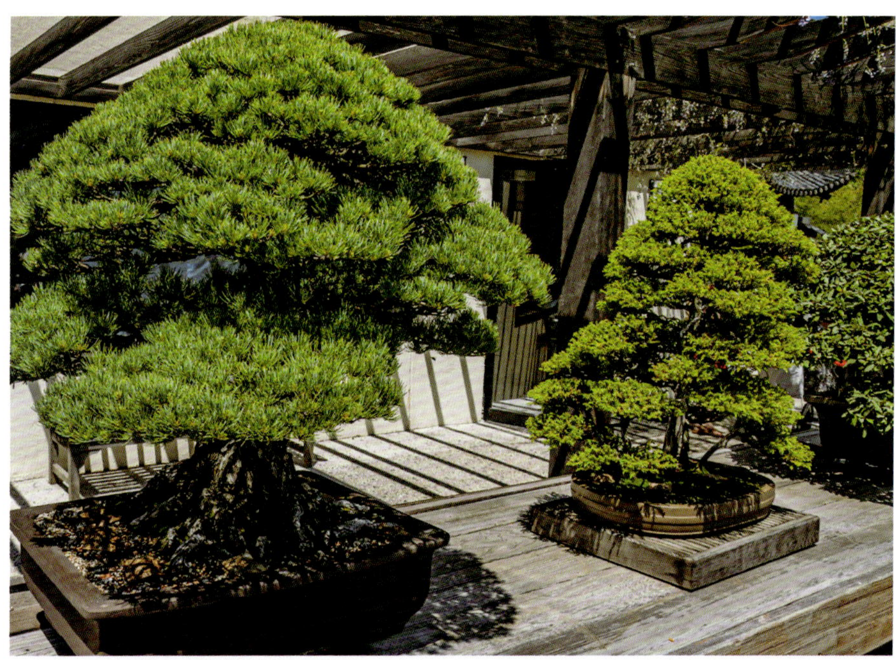

The museum's collection of bonsai trees now numbers over 300 specimens.

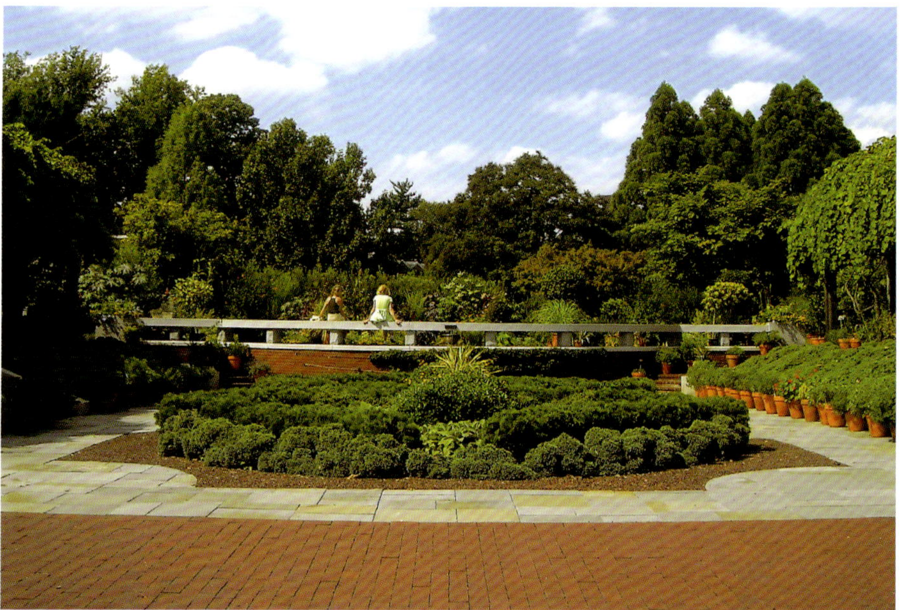

The National Herb Garden was dedicated in 1980. It is composed of herbal plants from around the world, organized into theme gardens, and was created for education and aesthetic enjoyment.

Worth Exploring in Florida

Arboretum of the University of Central Florida
Orlando, Florida

- The university encourages local volunteering, offering programs in their popular community garden
- Focused on sustaining and building pollinator populations, cultivating plants that attract bees and hummingbirds

Deerfield Beach Arboretum
Deerfield Beach, Florida

- Founded in 1995 with only 22 trees and palms
- Covers nine acres and features 325 species of palms, tropical fruit trees, bamboos, and flowering trees

Edison and Ford Winter Estates
Fort Myers, Florida

- Historic homes, laboratories, and grounds once used by Thomas Edison and Henry Ford
- The gardens contain 400 plant species from six continents

Flamingo Gardens
Davie, Florida

- A 60-acre botanical garden and wildlife sanctuary with one of the largest bird collections in the U.S.
- Showcases more than 3,000 species of tropical and subtropical plants

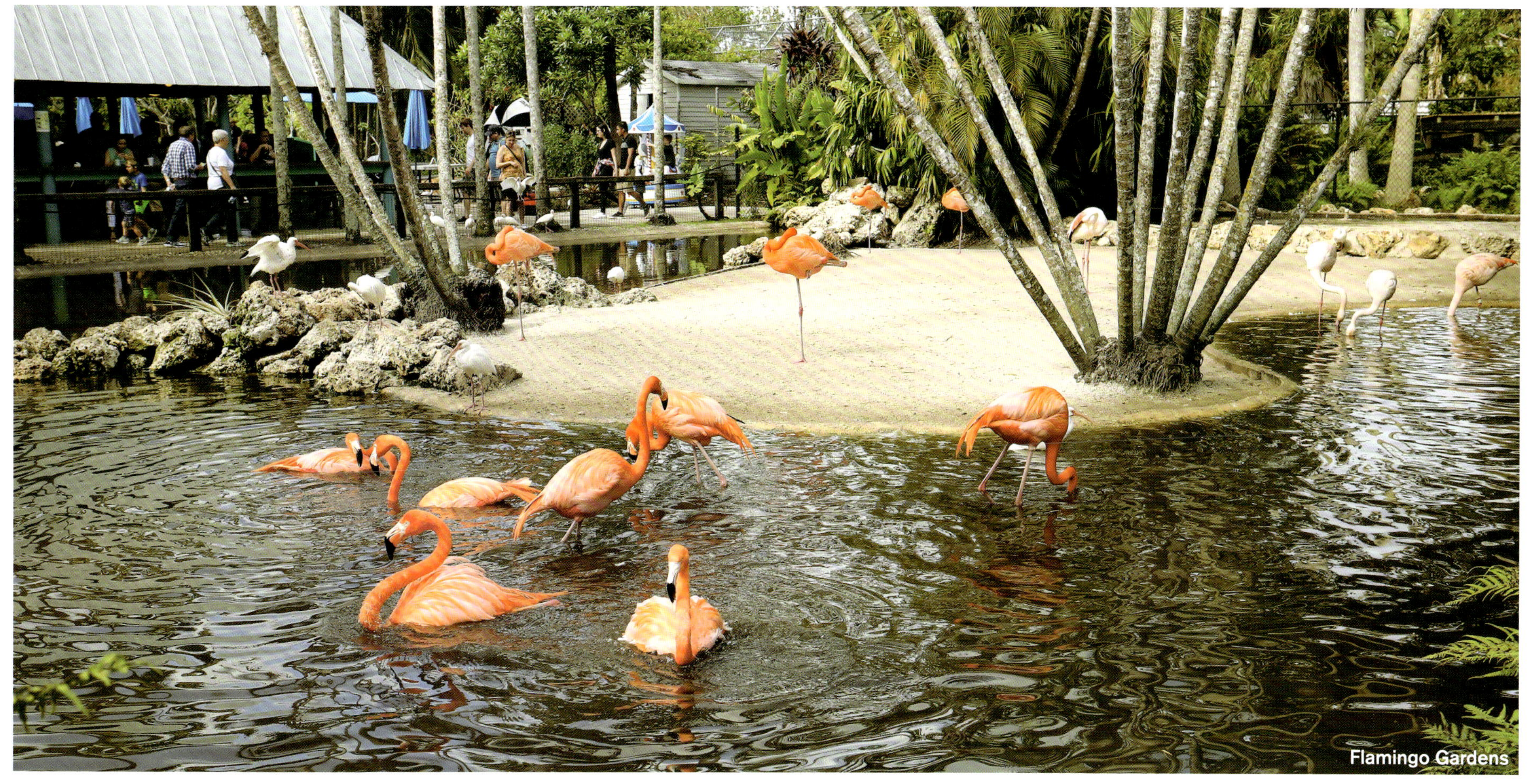

Flamingo Gardens

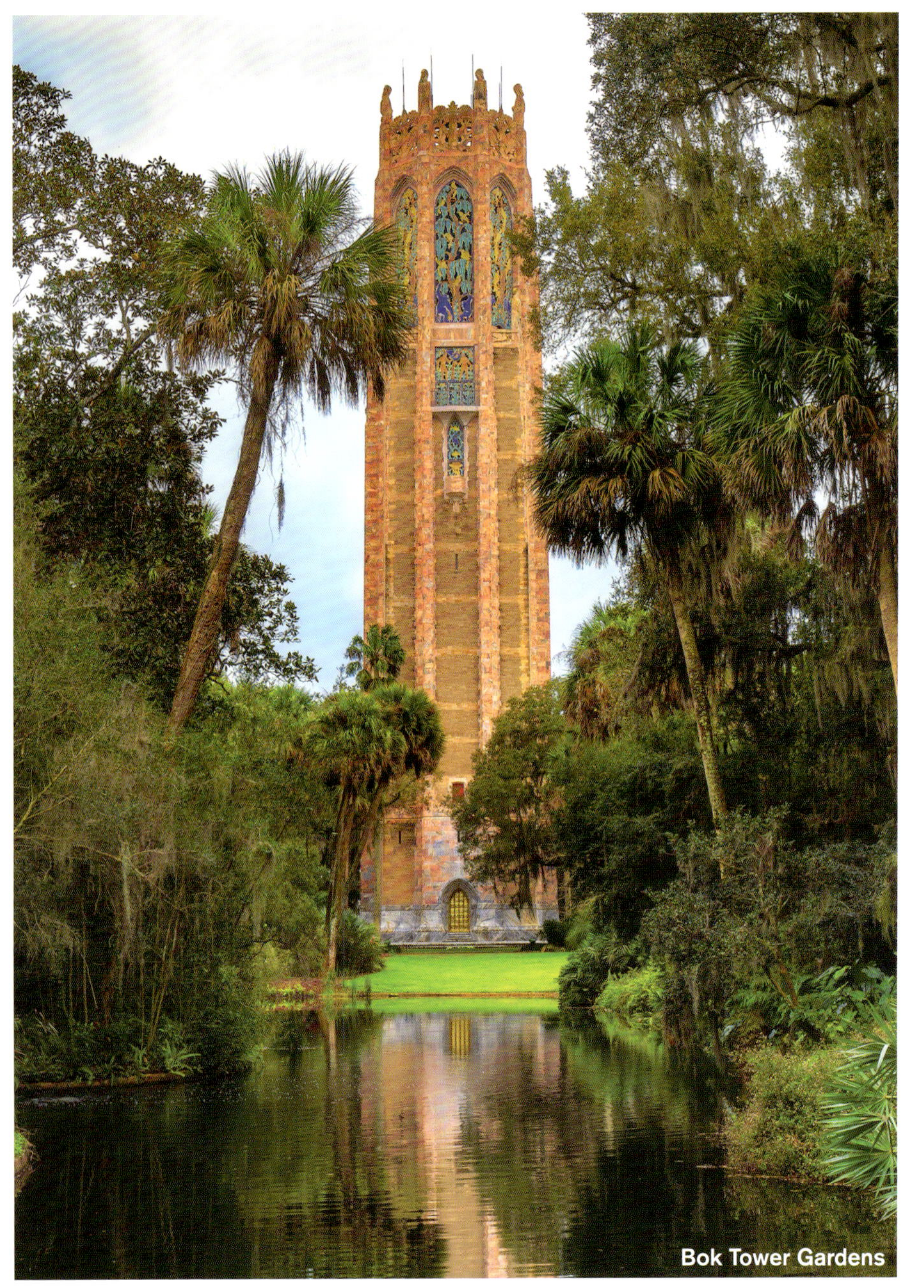
Bok Tower Gardens

Bok Tower Gardens
Lake Wales, Florida

This 250-acre contemplative garden and bird sanctuary was created by Pulitzer Prize-winning author Edward Bok in the 1920s. The garden's signature feature is its 60-bell Singing Tower. Highlights include the Olmsted Gardens (the work of famed landscape architect Frederick Law Olmsted Jr.), Hammock Hollow Children's Garden, the Wild Garden, Pine Ridge Nature Preserve, as well as several miles of trails.

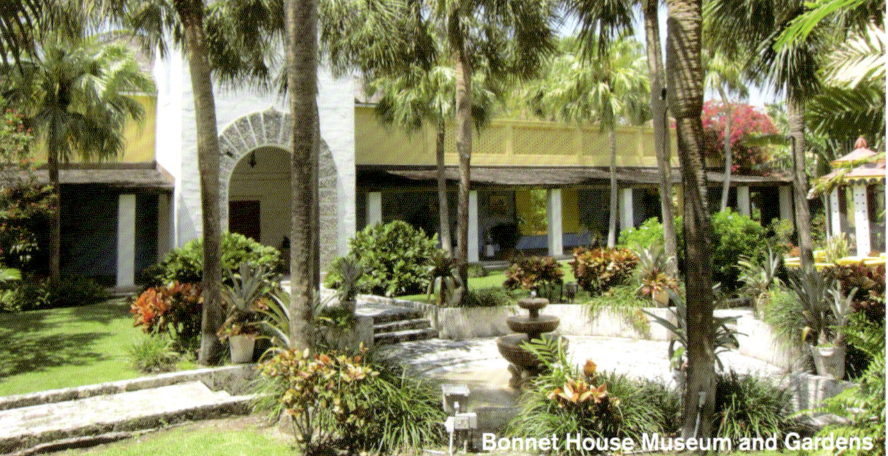
Bonnet House Museum and Gardens

Bonnet House Museum and Gardens
Fort Lauderdale, Florida

Dating back to 1920, and situated on the former estate of artist Frederic Clay Bartlett, this 35-acre property includes original buildings, 100 feet of beach, and several discrete ecosystems, including dunes, maritime forest, and mangrove wetlands. The grounds are important for preserving one of the last existing South Florida native barrier island habitats. There is also a Desert Garden, a hibiscus garden, and a courtyard featuring tropical vegetation.

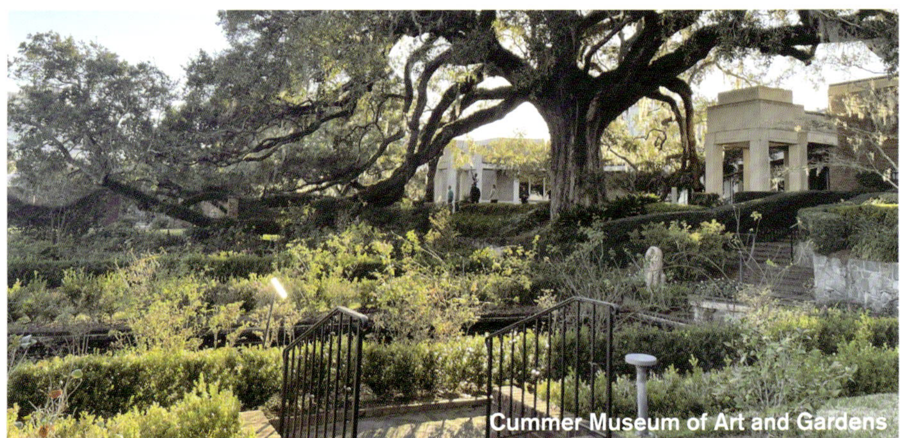
Cummer Museum of Art and Gardens

Cummer Museum of Art and Gardens
Jacksonville, Florida

Idyllically resting on the banks of the St. Johns River, this collection of unique gardens has a history stretching back more than 100 years. Though less than two acres in size, the gardens include the Sculpture Garden, Italian Garden, English Garden, and Olmsted Garden. They are made up of native Florida plants and trees, reflecting pools, fountains, and artwork.

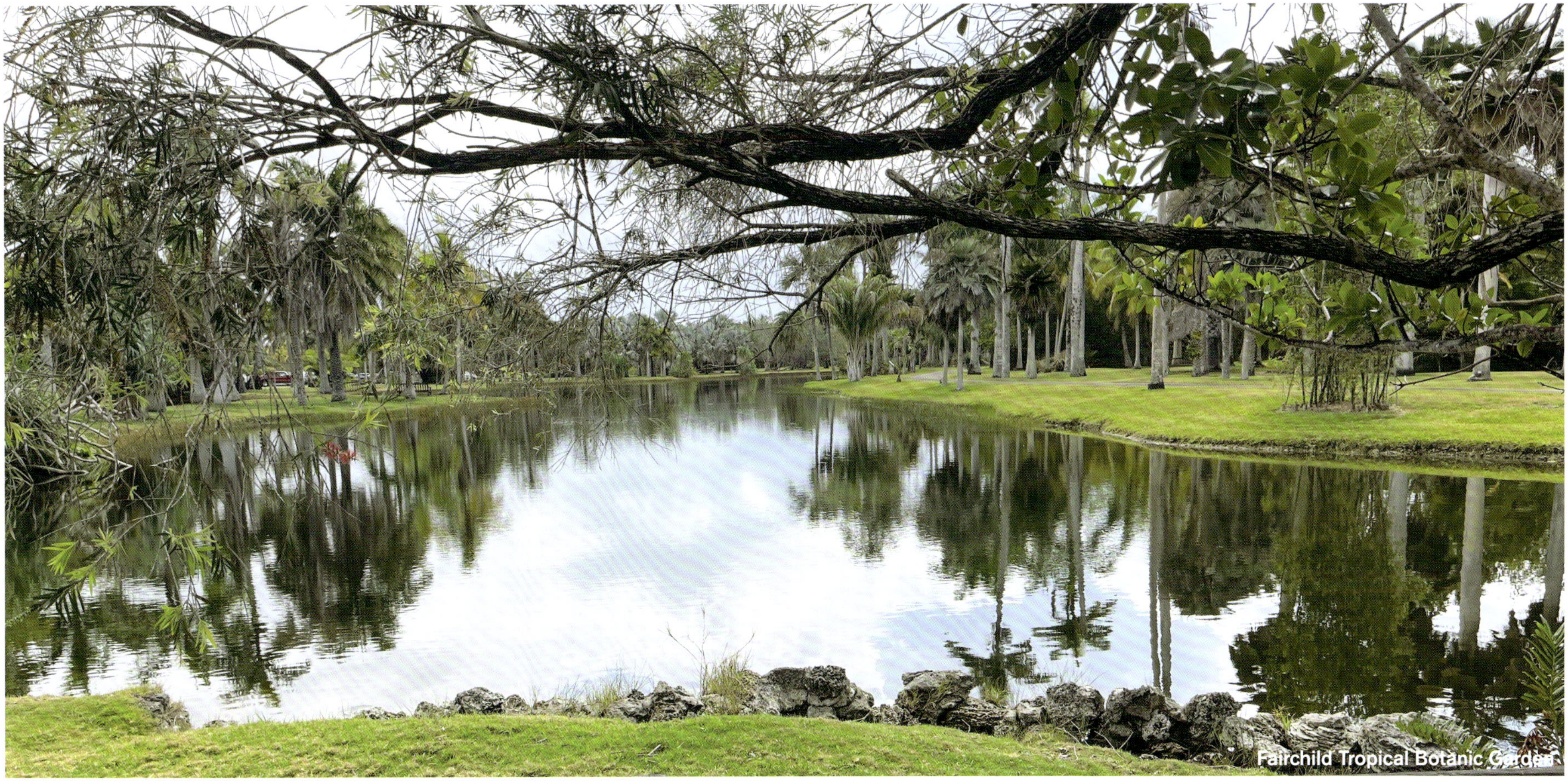

The grounds feature plenty of trails and vistas to stroll through and enjoy. Walking tours are led by well-informed volunteers.

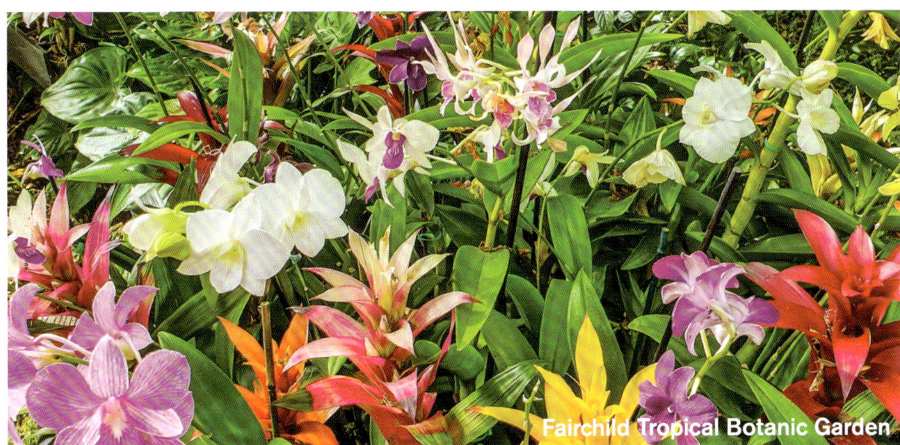

Visitors will discover a vast collection of flowering plants (more than 700 species) and more than 3,400 species of tropical plants in total.

Fairchild Tropical Botanic Garden
Coral Gables, Florida

Fairchild Tropical Botanic Garden was opened to the public in 1938. The 83-acre grounds feature extensive collections of rare tropical plants. The garden takes its name from the famous plant explorer, David Fairchild. He was renowned for traveling the world in search of new plants to bring back to the United States. Many of the plants growing on this site were collected by Fairchild, including a giant African baobab tree. Today the organization that runs the gardens also operates a museum, a learning center, and a conservation research facility.

The collection of plants here is incredibly rich and includes bromeliads, palms, cycads, orchids, bamboo, flowering vines, and exotic fruits. There is both an indoor butterfly house and outdoor butterfly garden. There is even a miniature rainforest, complete with waterfalls, cascades, and a misting system. Frequent art installations dot the outdoor areas.

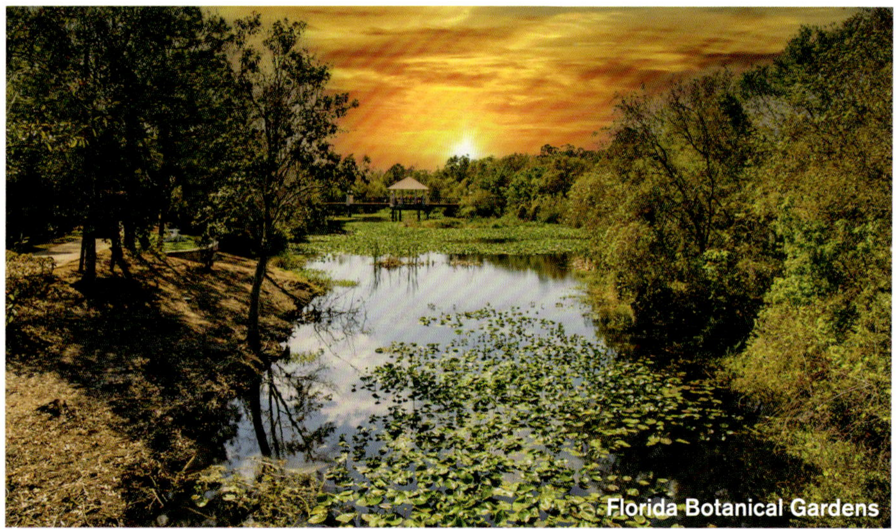

Elevated walks lead past lily pad-filled aquatic sections and lush Florida landscapes.

Florida Botanical Gardens
Largo, Florida

This garden, which spans more than 100 acres, is divided into 26 different sections that showcase beautiful botanical themes. Popular areas include the Herb Garden, Rose Garden, and Tropical Fruit Garden, as well as the Wedding Garden (also known as the Celebration Garden), which offers a lush backdrop for celebratory events. The Butterfly Garden features the colorful insects all year round, a benefit of the warm Florida climate.

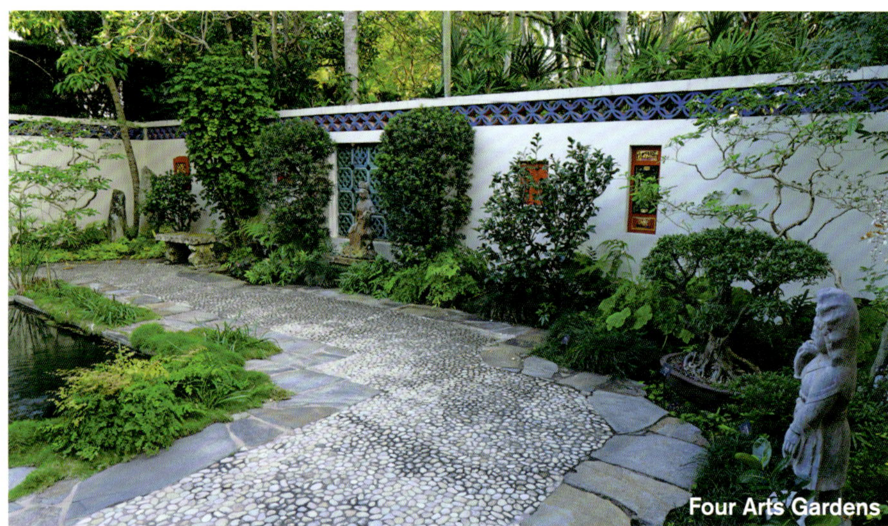

The garden features a small Chinese garden with a square water lily pool and carefully manicured surrounding vegetation.

Four Arts Gardens
Palm Beach, Florida

Maintained by the Palm Beach Garden Club, this garden is owned by the Society of the Four Arts, a nonprofit organization that also manages art galleries and libraries. The green oasis features themed gardens that teach visitors about South Florida's diverse plant life, including a Palm Garden, Formal Garden, and Tropical Garden. The property also contains the 2.2-acre Philip Hulitar Sculpture Garden, which was designed by Hulitar in 1979.

Fruit and Spice Park

This unique park offers both a variety of views and a variety of flavors!

Fruit and Spice Park
Homestead, Florida

As its name suggests, this unique park is known for its tropical fruits, spices, herbs, and nuts. More than 500 types of edible plants and trees grow on the 37-acre property, including 160 varieties of mangoes and more than 80 banana trees. Best of all, the park offers daily tasting tours of the gardens, where visitors can sample delicacies like star fruit, macadamia nuts, guava, and jackfruit.

Other Florida Gardens

John C. Gifford Arboretum
Coral Gables, Florida

- Named for a University of Miami professor of tropical forestry
- Home to more than 1,300 species of plants and trees

Key West Tropical Forest and Botanical Garden
Key West, Florida

- A 15.2-acre subtropical garden with native and rare flora and fauna
- Features several "champion trees"–the largest trees of their species

McKee Botanical Garden
Vero Beach, Florida

- Showcases award-winning orchids and a large collection of water lilies
- Contains more than 10,000 plants in an 18-acre jungle landscape

Nature Coast Botanical Gardens
Spring Hill, Florida

- Features 22 themed gardens on 3.5 acres, maintained by volunteers
- Highlights include an orchard, rose garden, and butterfly garden

Palm and Cycad Arboretum
Jacksonville, Florida

- Large variety of native and rare trees and shrubs
- Located on the campus of Florida State College at Jacksonville

Pan's Garden
Palm Beach, Florida

- A half-acre garden consisting of native plants, trees, and flowers
- A bronze statue of Pan, the Greek god of shepherds, stands at the garden's entrance

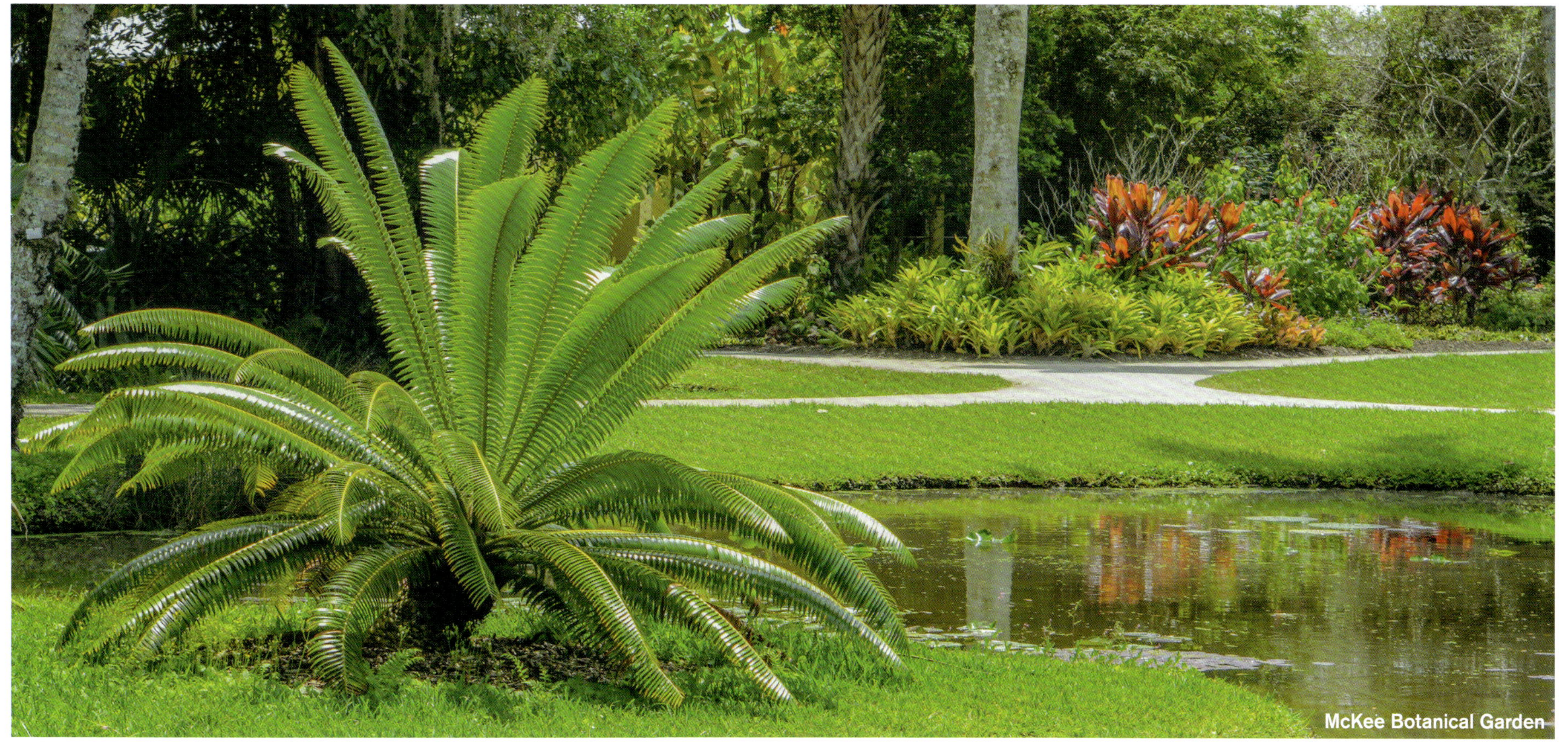

McKee Botanical Garden

Heathcote Botanical Gardens
Fort Pierce, Florida

A variety of specialty gardens awaits visitors at this five-acre subtropical property. Highlights include the Palm and Cycad Walk, which features a winding path amongst towering trees from around the world, and the Japanese Garden, with an entrance gate, pond, bridge, and a replica tea house. A beautiful Bonsai Gallery is located nearby.

Jacksonville Zoo and Botanical Gardens
Jacksonville, Florida

More than 1,000 plant species join the 2,000 animals at this zoo and botanical garden. The gardens, which are integrated amongst the animal exhibits, include the South African-themed Savanna Blooms, the tropical Gardens at Range of the Jaguar, and the pollinator-favorite Riverview Gardens, which attracts bees and butterflies.

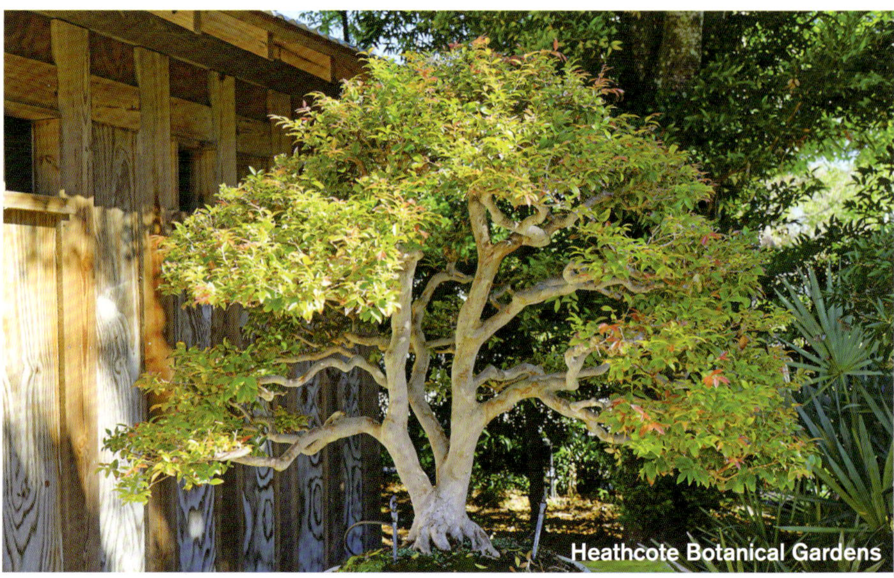

A bonsai nestles in a corner at Heathcote Botanical Gardens.

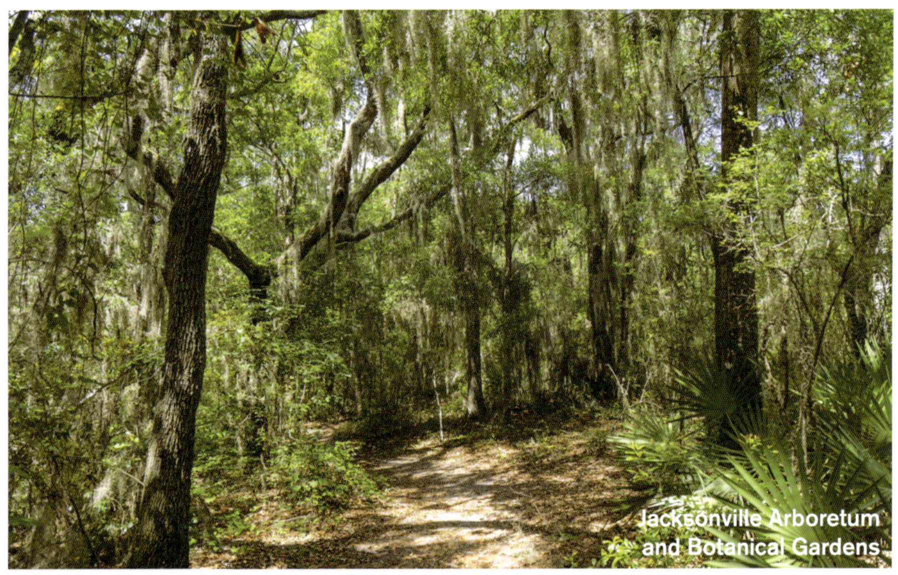

One of the site's many woodsy trails.

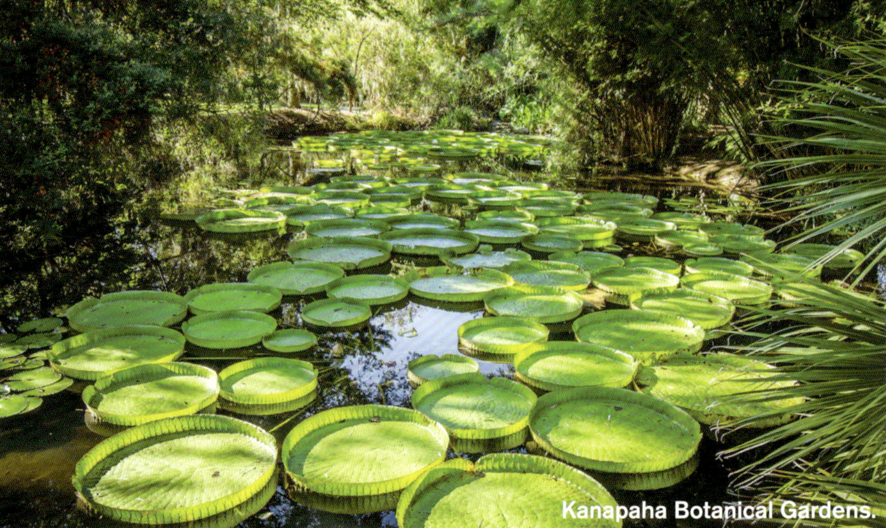

The amazing Victoria water lilies are a must-see at the Kanapaha Botanical Gardens.

Jacksonville Arboretum and Botanical Gardens
Jacksonville, Florida

With seven different hiking trails, 13 distinct ecosystems, and a variety of gardens, this 136-acre site is a true oasis in the city of Jacksonville. The tranquil property, which consists of tidal marshes, pine flatwoods, live oak hammocks, and more, is known for its Fernery, a garden with hundreds of plants including ferns, rhododendrons, and palms.

Kanapaha Botanical Gardens
Gainesville, Florida

Florida's largest public display of bamboos is found at this 68-acre property, which is made up of 24 individual plant collections. The site is also known for housing the largest herb garden in the southeastern United States, and, in the warmer months, for its impressive giant Victoria water lilies, which can grow up to 10 feet in diameter.

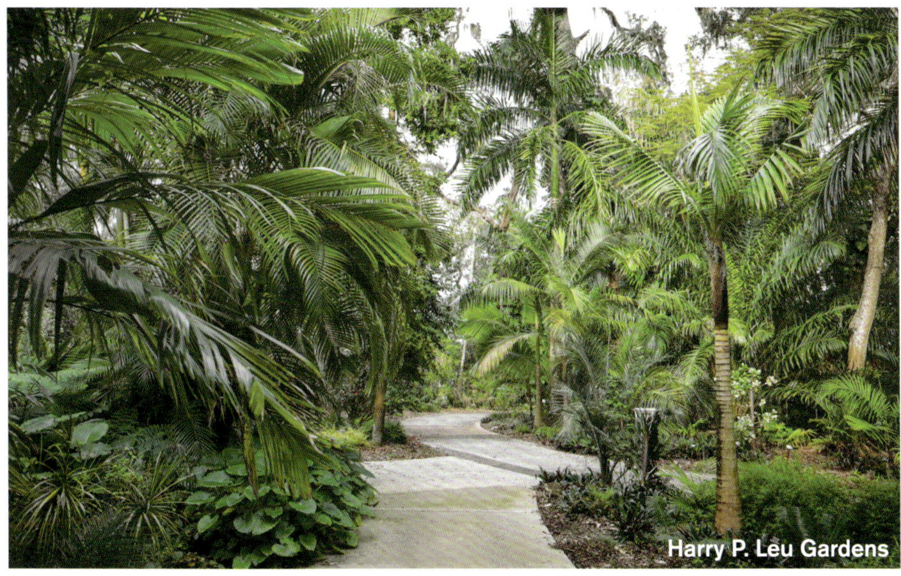

Meandering trails disappear among the palms, oaks, and camellias.

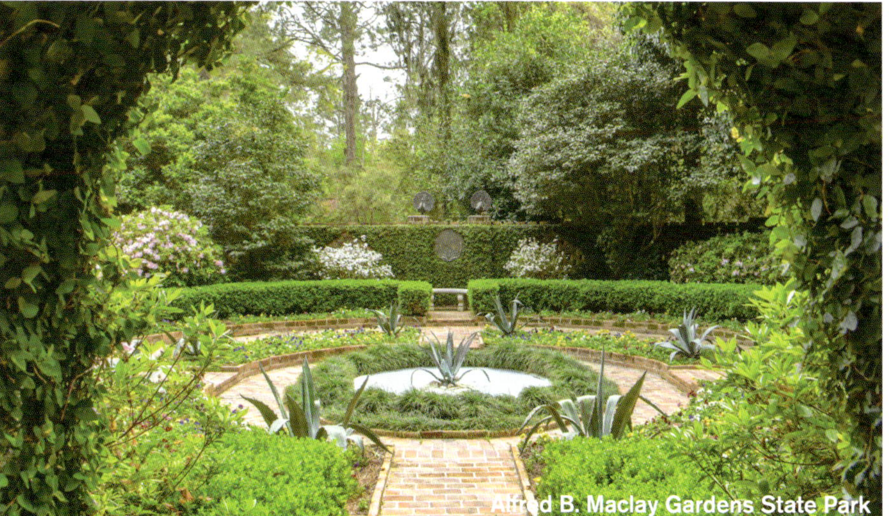

Walled areas and secret, tucked away places make exploring this garden a charming process of discovery.

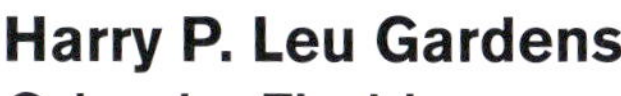

Harry P. Leu Gardens
Orlando, Florida

Named for the Orlando businessman who transformed the property into a tropical and subtropical oasis, this garden spans 50 acres and contains more than 3,500 plant species. The garden is famous for its collection of camellias, many of which were planted by Leu himself, and also features a Rose Garden, Tropical Fruit Collection, and much more.

Alfred B. Maclay Gardens State Park
Tallahassee, Florida

Alfred B. and Louise Maclay purchased the property this park now occupies in 1923, cultivating the first plants in this ornamental garden. Today, azaleas and camellias are especially abundant in the park, which also features a reflecting pool, paved brick walkway, and walled gardens. Peak blooming season is between January and April.

Mead Botanical Garden
Winter Park, Florida

This 47-acre garden contains hiking trails, a boardwalk, a creek, ponds, and a variety of native plants, including black-eyed Susans, wild petunias, and southern magnolias. The site also contains a community garden, butterfly garden, and an amphitheater, and is home to wildlife like wading birds, hawks, and hummingbirds.

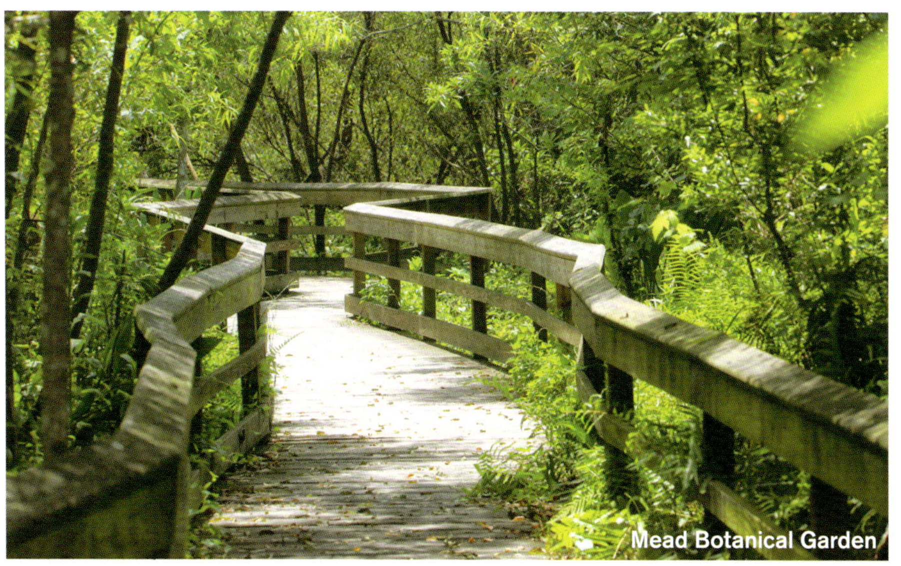

The garden is filled with plenty of lush trails and walkways.

Miami Beach Botanical Garden
Miami Beach, Florida

An urban oasis in the middle of the island city of Miami Beach, this garden covers just 2.6 acres but packs plenty of botanical beauty in the small space. Highlights include a Japanese Garden with bamboo, ponds, and lantern pagodas, and an Edible Garden that features papaya, pineapples, and a lychee tree.

Montgomery Botanical Center
Coral Gables, Florida

This botanical garden gathers seeds from wild palms and cycads around the world, cultivating them in its nursery before incorporating them into its tropical plant collections. The garden features a Cycad Walk and a Palm Walk, which each contain thousands of specimens sourced from more than 60 countries.

Mounts Botanical Garden
West Palm Beach, Florida

This 20-acre botanical garden, first opened in 1954, is the oldest and largest in Palm Beach County. It contains more than 7,000 species of tropical and subtropical plants, including Florida natives and specimens from around the world. Twenty-five gardens are located on the property, including a Tropical Forest Garden and Herb Garden.

Naples Botanical Garden
Naples, Florida

Established in 1993, Naples Botanical Garden became the youngest garden in history to win the prestigious Award for Garden Excellence in 2017. Its 170 acres of land represent seven different ecosystems and feature more than 1,000 species. The garden includes a tropical fruit collection, cacti and succulents, and two acres of ponds filled with aquatic plants.

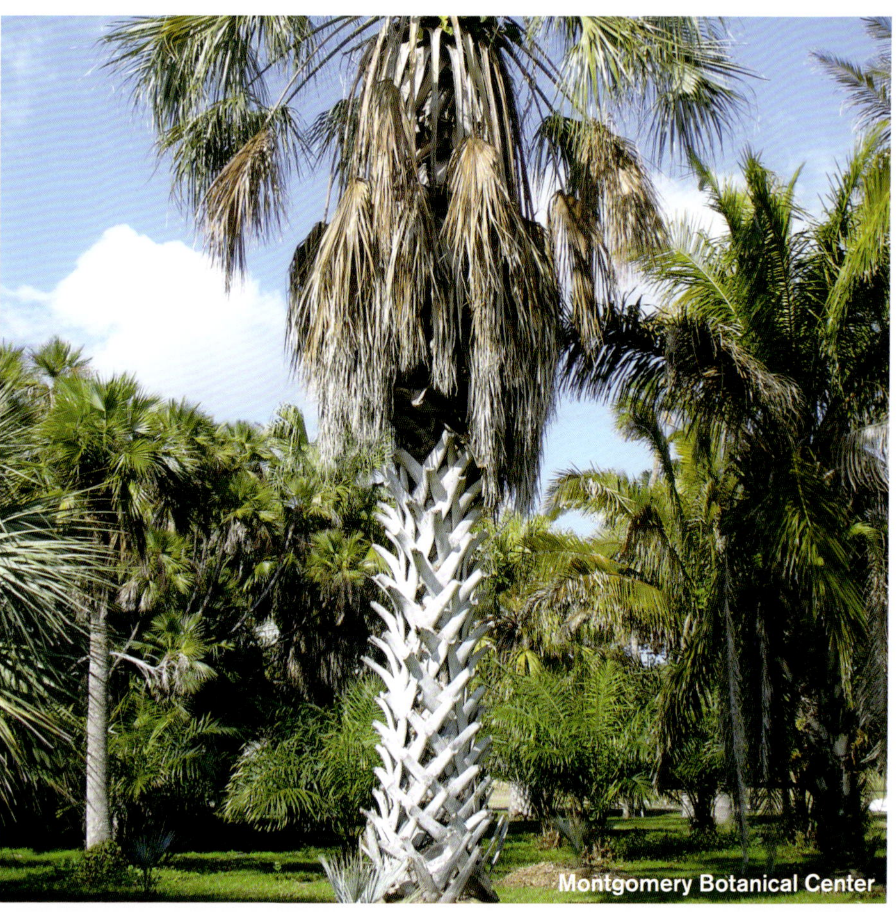

Montgomery Botanical Center

The site's majestic Sonoran palmetto is considered endangered. It is native to northwestern Mexico.

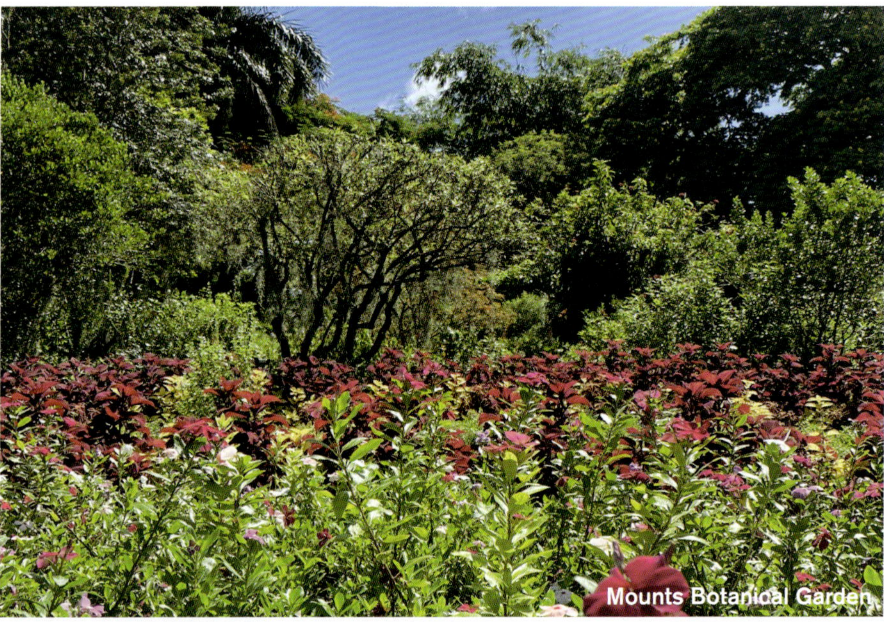

Mounts Botanical Garden

Tropical foliage and flowers fill every available space, making a walk through Mounts Botanical Garden a rich and vivid experience.

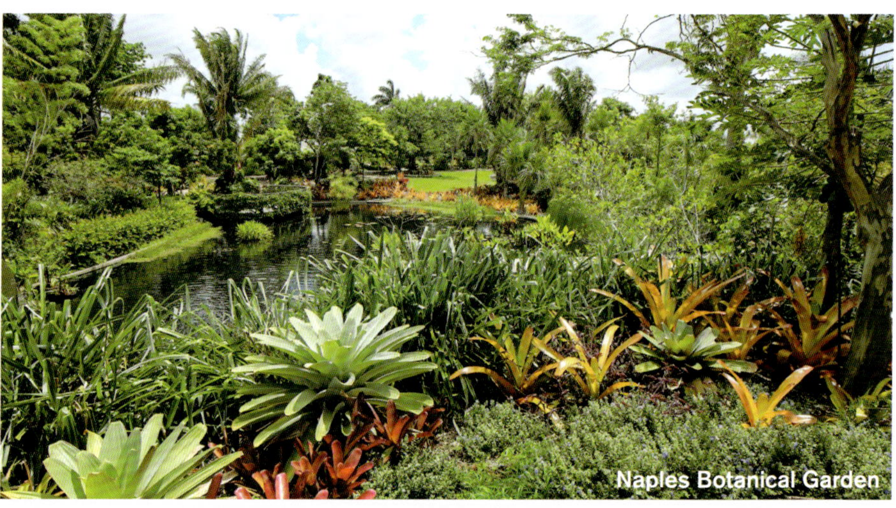

Naples Botanical Garden

The birds, flowers, plants, and landscape provide a paradise backdrop for visitors to wander through.

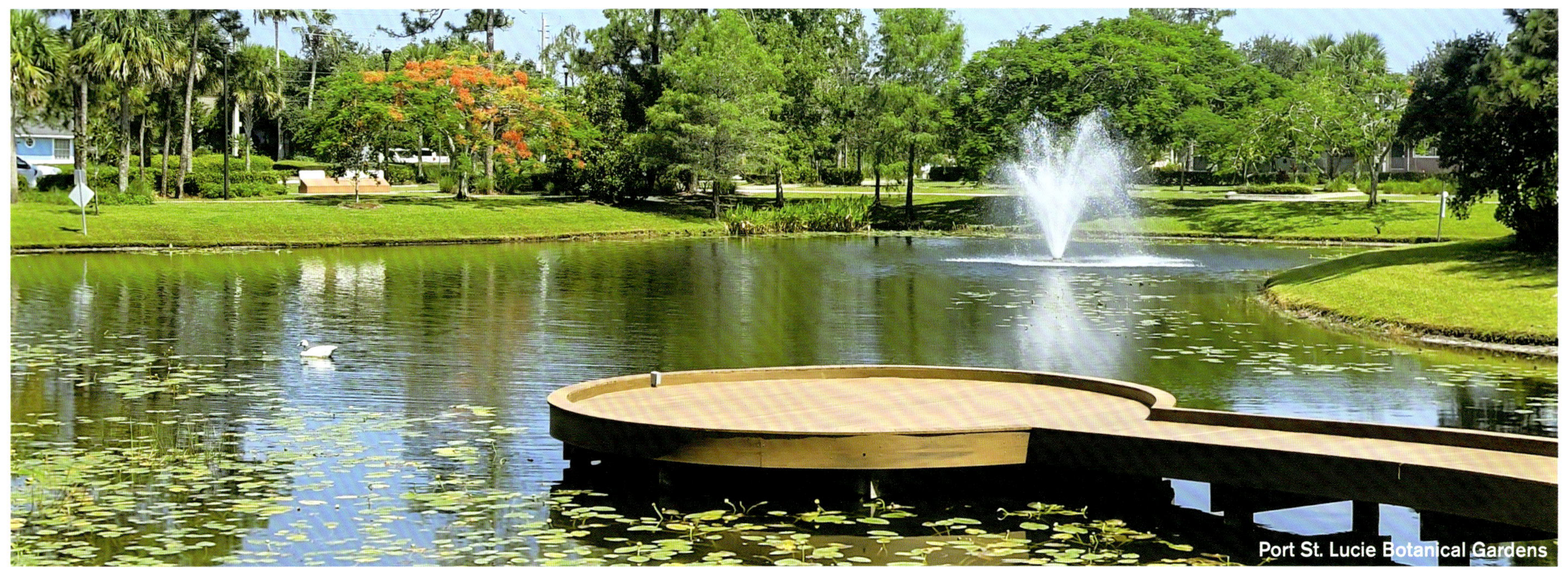
Port St. Lucie Botanical Gardens

The site provides a lush oasis in the heart of urban Port St. Lucie.

National Tropical Botanical Garden
Miami, Florida

Along with four gardens in Hawaii, this property, also known as The Kampong, is part of the National Tropical Botanical Garden. Thousands of tropical species from around the world are showcased here, with particular attention given to sustainability and scientific research. Both self-guided and guided tours are available through the garden.

Palma Sola Botanical Park
Bradenton, Florida

A free park that relies solely on donations, this garden prides itself on providing visitors with an interactive and educational natural environment. Highlights include a rare fruit trail featuring dragon fruit, African breadfruit, Surinam cherry, and more, as well as a nursery where guests can buy plants for their home gardens.

Port St. Lucie Botanical Gardens
Port St. Lucie, Florida

This relatively new 21-acre subtropical garden was established in 2010, using the site's natural native plants, including seven acres of mangrove wetlands, as a foundation. The property now boasts 16 separate gardens, including the Hibiscus Garden and the quiet, secluded Secret Garden. A 4,100-square-foot pavilion and an amphitheater are popular for weddings and events.

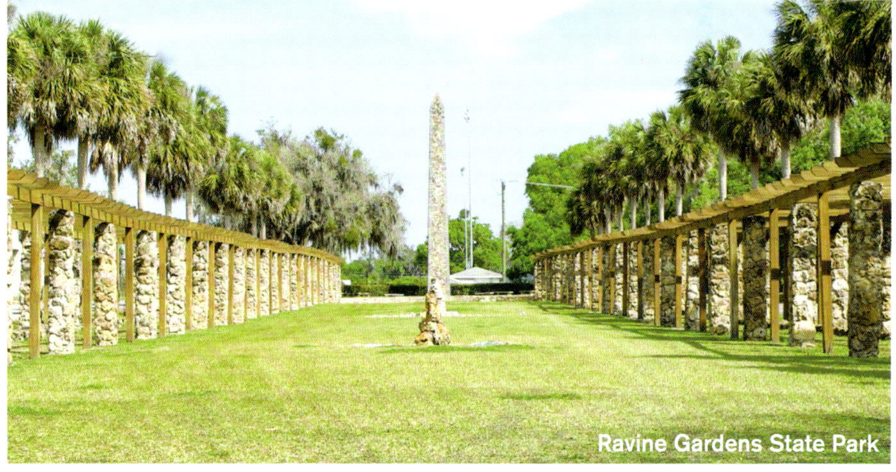
Ravine Gardens State Park

The obelisk stands 64 feet tall and is flanked by two rows of stone columns.

Ravine Gardens State Park
Palatka, Florida

Named for two 120-foot-deep ravines located on the property, this park was created during the New Deal era in 1933. An obelisk near the entrance is dedicated to Franklin D. Roosevelt, whose Works Progress Administration helped to establish the park. Today, it is best known for its 18 types of azaleas, most of which bloom between January and March.

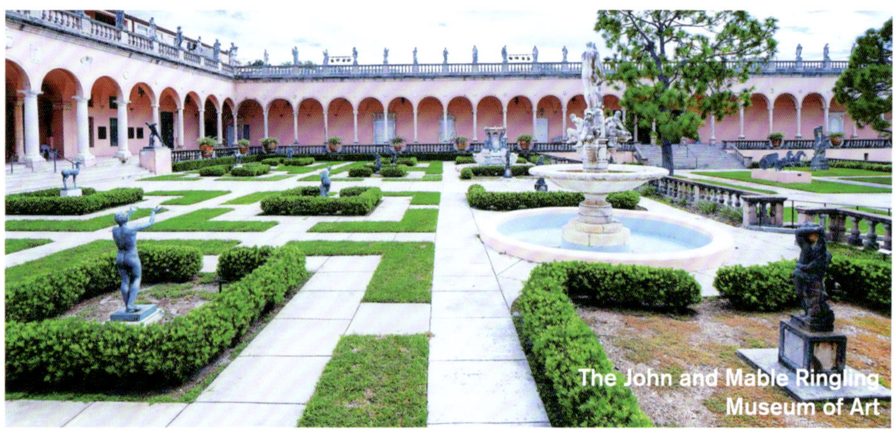

The courtyard, with its collection of sculptures, is an extension of the museum's interior galleries.

The John and Mable Ringling Museum of Art
Sarasota, Florida

John Ringling was one of the five Ringling brothers, the famous circus family who eventually purchased the Barnum and Bailey show. John and his wife, Mable, first used their Italian Renaissance-style mansion, constructed in 1926, as the winter headquarters of the circus. The prolific art collectors later opened the estate to the public as a museum in 1930. Today, the property not only features an art and circus museum, but also offers 66 acres of gardens, including a 27,000-square-foot Rose Garden with 1,200 roses and the peaceful Mable's Secret Garden, filled with bromeliads, succulents, and variegated bougainvillea.

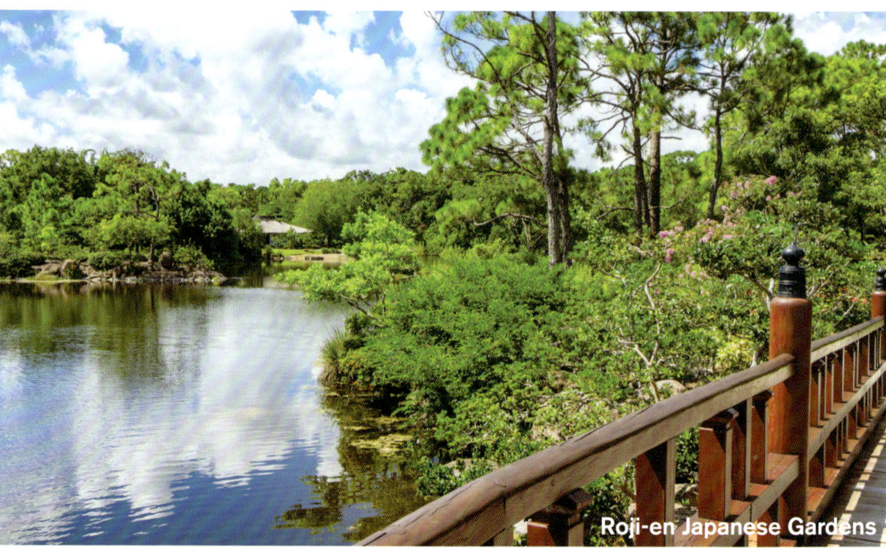

A stately, arched bridge provides access to two landscaped islands.

Roji-en Japanese Gardens
Delray Beach, Florida

The 16 acres of gardens within the Morikami Museum and Japanese Gardens, known as *Roji-en: Gardens of the Drops of Dew*, reflect garden styles popular in Japan between the eighth and twentieth centuries. Gardens include the Shinden Garden, an example of what early Kyoto nobility once enjoyed, and the Modern Romantic Garden, with echoes of Western influences.

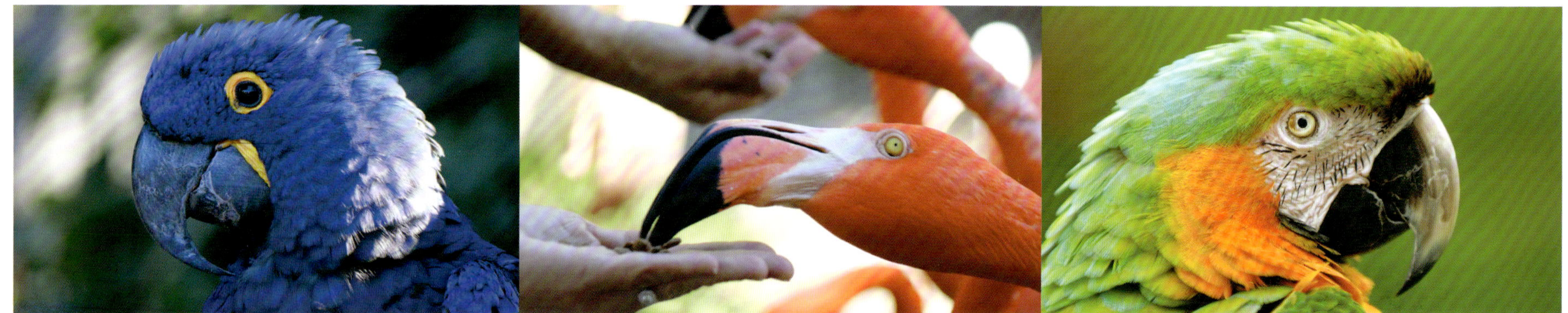
Colorful tropical birds are one of the main attractions at Sarasota Jungle Gardens.

Sarasota Jungle Gardens
Sarasota, Florida

Once a swampy banana grove, this property was transformed into a tropical botanical garden in 1939. Tropical plants from all over the world were imported to the location, including the rare Australian nut tree and the Peruvian apple cactus. Today, in addition to the gardens, this family-friendly attraction offers encounters with lemurs, parrots, and flamingos.

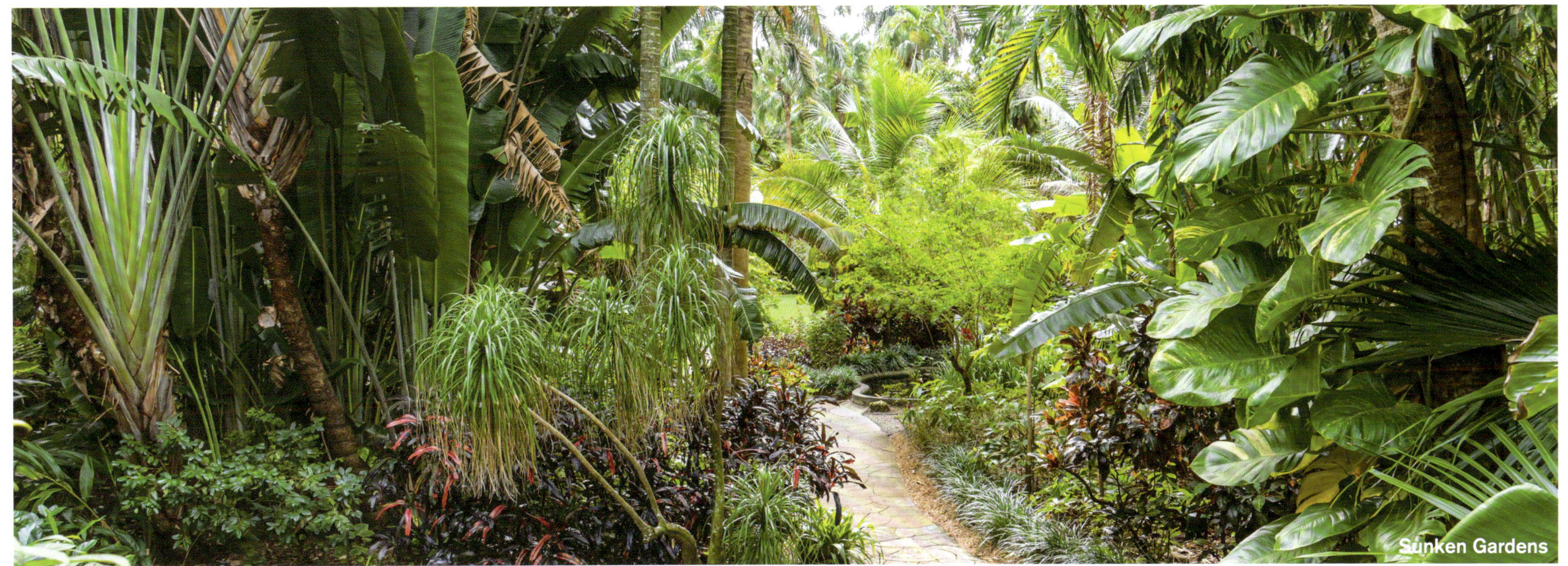

Several miles of maze-like trails crowded with tropical vegetation make visitors feel as if they're lost in a jungle.

Sunken Gardens
St. Petersburg, Florida

Considered one of the oldest roadside tourist attractions in the United States, this property began as a shallow lake ten feet below sea level. The property's owner, avid gardener George Turner Sr., drained the lake and planted tropical plants and trees to create a "sunken" garden. In the 1920s, he began charging visitors a nickel to wander through the lush garden. Now, more than a hundred years later, the gardens, filled with 500 species of tropical and subtropical plants, continue to draw visitors. Highlights include a grove of papaya and banana trees planted by Turner a century ago, an Orchid Arbor, and towering royal palms.

Marie Selby Botanical Gardens
Sarasota, Florida

This 15-acre property is the only botanical garden in the world dedicated to the study of epiphytes–plants that grow on other plants–including epiphytic orchids, bromeliads, gesneriads, and ferns. The garden prides itself on its conservation and environmental efforts and is home to the world's first net positive energy garden complex, generating more energy than it consumes. More than 150 expeditions to the tropics have resulted in a living plant collection that numbers in the tens of thousands and an herbarium with 115,000 specimens. Visitors can also peruse a butterfly garden, succulent garden, an edible garden, and a hardwood hammock.

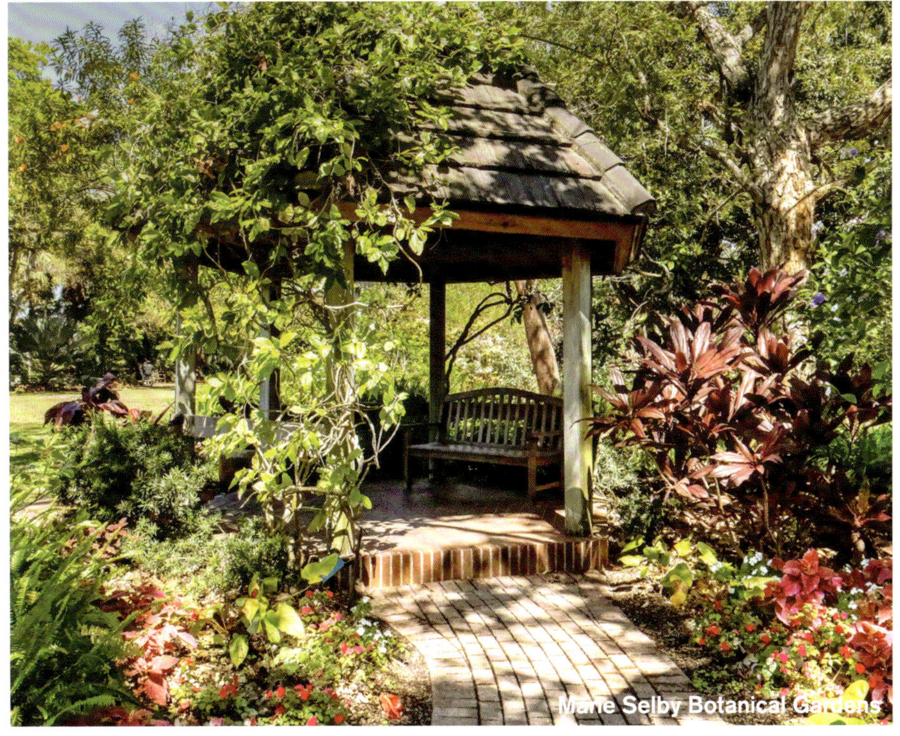

Visitors will find pavilions, gazebos, and other delightful spots tucked away on the grounds.

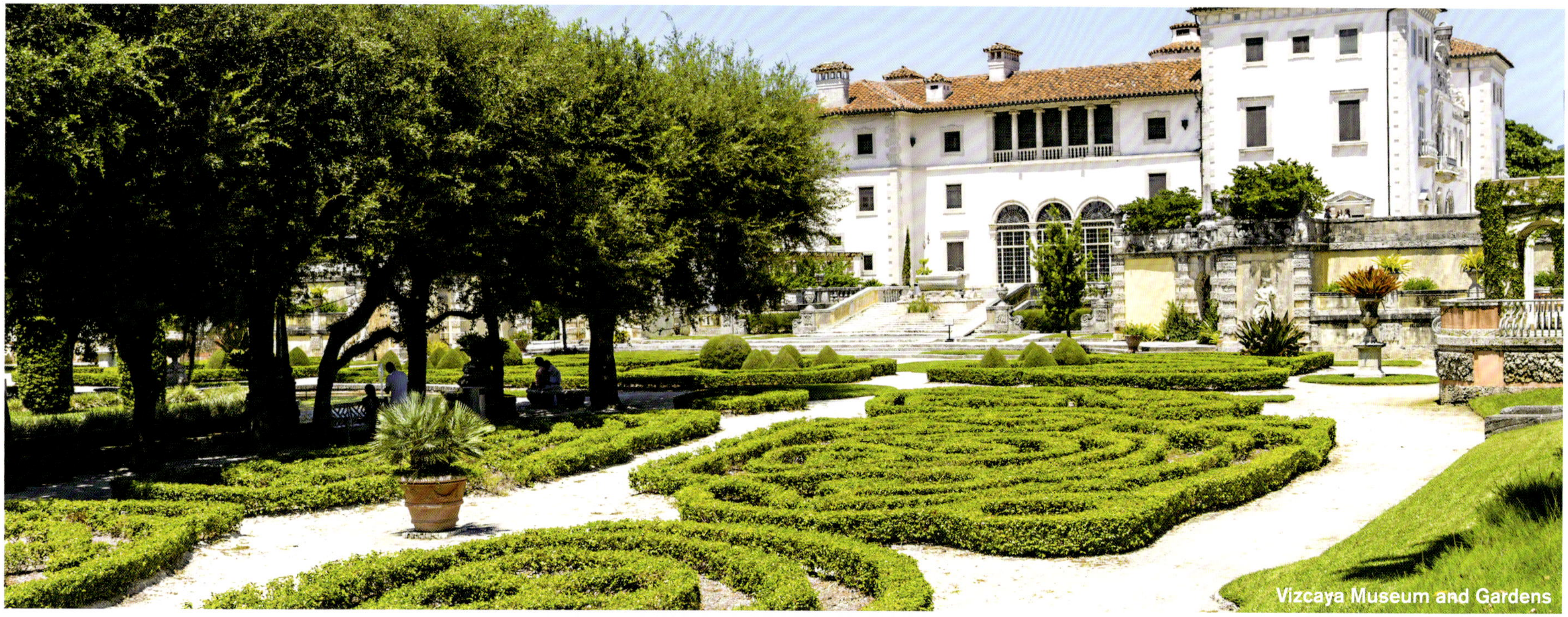

The formal gardens feature trimmed, patterned shrubs and classical statues.

University of South Florida Botanical Gardens
Tampa, Florida

Created in 1969 for use by the University of South Florida's biology department, this garden covers 16 acres on the campus. The property is evenly split between natural woodland and planted gardens, with an emphasis on native Florida plants. A medicinal herb garden, used by the USF College of Pharmacy for research, is also part of the collection.

Vizcaya Museum and Gardens
Miami, Florida

Villa Vizcaya, as it was previously known, looks as if it would be at home on the Italian Riviera. The Mediterranean Revival-style home was built between 1914 and 1922 and is surrounded by native forest and ten acres of formal gardens. The elaborate Italian Renaissance gardens include whimsical hedge mazes, endangered subtropical trees, and a collection of more than 2,000 orchids.

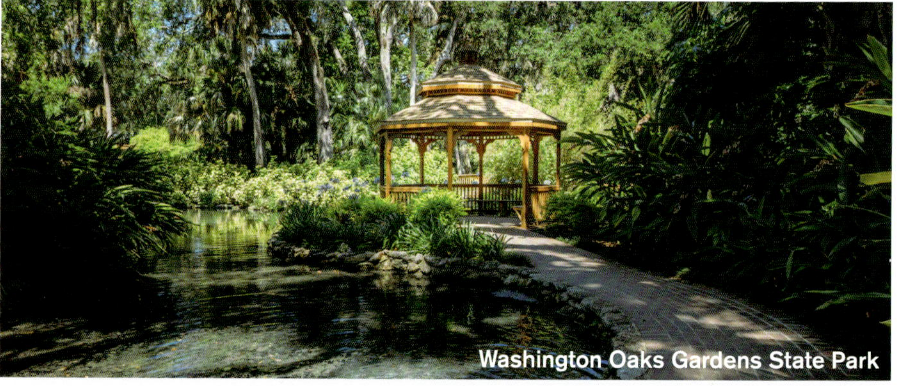

A trail leads to an enchanting gazebo set near a small pool.

Washington Oaks Gardens State Park
Palm Coast, Florida

This 425-acre park preserves the habitat–including beach, coastal scrub, coastal hammock, and marshes–of one of Florida's many barrier islands. But it is most well known for its manicured gardens, which contain colorful azaleas and camellias as well as gazebos, ponds, and walking paths. The park's 3,000-square-foot rose garden, which displays an average of 150 blooming bushes, is the largest on the Florida coast.

Atlanta Botanical Garden
Atlanta, Georgia

The very first 1976 office for the Atlanta Botanical Garden was a modest doublewide trailer set within a small plot of display gardens. But within ten years, more than 50,000 visitors flocked to the property, which quickly grew to the sprawling 30 acres it now occupies. An oasis in the middle of the bustling city, the garden is a popular destination for visitors and locals alike. One of the first Children's Gardens in the country opened at the site in 1999, becoming a favorite of visiting families. The award-winning garden contains a vegetable garden to demonstrate growing methods and stages of plant growth, a bog with carnivorous Venus flytraps and pitcher plants, and a buzzing beehive behind a glass case.

Other highlights include the Skyline Garden, which offers stunning views of Atlanta, the Rose Garden, which blooms between May and September, and Storza Woods, which contains the tallest trees on the property, tulip poplars. Two indoor gardens–the Dorothy Chapman Fuqua Conservatory and the Fuqua Orchid Center–round out the diverse attractions at the garden. Tropical ferns and palms, fruit and nut trees, and 2,000 species of orchids can be found in these temperature- and humidity-controlled areas.

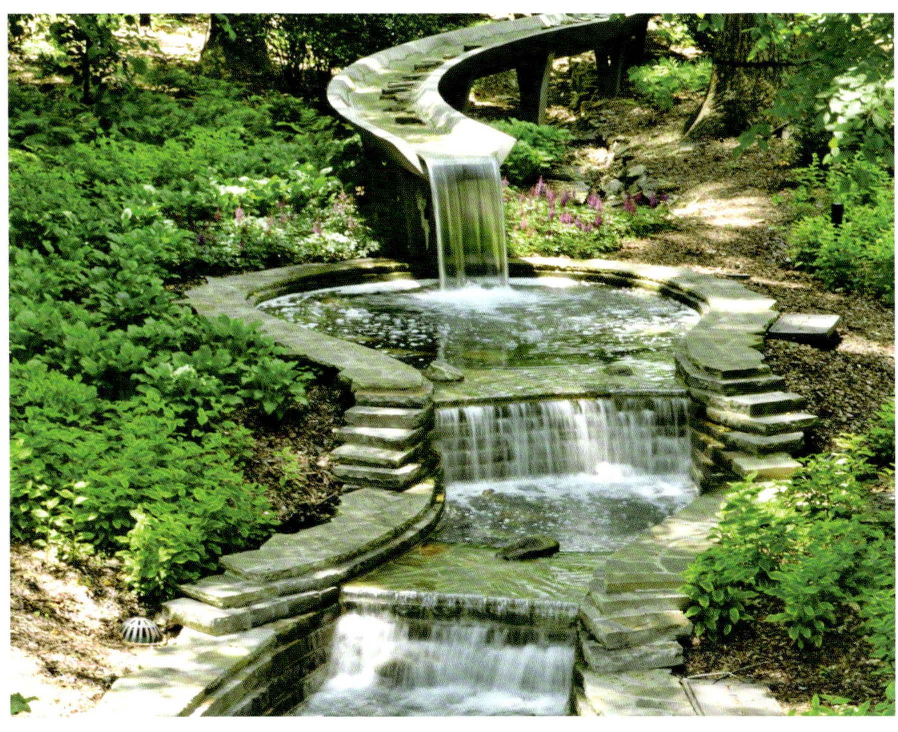

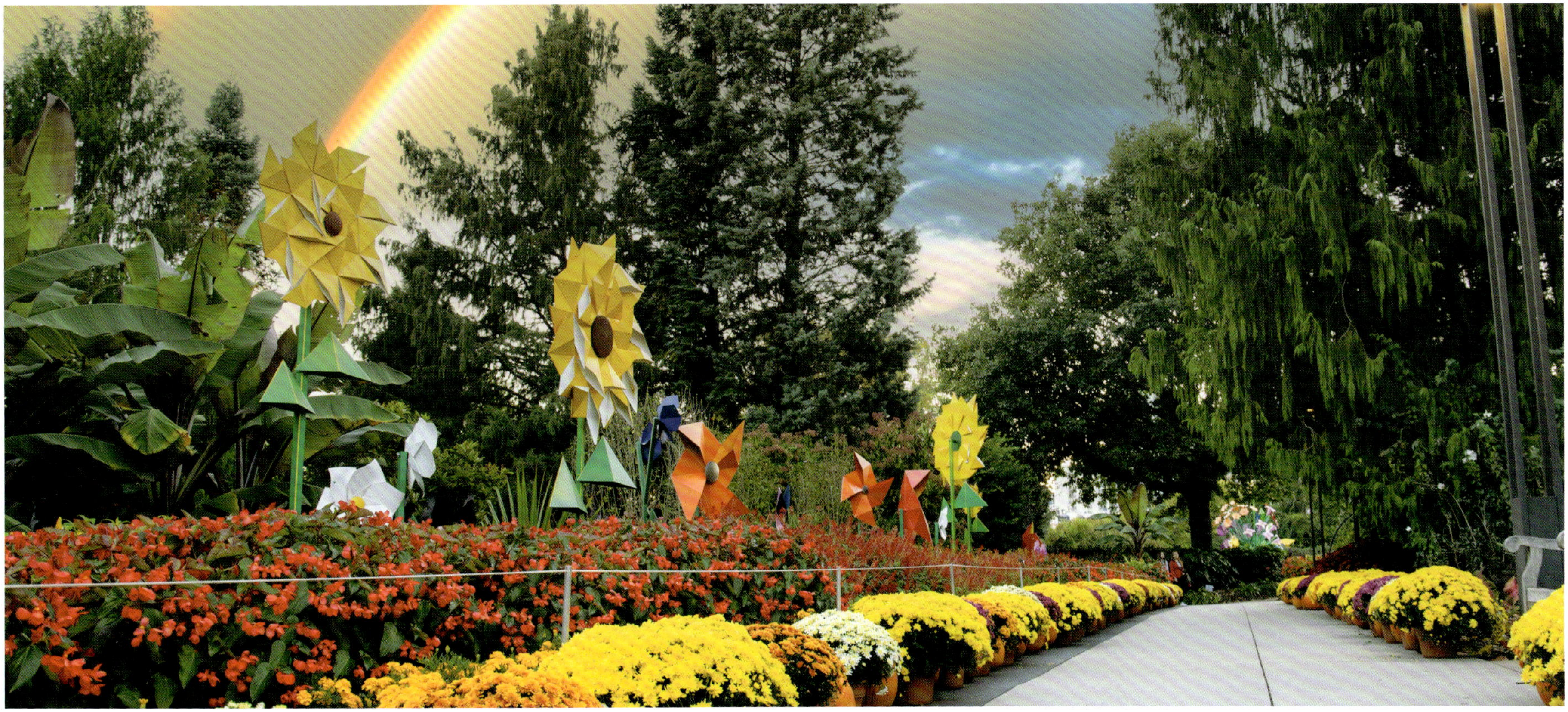

Worth Exploring in Georgia

Lockerly Arboretum
Milledgeville, Georgia

- Features 50 acres of gardens containing flowering shrubs and centuries-old trees
- Famous for Rose Hill, a Greek Revival-style home built in 1852

Savannah Botanical Gardens
Savannah, Georgia

- Contains formal gardens, a pond, nature trails, and an amphitheater
- Also known for its historic 1840 farmhouse, one of the only pre-Civil War homes in Savannah

Thompson Mills Forest and State Arboretum
Braselton, Georgia

- A 337-acre property considered the State Arboretum of Georgia
- Has nearly every example of Georgia's 215 native tree species

University of Georgia Campus Arboretum
Athens, Georgia

- Three walking tours of the arboretum are available in the North, Central, and South Campus areas
- 150 trees on the campus are marked with identifying plaques

Vines Botanical Garden
Loganville, Georgia

- Covers 79 acres and includes a lake, walking trail, pavilion, and 18,000-square-foot mansion
- Features annuals, perennials, and a rose garden

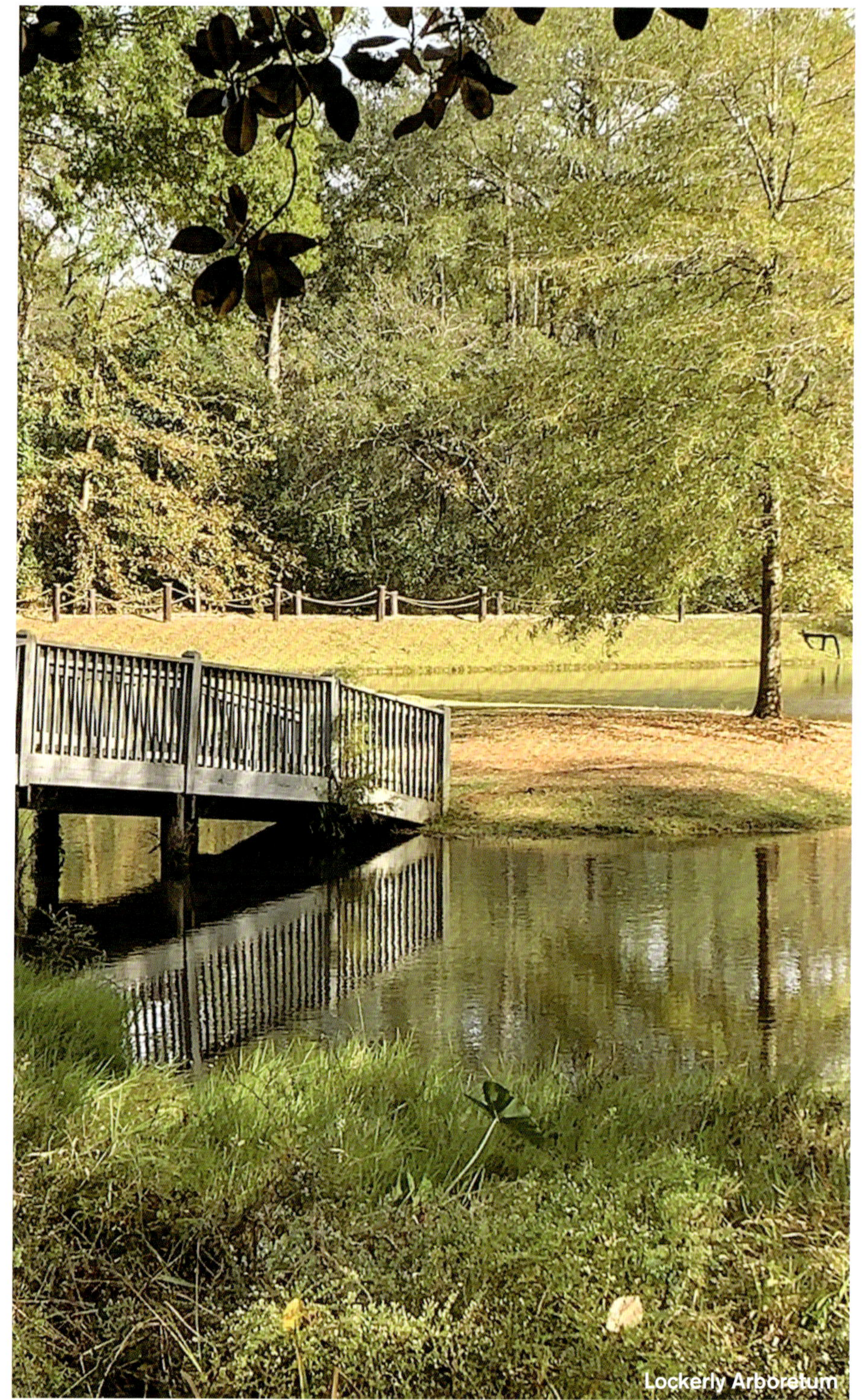

A footbridge connects to a small island at Lockerly Arboretum.

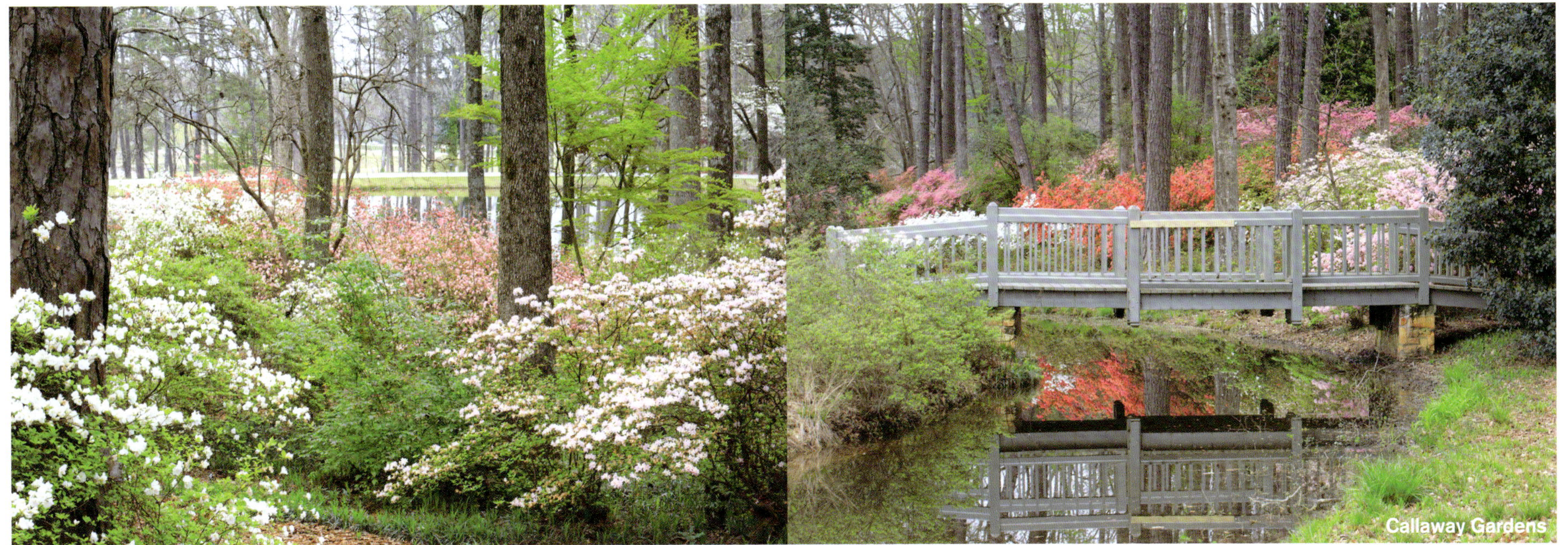
Callaway Gardens

Callaway Gardens
Pine Mountain, Georgia

The 2,500 acres of gardens at this resort property offer everything from quiet tranquility to heart-pumping excitement, drawing in more than 750,000 visitors annually. The garden may be best known for the 40-acre Callaway Brothers Azalea Bowl, a collection of more than 4,000 azaleas that burst with color every spring. Other highlights include the Cecil B. Day Butterfly Center, one of the largest tropical butterfly conservatories in North America, where more than 1,000 butterflies fly freely. The property also features biking paths, walking trails, and ten zip lines that soar up to 70 feet above the forest floor.

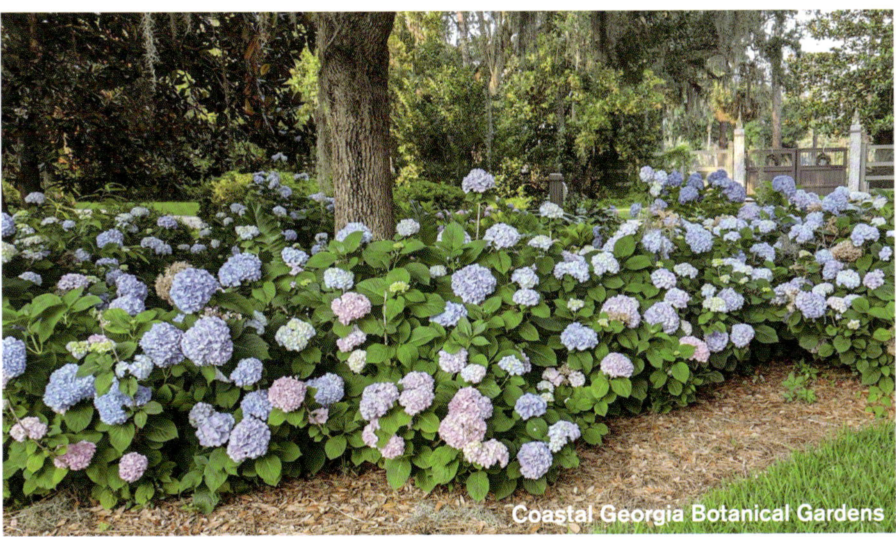
Coastal Georgia Botanical Gardens

The Coastal Georgia Botanical Gardens feature vigorous stands of hydrangeas—flowers that can withstand the local hot and humid climate.

Coastal Georgia Botanical Gardens
Savannah, Georgia

One of Savannah's most popular attractions, this botanical garden encourages education and provides community classes and school programs to teach the public about plants. The garden's collection began in the late 1880s with three giant Japanese timber bamboo plants, and has since grown to contain 70 different types of bamboo. The Barbour Lathrop Bamboo Collection showcases these fascinating specimens, many of which were brought back from China in the early 1900s. Other gardens include a Mediterranean garden, an orchid greenhouse, and the Rivers of Iris, where, after rain, visitors can observe the mesmerizing flow of "rivers" through the plants.

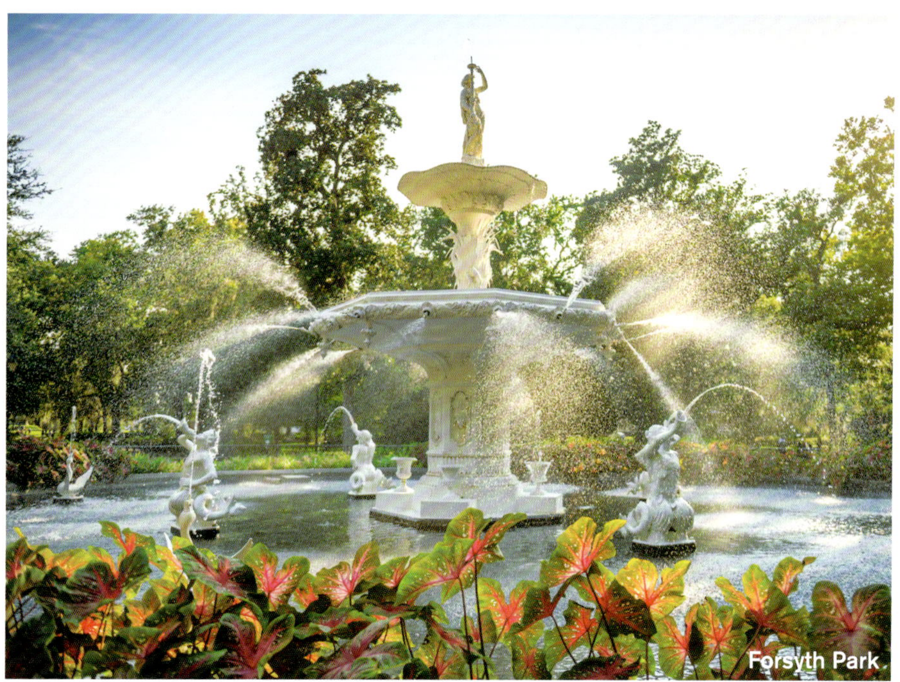

Forsyth Park

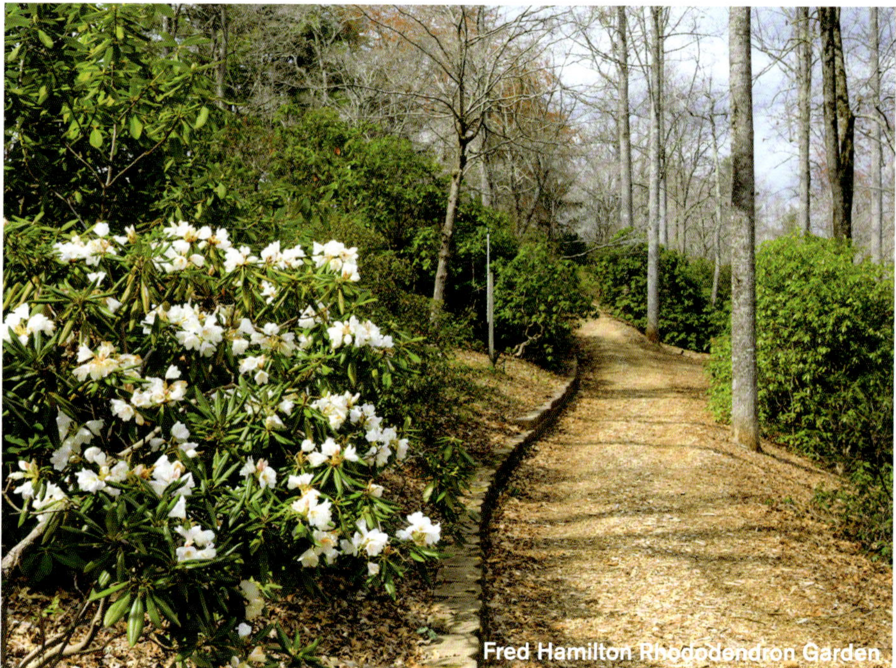

Fred Hamilton Rhododendron Garden

Forsyth Park
Savannah, Georgia

Located in Savannah's historic district, this garden was named in honor of the state's 33rd governor, John Forsyth. The park covers 30 acres and contains Savannah's most famous fountain, installed in 1858, which has been featured in several films. One of the park's most unique features is its Garden of Fragrance, filled with sweet-smelling plants.

Fred Hamilton Rhododendron Garden
Hiawassee, Georgia

It's not hard to guess what this 33-acre property is known for. But rhododendrons aren't the only plant visitors will find here! Azaleas, dogwood, trillium, ferns, and rare forest perennials line secluded winding trails. Along with the 400 varieties of rhododendron in the garden, there are more than 3,000 plants to enjoy.

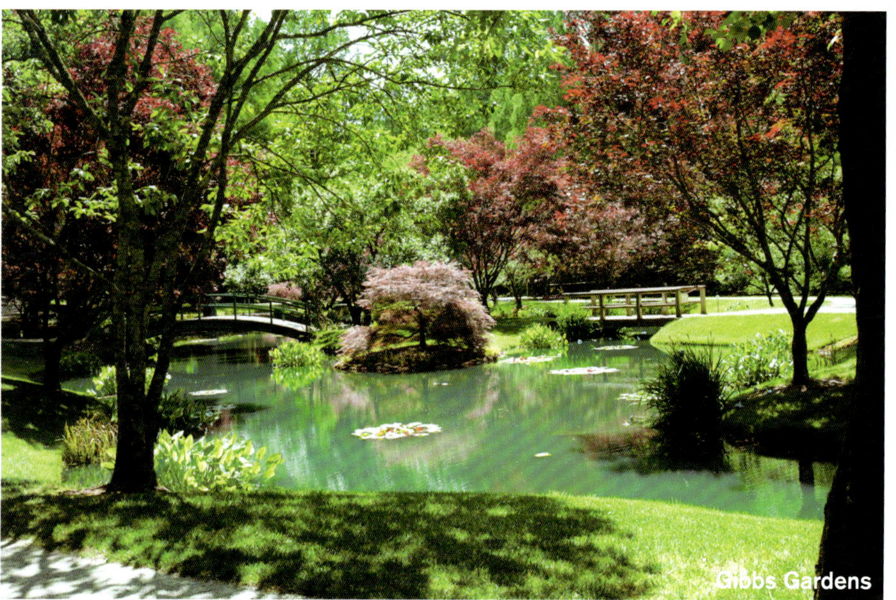

Gibbs Gardens

Gibbs Gardens
Ball Ground, Georgia

This 376-acre garden is named after Jim Gibbs, the founder of one of Atlanta's best-known landscaping companies, and much of the property's gardens, ponds, and waterfalls were designed by Gibbs himself. Popular features include the Le Jardin Color Garden, with thousands of colorful blooms, and the Inspiration Gardens, a peaceful sanctuary with conifers and flowering plants.

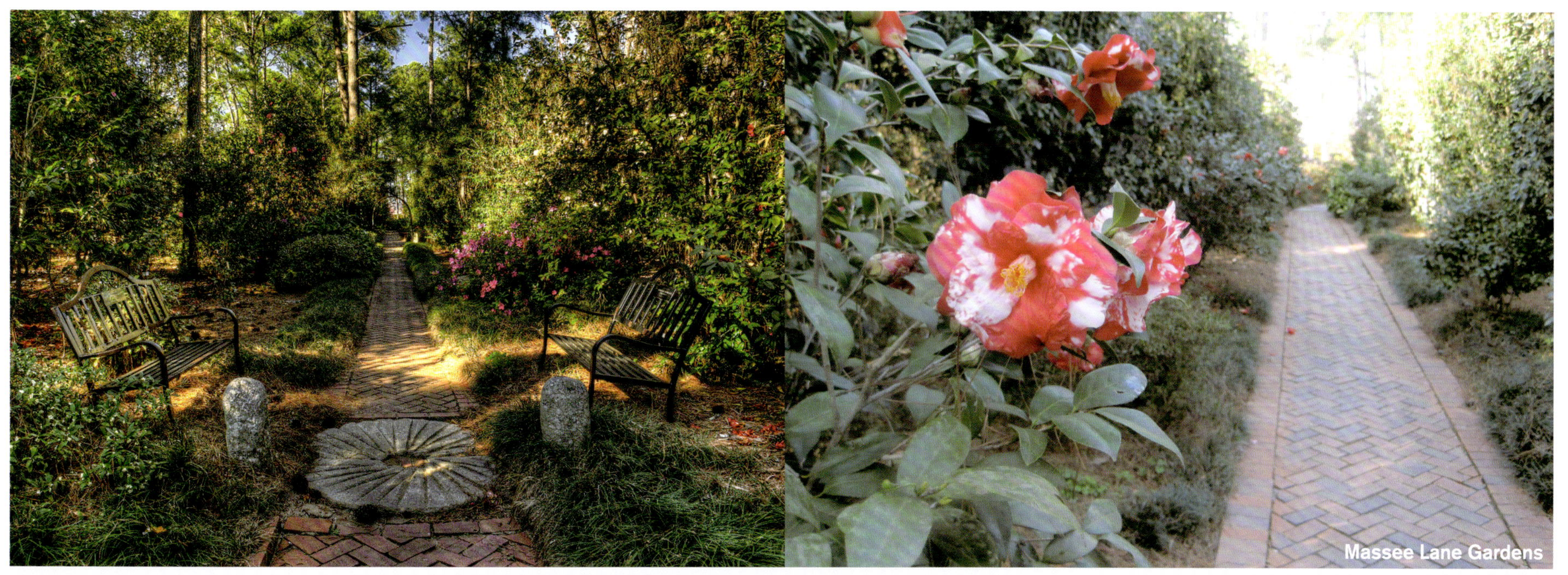

Charming brick lanes run past shrubs, arches, and walls of camellias.

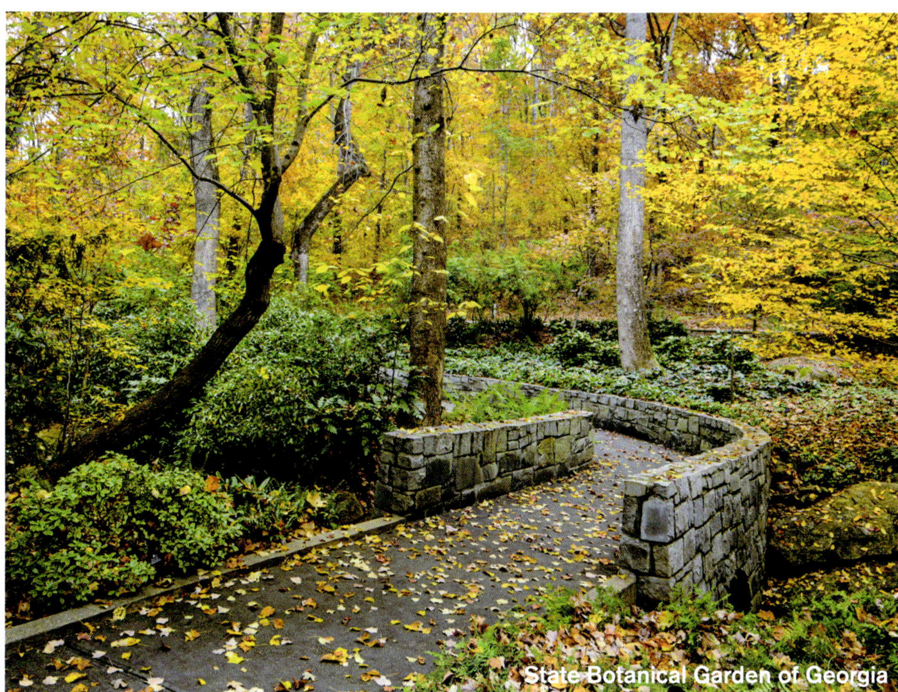

Spring and summer are popular times to visit, but the changing colors of autumn show off the grounds in another unique way.

Massee Lane Gardens
Fort Valley, Georgia

In the 1930s, this property was the private garden of David C. Strother, who then donated the land to the American Camellia Society in 1966. Now the location of the society's headquarters, the garden is still known for its camellia collection, but it also cultivates azaleas, daffodils, daylilies, chrysanthemums, and more than 150 kinds of roses. A tranquil Japanese garden features a koi pond and an *azumaya* (a traditional rustic shelter), and the Brown and Hall Environmental Garden is filled with plants native to the southeastern United States. Visitors enjoy searching for the dozens of millstones, which Strother collected, that have been incorporated into the garden's brick pathways.

State Botanical Garden of Georgia
Athens, Georgia

Operated by the University of Georgia, this 323-acre botanical garden strives to create an environment that encourages learning. As soon as visitors arrive at the property, they are greeted by the Discovery and Inspiration Garden, which coaxes guests young and old to explore, question, and discover. The property also includes the Alice H. Richards Children's Garden, a 2.5-acre area that encourages play and learning with kid-sized garden plots, edible plants, a treehouse, and other interactive exhibits. A Heritage Garden containing heirloom flowers and native species, a lush Tropical Conservatory, and an International Garden with plants from around the world round out the garden's attractions.

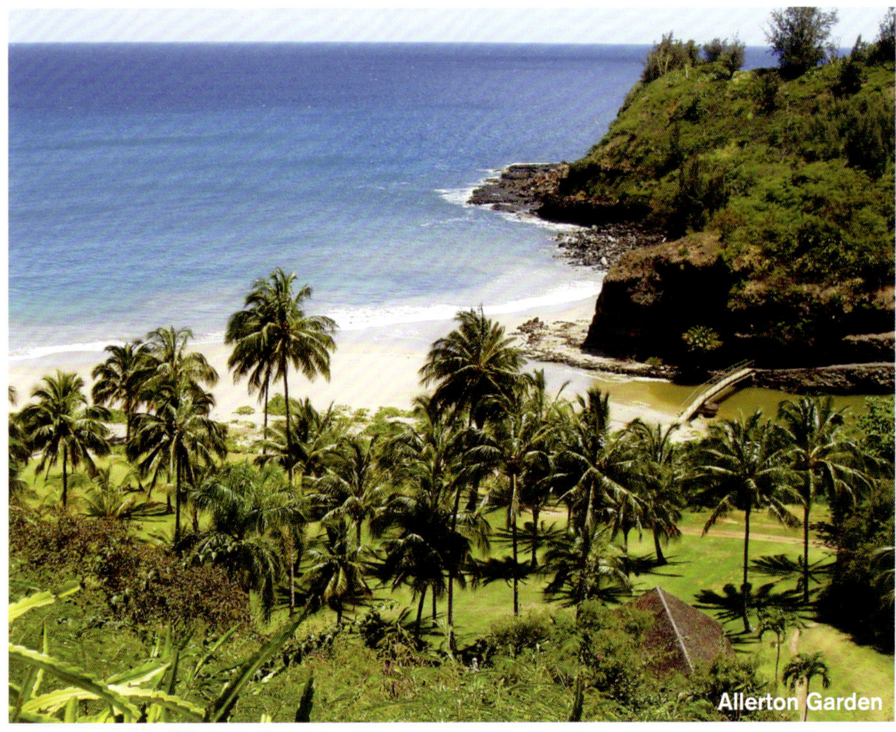

The oceanside setting of the garden is both breathtaking and serene.

Allerton Garden
Koloa, Hawaii

Part of the National Tropical Botanical Garden, Allerton Garden is located on the beautiful Hawaiian island of Kauai, fittingly known as the "Garden Isle." The garden is situated in the Lawa'i Valley, a culturally and historically significant region of the island. Queen Emma of Hawaii, who reigned from 1856 to 1863, once lived in this valley, and the modest house that was once her residence sits on the valley floor. The garden contains a large collection of Zingiberales, an order of large, flowering plants that includes ornamental plants like bird of paradise, food plants like banana, and spices like ginger, as well as exotic palms and other tropical plants.

Hawaii Tropical Botanical Garden
Papaikou, Hawaii

This 17-acre tropical oasis was established in 1984 on the Hamakua coast of the Big Island of Hawaii. Once an overgrown jungle choked with invasive species, the property was transformed by the garden's founder, Dan Lutkenhouse Sr., who was determined to preserve the native plants and botanical beauty of the land. Lutkenhouse and his assistants worked by hand, meticulously clearing invasive weeds while protecting valuable native species. Today, more than 2,500 tropical and subtropical plants, including native and exotic species, are featured at the garden. More than 100 of these were personally collected by Lutkenhouse on trips around the globe.

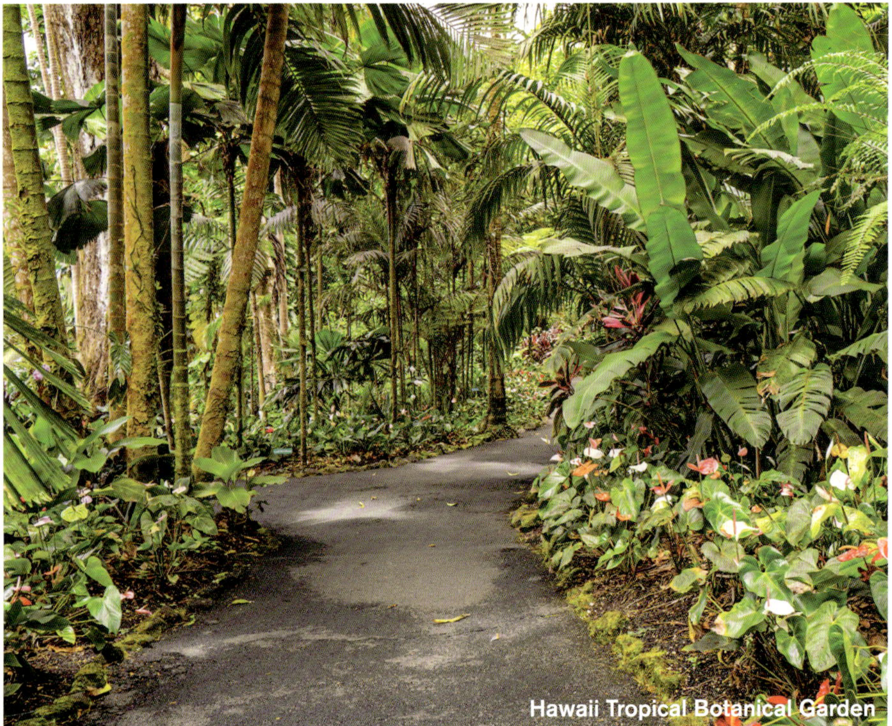

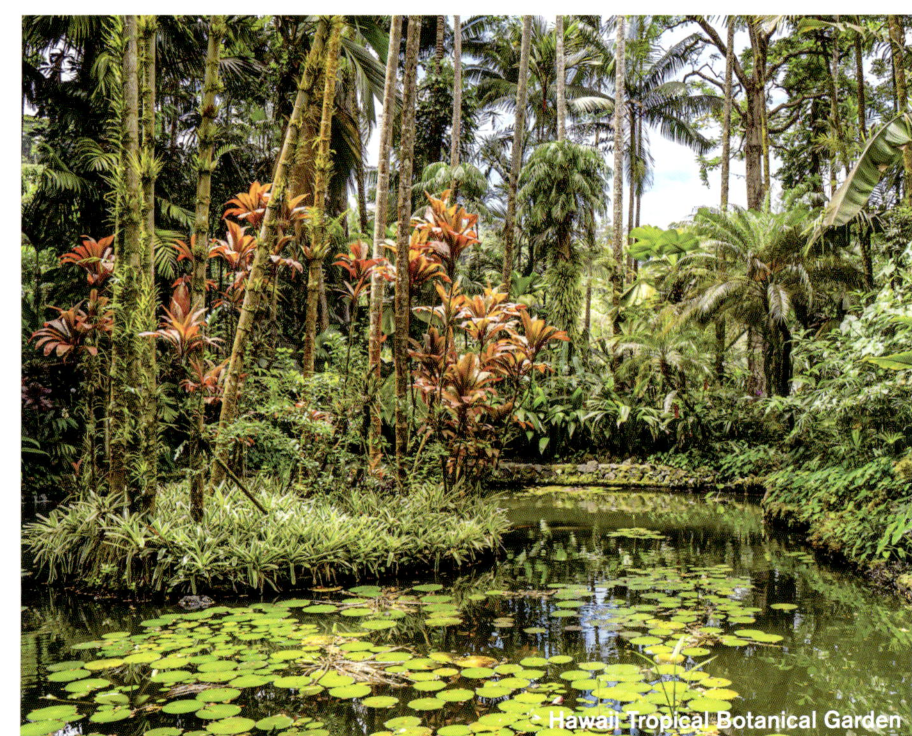

Worth Exploring in Hawaii

Foster Botanical Garden
Honolulu, Hawaii

- The oldest botanical garden in Honolulu, established in 1853
- The 13.5-acre garden features a conservatory, butterfly garden, palm garden, and a renowned orchid collection

Amy B. H. Greenwell Ethnobotanical Garden
Captain Cook, Hawaii

- Features more than 200 species of endemic, indigenous, and Polynesian plants that were growing in Hawaii prior to Captain James Cook's arrival
- Also includes a five-acre archeological site that preserves ancient Hawaiian agricultural lands

Kapi'olani Community College Cactus Garden
Captain Cook, Hawaii

- Created by Moriso Teraoka, a member of the 100th Infantry Battalion during World War II
- Contains a variety of cacti and succulents, which are maintained by volunteers

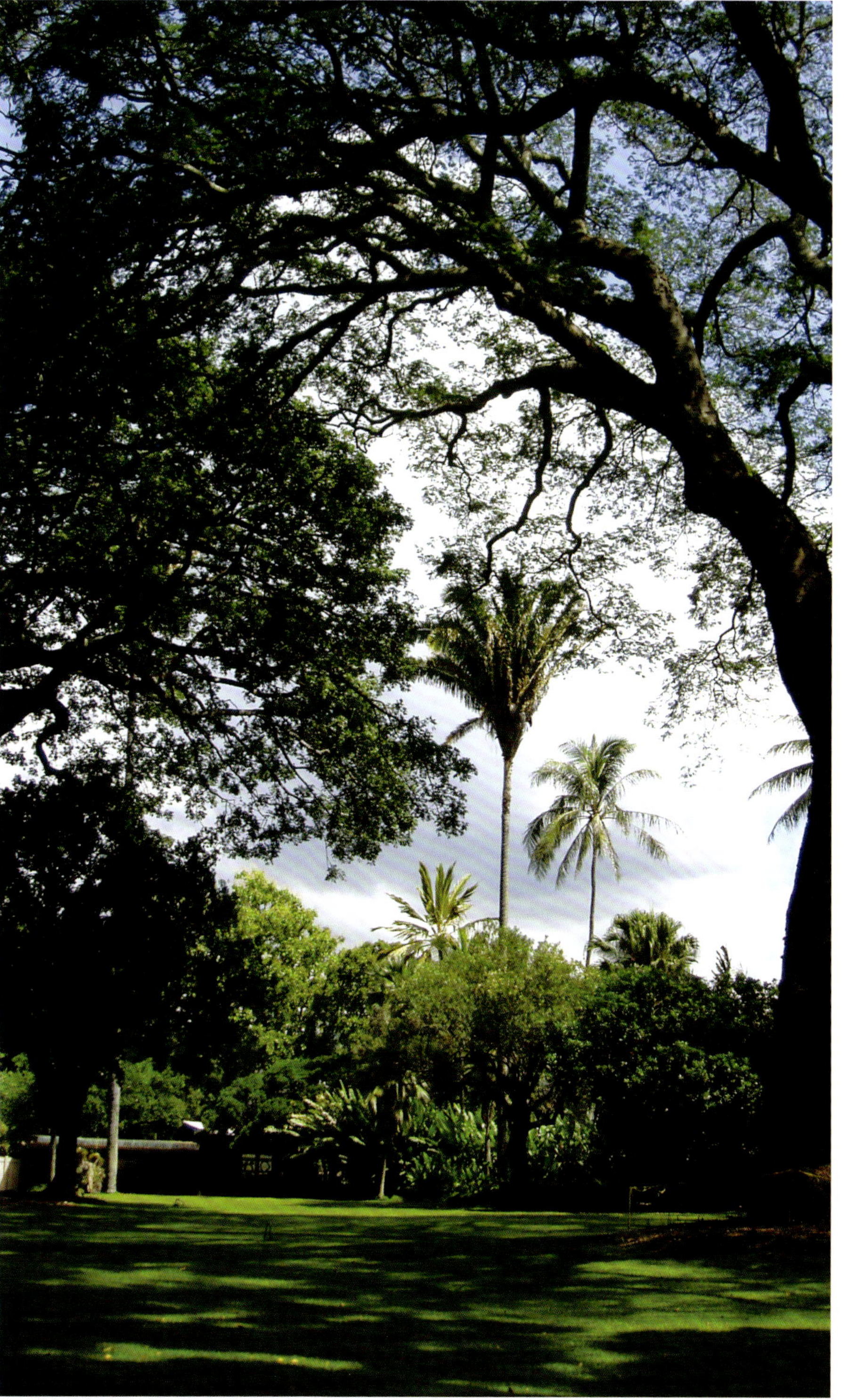

The grounds at Foster Botanical Garden.

Honolulu Botanical Gardens
Oahu, Hawaii

Not just one, but five unique gardens make up the Honolulu Botanical Gardens on the island of Oahu. Collectively, the gardens cover 650 acres and contain more than 5,000 different types of trees and plants from around the world. Emphasizing Hawaii's rare flora, the gardens cultivate, study, and conserve the plants under their care.

Ke'anae Arboretum
Kula, Hawaii

Located along the popular Hana Highway, a scenic, winding road that connects the towns of Kahului and Hana on the island of Maui, this six-acre garden occupies a group of leveled terraces that were once used for growing taro, a staple of traditional Hawaiian culture. Today, visitors can see 150 varieties of tropical plants, including hibiscus and papaya.

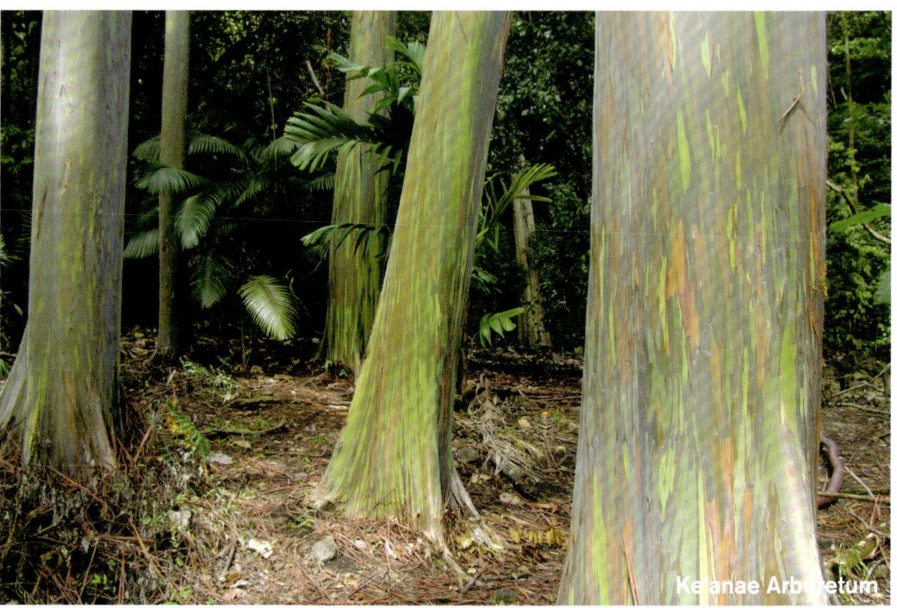
Ke'anae Arboretum

The park includes stands of rainbow eucalyptus trees with their surprisingly colorful trunks.

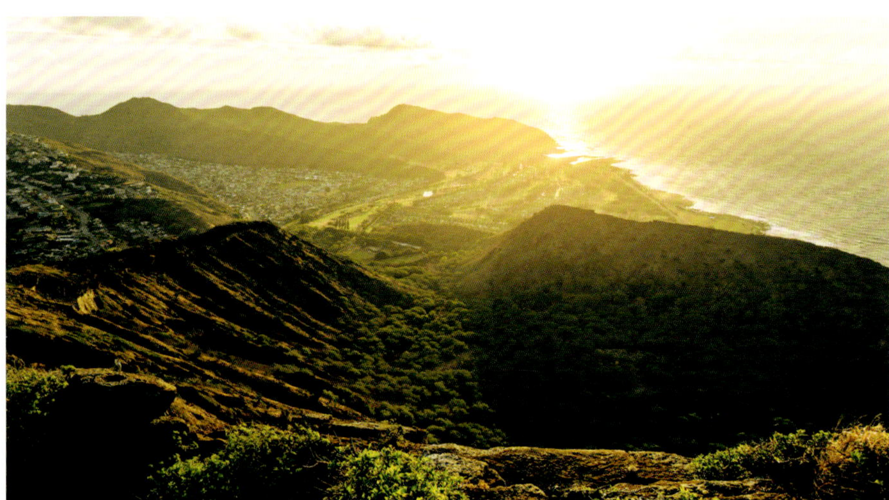

Koko Crater Botanical Garden's unusual location gives visitors a one-of-a-kind experience in a unique habitat.

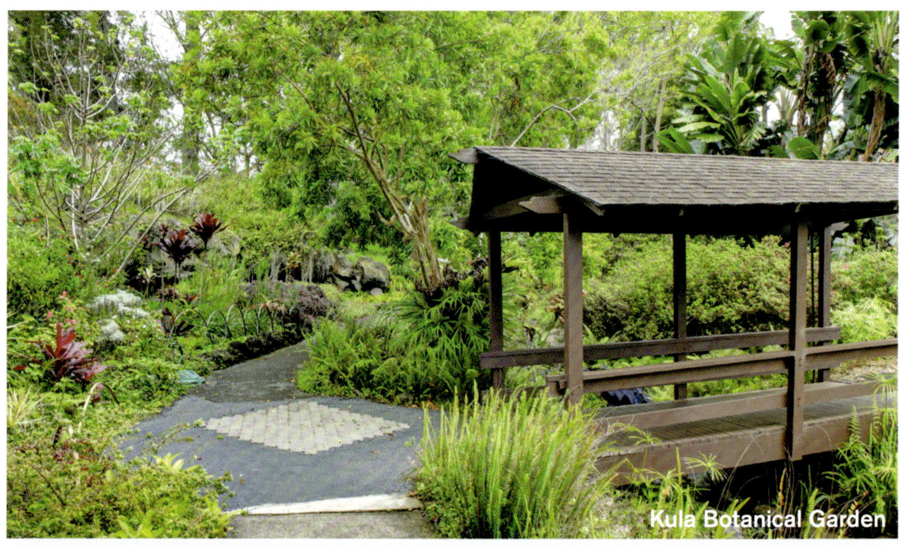
Kula Botanical Garden

In addition to the many native plants, the garden includes an aviary, koi pond, and covered bridge.

Koko Crater Botanical Garden
Honolulu, Hawaii

Koko Crater is an extinct volcanic cone that rises about 1,208 feet above sea level. What was once filled with lava is now teeming with life, including plumeria, bougainvillea, trees, aloes, cacti, and other plants suitable to the dry conditions inside the crater. This 60-acre garden protects the rare flora of this once-volcanic area.

Kula Botanical Garden
Kula, Hawaii

This native Hawaiian plant reserve was the first public garden on the island of Maui, established in 1971. The property covers six acres on the slopes of Maui's massive shield volcano, Haleakala. Almost 2,000 types of plants, including orchids, bromeliads, and native Hawaiian trees like koa and kukui, are featured within the garden.

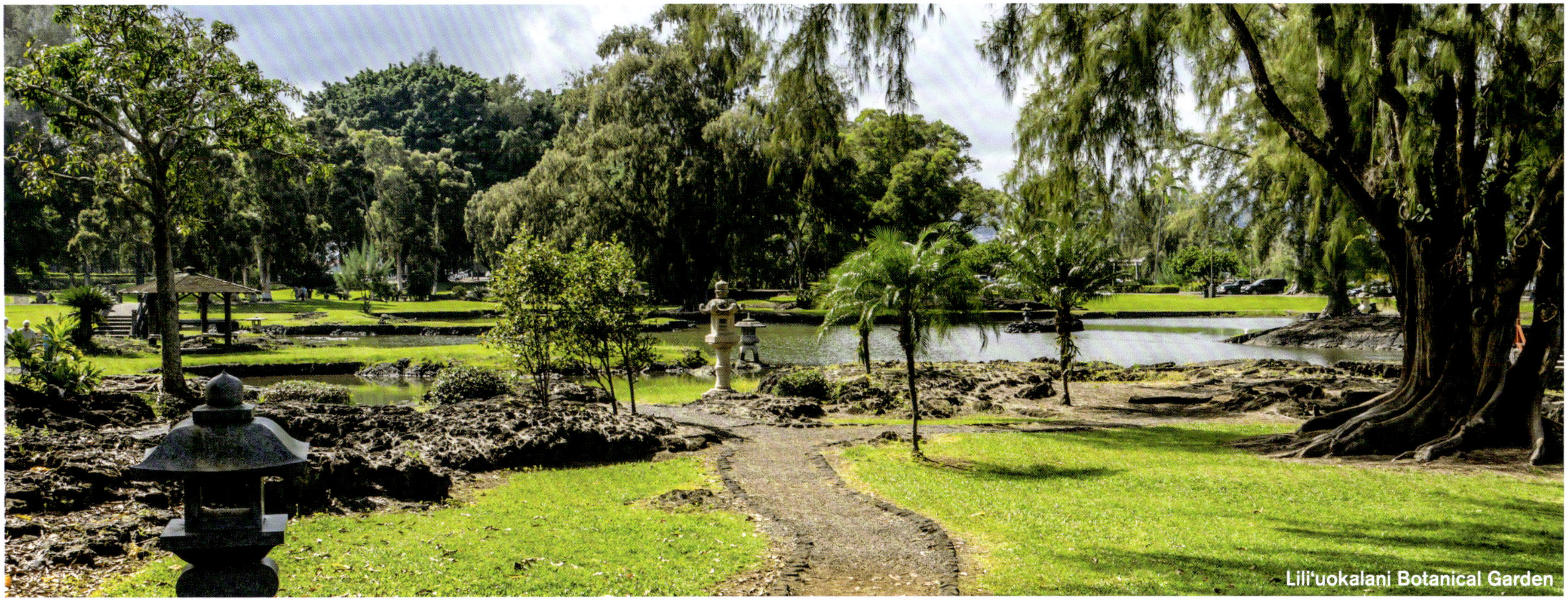

Lili'uokalani Botanical Garden

The garden provides an oasis for urban locals from Honolulu.

Lili'uokalani Botanical Garden
Honolulu, Hawaii

The land on which this seven-acre garden sits was given to the city of Honolulu by Queen Lili'uokalani, Hawaii's last reigning monarch. The garden, situated near the picturesque Nu'uanu Stream and Waikahalulu waterfall, is devoted solely to native plants, including banyan, kukui, and royal palm trees.

Harold L. Lyon Arboretum
Honolulu, Hawaii

This garden, which was established in 1918 and is managed by the University of Hawaii, spans almost 200 acres in the Manoa Valley. Much of the site consists of a man-made rainforest, created by the arboretum's first director, botanist Harold L. Lyon. More than 5,000 species of tropical plants now thrive in the garden.

Maui Nui Botanical Gardens
Kahului, Hawaii

Covering five acres on the island of Maui, this garden features not only native Hawaiian plants, but also those introduced to the islands from Polynesia. Special emphasis is placed on native plants found on the coastline, and the garden maintains a seed bank to protect these species in case of fires or other disasters.

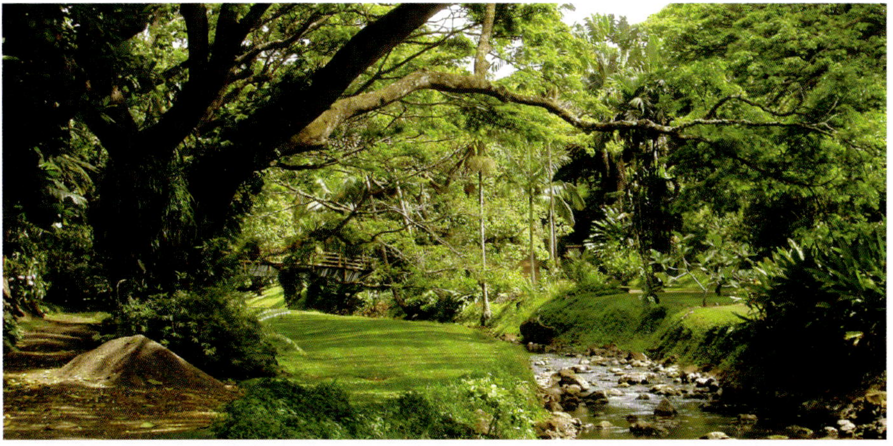

McBryde Garden comprises about 200 acres on the south shore of Kauai.

McBryde Garden
Koloa, Hawaii

McBryde Garden prides itself on cultivating the largest collection of native Hawaiian plants in existence, including rare and endangered species. Most notable is the alula plant, which has been extinct in the wild since 2020, and a collection of plants brought to the islands in canoes by the Polynesians, lending their nickname, "canoe plants."

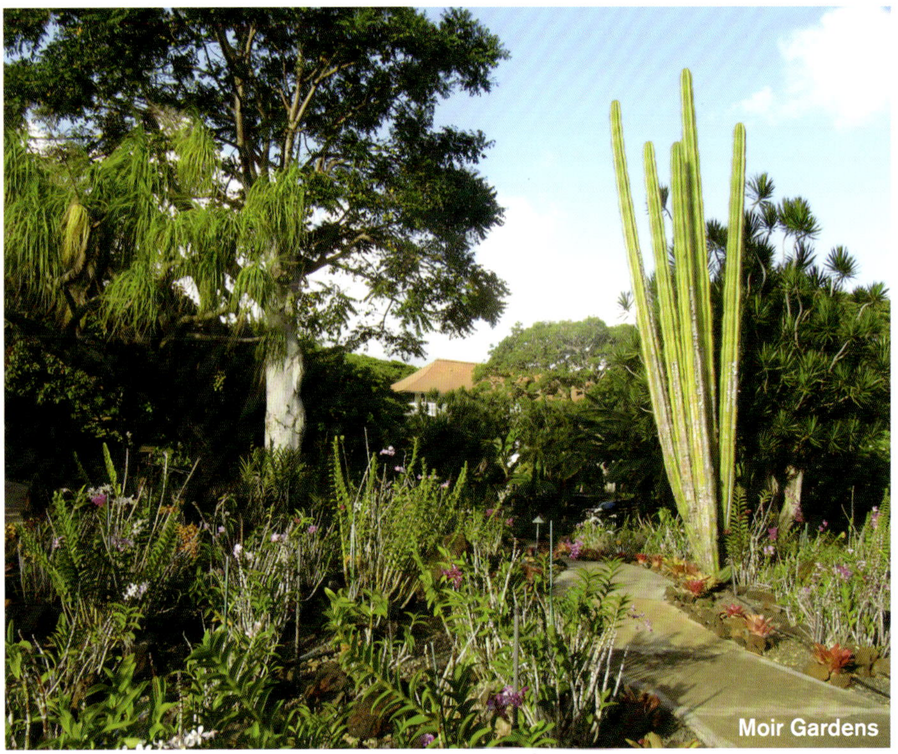

Moir Gardens

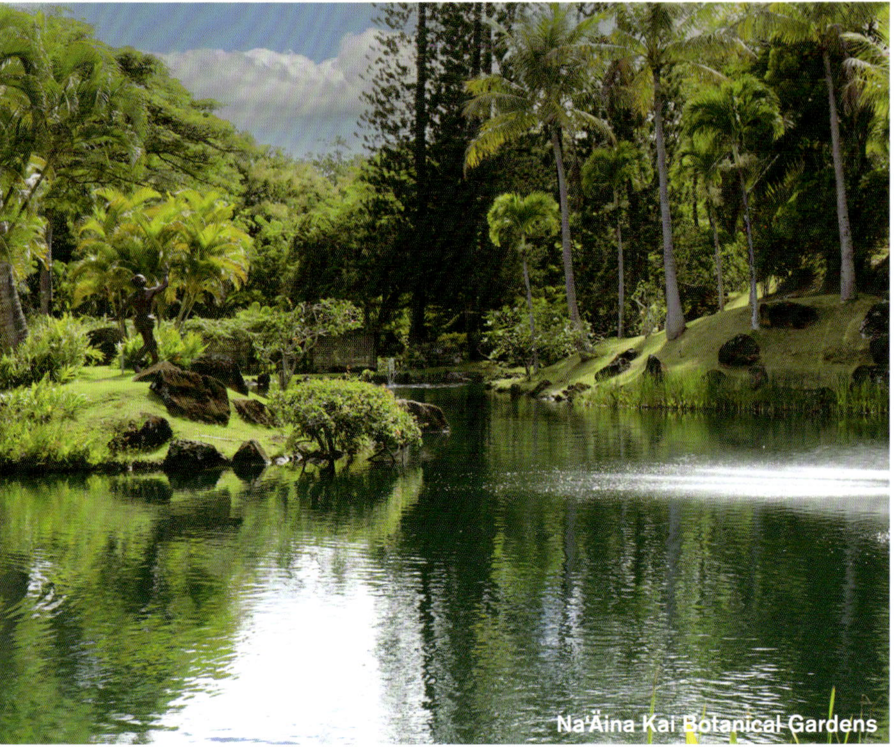

Na'Āina Kai Botanical Gardens

Moir Gardens
Poipu, Hawaii

This 35-acre garden was established in 1954 by Alexandra Moir, whose husband, Hector, was the manager of Kiahuna Plantation, Hawaii's first sugarcane plantation. Alexandra began adding drought-tolerant plants to the grounds in the 1930s, including succulents, cacti, orchids, and coconut trees. Today, the gardens are adjacent to an oceanfront resort property, making them a perfect spot for a quiet pre-dinner stroll.

Na'Āina Kai Botanical Gardens
Kilauea, Hawaii

Na'Āina Kai, meaning "lands by the sea," was created in 1982 to not only conserve the trees and plants of the property, but also to be a venue for artists to display their work. The 240-acre garden features more than 200 bronze sculptures throughout the grounds, which includes an International Desert Garden, a Wild Forest Garden, a hedge maze, and a children's garden.

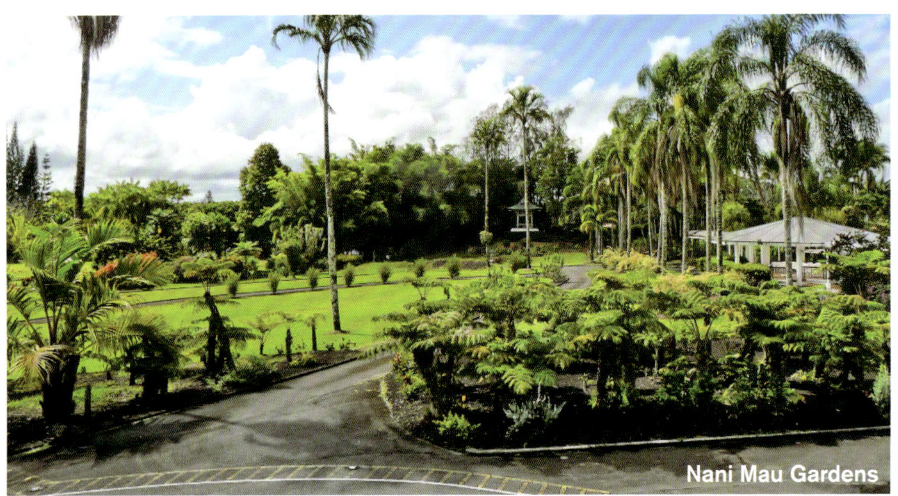

Nani Mau Gardens

Nani Mau Gardens
Hilo, Hawaii

Before this 23-acre property was transformed into a botanical garden, it was used to grow papayas. Today, papayas are just one of the 2,000 plant varieties cultivated at Nani Mau, which means "beautiful forever." The garden features more than 200 types of flowering plants–including 2,300 orchids–and 100 species of fruit trees. The site also contains a Japanese garden, butterfly house, and a European garden.

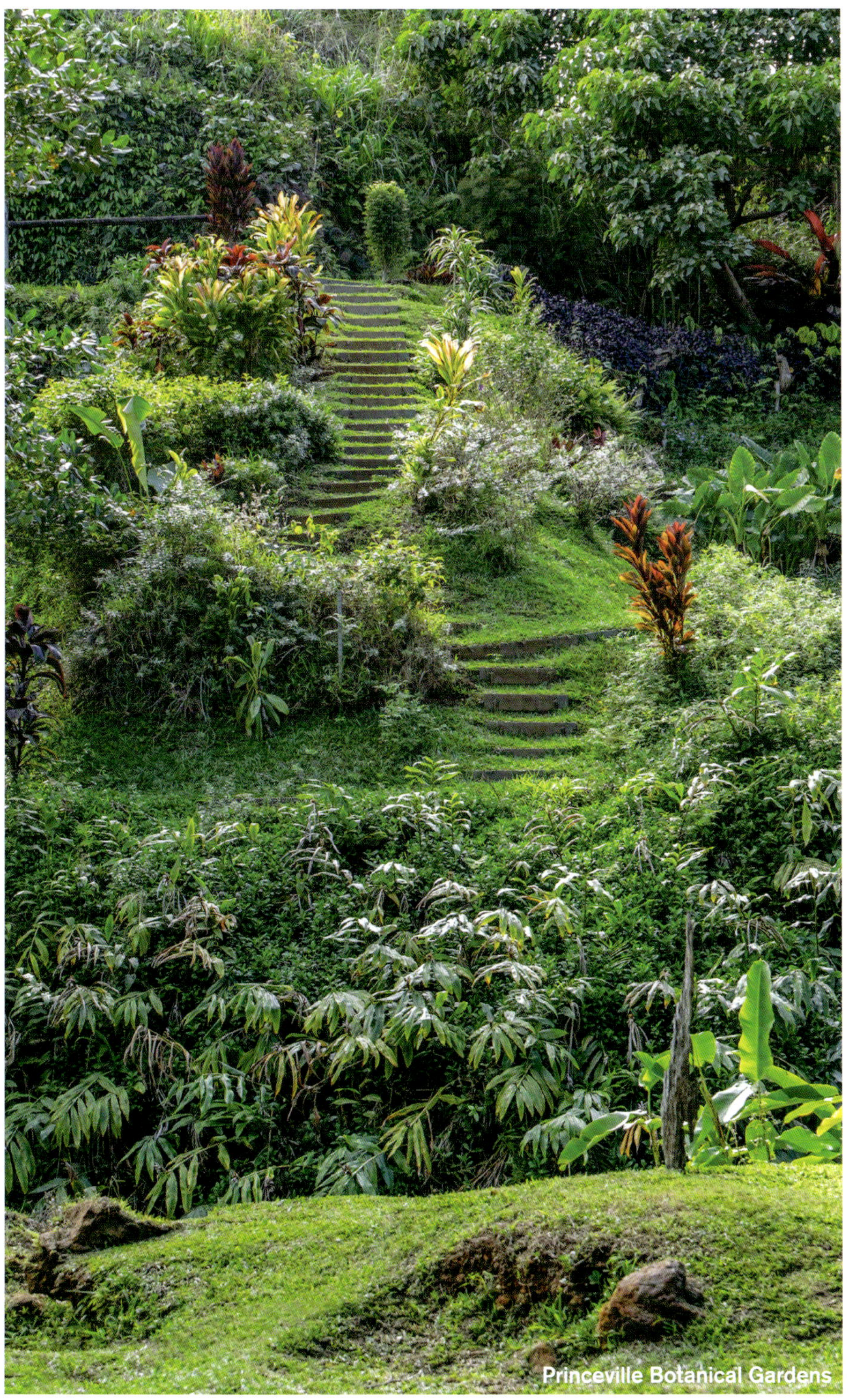
Princeville Botanical Gardens

Ravines, bridges, and a terraced topography give the gardens an adventurous feel.

Princeville Botanical Gardens
Princeville, Hawaii

This relatively young botanical garden began as a hobby for founders Bill and Lucinda Robertson, who officially opened the property to the public in 2010. The unique garden now cultivates chocolate, honey, and fruits, in addition to other tropical plants, and offers reservation-only walking tours of the property. A three-hour tour guides visitors through the entire garden, where they can learn about the history of chocolate and view the cacao trees where the process of making this candy begins. Gourmet chocolates from around the world–as well as fruit and honey–are offered for tasting, making this garden a favorite for chocoholics!

Other Hawaii Gardens

Sadie Seymour Botanical Gardens
Kailua-Kona, Hawaii

- Features plants from Hawaii, Australia, New Zealand, Indonesia, Africa, and Central America
- Is also an archeological site containing a *heiau*, or Hawaiian temple

Spirit of Aloha Oceanfront Botanical Gardens
Haiku, Hawaii

- An 11-acre nature preserve and Historic Hawaiian Site dedicated to protecting native Hawaiian plants
- A National Wildlife Federation-certified bird sanctuary

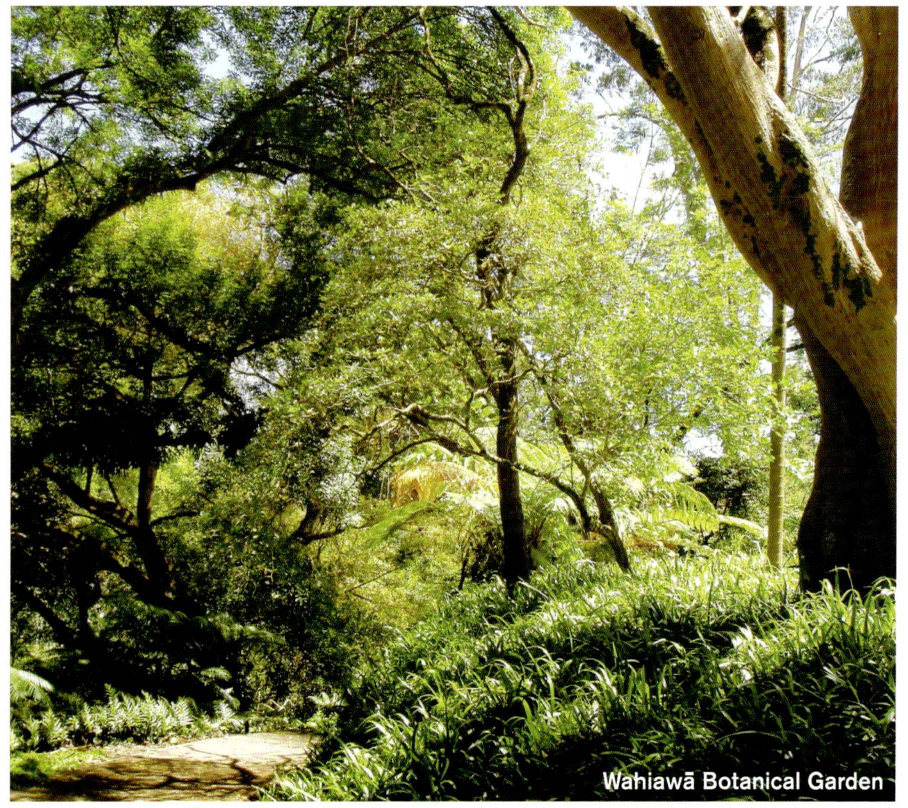
Wahiawā Botanical Garden

University of Hawaii at Hilo Botanical Gardens
Hilo, Hawaii

Curiosity was the catalyst that led to the creation of this garden on the University of Hawaii campus. In the 1990s, UH-Hilo biology professor Dom Hemmes was taken aback when a student said they'd never seen a pine tree. Hemmes immediately began planning and creating a garden where future students could study and learn about plants they may not have had an opportunity to see. Whereas most botanical gardens in Hawaii focus on protecting native plants, Hemmes designed his garden to showcase specimens from all over the world. The garden is now best known for its impressive collection of more than 120 cycads.

Wahiawā Botanical Garden
Wahiawa, Hawaii

Considered the "tropical jewel" of the Honolulu Botanical Gardens, this 27-acre garden's origins stretch back to the 1920s, when the property was used by the Hawaiian Sugar Planters' Association for experimental tree planting. The botanical garden was officially opened in 1957, but many of its trees date back more than a hundred years. Wahiawā is considered a rainforest garden, and requires temperatures that are relatively cool compared to other gardens on the islands. The garden features a self-guided tour that directs visitors past dozens of significant trees and plants, including colorful Rainbow Eucalyptus, fragrant Arabian Coffee shrubs, and the native Hawaiian Tree Fern.

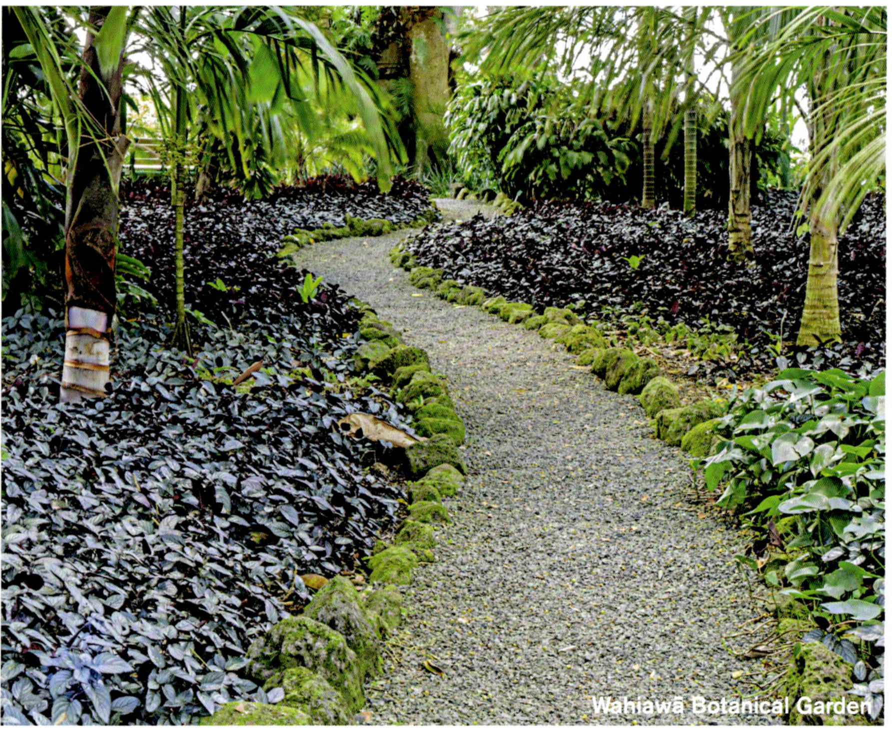
Wahiawā Botanical Garden

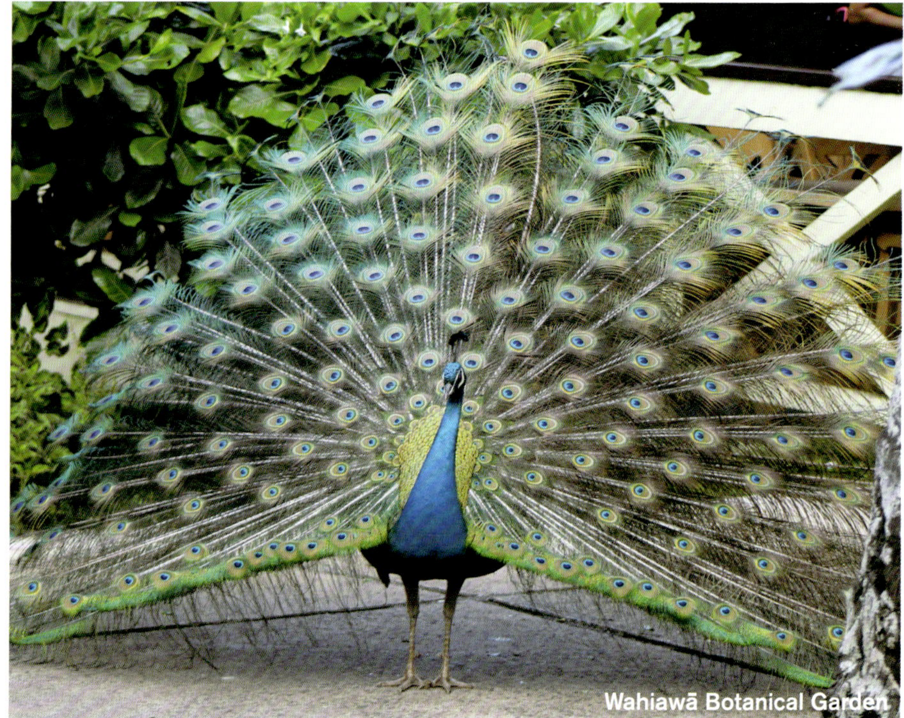
Wahiawā Botanical Garden

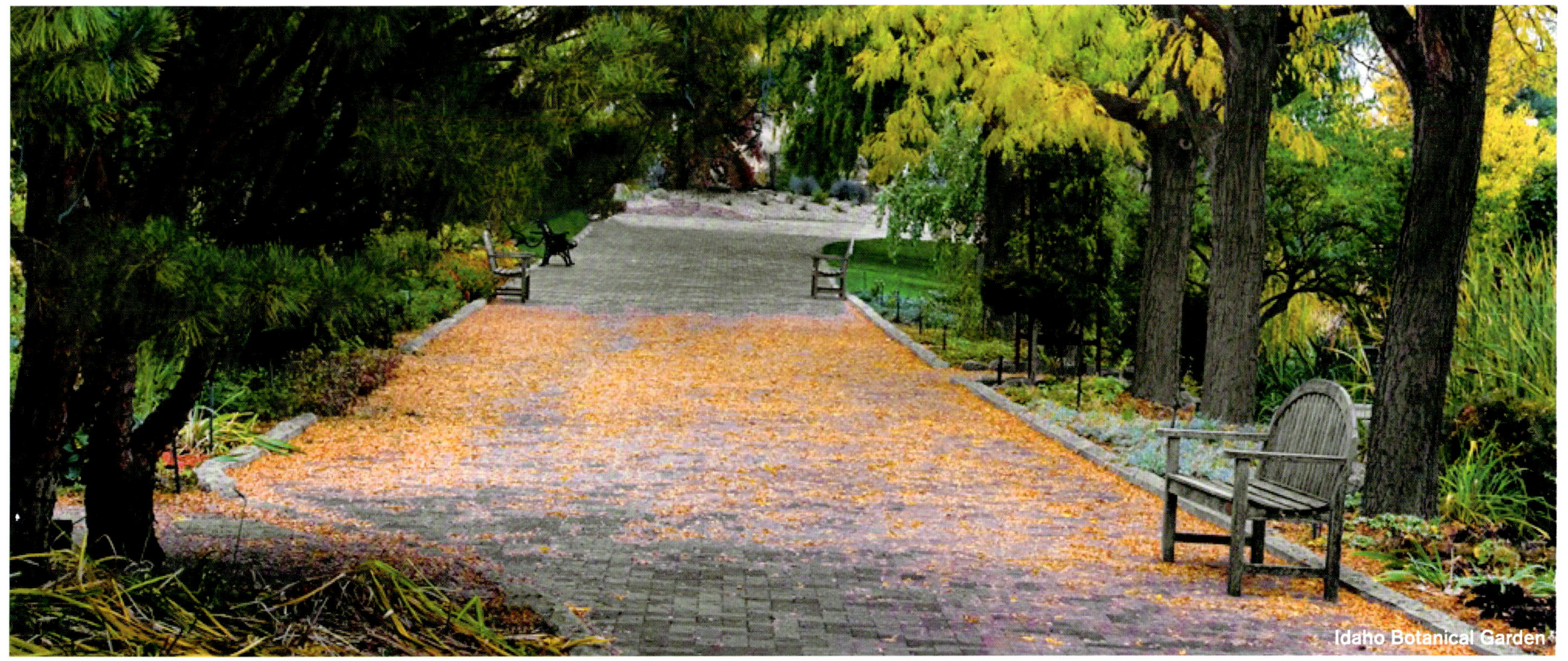

A brick pathway circles the herb garden.

Idaho Botanical Garden
Boise, Idaho

This 15-acre garden prides itself on being a "museum" for plants. Meticulous records are kept for every specimen in the garden, lending the plants historical, educational, and scientific value along with their aesthetic beauty. Collections include a Rose Garden with modern and antique roses, an Herb Garden featuring thyme, rosemary, sorrel, and comfrey, and an Idaho Native Plant Garden showcasing the state's diverse plant life. Of particular significance to the area is the Lewis and Clark Native Plant Garden, which contains 145 species collected by the famed explorers, who traveled through Idaho on their journey from the Mississippi River to the Pacific Ocean between 1804 and 1806.

Worth Exploring in Idaho

Idaho State Arboretum
Pocatello, Idaho

- Open daily, with free admission and guided tours
- Plants include yellow-bloomed forsythia, several species of pine, and magnolia

Sawtooth Botanical Garden
Ketchum, Idaho

- Represents the five biomes found within Idaho: sagebrush steppe, lava, alpine, montane, and riparian
- Features educational and meditative spaces, and children's gardens

University of Idaho Arboretum and Botanical Garden
Moscow, Idaho

- Spans 63 acres and contains more than 800 species of plants and trees
- Cultivates conifers, ornamental plants, and a giant sequoia

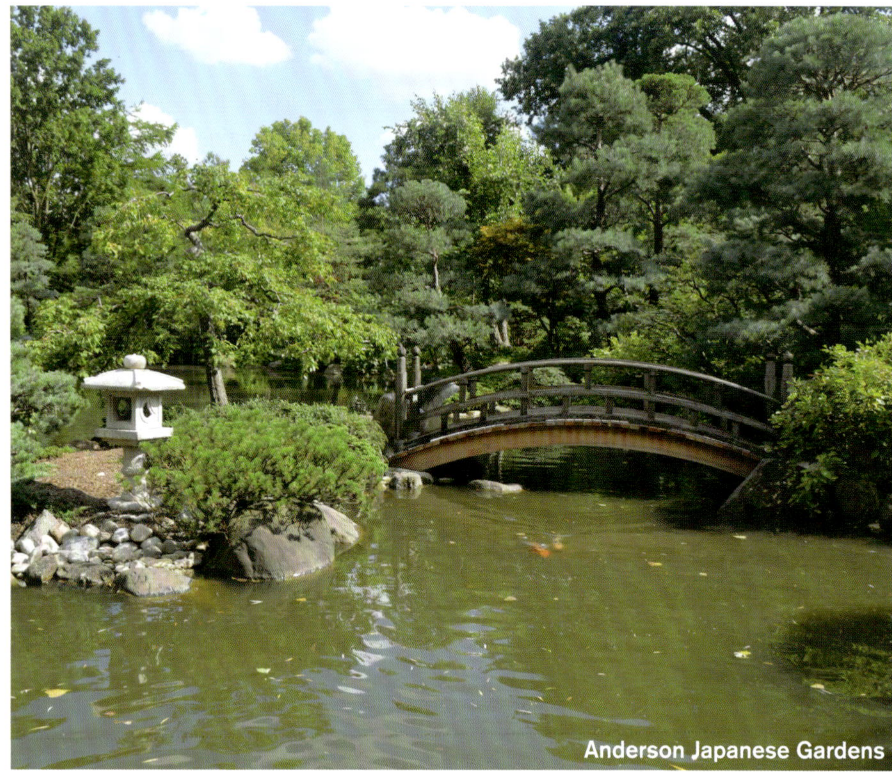
Anderson Japanese Gardens

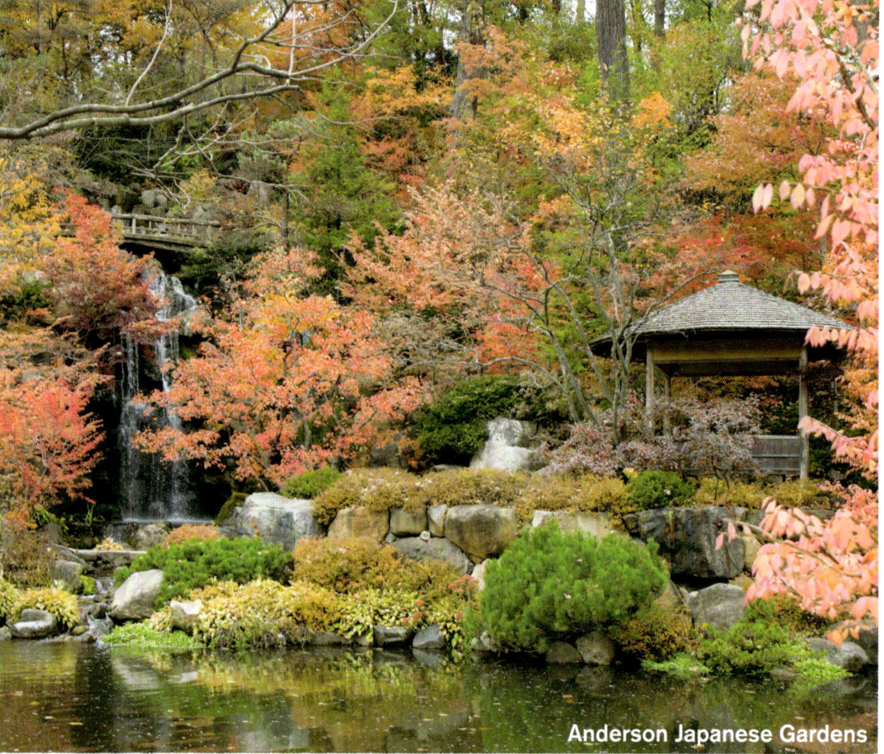
Anderson Japanese Gardens

Anderson Japanese Gardens
Rockford, Illinois

Welcoming nearly 100,000 guests every year, this garden strives to be a unique, world-class experience. Businessman John Anderson was inspired to create the property in 1978 after a trip to a Japanese-style garden in Oregon, and he carefully planned out the garden to exude authenticity. Today, Anderson Japanese Gardens is considered one of the finest Japanese gardens in the world. From the carefully pruned trees and shrubs to the pagodas, stone lanterns, ponds, and bridges, every detail has been cultivated into a work of art. The property is highly sought after for weddings and other events, and in the summer offers concerts and outdoor musical performances in its tranquil setting.

Worth Exploring in Illinois

Mabery Gelvin Botanical Garden
Mahomet, Illinois

- An eight-acre garden located in the Lake of the Woods Forest Preserve
- Features a Japanese garden with waterfalls and a koi pond

Don Opel Arboretum
Freeport, Illinois

- Located on the campus of Highland Community College
- Contains 200 varieties of trees and shrubs and 150 perennials

Quad City Botanical Center
Rock Island, Illinois

- An indoor tropical atrium and outdoor gardens situated next to the Mississippi River
- Collections include irises, daylilies, mums, and ornamental grasses

University of Illinois Arboretum/Plant Biology Greenhouse and Conservatory
Urbana, Illinois

- 160 acres of gardens, plant collections, and habitats
- The 2000-square-foot conservatory houses more than 200 species of tropical and subtropical plants

Wilder Park Conservatory
Elmhurst, Illinois

- Features prairie grasses, forbs, and woodland flowers
- Has grown from 500 types of plants at its founding in 1923 to nearly 12,000 today

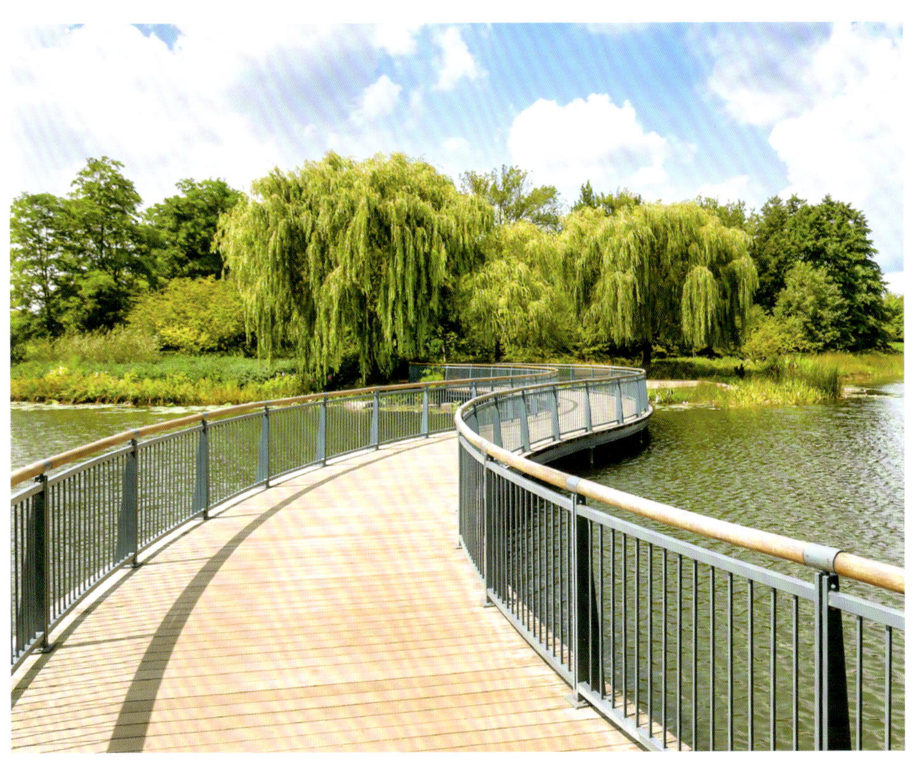

Chicago Botanic Garden
Glencoe, Illinois

This garden can trace its origins back to 1890, when the Chicago Horticultural Society regularly hosted flower and horticultural shows, including a show during the 1893 World's Fair. But it wasn't until 1962 that the society helped to plan and then create a new public garden, officially opening the Chicago Botanic Garden in 1972.

Today, the 385-acre garden sits within the Cook County Forest Preserves and contains 27 display gardens and five natural habitats. Visitor favorites include the Sensory Garden, where colorful, sweet-smelling blossoms delight the senses, the Buehler Enabling Garden, which features raised beds and adaptive gardening tools to demonstrate how gardening can be accessible for everyone, and the Heritage Garden, dedicated to Carl Linnaeus, the "father of modern taxonomy." Other gardens include the Krasberg Rose Garden, which features more than 5,000 roses and is one of the largest public rose display gardens in the country. Also notable is the four-acre Regenstein Fruit and Vegetable Garden, featuring 700 types of berries, fruits, vegetables, and herbs that grow well in the Chicago climate, showing visitors what's possible in their own home gardens. The Graham Bulb Garden, full of tulips and lilies, and the Elizabeth Hubert Malott Japanese Garden round out the spectacular spaces at this impressive destination.

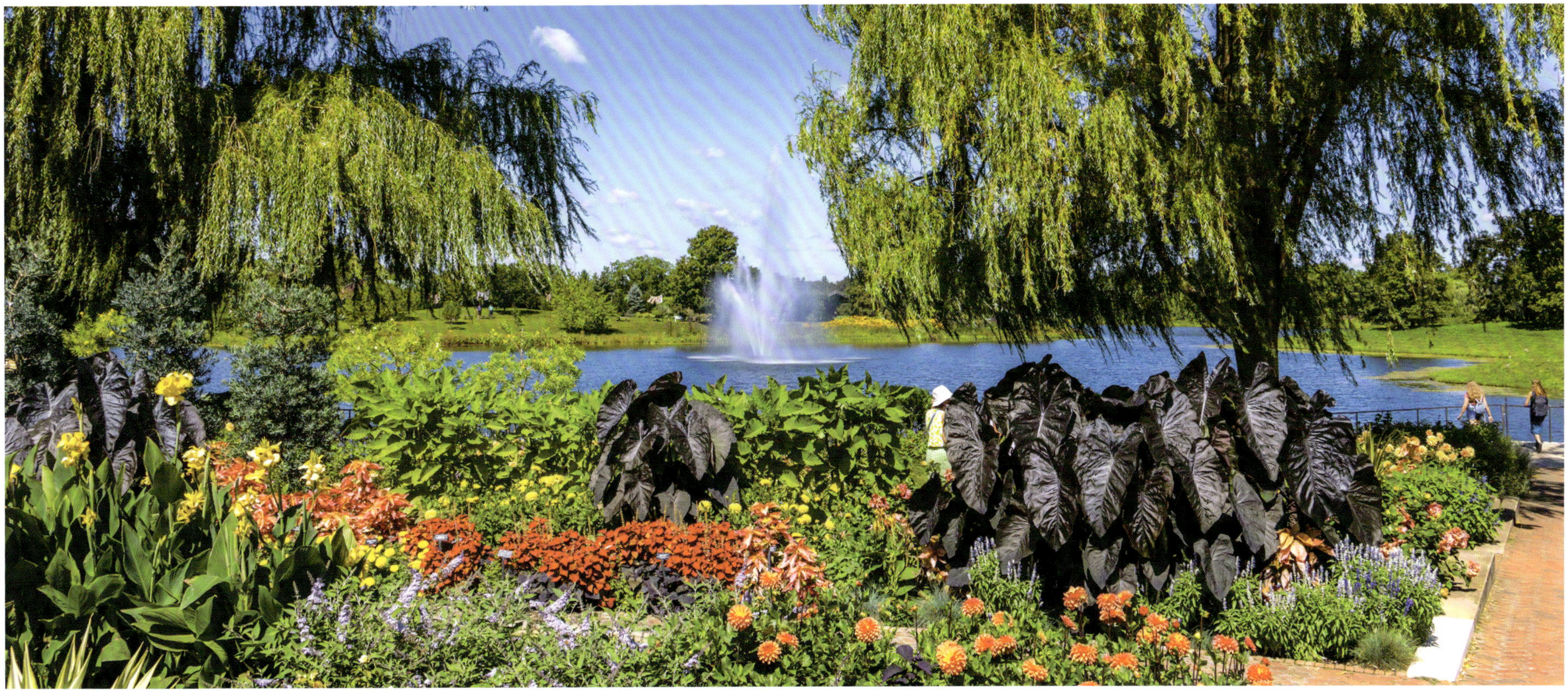

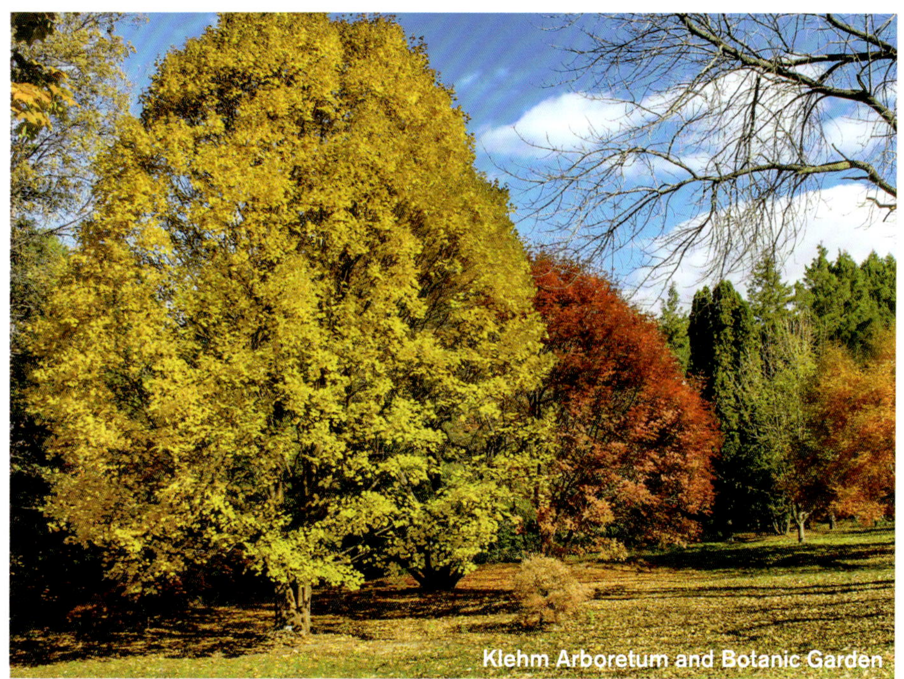
Klehm Arboretum and Botanic Garden

The Gardens at SIUE
Edwardsville, Illinois

Located on the campus of Southern Illinois University Edwardsville, this 36-acre garden began its life as a modest arboretum in 1990. The site has since grown, adding scenic paths, a butterfly garden, bridges, and event spaces. Every April, the gardens welcome *Art for the Earth*, artwork installed in honor of Earth Day.

Klehm Arboretum and Botanic Garden
Rockford, Illinois

An interactive children's garden, a fountain garden, and a vibrant pollinator garden are a few of the features that draw families to this 155-acre property in northern Illinois. The arboretum contains more than 50 species of conifers, as well as maple, elm, beech and dozens more trees from around the world.

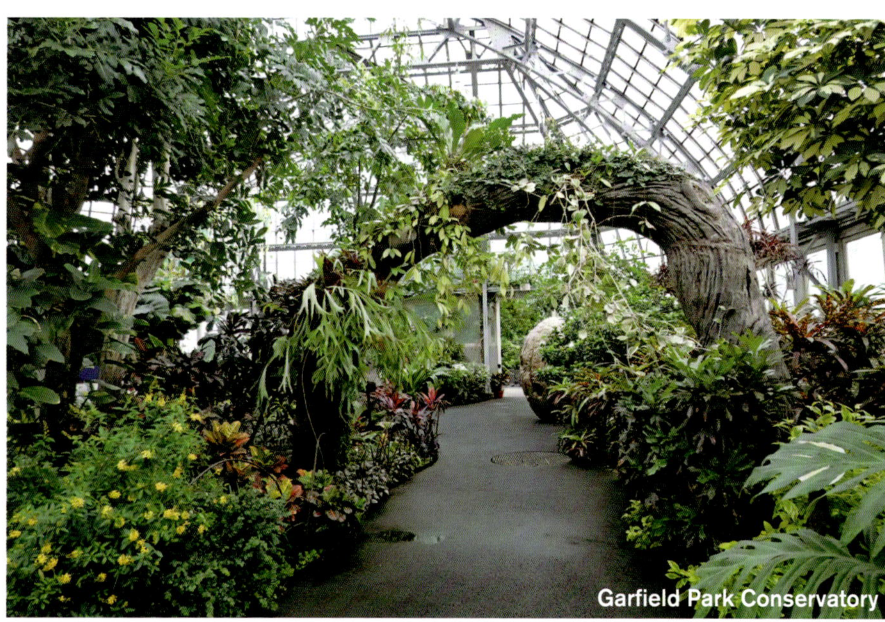
Garfield Park Conservatory

Garfield Park Conservatory
Chicago, Illinois

A two-acre greenhouse and ten-acre outdoor space make up this urban oasis, one of the largest conservatories in the country. Highlights include the Palm House–which, at 65 feet high and 90 feet wide, is the largest room in the conservatory–and the Show House, the site of colorful annual flower shows.

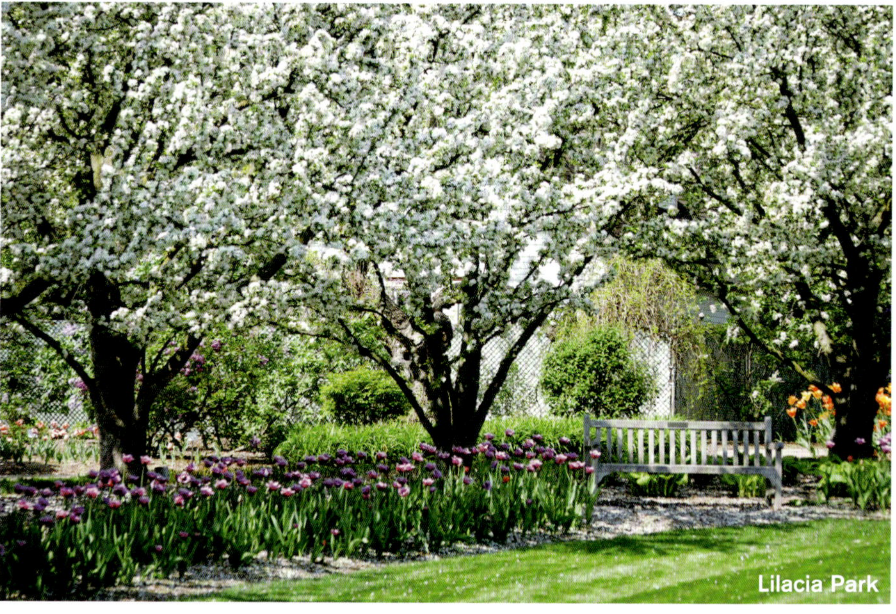
Lilacia Park

Lilacia Park
Lombard, Illinois

This park, which was added to the National Register of Historic Places in 2019, is best known for its spectacular lilacs and tulips. The 8.5-acre park was established in 1927 using lilac cuttings that were collected in the 1800s. Today, the gardens showcase more than 200 varieties of lilacs and 50 varieties of tulips.

Abraham Lincoln Memorial Garden
Springfield, Illinois

Named in honor of the president who spent much of his time in Springfield before he was elected the sixteenth president, this garden is made up of several sections that span 100 acres. Highlights include an interactive indoor Nature Center, a colorful native wildflower garden, and the playful Children's Woodland Garden.

Morton Arboretum
Lisle, Illinois

More than 4,100 plant species are cultivated on this 1,700-acre property, which is also the home of the Center for Tree Science. In addition to the garden's numerous trees and plants, it also contains the Schulenberg Prairie, a restored tallgrass prairie. The arboretum offers educational content for children and adults, including classroom and online courses.

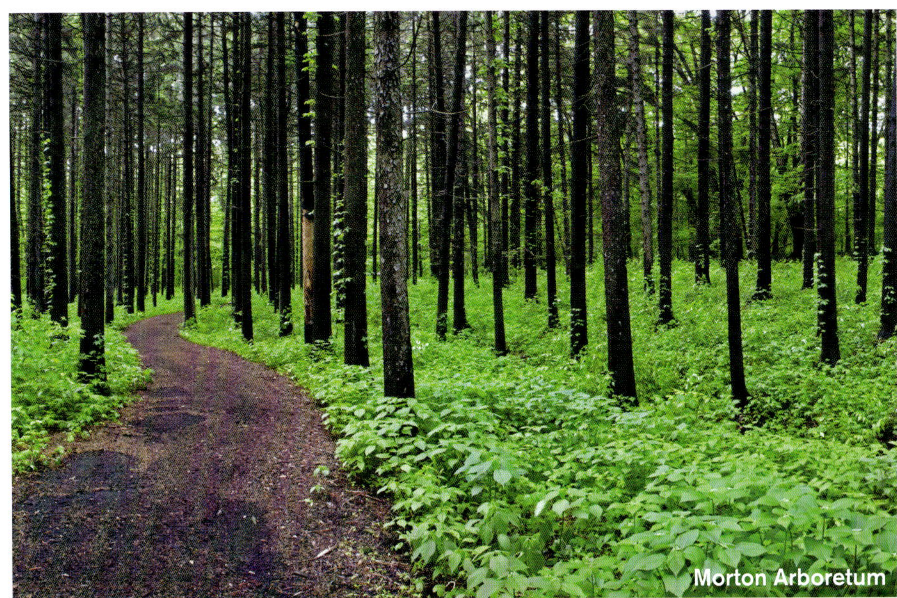

A trail winds through the arboretum's Spruce Plot.

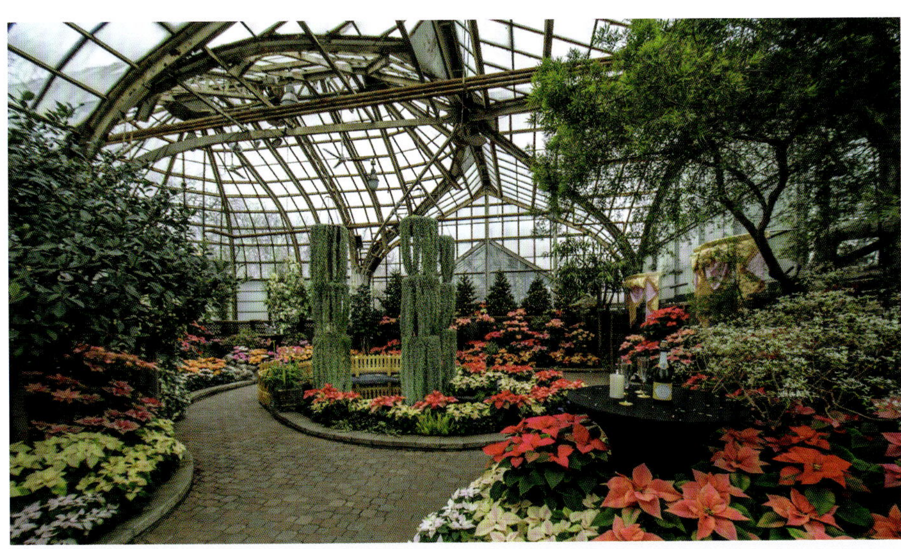

The Lincoln Park Conservatory offers urbanites a botanical retreat in the heart of the city.

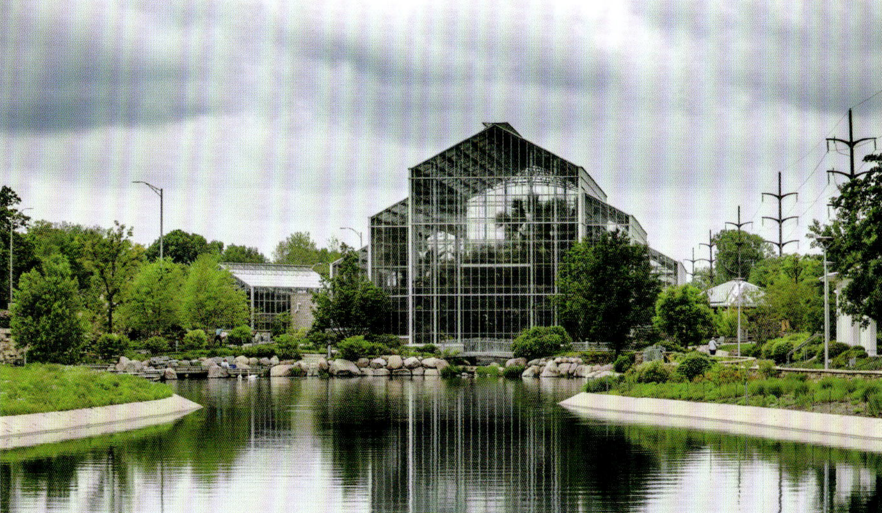

The Nicholas Conservatory and Garden is set on the banks of the Rock River.

Lincoln Park Conservatory
Chicago, Illinois

This three-acre, Victorian-era glass greenhouse was originally built between 1890 and 1895, and contains four display houses. The conservatory not only showcases exotic and tropical plants, but also grows plants used within the 1,208-acre Lincoln Park. Display halls include the Palm House, Orchid House, Fern Room, and Show House.

Nicholas Conservatory and Garden
Rockford, Illinois

At 11,000 square feet, this conservatory is the third largest in Illinois and contains water features, murals, and sculptures. Plants include tropical palms, orchids, and bromeliads, which are cultivated in an environmentally friendly way. A clever Green Roof Garden grows above the lobby, keeping the facility warm in the winter and cool in the summer.

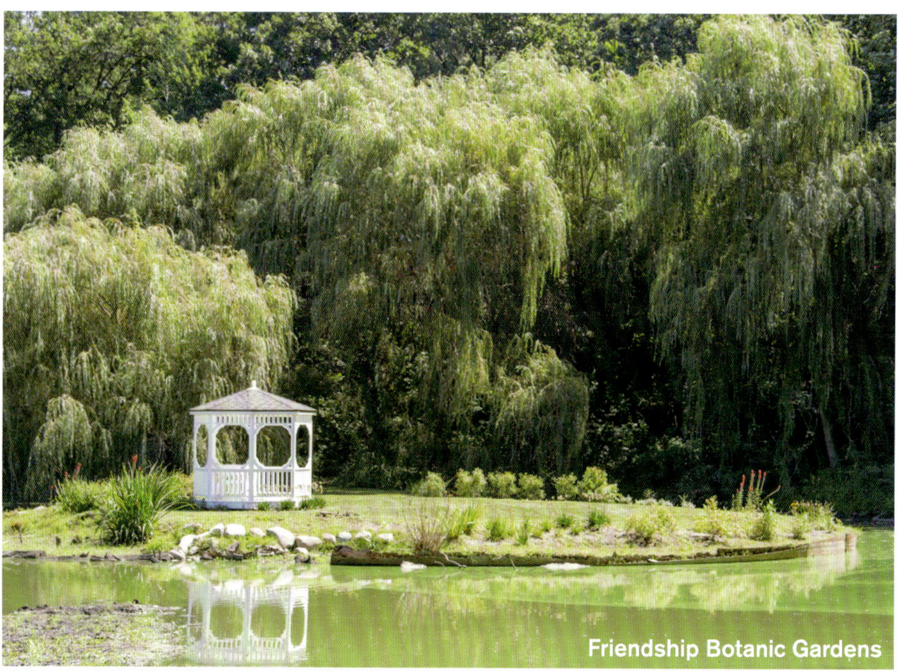

A small island with a gazebo framed by willows is tucked away on the grounds.

Friendship Botanic Gardens
Michigan City, Indiana
Spanning 105 acres of wooded landscape, this garden is home to several "legacy" trees, the oldest of which is a 215-year-old spruce tree. The property is known for its winding nature trails, including the Symphony Loop, the Wilderness Trail, and the Pottawatomie Trail, which feature numbered markers with descriptions of the garden's vegetation. The site's historic Heritage Gardens highlight garden culture from around the world, containing a Native American Garden, Romanian Garden, African-American Garden, English Tea House Garden, and much more. The garden is also renowned for its bird-watching opportunities, with keen-eyed visitors spotting herons, falcons, hummingbirds, woodpeckers, and dozens more species.

Worth Exploring in Indiana

Brincka Cross Gardens
Michigan City, Indiana
- A 61-acre property with a home that can be used as an event space
- Contains 450 varieties of hostas, daffodils, and magnolias

Christy Woods
Muncie, Indiana
- Located on the campus of Ball State University
- Established in 1918 and covered with forest of oak, hickory, maple, ash, and walnut

Foellinger-Freimann Botanical Conservatory
Fort Wayne, Indiana
- 100,000 square feet of gardens, including tropical plants and a Sonoran Desert display
- Contains 1,200 plants and 72 types of cacti

Hayes Arboretum
Richmond, Indiana
- Contains wild plants native to the region, including 450-year-old trees
- Features a geology collection with every type of rock native to Indiana

Potawatomi Conservatories
South Bend, Indiana
- Includes the Ella Morris Conservatory, the Muessel-Ellison Botanical Conservatory, and the Muessel-Ellison Desert Dome
- Features tropical, subtropical, and desert flora

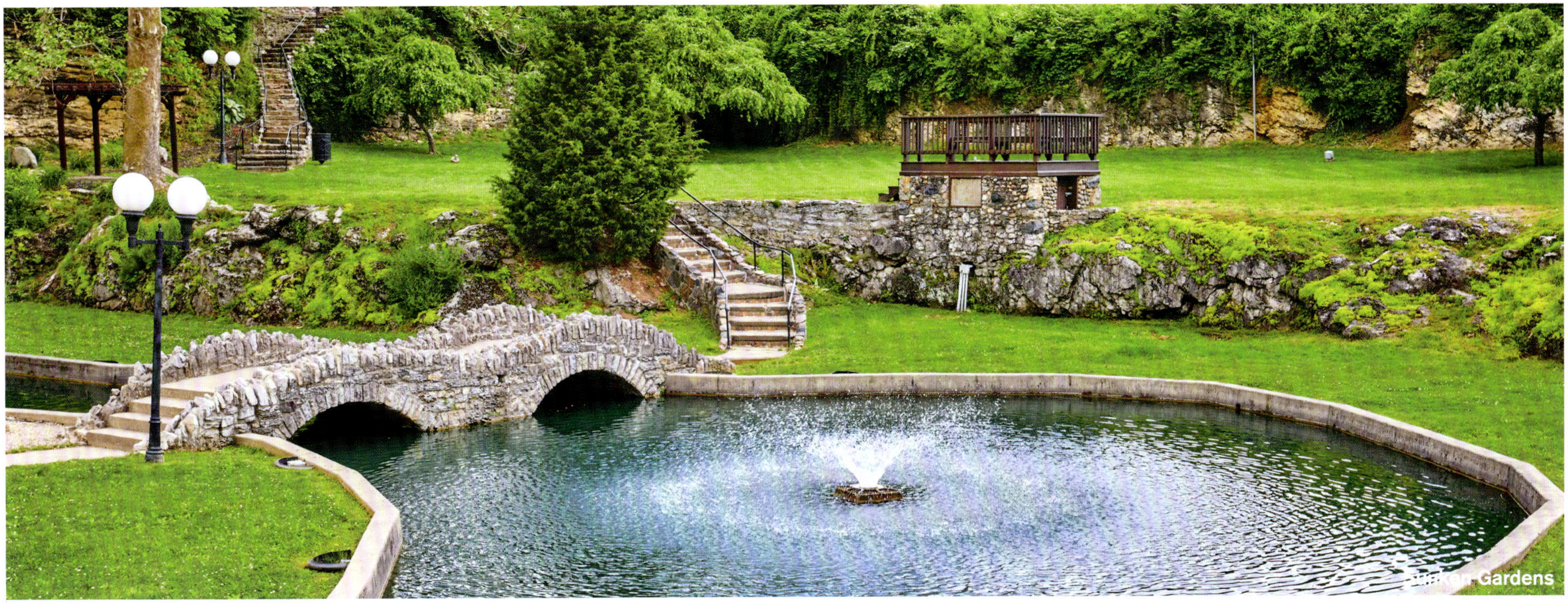

Stonework at the gardens includes a graceful fieldstone bridge, stairs, and natural-looking walls.

Gabis Arboretum at Purdue Northwest
Valparaiso, Indiana

An award-winning garden railway is one of the standout features of this 300-acre property, which also contains the largest collection of oak trees in Indiana. The arboretum offers a Native Plant Garden that is registered as a Monarch Waystation, an Adventure Garden demonstrating eco-friendly gardening methods, and several beautiful rose gardens.

Purdue University Horticulture Gardens
West Lafayette, Indiana

Also known as the Jules Janick Horticulture Garden in honor of the donor, a long-tenured faculty member, who helped to fund its 2019 revitalization, this garden was first established in 1982. It is home to hundreds of ornamental plants, with a particular emphasis on herbaceous perennials, mixed with annuals and woody plants.

Sunken Gardens
Huntington, Indiana

In the early 1900s, the property where this garden now sits was an abandoned quarry. But in 1923, the Chicago Landscape Company transformed it into a beautiful natural setting, complete with gardens, footbridges, fountains, and a horseshoe-shaped pool. Instead of being an eyesore, the former quarry's rock walls provide a unique backdrop.

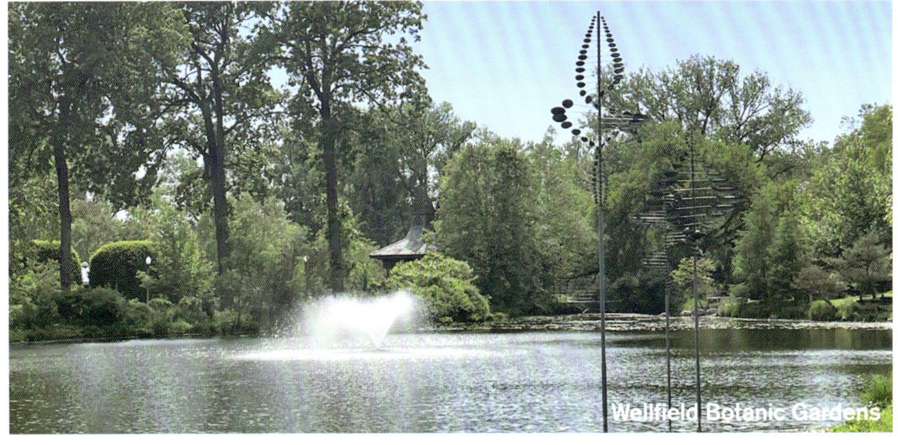

Sights at the garden include lakes, streams, waterfalls, and a fountain.

Wellfield Botanic Gardens
Elkhart, Indiana

This 36-acre property is known for more than just botanical beauty; it's also a source of hydropower and drinking water for the surrounding communities. The gardens are located on the site of the Main Street Well Field, the primary source of water for Elkhart since the 1800s. Features include an English-style garden and a children's garden.

Worth Exploring in Iowa

Bickelhaupt Arboretum
Clinton, Iowa

- Hundreds of types of trees, grouped by genus
- Also contains a wildflower garden, butterfly garden, and daylily collection

Brenton Arboretum
Dallas Center, Iowa

- A collection of 2,600 trees and plants, including 175 native Iowa species
- Contains a lake, pond, streams, walking paths, and wildflowers

Forest Park Museum and Arboretum
Perry, Iowa

- Contains 100 species of native trees and shrubs
- The property features an 1867 schoolhouse, an 1860s cabin, historical exhibits, and transportation memorabilia

Iowa Arboretum and Gardens
Madrid, Iowa

- 170 acres of trees and shrubs, as well as trails, streams, and prairies
- Features a founder's garden, herb garden, children's garden, and butterfly garden

Lilac Arboretum and Children's Forest
Des Moines, Iowa

- Also known as the Ewing Lilac Arboretum
- Contains more than 1,400 lilac bushes consisting of 120 varieties

Newton Arboretum and Botanical Gardens
Newton, Iowa

- Contains six acres of cultivated gardens and 13.5 acres of seedling prairie
- Home to 280 individual trees and shrubs

Stampe Lilac Garden
Davenport, Iowa

- A lilac garden, gazebo, and lodge in a picturesque location
- Vibrant blooms make for a perfect wedding backdrop

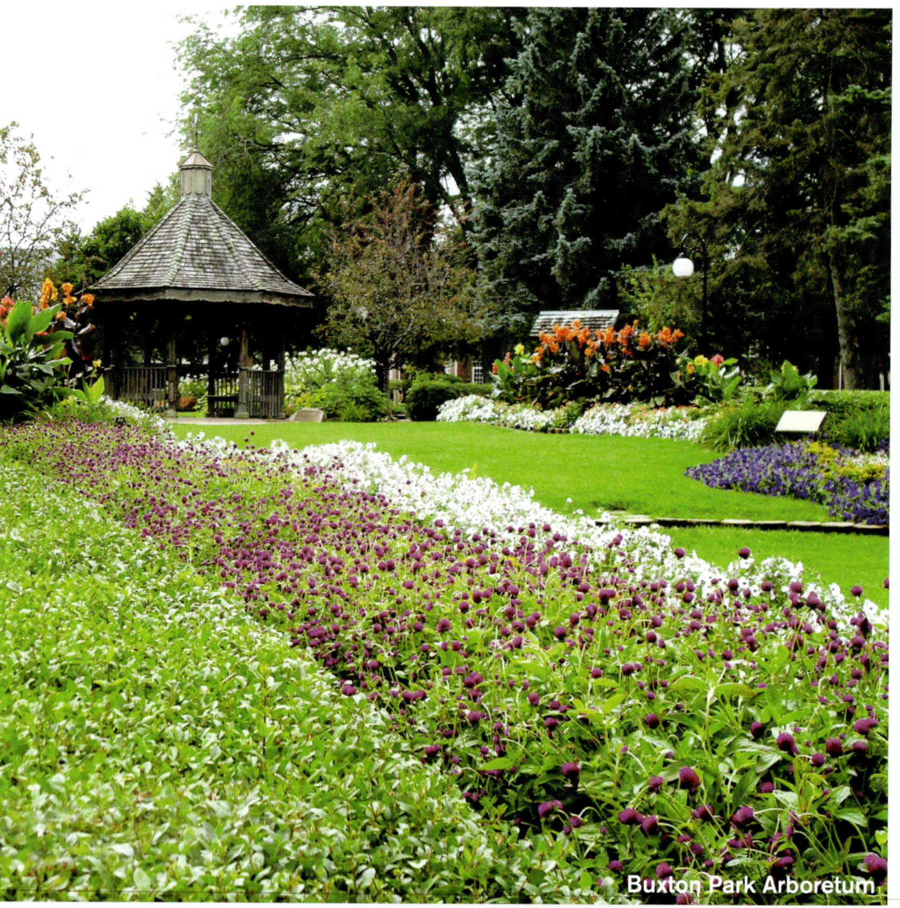
Buxton Park Arboretum

This small-town park is quaint, colorful, and charming.

Buxton Park Arboretum
Indianola, Iowa

When William Buxton Sr. donated this park to Indianola in December 1905, he called it a "Christmas gift to the public." The "gift" became the first park established in the city, and today it is a 5.4-acre arboretum and botanical garden with 12 flowerbeds, an arboretum, a butterfly garden, an ornamental fountain, and public art. The tranquil property is always open, free of charge, and offers a self-guided tour pamphlet for those wishing to know more about the trees in the park. In 2019, the park added a children's garden, where little ones can play and explore kid-sized garden plots.

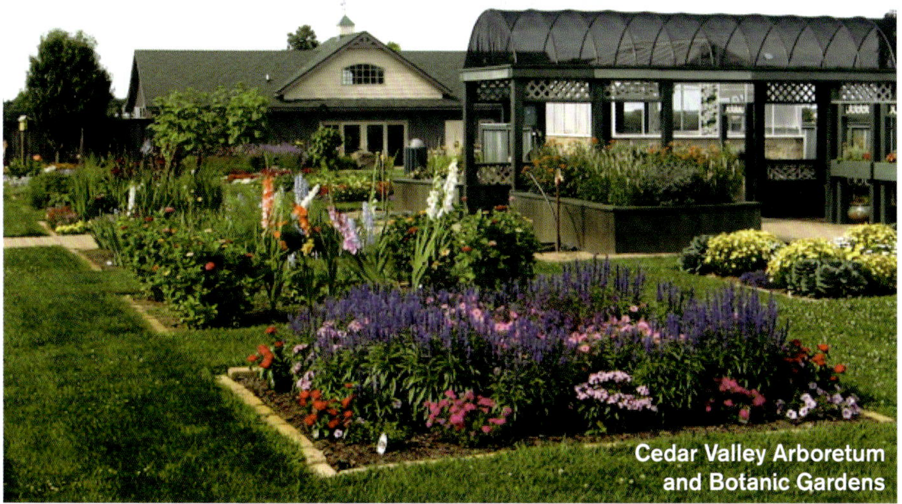
Cedar Valley Arboretum and Botanic Gardens

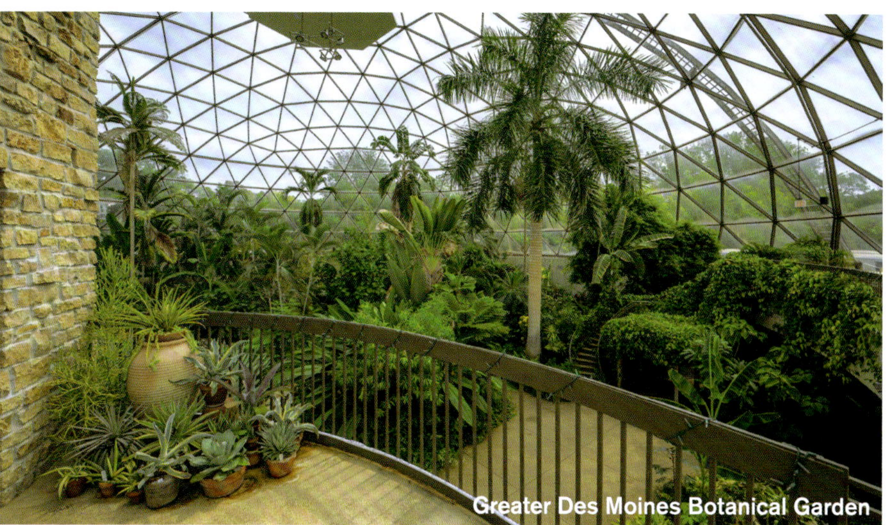
Greater Des Moines Botanical Garden

Cedar Valley Arboretum and Botanic Gardens
Waterloo, Iowa

More than 20 gardens are cultivated on this 40-acre property, which was once an expanse of farmland. The garden was established in 1996 with a planting of 150 native Iowa trees, in what is now known as the Sesquicentennial Forest. Other gardens include a rose garden, children's garden, and daylily collection.

Greater Des Moines Botanical Garden
Des Moines, Iowa

Located near downtown Des Moines, this garden traces its origins back to 1929, but the property did not officially open for another 50 years. Today, the site contains a conservatory with 1,200 different varieties of plants, and several outdoor gardens, some of which overlook downtown, like the *Principal Belvedere*–Italian for "beautiful view."

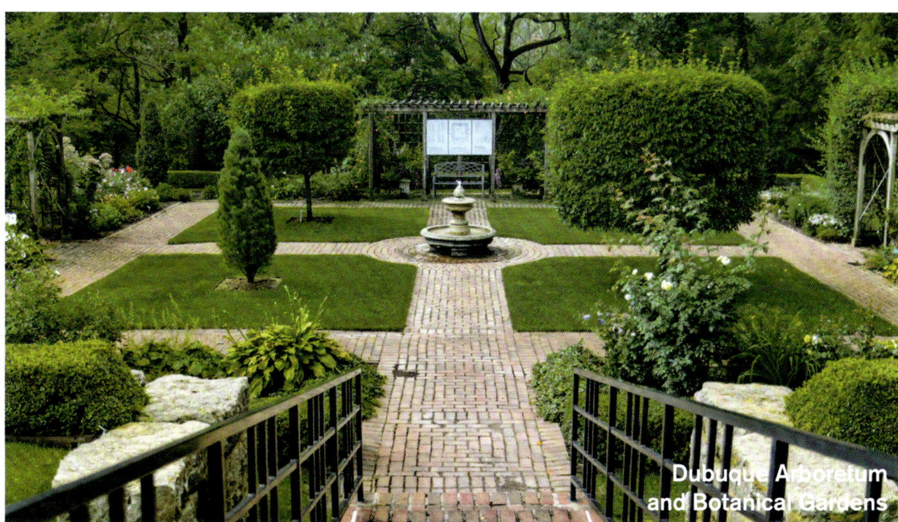
Dubuque Arboretum and Botanical Gardens

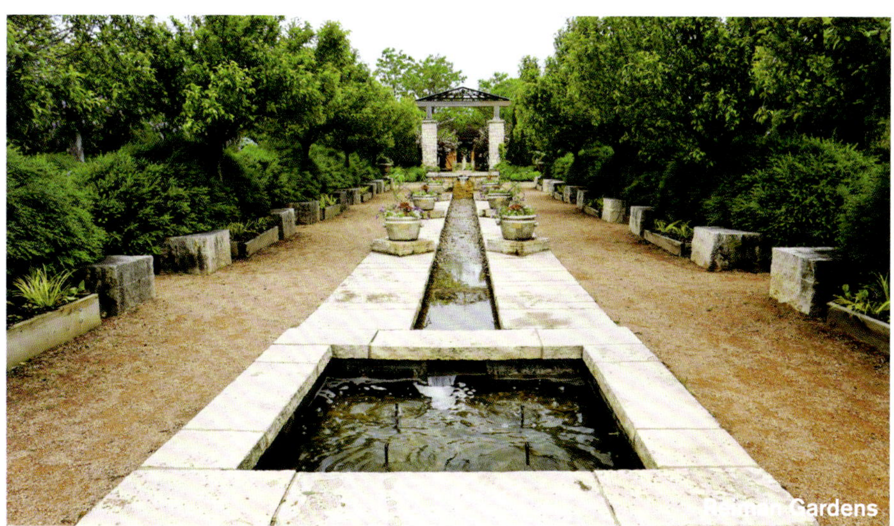
Reiman Gardens

Dubuque Arboretum and Botanical Gardens
Dubuque, Iowa

This 56-acre arboretum and botanical garden is the largest in the country that is managed entirely by volunteers. Highlights include the perfectly manicured Hardie Formal English Garden, an edible garden filled with vegetables and herbs dubbed the Garden of Eat'n, and a shaded wildflower area featuring trillium, hepatica, and other perennials.

Reiman Gardens
Ames, Iowa

This 17-acre garden, located on the Iowa State University campus, is home to more than 20 separate garden areas and 6,000 types of plants. Collections include the Helen Latch Jones Rose Garden, the Trial and Display Gardens, and several "demonstration" gardens to give visitors inspiration for their home gardens.

Bartlett Arboretum
Belle Plaine, Kansas

This 20-acre arboretum is open seasonally and for special events, often hosting weddings and corporate outings. The property contains almost ten State Champion trees, including a Japanese Maple, Southern Magnolia, and a Virginia Pine that is both a state and national champ. The site also maintains an apiary to facilitate pollination.

Dyck Arboretum of the Plains
Hesston, Kansas

Established in 1981 on a 13-acre plot of land, this arboretum now spans 29 acres and contains 1,000 varieties of trees, shrubs, wildflowers, and grasses. The property's creators, Harold and Elva Mae Dyck, purposely placed the site between a college and a retirement community, giving visitors of all ages access to the arboretum's beauty.

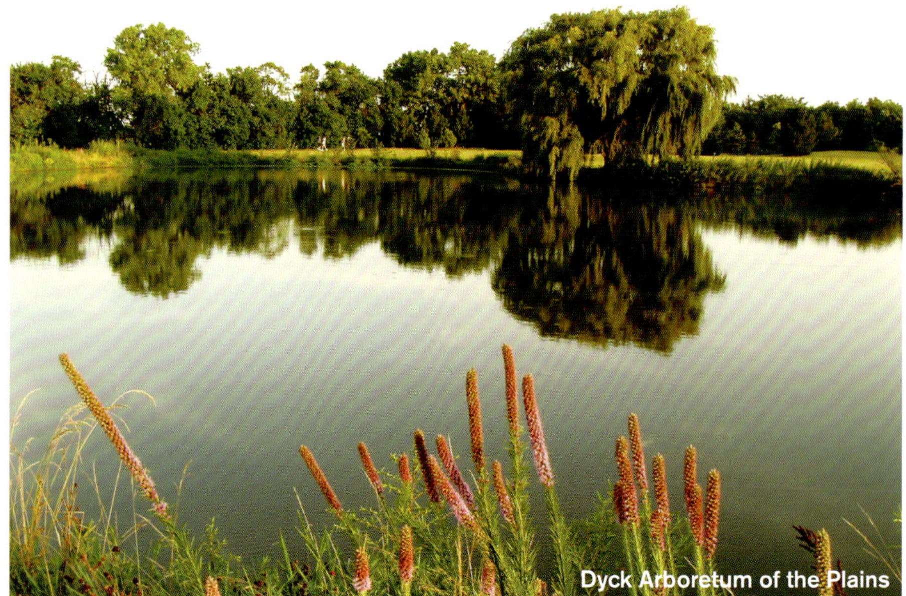

Dyck Arboretum of the Plains

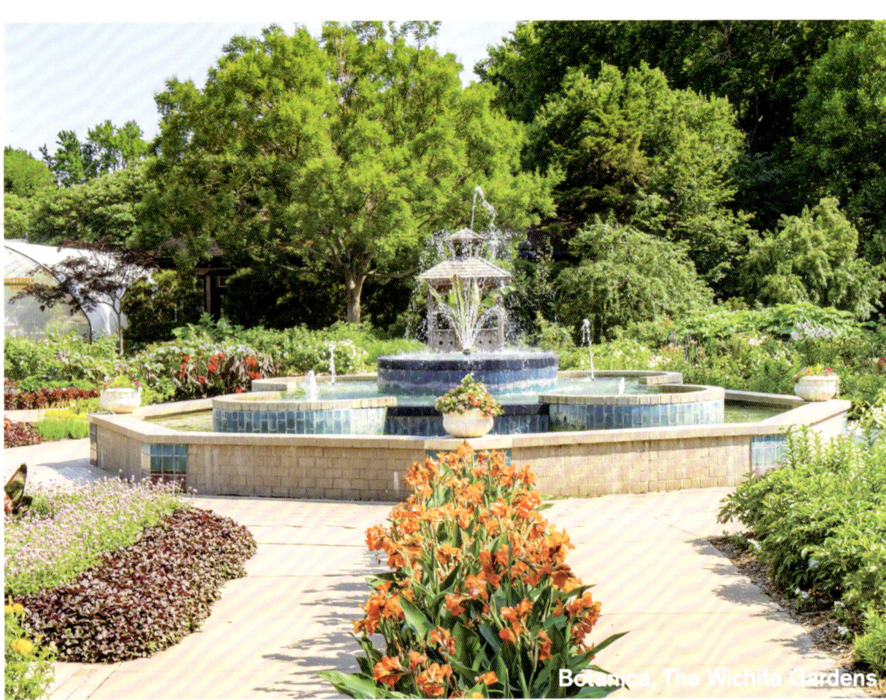

Botanica, The Wichita Gardens

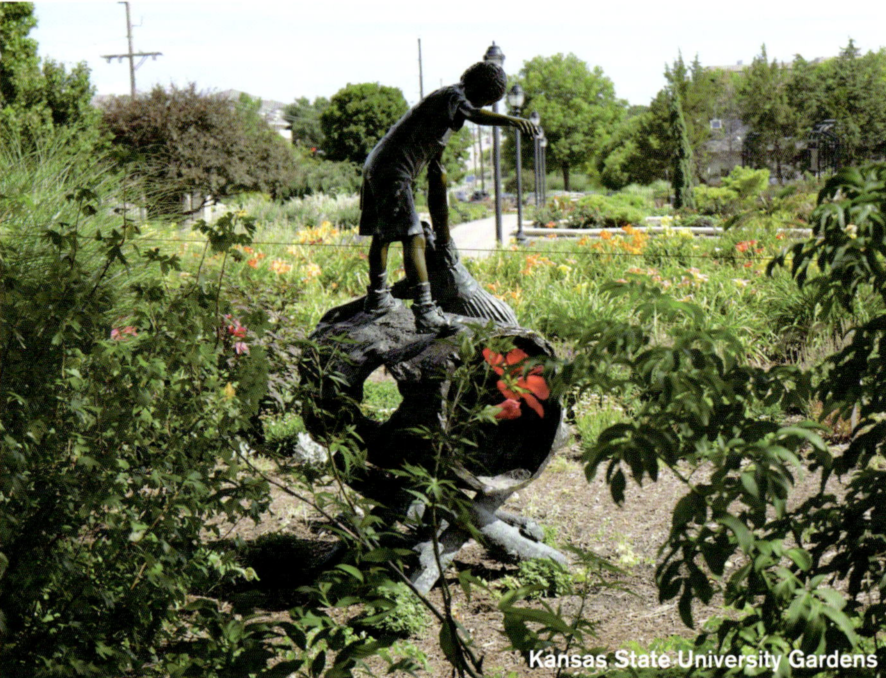

Kansas State University Gardens

Botanica, The Wichita Gardens
Wichita, Kansas

More than 4,000 plant species are on display at this 20-acre garden, which contains one-of-a-kind features like the Koch Carousel Gardens, an outdoor game plaza with a carousel and a sensory garden. Other highlights include the Chinese Garden of Friendship and the Butterfly Garden, which is continually in bloom throughout the summer and fall.

Kansas State University Gardens
Manhattan, Kansas

Informally known as the K-State Gardens, these free gardens have been on the university campus since 1875. Along with vibrant collections of daylilies, roses, irises, and peonies, the property includes a Cottage Garden, an Adaptive and Native Garden, and a Butterfly Garden that serves as a Monarch Waystation.

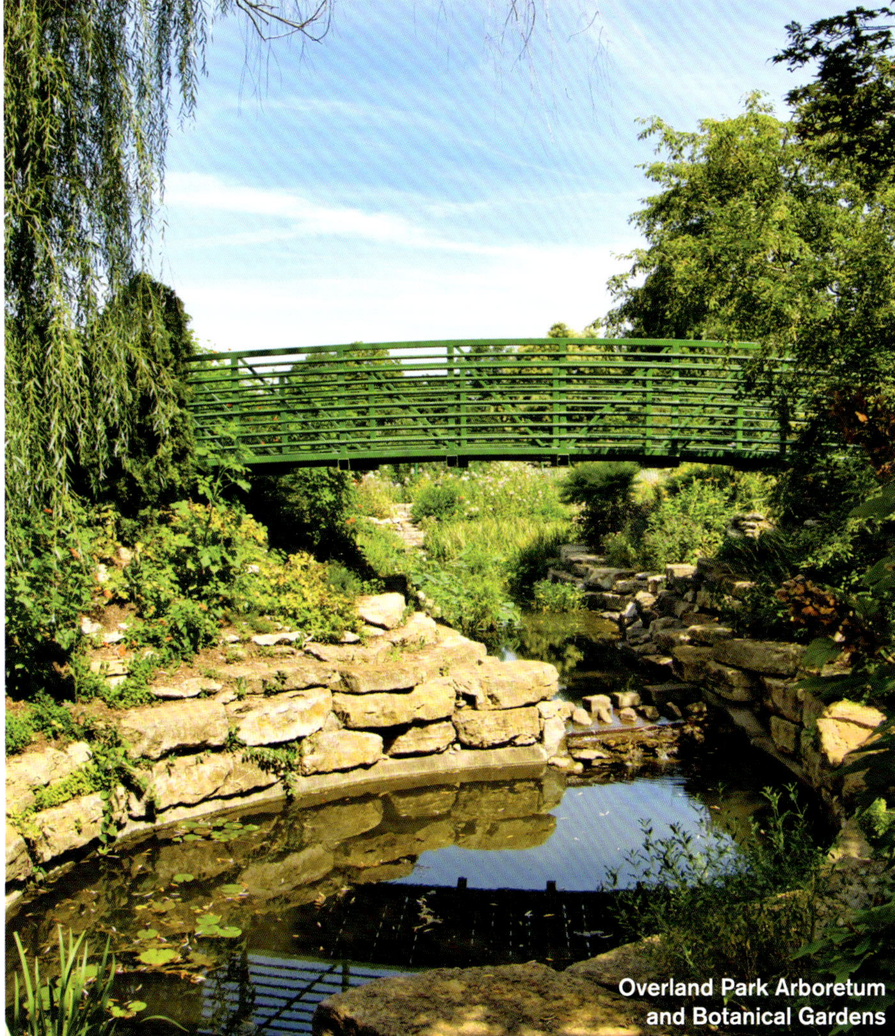

Six miles of winding trails, two bridges, limestone bluffs, and miniature garden ecosystems allow visitors to make new discoveries around every turn.

Overland Park Arboretum and Botanical Gardens
Overland Park, Kansas

This 300-acre arboretum and botanical garden is home to eight different ecosystems, including dry-mesic prairie, which contains grasses like big and little bluestem and Indian grass, and riparian woodland, with trees like silver maple, black walnut, and sycamore. More than 1,700 species of trees and plants are found throughout the property in more than a dozen themed gardens. Highlights include the Cohen Iris Garden, featuring 300 types of irises; the Train Garden, which surrounds model trains, a full-size railroad crossing gate, and a real caboose; and the Legacy Garden, which contains four time capsules that are opened every 25 years.

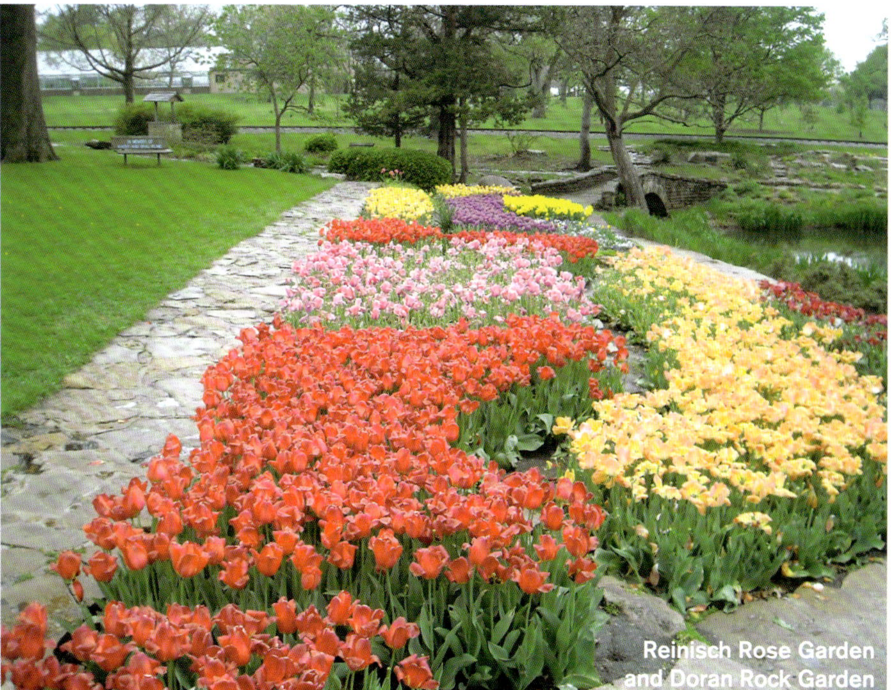

Peak blooming times are late May through early June.

Reinisch Rose Garden and Doran Rock Garden
Topeka, Kansas

Don't be fooled by the name: Although this garden contains hundreds of varieties of roses–which number in the thousands–it is home to so much more! More than 6,500 types of plants are found within the garden, which was first opened in 1930, and the property is one of 23 test gardens in the country that experiments with hybrid species. The Logan Test Garden displays these plants, many of which have been chosen as All-America Rose Selections. Nearby is the Doran Rock Garden, featuring natural rocks, a reflecting pool, and a stone footbridge, and filled with Japanese maples, willow oaks, and flowering annuals.

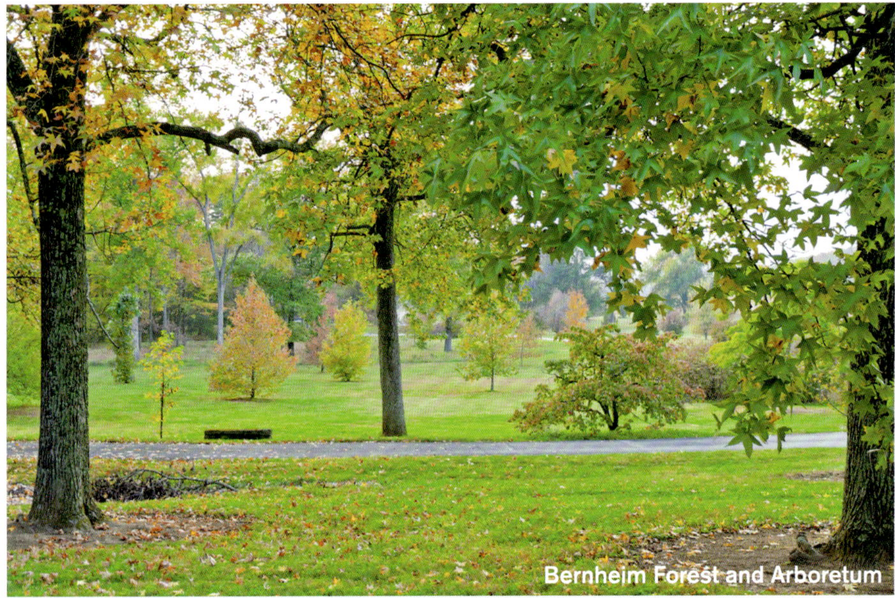

The sprawling property provides plenty of places to stop and take in the view.

Worth Exploring in Kentucky

Baker Arboretum
Bowling Green, Kentucky

- Contains 1,200 varieties of plants and 600 different species
- Collections include conifers, Asian maples, flowering trees, and shrubs

University of Kentucky Arboretum
Lexington, Kentucky

- A 100-acre property with 18 Kentucky-native tree species
- Gardens include a rose garden, vegetable garden, and the Kentucky Children's Garden

Yew Dell Botanical Gardens
Crestwood, Kentucky

- The historic property was once owned by farmer and gardener Theodore Klein
- Collections include a Cottage Garden, Cut Flower Garden, and an arboretum

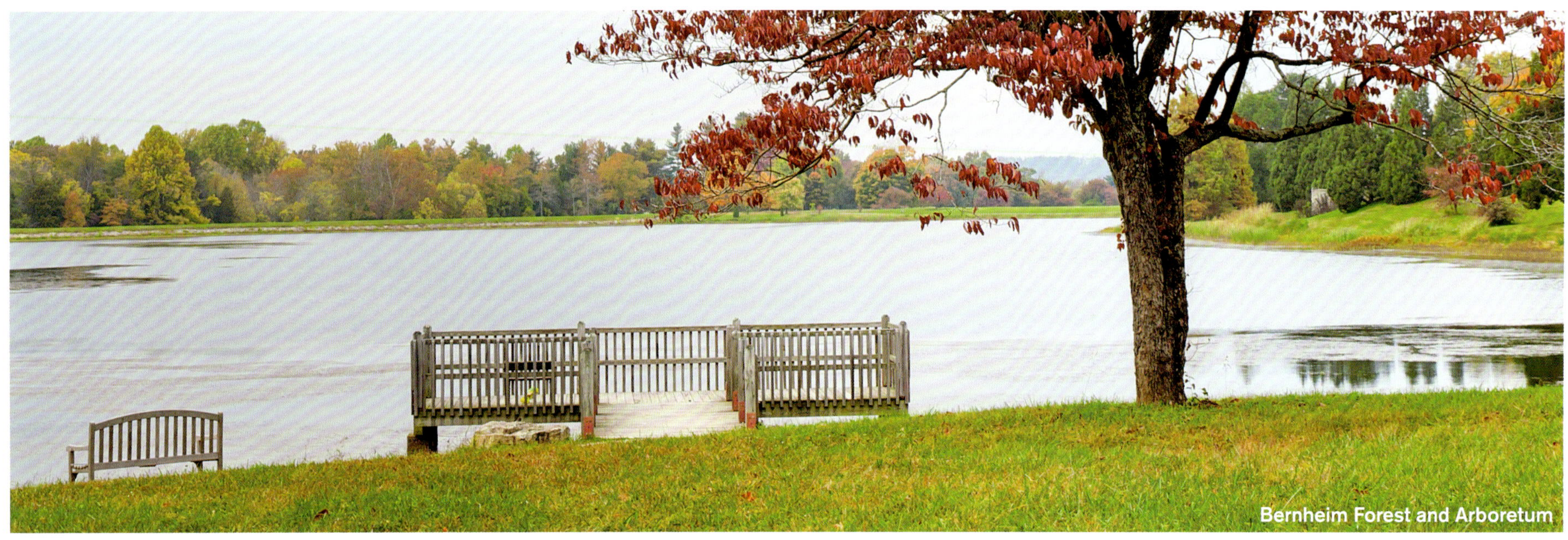

Bernheim Forest and Arboretum
Clermont, Kentucky

Founded in 1929 by Isaac W. Bernheim, this expansive property covers 16,346 acres and includes an arboretum and wild forest. The natural forest is made up of mostly beech and maple, and contains more than 40 miles of hiking and biking trails. Other points of interest in the forest include the Canopy Tree Walk, a boardwalk suspended 75 feet over the forest floor, and the unique Playcosystem, a 17-acre natural playground that provides children with endless, unstructured, outdoor play opportunities. A tranquil Meditation Trail, a four-acre Edible Garden, and art created by local and national artists make this a truly special destination.

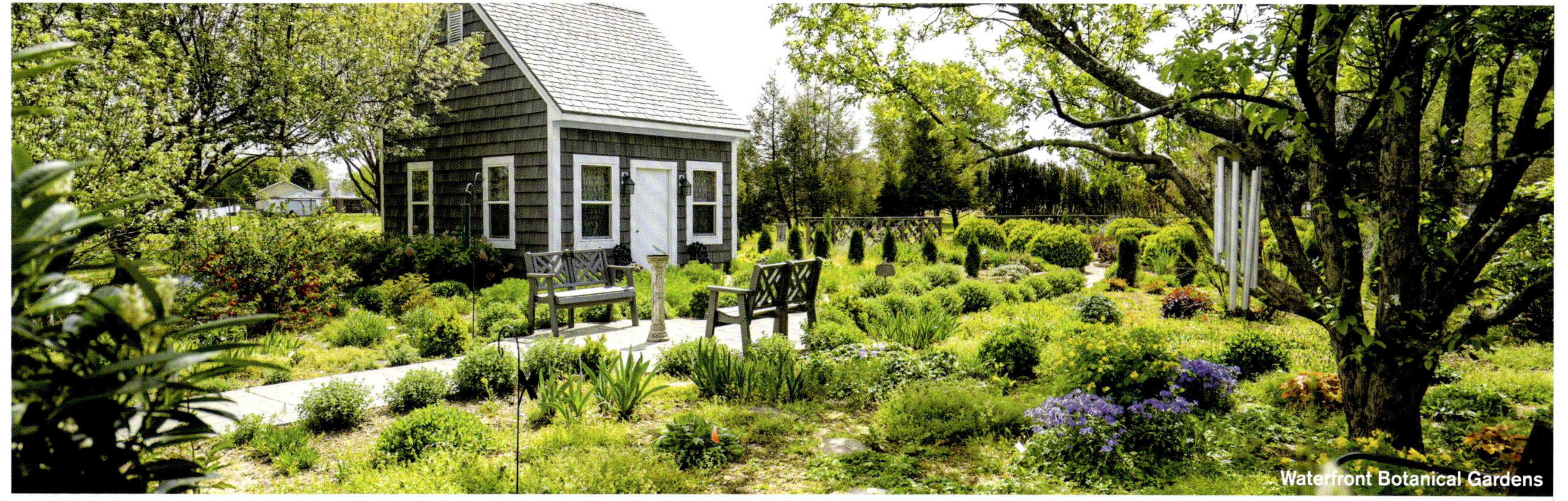

The gardens are a popular destination for social gatherings and events.

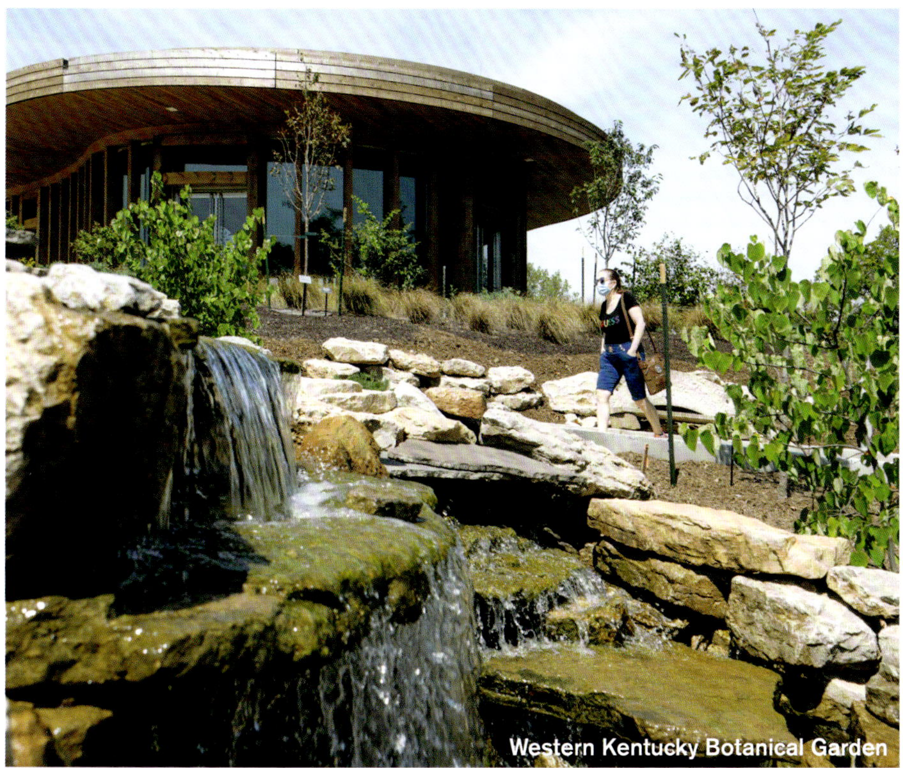

The on-site education center hosts classes and workshops that explore environmental issues, horticulture and gardening, local history, and health.

Boone County Arboretum
Union, Kentucky

This 121-acre property is sometimes known as Central Park, and for good reason: It was the first arboretum in the country set within a recreational park. Twelve athletic fields, connected by two miles of hiking and biking trails, are located in the park, which also contains more than 1,400 trees and 1,900 shrubs. All plants are recorded by GPS, making them easy to find on the arboretum's maps.

Waterfront Botanical Gardens
Louisville, Kentucky

The site of this beautiful botanical garden just outside downtown Louisville was once an unsightly city dump. Its transformation, which started in 2014, has been a lovely example of repurposing land for beneficial uses. Today, the 23-acre garden is home to a native plant garden, a pollinator garden, and an edible garden, as well as art and sculptures, with more–including a Japanese garden–planned for the future.

Western Kentucky Botanical Garden
Owensboro, Kentucky

Established in 1993, this 8.5-acre property is a local favorite for weddings and outdoor events. The garden is especially loved for its impressive collection of daylilies, which are celebrated every year with the week-long Dazzling Daylily Festival, considered one of the best festivals in the Southeast. Other highlights include a rose garden, an English cottage garden, a fruit and berry garden, and several historical buildings.

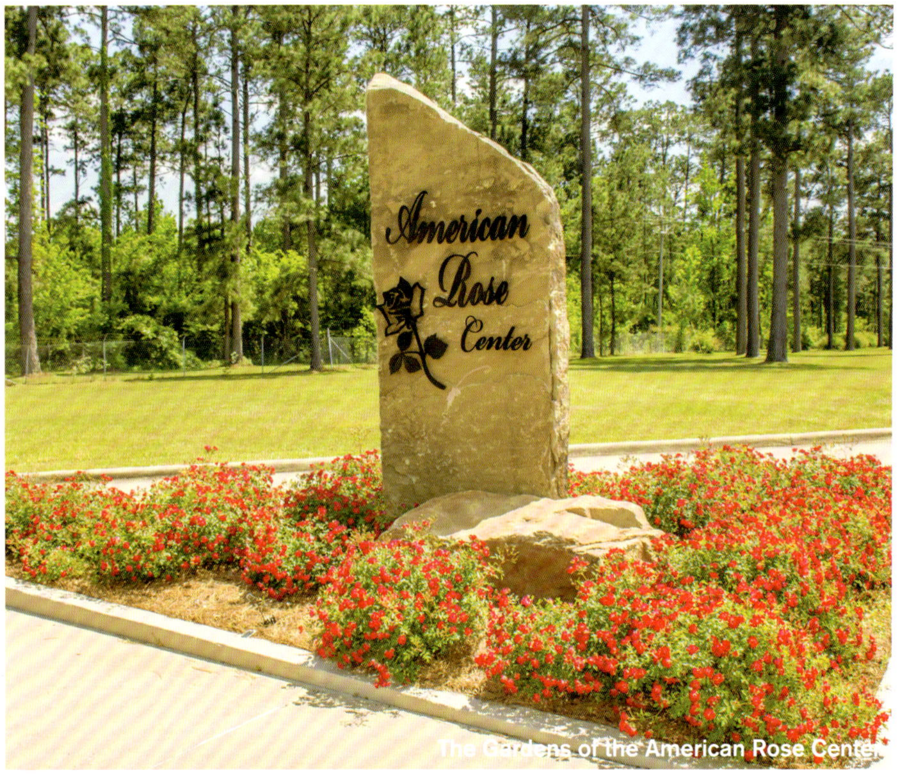

The Gardens of the American Rose Center

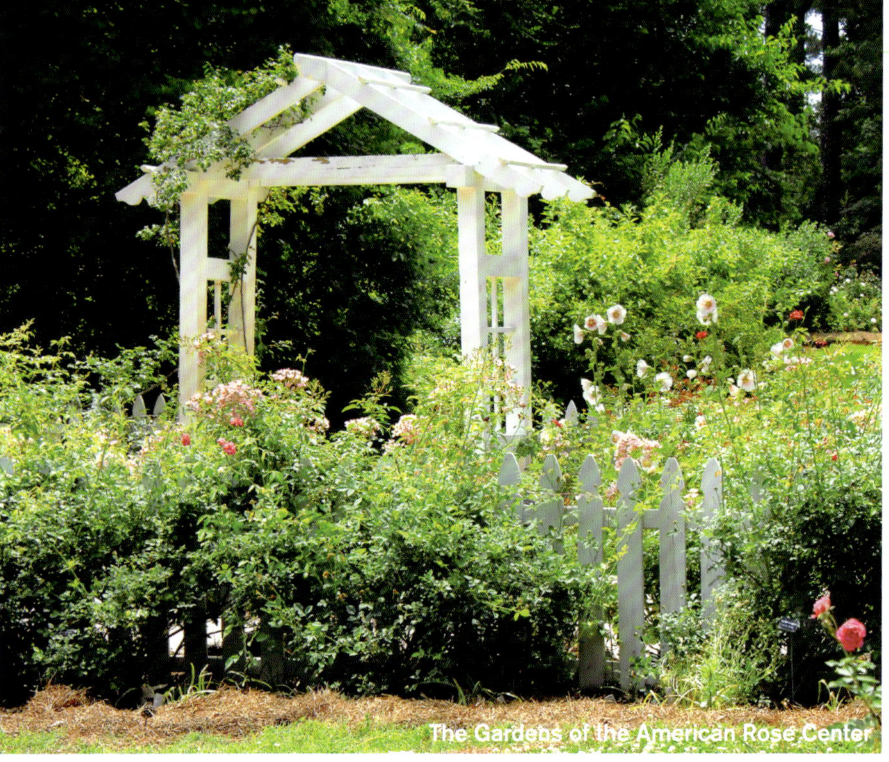
The Gardens of the American Rose Center

Worth Exploring in Louisiana

Laurens Henry Cohn Sr. Memorial Plant Arboretum
Baton Rouge, Lousiana

- More than 120 species of native and adaptable trees and shrubs
- Collections include Japanese maples, conifers, and crape myrtles, as well as orchids and camellias

Independence Park Botanic Gardens
Baton Rouge, Louisiana

- Highlights include a daylily garden, a rose garden, and a Louisiana Iris garden
- Contains the Baton Rouge Garden Center, where flower shows and special events are held

Louisiana State Arboretum
Ville Platte, Louisiana

- More than 600 acres of natural growth and additional plantings, including 150 native species
- The first state-supported arboretum in the United States

Louisiana Tech University Arboretum
Ruston, Louisiana

- Used for research by students studying biology, forestry, and environmental and agricultural sciences
- Spans about 50 acres and includes walking trails and informational signage about each species

Biedenharn Museum and Gardens
Monroe, Louisiana

A Coca-Cola museum, a Bible museum, and an English garden may seem like unlikely partners, yet all three are found at this unique property. Once the home of Joseph Biedenharn, the first bottler of Coca-Cola, and his daughter, Emma, who loved art, gardening, and the Bible, the site now lovingly reflects the home's history.

The Gardens of the American Rose Center
Shreveport, Louisiana

It's not hard to guess what this 118-acre property is best known for. Showcasing 100 varieties of roses in 65 separate gardens, this site is the headquarters for the American Rose Society. Towering, cathedral-like pines surround the 20,000 rose bushes in the gardens, which, depending on variety, bloom from April to October.

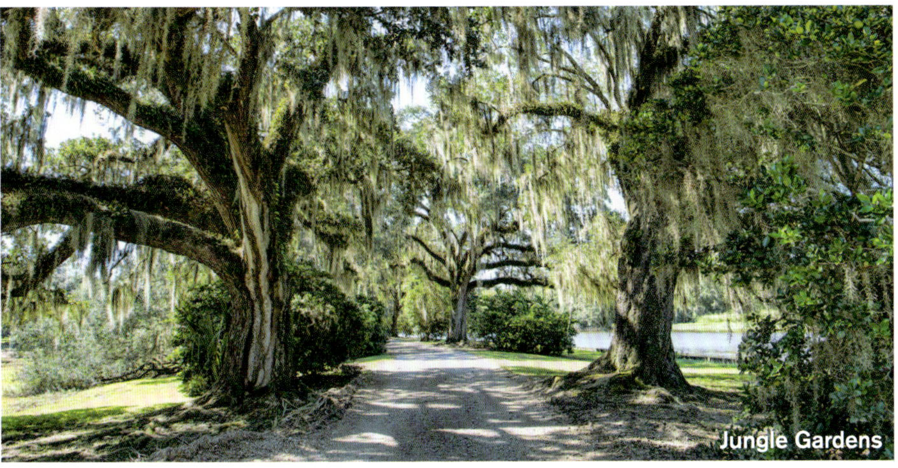

The grounds feature four miles of gravel roads sheltered by live oak trees and Spanish moss.

Jungle Gardens
Avery Island, Louisiana

Ned McIlhenny, son of Tabasco sauce inventor Edmund McIlhenny, founded this garden in the 1920s to share his love of nature and conservation. McIlhenny filled the 170-acre property with botanical specimens from around the world, including 64 varieties of bamboo, now one of the oldest collections of bamboo in the country. The garden is also home to "Bird City," a nesting site for thousands of water birds.

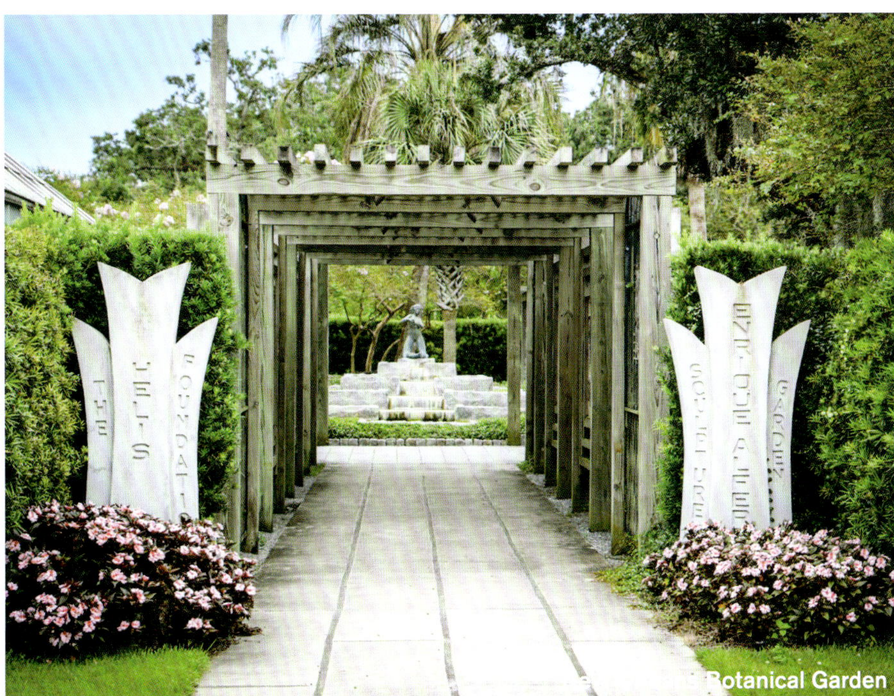

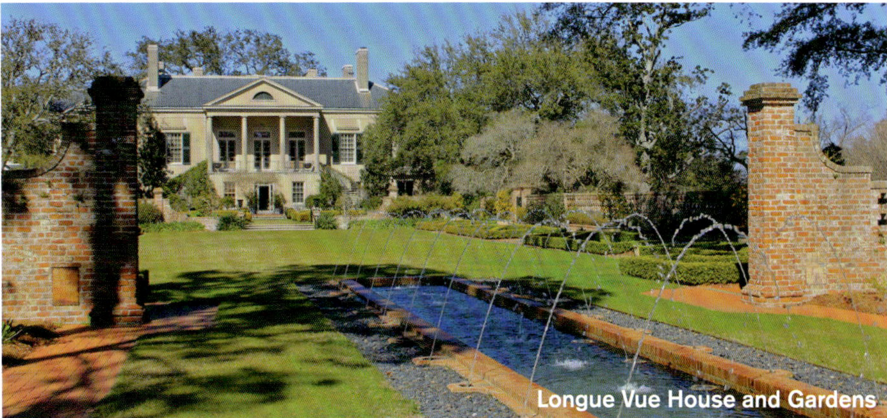

A view of the back of the house. The gardens were designed by landscape architect Ellen Biddle Shipman.

Longue Vue House and Gardens
New Orleans, Louisiana

The house on the grounds of this U.S. National Historic Landmark was constructed deliberately to complement the property's gardens. Each side of the house features a different façade, looking out on a different garden: the Pan Garden, the East Lawn, the Spanish Court, and the Oak Allée. Other highlights include the Canal Garden, the Discovery Garden, the Wild Garden, and the Overlook Pond.

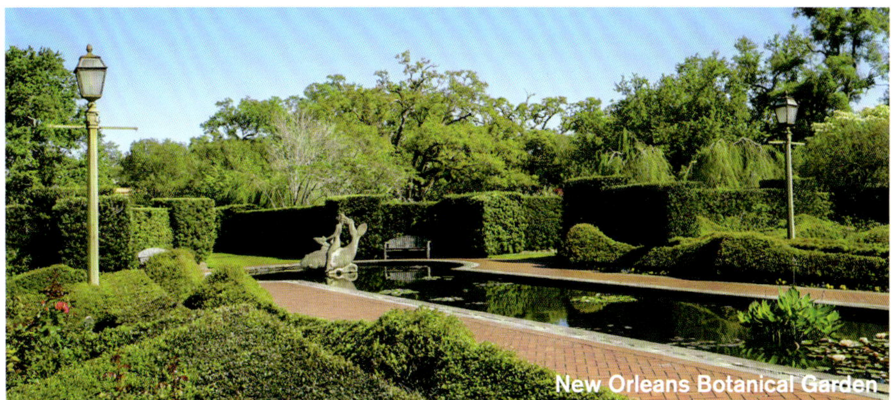

New Orleans Botanical Garden
New Orleans, Louisiana

This ten-acre garden in the heart of New Orleans was funded by the Works Progress Administration (WPA) in 1936, and is one of the last examples of WPA public garden design left in the country. The Art Deco-style garden is made up of several different sections, including an azalea and camellia garden, the Original Garden–which is the original 1936 rose garden–and the fragrant Butterfly Walk.

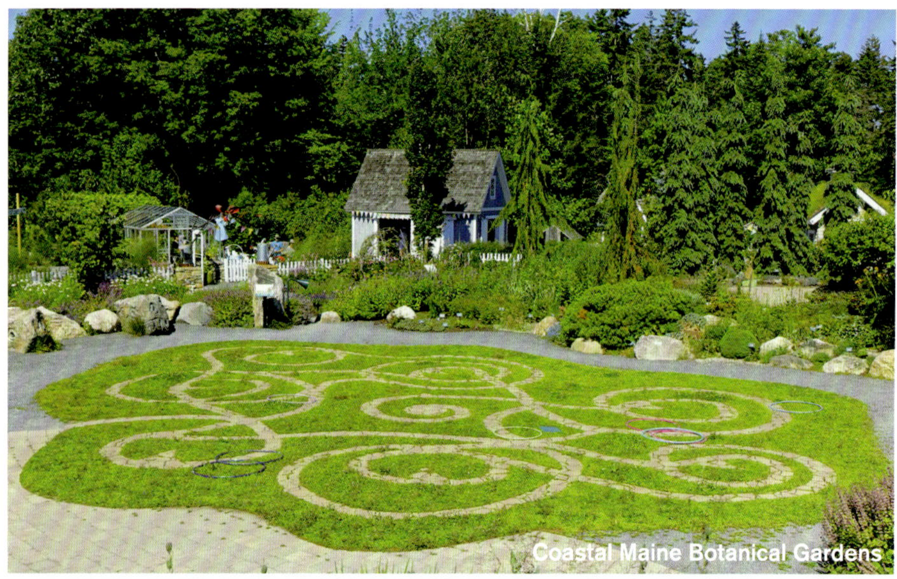

The grounds include a quaint children's garden.

Coastal Maine Botanical Gardens
Boothbay, Maine

Welcoming more than 300,000 visitors a year, this 300-acre botanical garden is the largest in New England and is considered one of Maine's top tourist attractions. The garden was established in 2007 on 128 acres of land, and has grown to encompass 295 acres today. The property's first planned garden was the Giles Rhododendron and Perennial Garden, which today contains more than 1,000 rhododendrons. Drawing inspiration from formal European rose gardens is the Arbor Garden, a tranquil oasis with climbing roses, wisteria, and honeysuckle. The garden makes plenty of space for beneficial pollinators, and features a 2,160-square-foot, Gothic-style, Native Butterfly House. The butterfly house supports native New England species throughout their life cycles, from caterpillar to butterfly. Also found in the garden are 16 honeybee hives in the Learning Apiary, where visitors can watch and learn about these important insects.

Coastal Maine Botanical Gardens

A tiny house lurks among the flowers.

Worth Exploring in Maine

Ecotat Gardens and Arboretum
Hermon, Maine

- Contains more than 55 different gardens on 88 acres
- Several miles of trails traverse the property and are popular for hiking and cross-country skiing

Fay Hyland Botanical Plantation
Orono, Maine

- Established in 1934 on the campus of the University of Maine
- A ten-acre garden featuring both native and non-native species

Harvey Butler Memorial Rhododendron Sanctuary
Springvale, Maine

- Site of a 5.3-acre stand of wild rhododendron, which is in peak bloom in mid-July
- Also features more than 35 species of wildflowers

Perkins Arboretum
Waterville, Maine

- Established in 1946 in memory of Colby College professor Edward Perkins
- The 128-acre arboretum contains beech, oak, maple, birch, and more

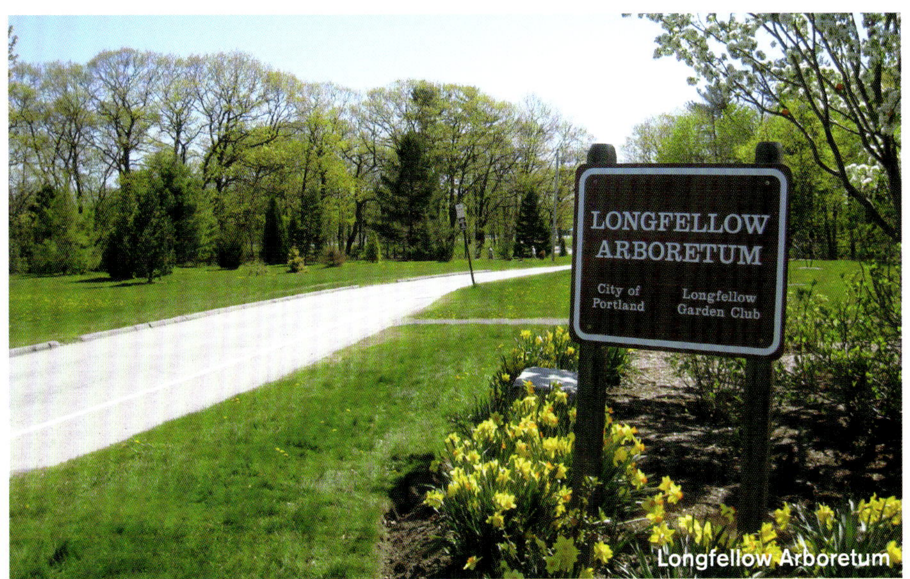

Longfellow Arboretum

Longfellow Arboretum
Portland, Maine

When this arboretum was established in 1976, it contained 11 trees collected from three different continents. Today, the property is home to more than 100 trees, both native and exotic, as well as shrubs like lilac, hydrangea, dogwood, and azalea. Notable species include the Chinese-native dawn redwood, the weeping European beech, and the yellow birch, a native Maine tree often used to make furniture and cabinets.

Shoreway Arboretum
South Portland, Maine

This arboretum, located on the campus of Maine's largest and oldest community college, Southern Maine Community College, gets its name from the Spring Point Shoreway, a 21-acre stretch of coastline along Simonton Cove. Due to its proximity to the sea air, the property, set along the sand- and pebble-filled Willard Beach, contains specimens of salt-tolerant trees and shrubs, including a Swiss stone pine tree.

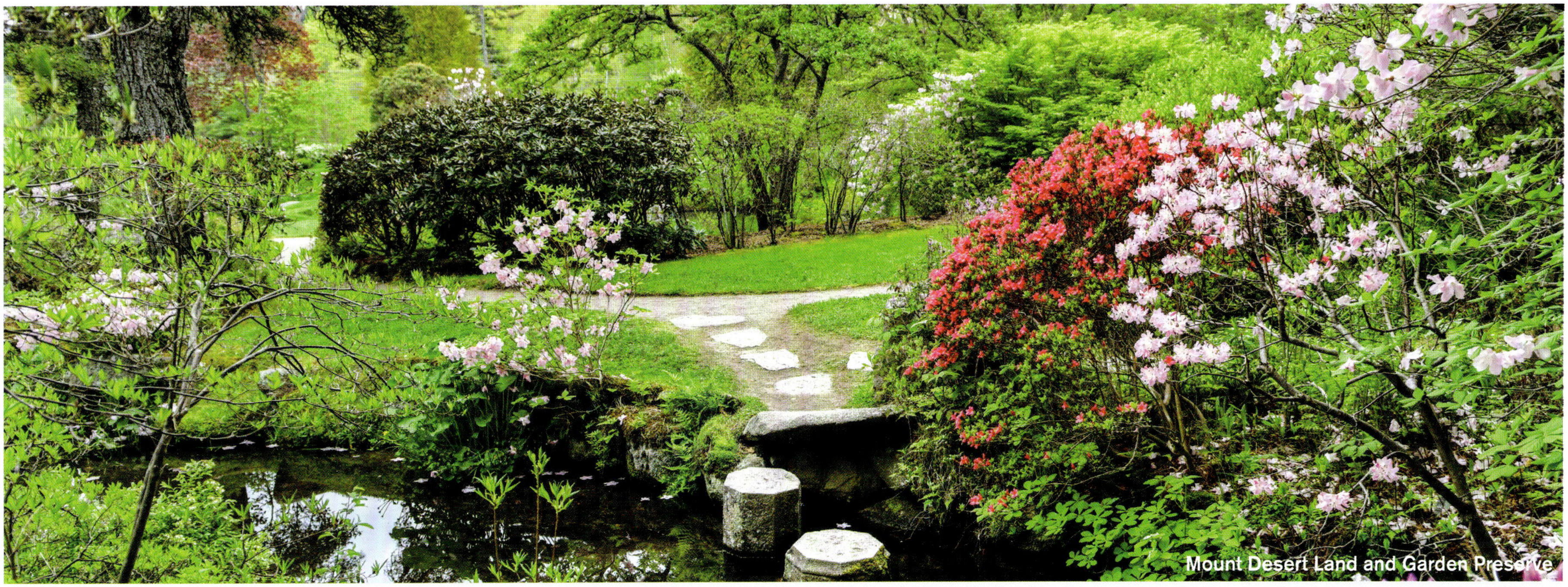

Mount Desert Land and Garden Preserve

The Asticou Azalea Garden incorporates design elements taken from classic Japanese gardens.

Mount Desert Land and Garden Preserve
Mount Desert, Maine

Located adjacent to the wild beauty of Acadia National Park, this garden preserves 1,400 acres of historic natural land, gardens, and trails. The gardens, including the Abby Aldrich Rockefeller Garden, Asticou Azalea Garden, and Thuya Garden, are open mostly throughout the summer and fall months, whereas the hiking trails and quiet roads of the Little Long Pond Natural Lands are accessible year-round.

Adkins Arboretum
Ridgely, Maryland

Established in 1980 with a mission to showcase all of Maryland's forest types, this arboretum has since embraced the study of the indigenous plant communities of the Delmarva Peninsula. The property is home to more than 600 species of shrubs, trees, wildflowers, and grasses found in the Chesapeake Bay region, and offers guided walks, adult and youth educational programs, and numerous art exhibits.

Brookside Gardens
Wheaton, Maryland

The first botanical garden in the state of Maryland, this 50-acre property contains dozens of distinct areas to explore. Visitor favorites include the Azalea Garden, which contains 2,000 azaleas, the Rose Garden, with dozens of different types of roses, and the Japanese-style Gude Garden, featuring a teahouse overlooking a pond. The garden also offers a seasonal Butterfly Experience, with hundreds of butterflies from around the world.

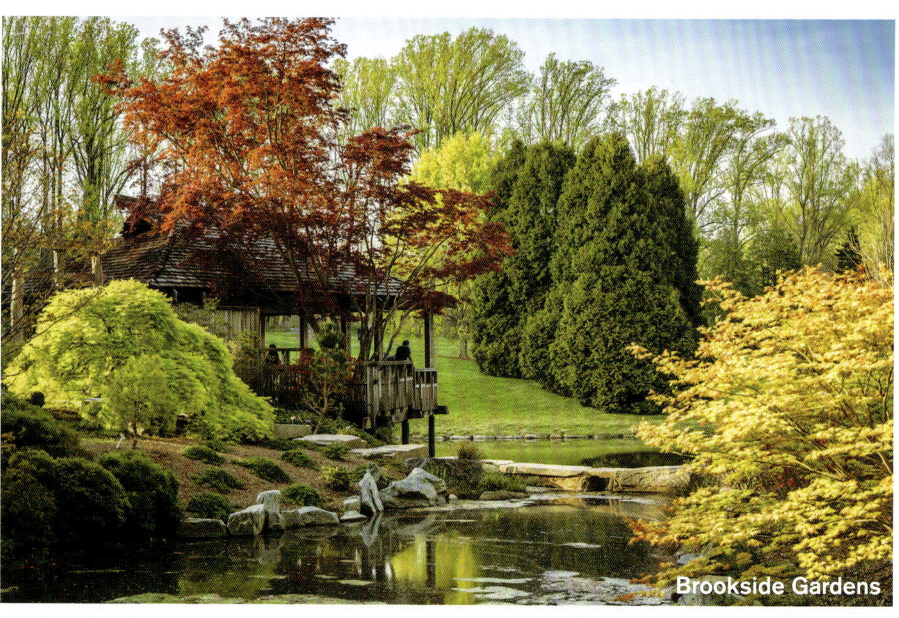

Brookside Gardens

The property provides winding trails and plenty of places to stop and admire the views.

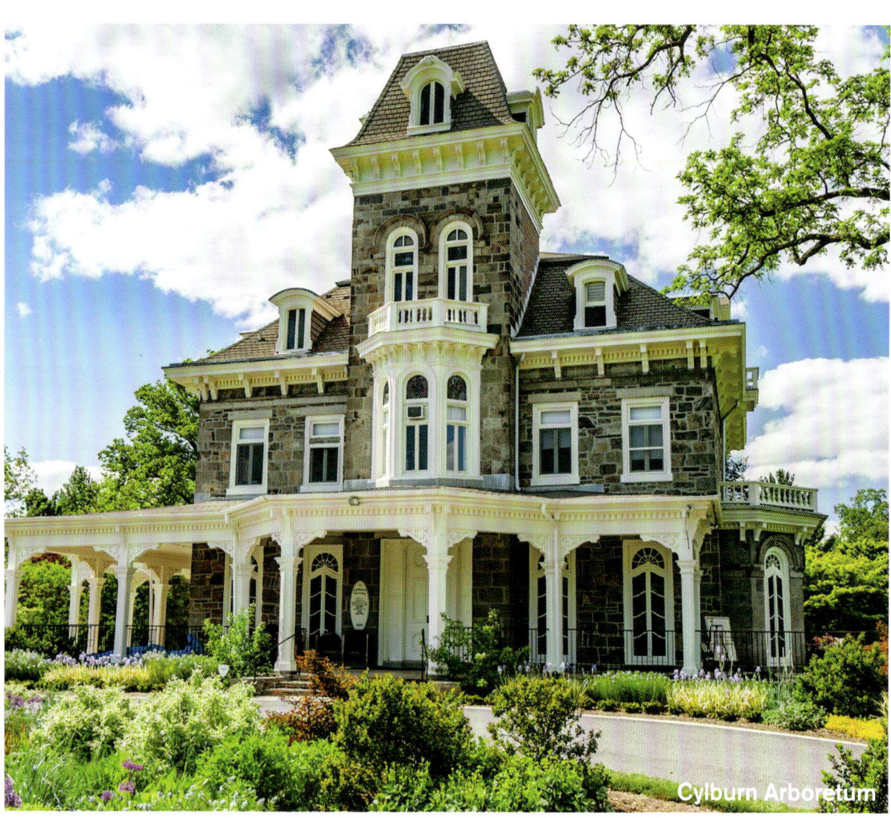

Cylburn Arboretum

A stately mansion and manicured walkways await visitor discovery.

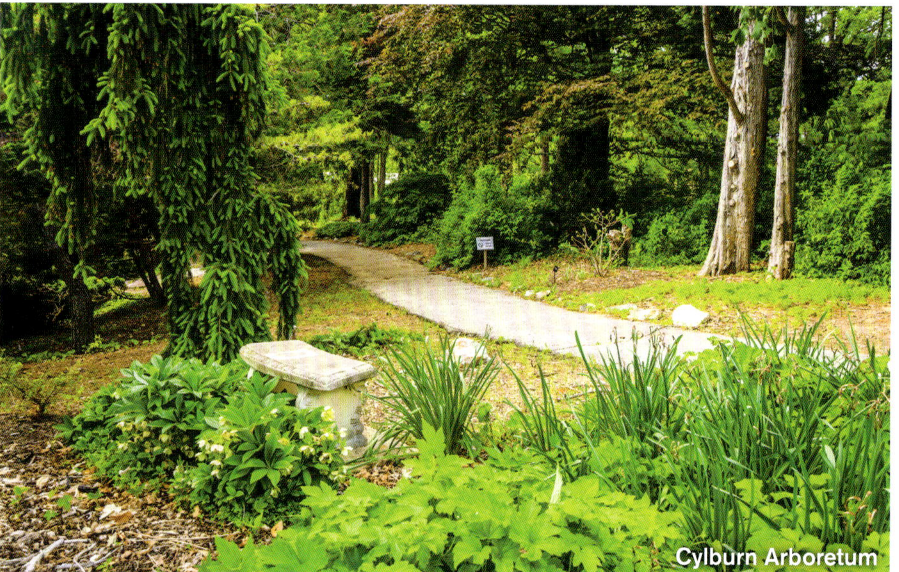

Cylburn Arboretum

Cylburn Arboretum
Baltimore, Maryland

This 200-acre property is located just outside downtown Baltimore, providing city dwellers with an urban oasis to hike, wander, and recharge. Collections include maple, boxwood, magnolia, and spruce trees, as well as a wide variety of planted flower and vegetable gardens surrounding the imposing Cylburn Mansion. The mansion, which was completed in 1888, now houses a collection of watercolor paintings depicting Maryland wildflowers.

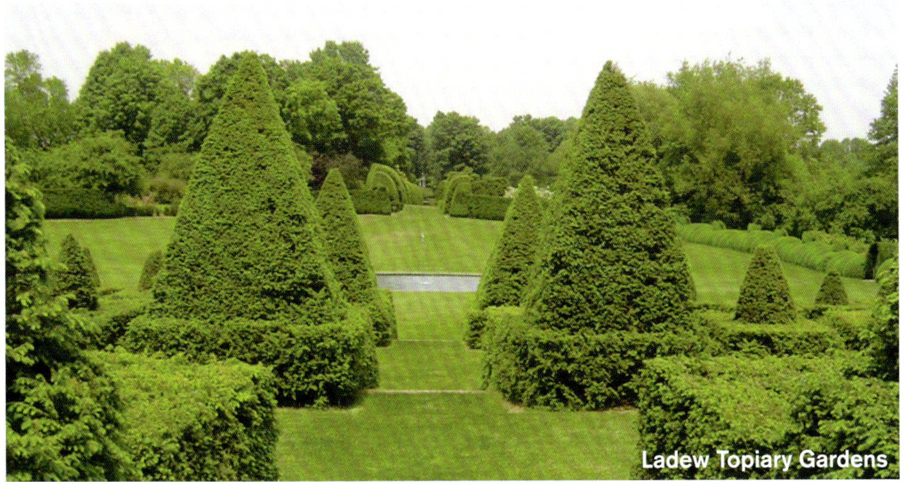
Ladew Topiary Gardens

Ladew Topiary Gardens
Monkton, Maryland

The 100-plus topiary sculptures at this 22-acre garden are only a small part of what makes the property special. Numerous "garden rooms" are located throughout the grounds, including a rose garden, waterlily garden, and a Victorian garden. Also notable is the Manor House, built in 1749 and filled with antiques and 2,500 books.

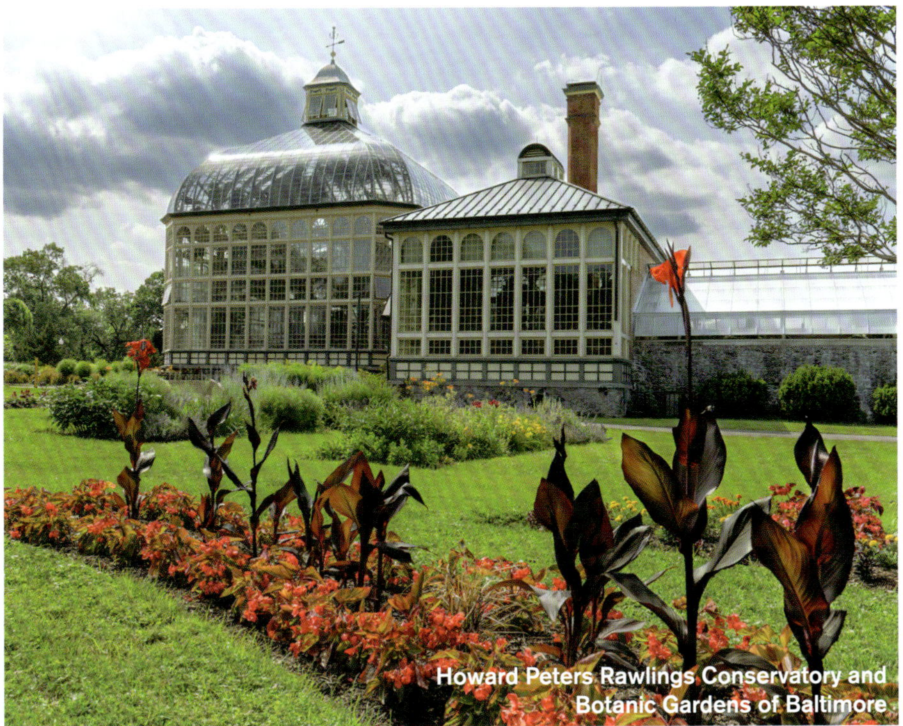
Howard Peters Rawlings Conservatory and Botanic Gardens of Baltimore

Flowerbeds surround the conservatory in a kaleidoscope of colors.

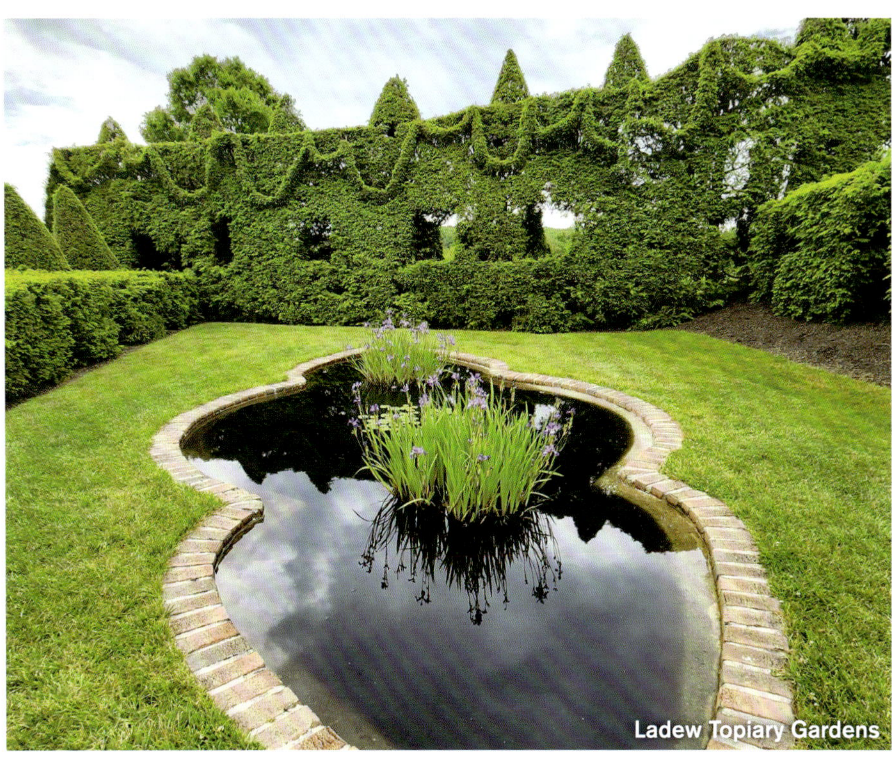
Ladew Topiary Gardens

Howard Peters Rawlings Conservatory and Botanic Gardens of Baltimore
Baltimore, Maryland

Dating back to 1888, this 1.5-acre property features five unique areas, including the 1888 Palm House, the Orchid Room, the Mediterranean House, the Tropical House, and the Desert House. The steel and glass conservatory is the second oldest building of its kind still in use in the country, and is on the National Register of Historic Places.

Salisbury University Arboretum
Salisbury, Maryland

In 1988, the entire campus of Salisbury University was declared an arboretum by the American Association of Botanical Gardens and Arboreta. Today, more than 2,000 species can be found on the property, accentuated by water features and a sculpture collection. A walk through campus reveals roses, magnolias, Japanese maples, and much more.

University of Maryland Arboretum and Botanical Garden
College Park, Maryland

This university campus arboretum has been given the honor of "Tree Campus Higher Education" by the Arbor Day Foundation 15 years in a row. And it's no wonder: The campus is home to more than 17,000 trees, including 16 County Champion Trees, and a wide variety of pollinator and native plant gardens.

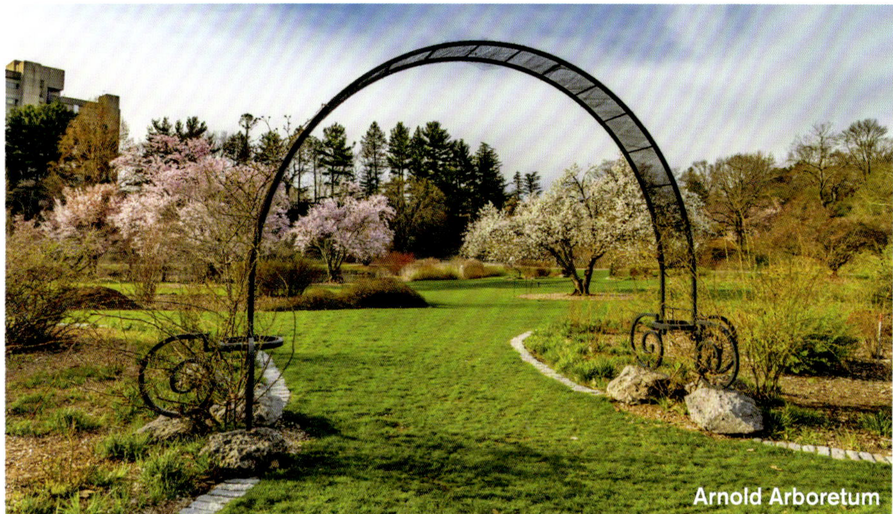

Arnold Arboretum

Arnold Arboretum
Boston, Massachusetts

Encompassing 281 acres on the campus of Harvard University, this preserve contains one of the most comprehensive and well-documented collections of woody plants in the world. It was founded in 1872, making it the oldest public arboretum in the U.S. Collections include maples, hemlocks, azaleas, and conifers, and total plants number at least 16,000.

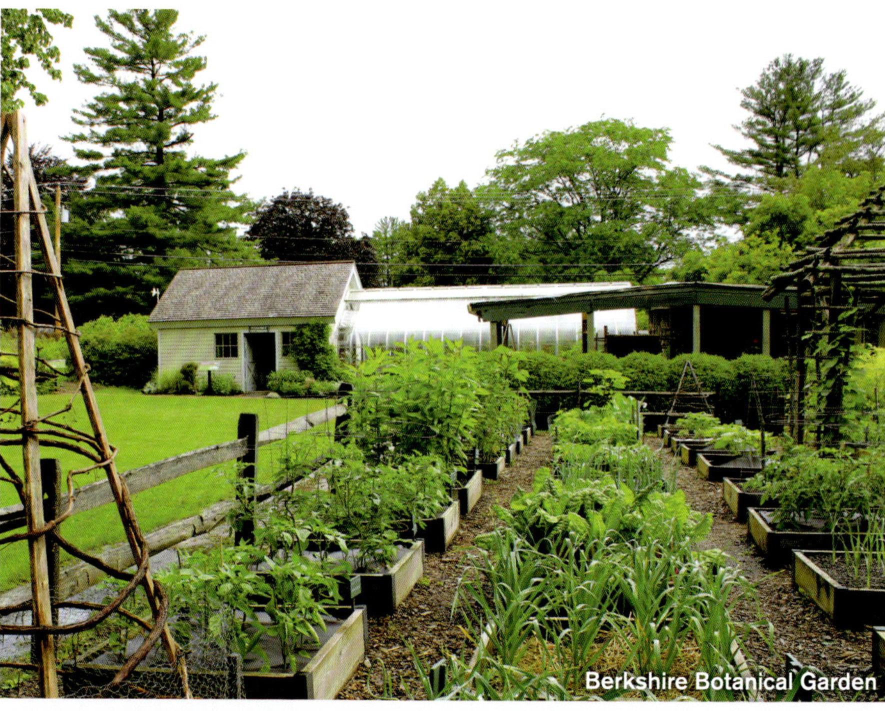

Berkshire Botanical Garden

The site's focus on functional plants attracts horticulturalists and home gardeners.

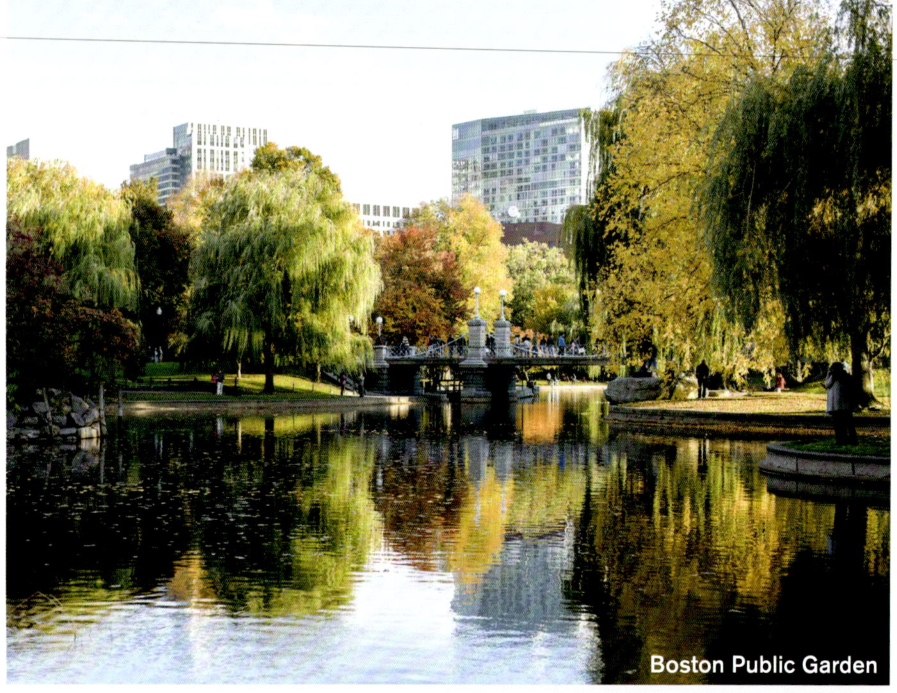

Boston Public Garden

The garden's pond provides a focal point for strollers and picnickers.

Berkshire Botanical Garden
Stockbridge, Massachusetts

This 24-acre garden, established in 1934, is considered one of the oldest public botanical gardens in the Northeast. Showcasing plants that thrive in the area's climate, the property features a Historic 1937 Herb Garden, a colorful Daylily Walk, a Children's Discovery Garden, and dozens more collections aimed at inspiring home gardeners.

Boston Public Garden
Boston, Massachusetts

The early days of this garden (established in 1837), were influenced by the Victorian styles of the day. Today, that influence is carefully maintained in the colorful, vibrant flowerbeds and stands of native and European trees throughout the park. Tourists love the four-acre pond with its fleet of Swan Boats, which have been operating since 1877.

Botanic Garden of Smith College
Northampton, Massachusetts

This garden was founded by the first president of Smith College, Laurenus Clark Seelye, who envisioned a campus that would not only be beautiful, but educational as well. The 127-acre property contains an arboretum, six acres of manicured gardens, and the 12,000-square-foot Lyman Conservatory, home to 2,200 plant species.

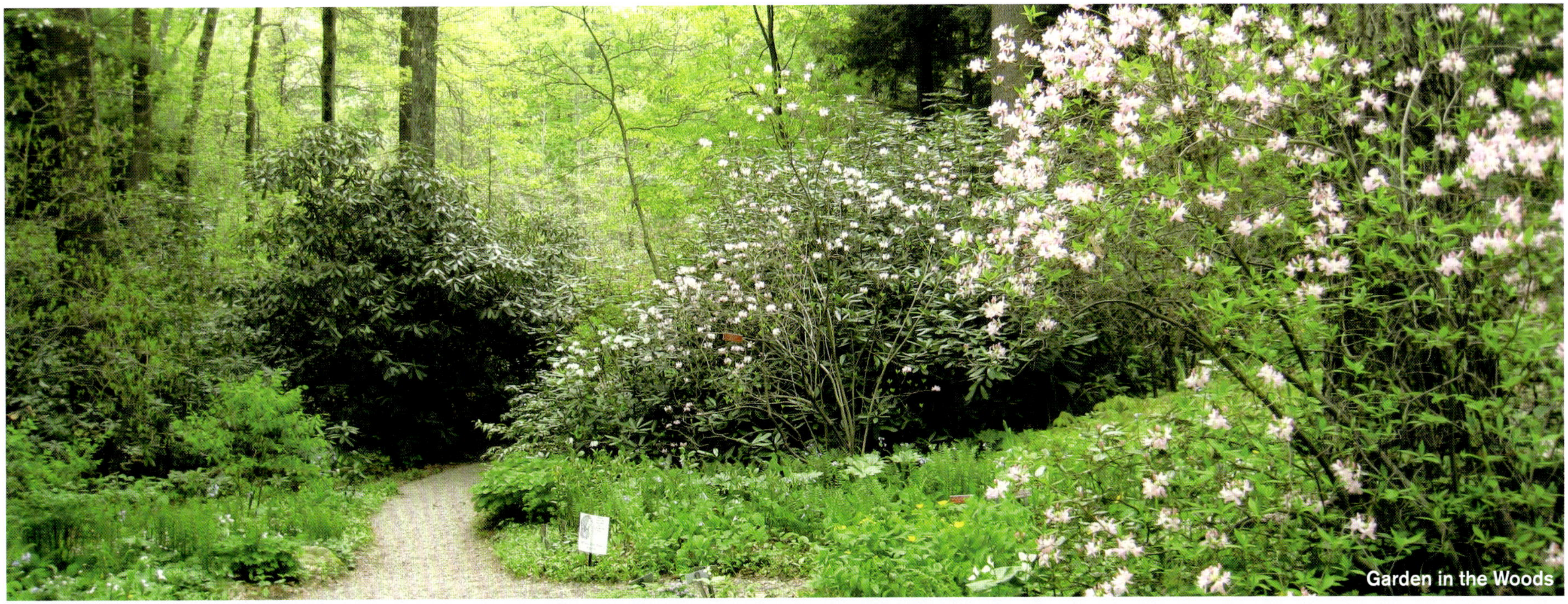

The main garden path is about a mile in length.

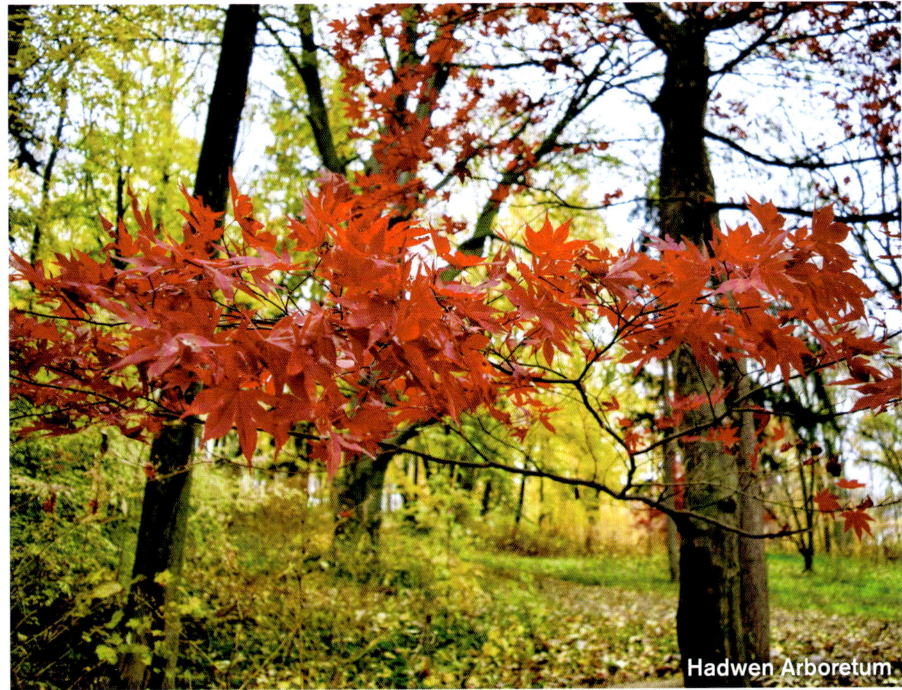

Along the trail, visitors will discover many unique tree species, like this Japanese Maple.

Garden in the Woods
Framingham, Massachusetts

As its name suggests, this 45-acre botanical garden sits within a mature oak forest, where it highlights the dramatic natural beauty of the region. More than 1,000 species of native plants are represented on the property, which is also the headquarters of the Native Plant Trust, the nation's first plant conservation organization. The native species collection is the largest in New England and includes an impressive number of wildflowers. One of the garden's highlights is its bog area, which replicates the natural bogs found in New England. Here, visitors may encounter pitcher plants, wild orchids, trillium, and sundew, and gain inspiration for their own home gardens.

Hadwen Arboretum
Worcester, Massachusetts

The 26 acres of this arboretum are located just a short walk from the campus of Clark University, and about midway through the East-West Trail, a 14-mile, cross-city hiking path. The property is named after its first caretaker, Obadiah Hadwen, who planted many of the heritage trees now located in the park, including rare species not often found in New England. At least 66 species of trees have been identified in the arboretum, and a network of trails guides visitors past woody and herbaceous plants and wildflowers. Notable species include cucumber magnolia, American yellowwood, and Japanese koyamaki trees.

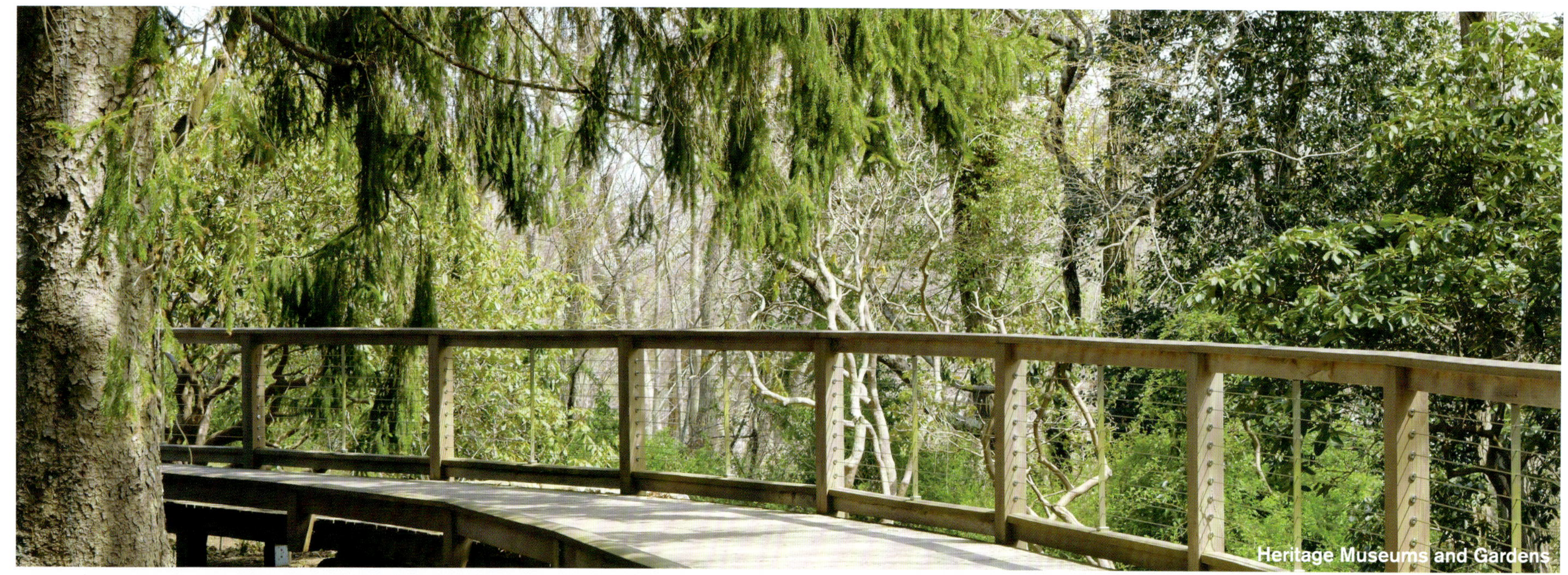

Several miles of trails snake through the grounds. Shaded benches and tucked away groves give the gardens a quiet and contemplative feel.

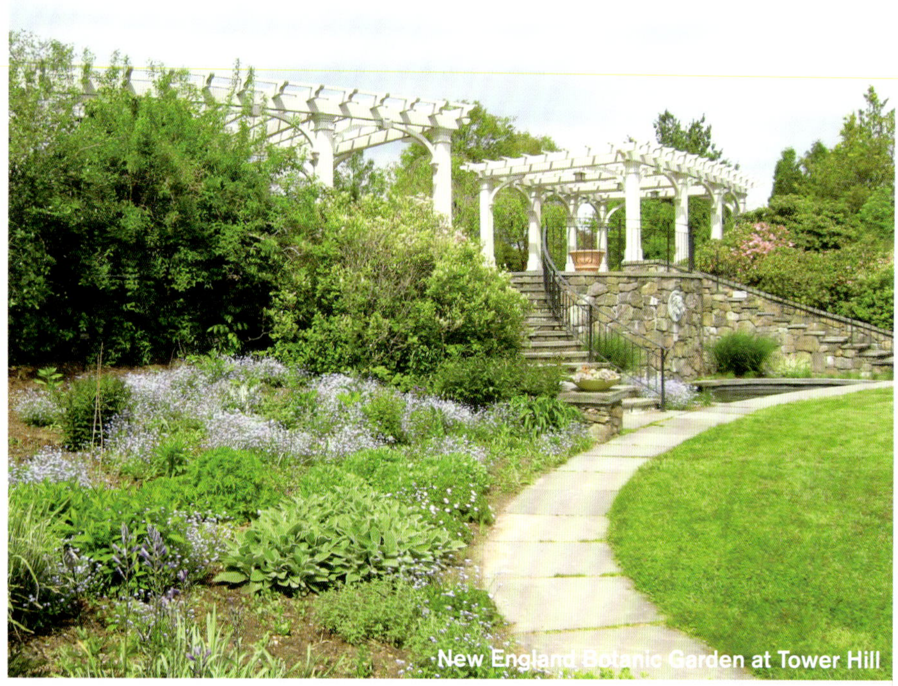

One of the harder to find gardens is the aptly named Secret Garden, which is nestled below the Lawn Garden.

Heritage Museums and Gardens
Sandwich, Massachusetts

Often considered a "must-see" destination for visitors to the area, this 100-acre public garden was once the home of noted rhododendron hybridizer Charles O. Dexter. The garden's pride and joy is its extensive collection of rhododendrons, including 125 cultivars that were created by Dexter between 1921 and 1943. Other highlights include the Hydrangea Display Garden, the Herb Garden, and the Daylily Garden featuring more than 1,000 varieties. The property also contains several miles of nature trails, three gallery buildings showcasing American folk art and collectibles, a 1919 working carousel, and a collection of classic American automobiles.

New England Botanic Garden at Tower Hill
Boylston, Massachusetts

Spanning 200 acres of formal and natural gardens and conservatories, this property welcomes more than 230,000 annual visitors to its year-round garden spaces. The site contains 18 distinct gardens, including the diverse Cottage Garden, the subtropical *Limonaia*–or Lemon House–and a stunning Field of Daffodils with 25,000 flowers. Other favorites include the Vegetable Garden, which is the oldest garden on the property, and the Frank L. Harrington Sr. Apple Orchard, which contains 250 apple trees, including 119 heritage varieties that date back to the nineteenth century. The garden also contains miles of walking trails, perfect for exploring this urban oasis.

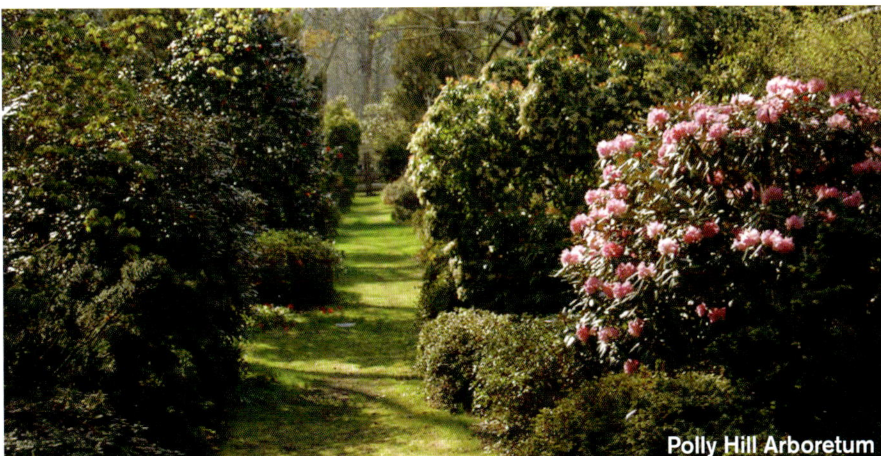

Polly's Play Pen is a fenced section of the garden containing rare plants needing protection from rabbits and deer.

Polly Hill Arboretum
West Tisbury, Massachusetts

The island of Martha's Vineyard is home to this botanical landmark, named for horticulture specialist Polly Hill. The property contains 20 acres of cultivated gardens and an additional 40 acres of natural woodland, and features rare trees and shrubs from around the world. The garden is perhaps best known for a collection of Hill's North Tisbury azaleas, but also includes camellias, conifers, magnolias, and more.

Wellesley College Botanic Gardens
Wellesley, Massachusetts

This 22-acre garden contains thousands of diverse specimens representing more than 150 different plant species. Gardens include the Alexandra Botanic Garden, the H.H. Hunnewell Arboretum, and the unique Edible Ecosystem Teaching Garden, which includes an outdoor classroom space. The property also features several greenhouses, including the Global Flora conservatory, with plants from around the world.

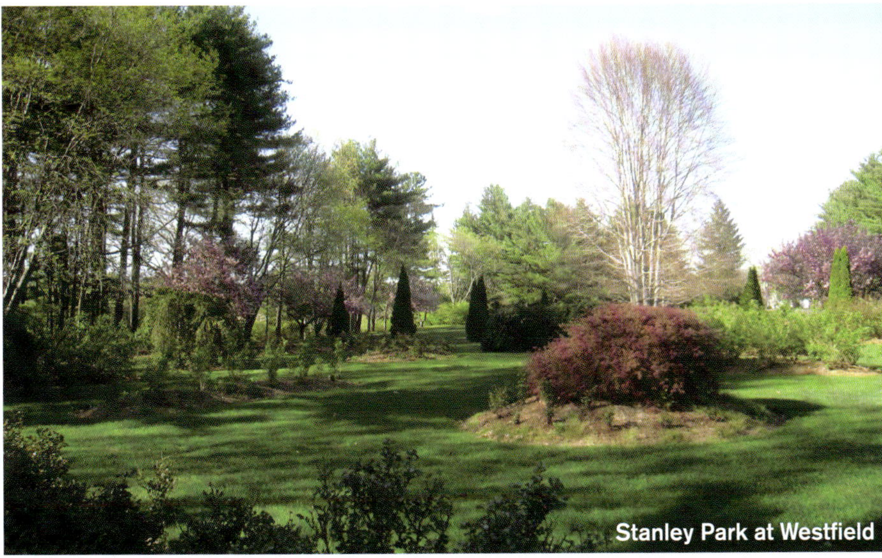

The five-acre arboretum features a landscaped array of trees and shrubs, along with a 30-foot fountain.

Stanley Park at Westfield
Westfield, Massachusetts

Named for founder Frank Stanley Beveridge, this park spans 300 acres of trails, recreation areas, woods, and gardens. Highlights include the Rhododendron Display Garden, the Rose and Flower Garden, the Asian Garden, and the Arboretum. The property also features a wildlife sanctuary, a 98-foot-high carillon tower, a Colonial-era village, and a beloved duck pond, home to ducks, geese, and swans.

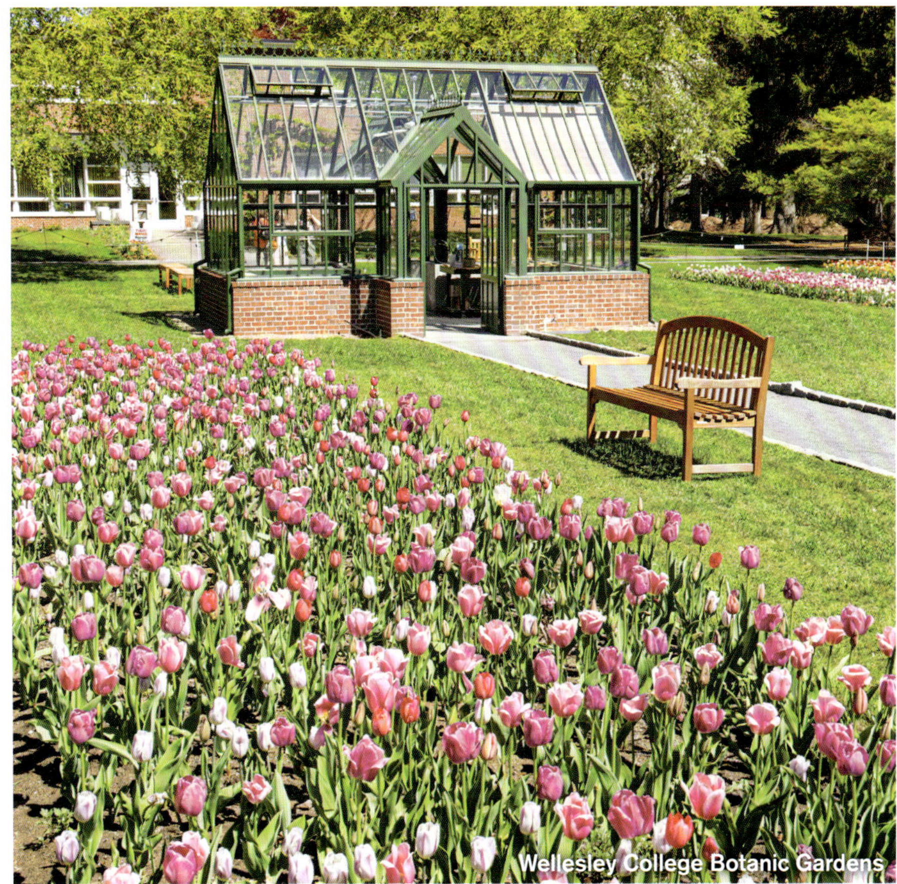

Beds of tulips erupt in multiple colors in the spring.

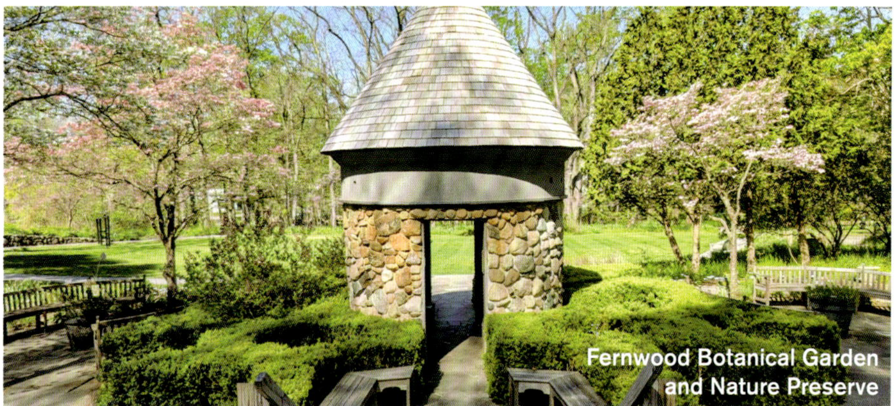

A stone dovecote—a structure historically used to house domesticated pigeons—occupies the center of the Herb and Sensory Garden.

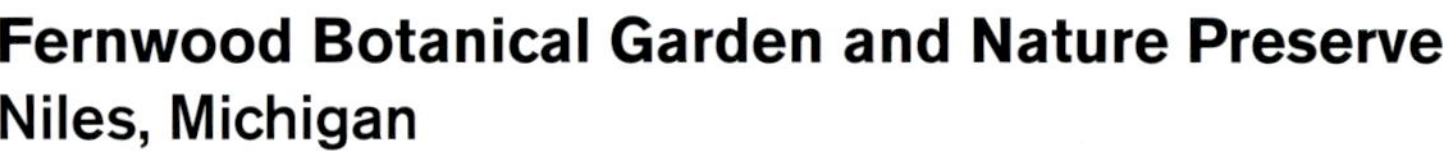

Fernwood Botanical Garden and Nature Preserve

Niles, Michigan

Situated along the St. Joseph River, this garden protects at least ten different ecosystems. The property spans 105 acres and contains miles of hiking trails, an arboretum, and a reconstructed tallgrass prairie. Gardens include the Herb and Sensory Garden, the Japanese Garden, and the Moore Woodlot and Daffodil Bowl.

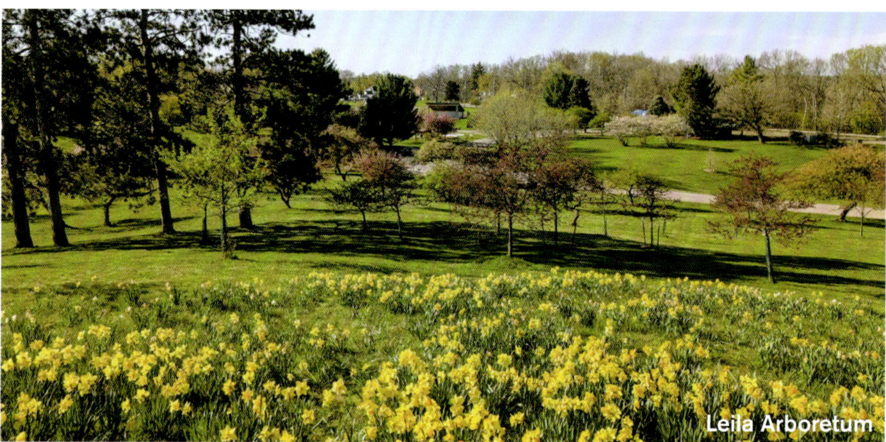

The site features plenty of open space to enjoy.

Leila Arboretum

Battle Creek, Michigan

This 72-acre property was named in honor of Leila Post Montgomery, the widow of famed cereal magnate C.W. Post. The garden oasis is filled with 25,000 different plants, including lilacs, daylilies, tulips, and daffodils. The site is also home to a community vegetable garden, public art, and a 6,000-square-foot greenhouse.

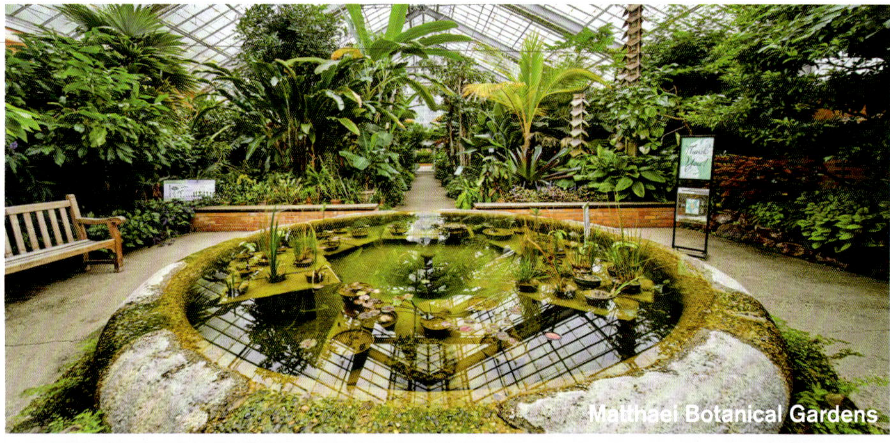

The conservatory includes the arid house, temperate house, and tropical house (pictured).

Matthaei Botanical Gardens

Ann Arbor, Michigan

Managed by the University of Michigan, this property spans 841 acres across four sites, including an arboretum, bog, nature area, and gardens. Highlights include a conservatory with three separate climate zones, a fragrant Magnolia Glade, and the Centennial Shrub Collection. Miles of trails guide visitors through the numerous botanical attractions.

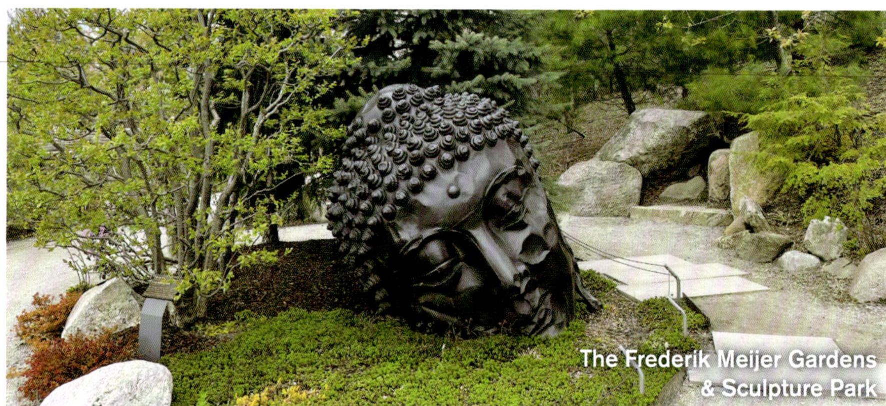

The sculptures alone are worth a long visit. The permanent collection features more than 200 works.

The Frederik Meijer Gardens & Sculpture Park

Grand Rapids, Michigan

Containing one of the most visited art museums in the world and ranked among the best sculpture parks in the country, this property offers more than just natural beauty. Gardens on the 158-acre site include a Japanese garden, the Michigan's Farm Garden, the Lena Meijer Children's Garden, and an indoor carnivorous plant house.

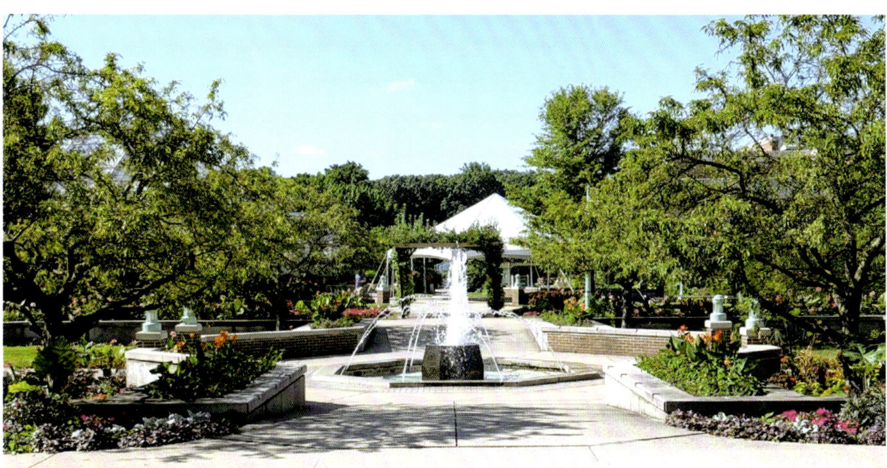

MSU Horticulture Garden
East Lansing, Michigan

A 14-acre garden used for both education and inspiration by the Michigan State University Department of Agriculture and Natural Resources, this property is open to the public daily, free of charge. The gardens surround the university's teaching greenhouses and feature a perennial garden with 400 species, an annual garden with 1,000 varieties, an arboretum used by landscape students, and the Michigan 4-H Children's Garden.

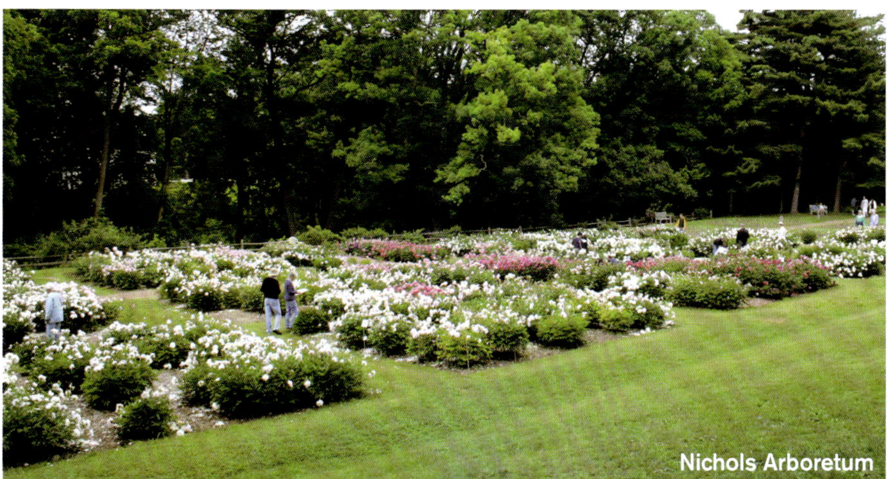
Nichols Arboretum

Nichols Arboretum
Ann Arbor, Michigan

Colloquially known as "the Arb," this site on the University of Michigan campus is located on the banks of the Huron River. The 128-acre arboretum was established in 1907 and contains 110 species of trees, including many originally planted in the early 1900s. The property includes landscaped areas with small trees and ornamental flowers, as well as natural areas of oak-hickory forest and wet meadows.

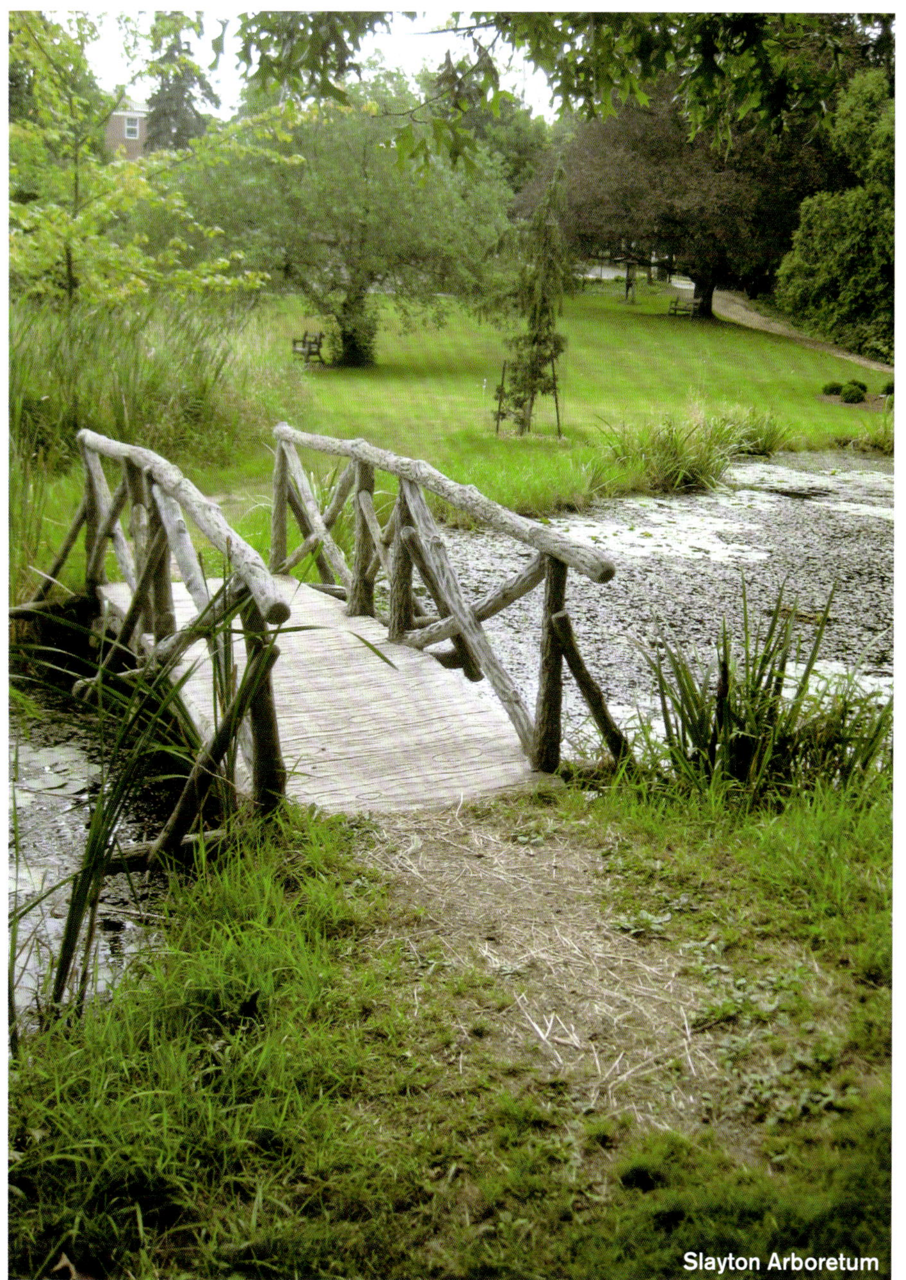
Slayton Arboretum

Slayton Arboretum
Hillsdale, Michigan

Hillsdale College alumni Mr. and Mrs. George A. Slayton donated the 14 acres of this arboretum in 1922 to celebrate the 50th anniversary of their own graduation. Today, the grounds are used as an outdoor laboratory for students as well as a tranquil gathering place for the public. The property contains fieldstone buildings, bridges, waterfalls, nature trails, ponds, and a children's garden.

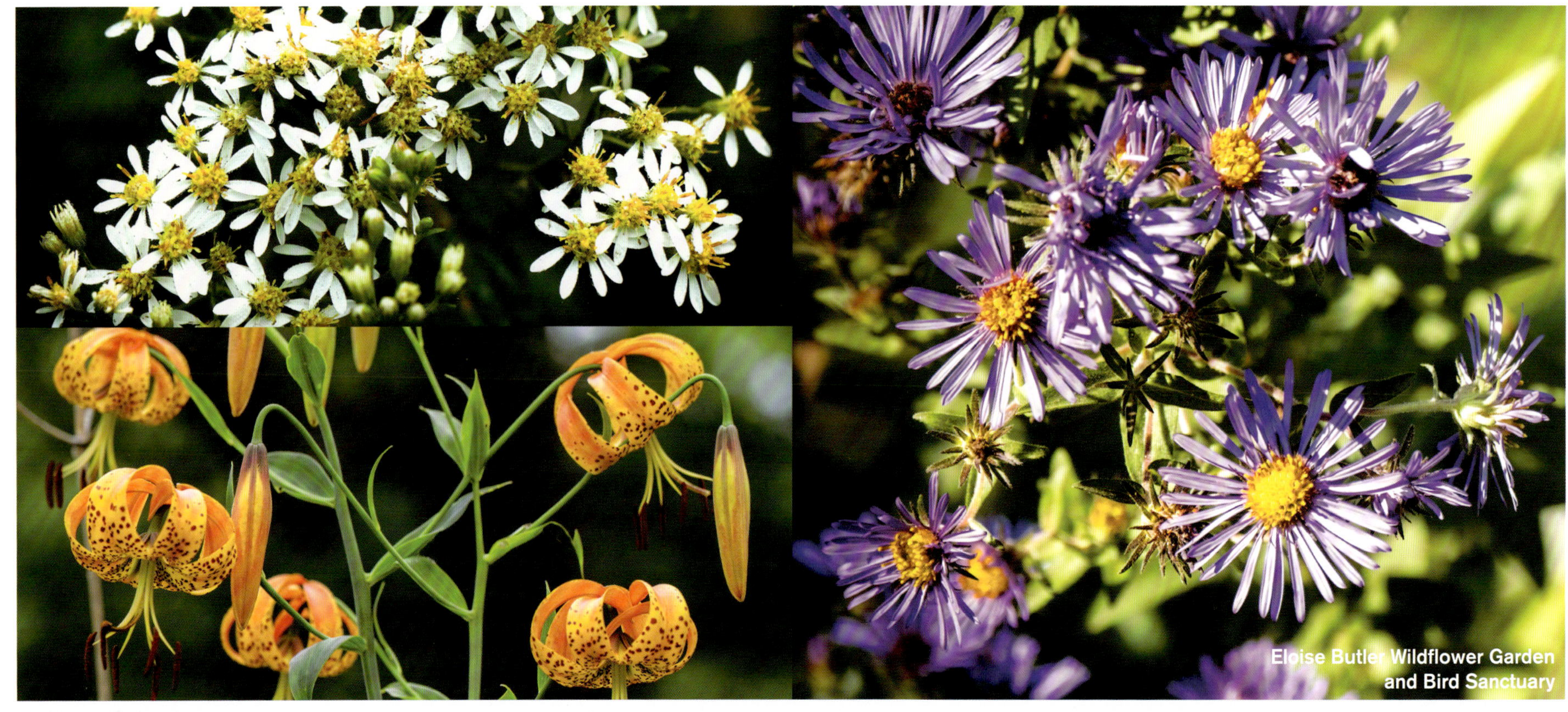

Hundreds of wildflowers show off their colors, including daylilies, asters, daisies, cardinal flowers, and rudbeckia.

Eloise Butler Wildflower Garden and Bird Sanctuary
Minneapolis, Minnesota

Established in 1907, this 18-acre site is the oldest public native plant garden in the United States. The grounds are not only home to more than 600 native plant species, but also to at least 130 migratory and resident bird species. Woodland, wetland, and meadow areas showcase stunning examples of nature's beauty year-round, from irises and sunflowers in the summer, to colorful leaves in the fall.

Leif Erikson Park and Rose Garden
Duluth, Minnesota

Lake Superior provides a scenic backdrop to this park and its 4.5-acre garden, which contains more than 3,000 rose bushes. The property also features a statue of the park's namesake, Leif Erikson, a Norse explorer believed to be the first known European to set foot in North America, almost 500 years before Christopher Columbus. The park's picturesque marble gazebo is a popular spot for weddings.

The Arboretum at Gustavus Adolphus College
St. Peter, Minnesota

Three ecosystems–coniferous forest, tallgrass prairie, and deciduous forest–are found within this arboretum, representing the major ecosystems found in the state of Minnesota. In addition, the property contains formal gardens and trees from around the world. Highlights include flowering bulbs and chrysanthemums in the Thornberg Garden, the Uhler Prairie, which features native grasses, and the ironwood trees of the Esbjornson Ironwood Grove.

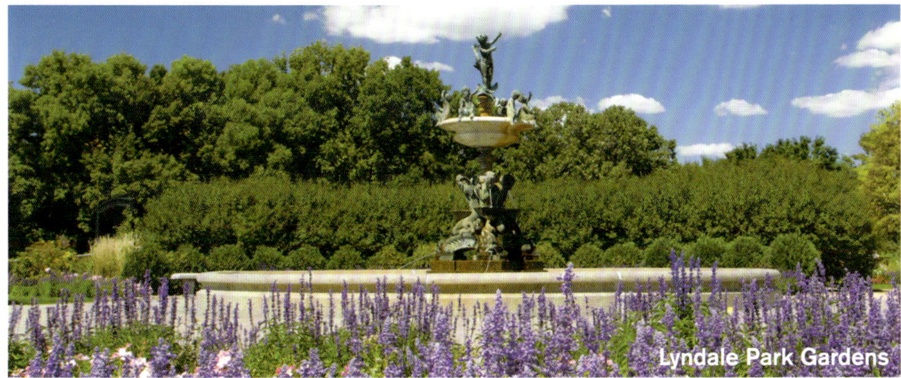

The upper portion of the Rose Garden features a bronze and marble fountain built in the late 1500s in Italy.

Lyndale Park Gardens
Minneapolis, Minnesota

This property traces its origins back to 1906, when the park's superintendent, Theodore Wirth, wanted to create a garden area that would be both beautiful and educational. The result was a 61-acre garden with four distinct spaces: The Peace Garden, the Rose Garden, the Perennial Garden, and the Perennial Trial Garden. Roses and crabapple trees are especially prolific on the grounds, with many examples surviving from their original early-1900s plantings.

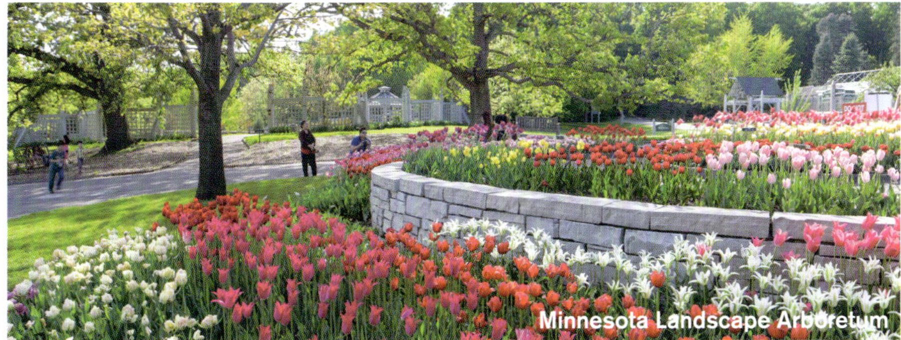

Tulips are a big attraction in the spring.

Minnesota Landscape Arboretum
Chaska, Minnesota

Attracting almost 700,000 visitors per year, this 1,200-acre property contains 28 specialty gardens, 44 plant collections, and more than 5,900 species and cultivars of plants. The garden is dedicated to education, and features numerous demonstration areas to teach visitors about eco-friendly practices. The site is also home to more than 100 works of art, and provides guided tours of the grounds.

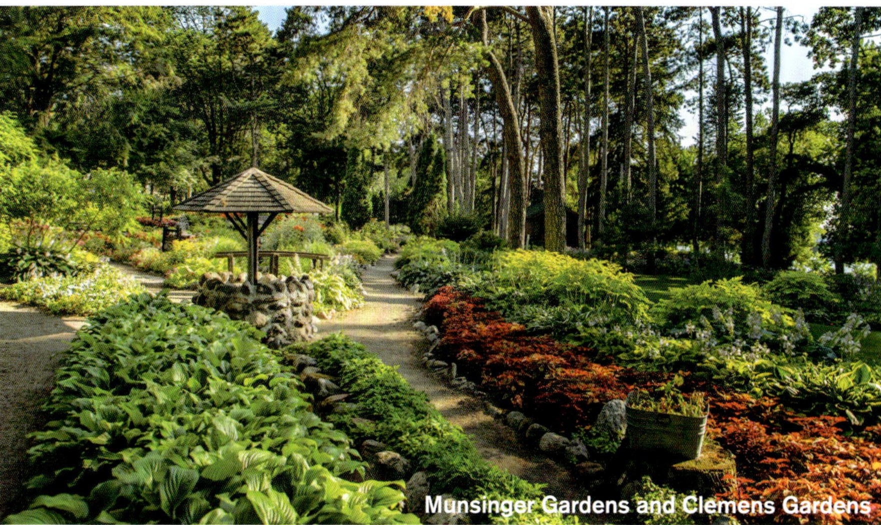

Munsinger Gardens.

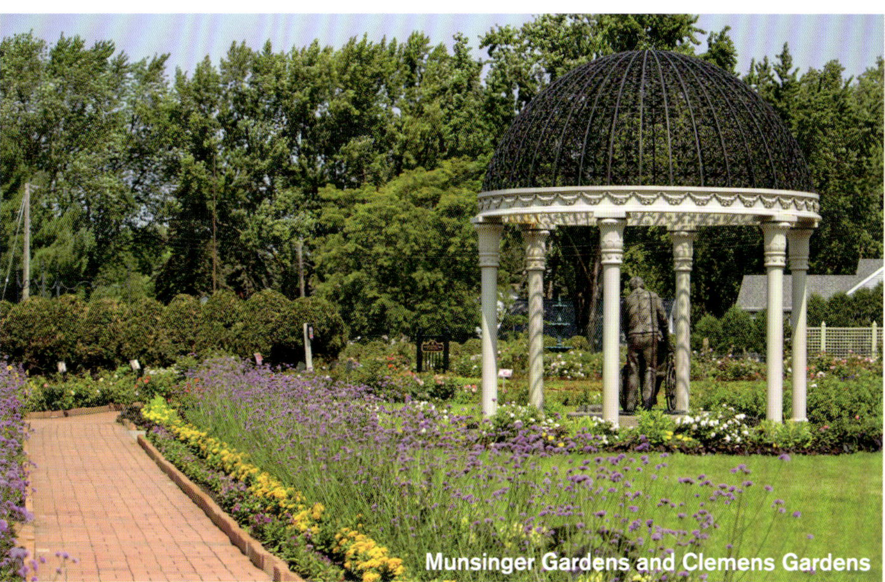

Clemens Gardens.

Munsinger Gardens and Clemens Gardens
St. Cloud, Minnesota

These two separate gardens are next-door neighbors, occupying a combined 21 acres on the banks of the Mississippi River. Munsinger, established in 1915, contains informal gardens, winding paths, a lily pond, and tall pine trees, perfect for quiet reflection. Clemens was founded in the 1990s, and appeals to those who prefer a more formal setting, with European-style flower gardens, brick walkways, and fountains.

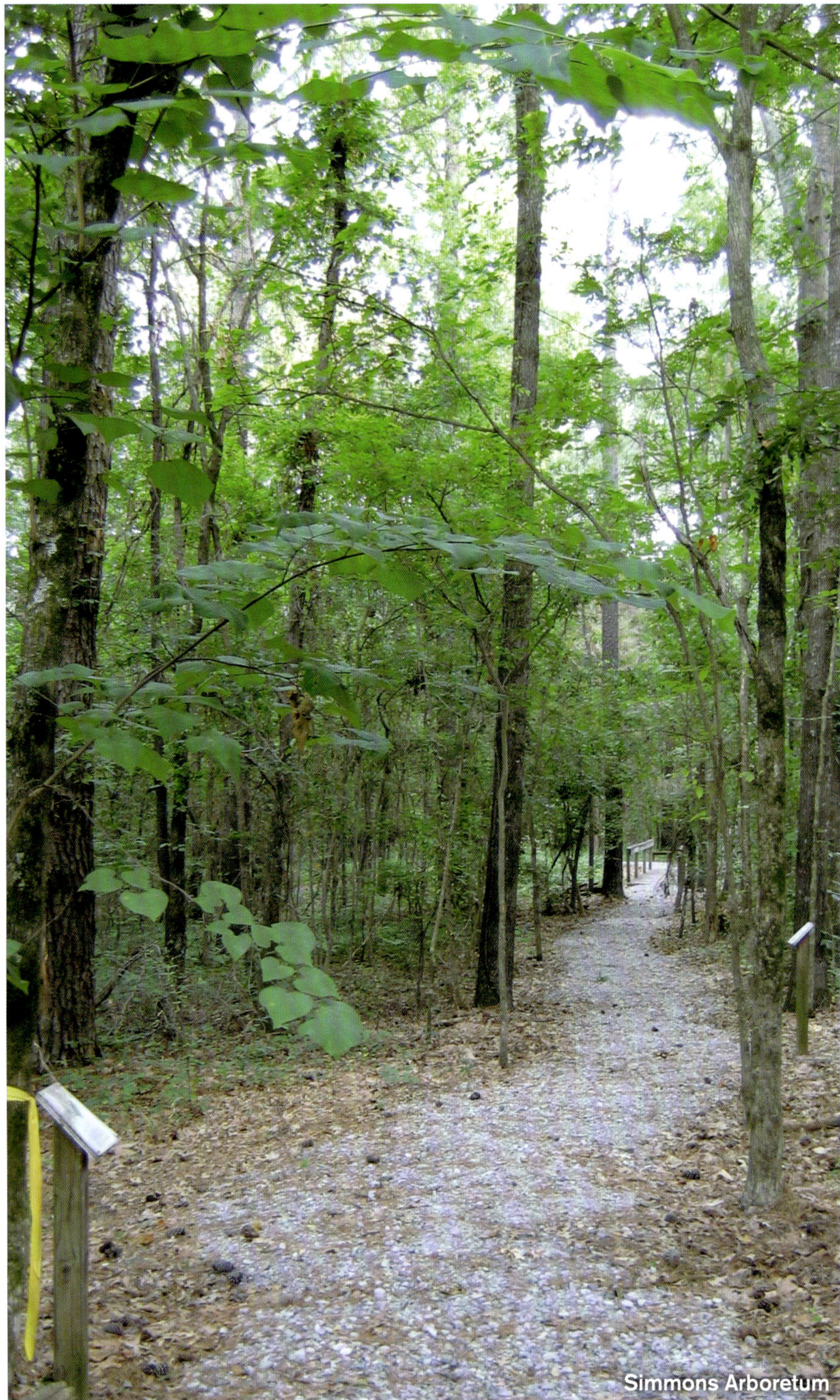

Visitors will find winding, woody trails at Simmons Arboretum.

Crosby Arboretum
Picayune, Mississippi

Established with a mission to preserve the natural heritage and biological diversity of the area, this arboretum showcases plants that are native to Mississippi's Pearl River drainage basin. These include the common vegetation found in pine forests, savannas, hillside bogs, bottomland hardwoods and more. A 64-acre interpretive center and 700 acres of natural landscapes give visitors plenty to explore and discover. Highlights include a collection of carnivorous pitcher plants in the Savanna Exhibit, 12,000 trees and shrubs in the Woodland Exhibit, and the Pinecote Pavilion, a Frank Lloyd Wright-inspired structure considered one of Mississippi's architectural jewels.

Worth Exploring in Mississippi

Jackson State University Botanical Garden
Jackson, Mississippi

- A diverse collection of plant species located in the Presidential Complex on campus
- Educational guided tours offer insights into conservation

The Gardens at Mississippi Museum of Art
Jackson, Mississippi

- A 1.2-acre park in downtown Jackson, known as the Art Garden
- Features the second-largest native plant display in the state

Mynelle Gardens
Jackson, Mississippi

- Contains azaleas, daylilies, camellias, and hundreds of perennials and annuals
- Also a sanctuary for wildlife and songbirds

Simmons Arboretum
Madison, Mississippi

- A ten-acre oasis with walking trails and native trees and plants
- Signs provide information and identification of plants on the trail

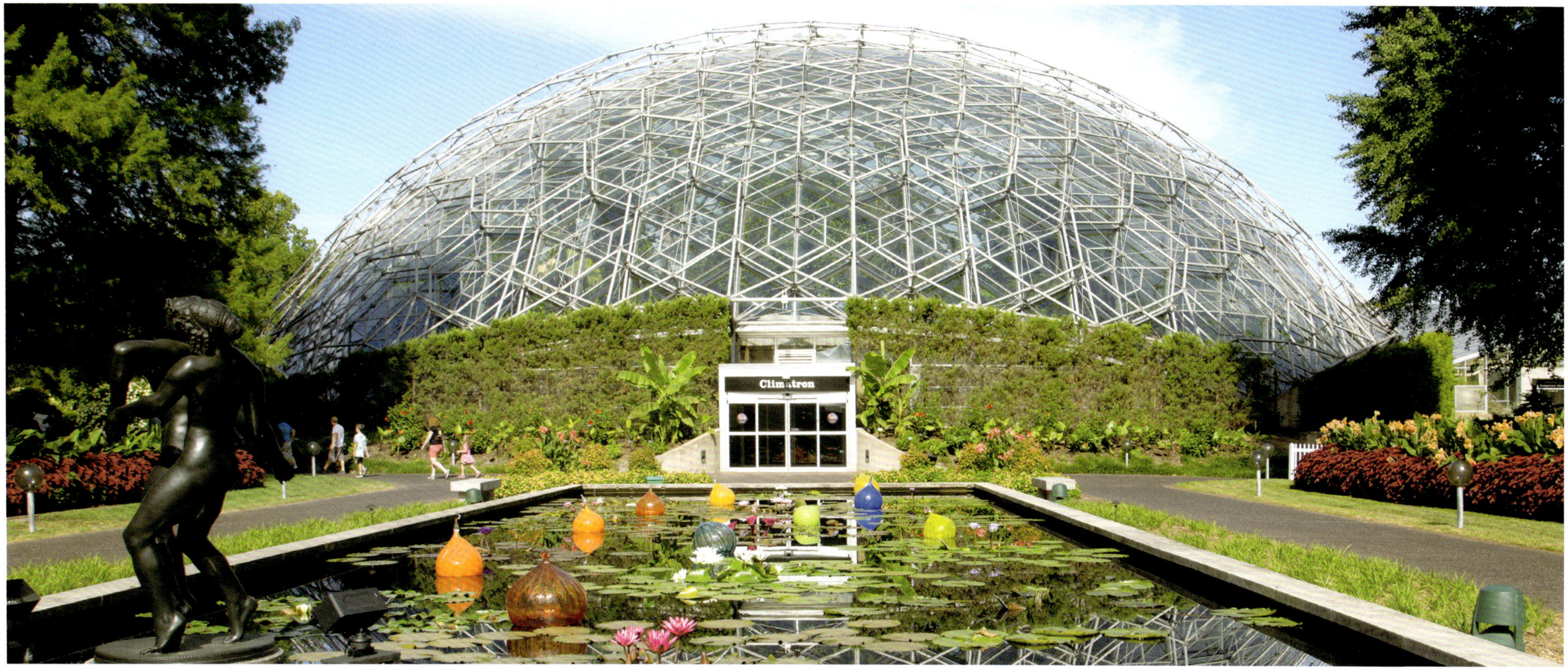

The Climatron greenhouse rises 70 feet and houses a simulated tropical rainforest.

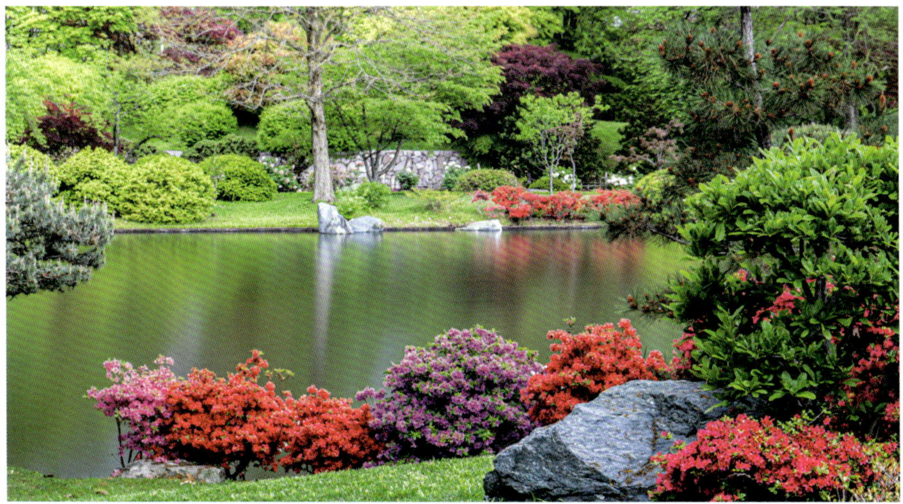

The name *Seiwa-en* can be translated as "garden of pure, clear harmony and peace." And a leisurely stroll past the plants, waterfalls, and islands of this garden can make anyone understand why. In addition to the traditional features, the garden hosts a yearly Japanese Festival—one of the oldest and largest in the country.

Missouri Botanical Garden
St. Louis, Missouri

A green oasis in the middle of the hustle and bustle of St. Louis, this garden is informally known as "Shaw's Garden" in honor of its founder, Henry Shaw. Shaw established the garden on his property in 1859, making it one of the oldest botanical gardens in the United States and a National Historical Landmark.

The property spans 79 acres and includes more than 4,800 trees, some of which were planted by Shaw in the nineteenth century. The property is also known for the William T. Kemper Center for Home Gardening, an area comprised of 23 demonstration gardens that provide endless inspiration for home gardeners. Another highlight is the 14-acre *Seiwa-en*, one of the largest Japanese strolling gardens in North America. A Chinese Garden, English Woodland Garden, and a tropical conservatory are more of the spaces that make this a must-see destination. In addition to the main property, the garden oversees two other sites outside of the city: the Sophia M. Sachs Butterfly House, which is home to 60 tropical butterfly species and 150 tropical plants, and the 2,400-acre Shaw Nature Reserve, featuring 18 miles of hiking trails through woods, glades, prairies, savannas, and wetlands.

The 100-foot Memorial Bell Tower stands at the end of the Tower Trail. There are three designated trails that pass through campus trees.

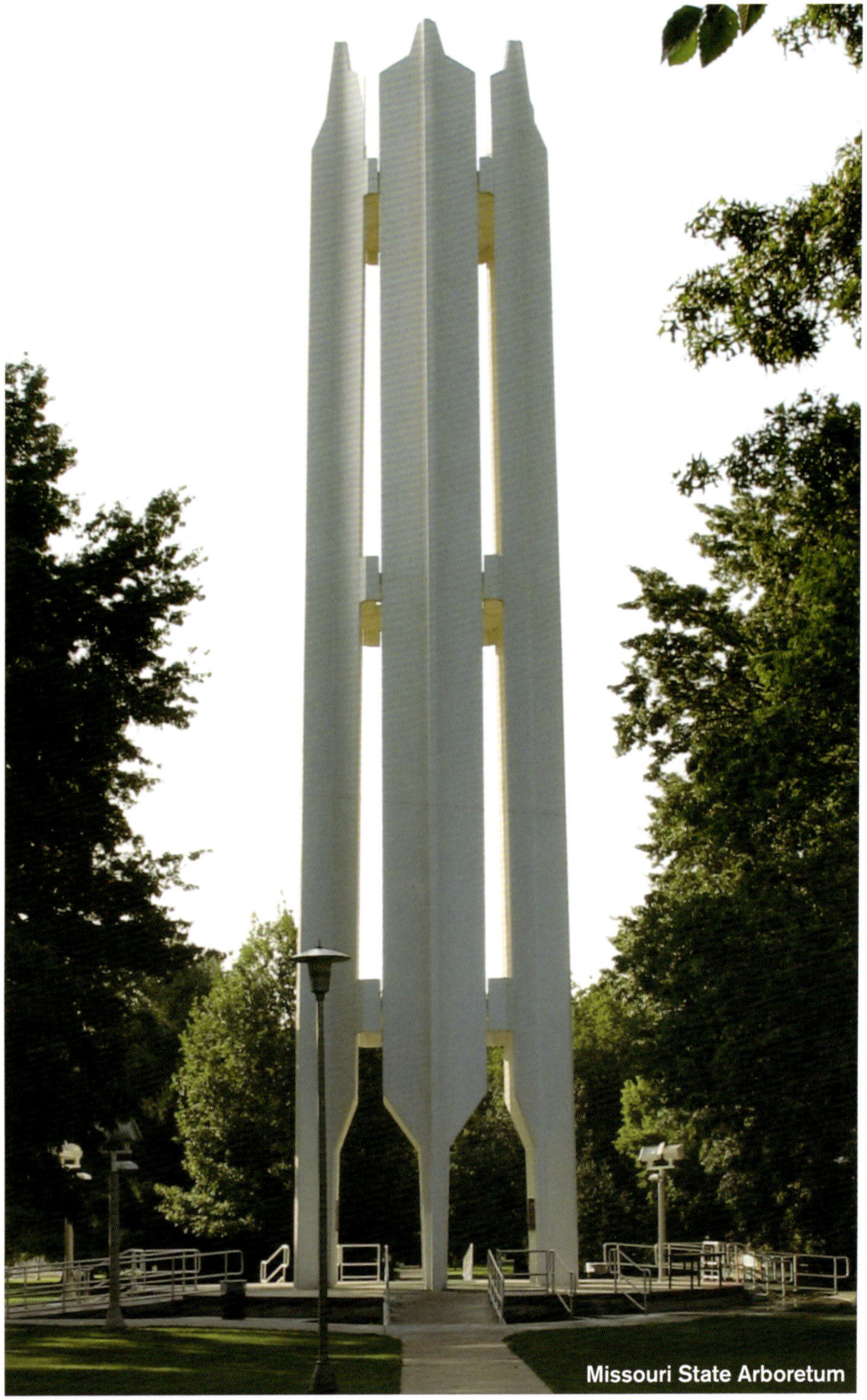

Missouri State Arboretum
Maryville, Missouri

Established by the Missouri State Legislature in 1993, this 452-acre arboretum is home to 1,700 trees representing more than 160 species. The property is located on the campus of Northwest Missouri State University, which is often considered the "most beautiful state university campus," thanks to its beautiful botanical diversity.

Mizzou Botanic Garden
Columbia, Missouri

This garden on the campus of the University of Missouri contains numerous specialty areas containing thousands of plants. Visitor favorites include the Peony Garden, the Daylily Garden, the Native Missouri Tree Collection, and the Jefferson Garden, which contains the original obelisk tombstone that once sat next to Thomas Jefferson's grave.

Powell Gardens
Kingsville, Missouri

The 970 acres of this botanical garden seek to highlight the region's most iconic landscape, the prairie. Before its 1984 founding, the land was, unsurprisingly, an expanse of agricultural farmland. Today, the garden showcases 6,000 varieties of plants and preserves part of the one percent of Missouri's tallgrass prairie that still remains.

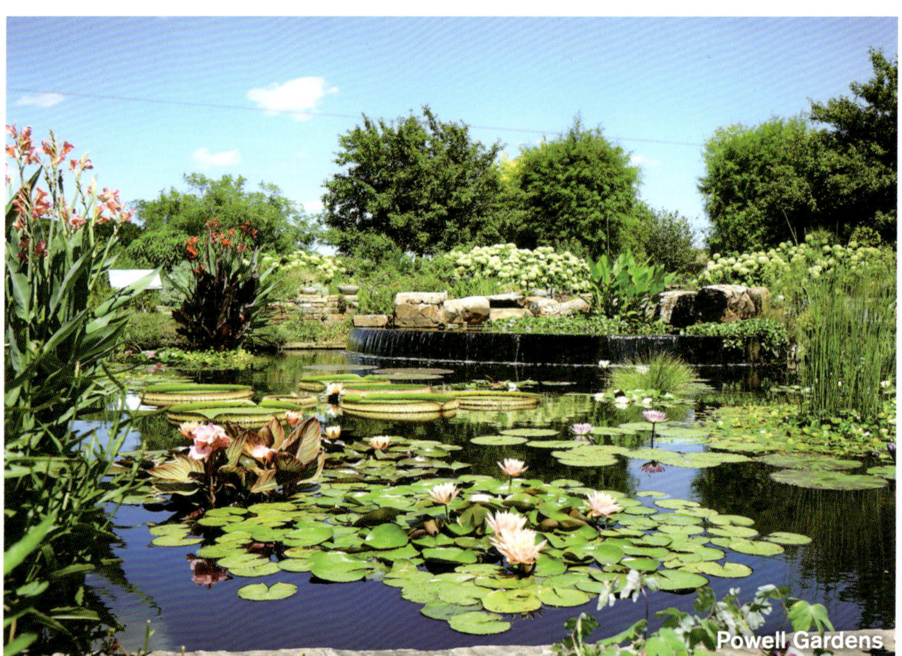

Lush aquatic plants are part of Powell Gardens' allure, with a series of pools presenting cannas, lotus, papyrus, and waterlilies.

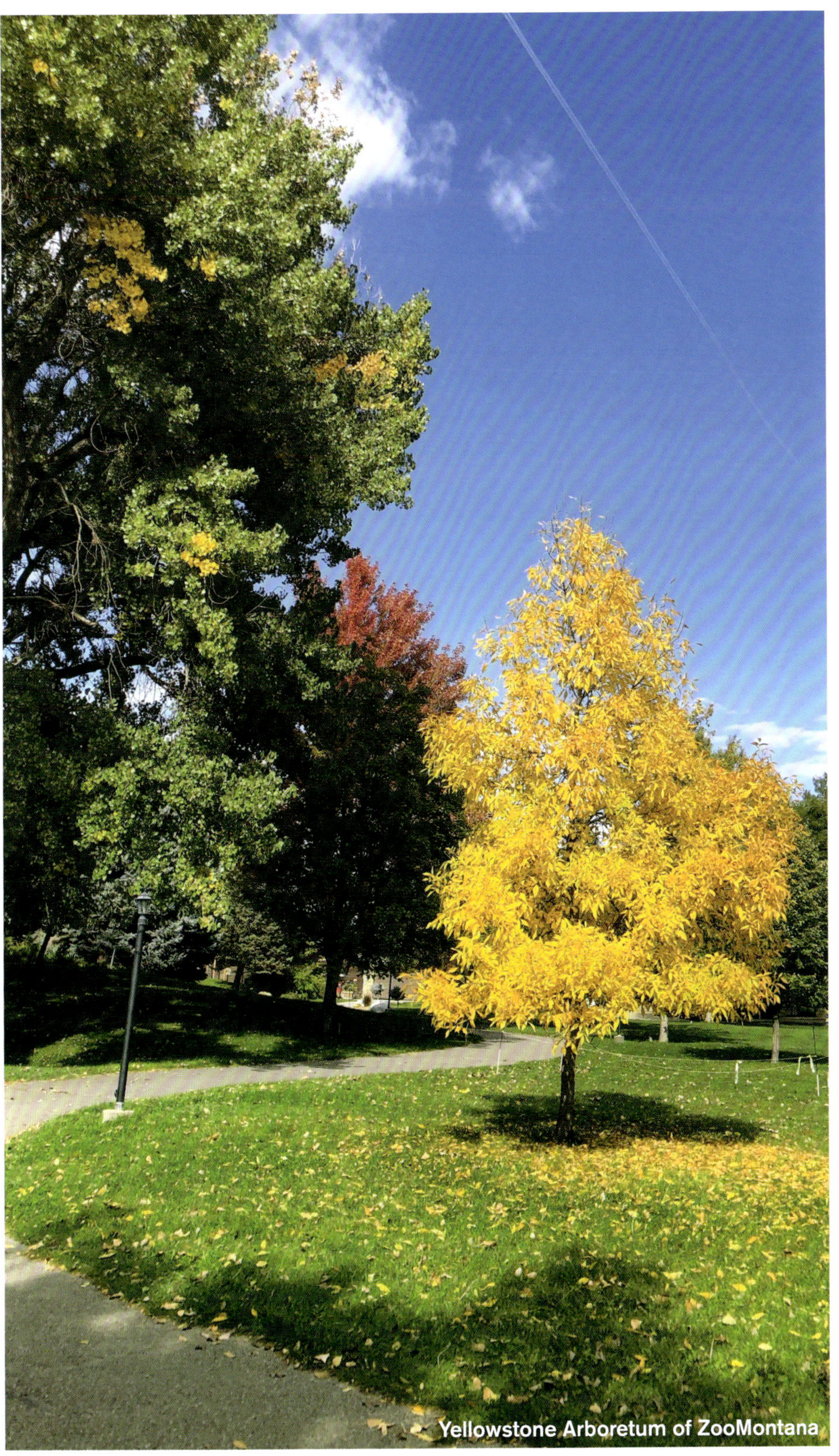
Yellowstone Arboretum of ZooMontana

Worth Exploring in Montana

Gatiss Gardens
Kalispell, Montana
- A five-acre English cottage-style garden
- Colorful, showy flowers include irises, poppies, sweet peas, and trumpet gentian

Lackschewitz-Preece Montana Native Botanic Garden
Missoula, Montana
- Established in 1967 on the University of Montana campus
- Ecosystem sections have included alpine, wet meadows, lowland moist forest, aspen grove, shrub lands, mixed coniferous forest, and riparian shrub lands

Missoula Botanical Gardens
Missoula, Montana
- Consists of garden spaces with sustainability in mind
- Highlights include a conservatory, sensory garden, and a native plants garden

Montana Arboretum and Gardens
Bozeman, Montana
- Official state arboretum located on the campus of the University of Montana
- Contains more than 2,000 trees representing eight forest regions

Rocky Mountain Gardens
Missoula, Montana
- First opened to public in 2024 and now covers 2.75 acres
- Areas include distinct growing areas, such as vegetable, medicinal herb, rose, pollinator-friendly, and ornamental garden beds
- The Beautiful Blooms garden changes colors and themes annually

Tizer Botanic Gardens and Arboretum
Jefferson City, Montana
- The only botanical garden in Montana to operate year-round
- Contains a Wildflower Walk, Herb Garden, Rose Garden, and more

Yellowstone Arboretum of ZooMontana
Billings, Montana
- Located on the grounds of ZooMontana, a zoo and botanical park
- Contains many trees and plants discovered by the Lewis and Clark Expedition

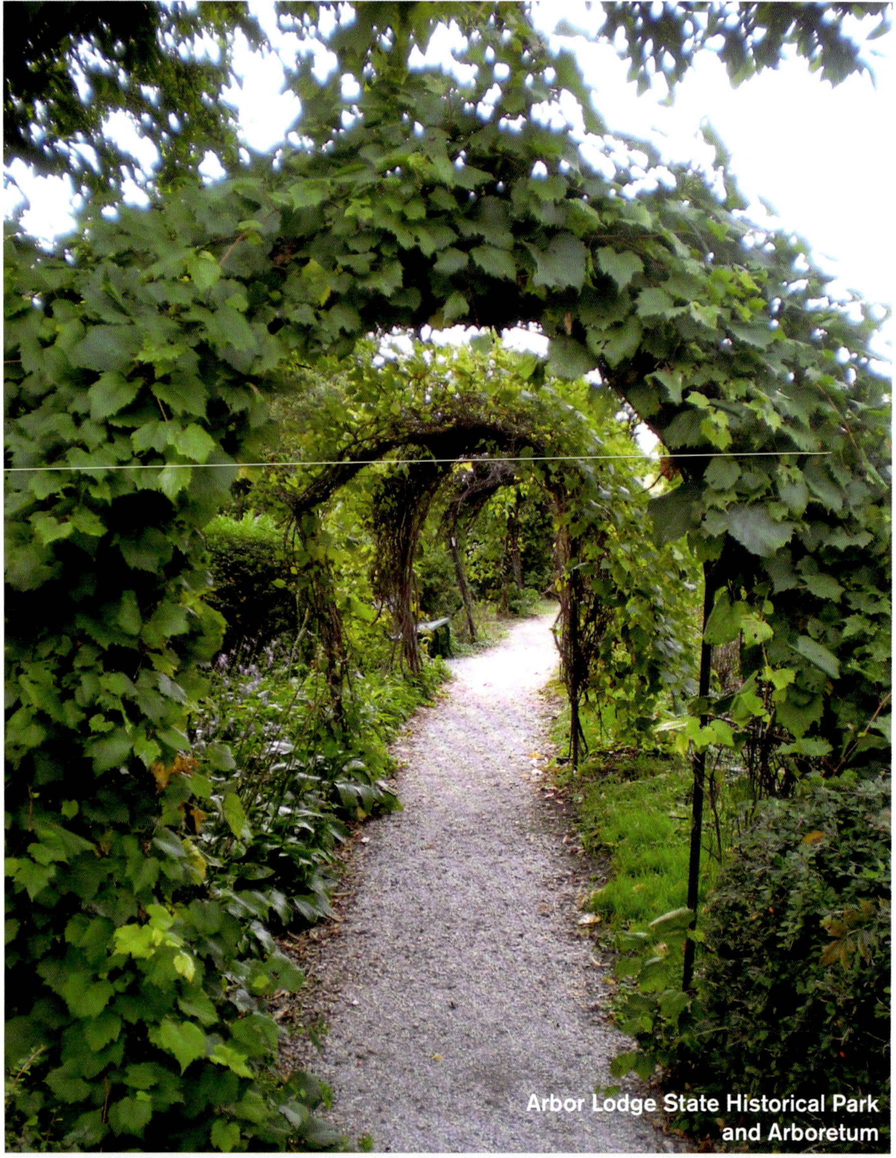

Leafy arches lead through the rose garden.

Arbor Lodge State Historical Park and Arboretum
Nebraska City, Nebraska

The idea for Arbor Day, now recognized every year on the last Friday in April, originated on the grounds of this 72-acre park. A 52-room historic mansion is the centerpiece of the property, where Arbor Day creator J. Sterling Morton, as well as his son, Joy–founder of the Morton Salt Company–once lived. Morton's love of trees is obvious throughout the property, which contains 270 varieties of trees and shrubs, including at least 10 state champion trees. The site is also home to several apple orchards, almost 2.5 miles of walking trails, and one of the country's largest and most diverse collections of lilacs.

Worth Exploring in Nebraska

Alice Abel Arboretum
Lincoln, Nebraska

- Located on the campus of Nebraska Wesleyan University
- Contains more than 100 species of trees, shrubs, and plants on 25 acres

Doane University Osterhout Arboretum
Crete, Nebraska

- Named for 1937 graduate M. David Osterhout, who initiated efforts to landscape the university campus
- Contains more than 200 varieties of trees and shrubs

Gilman Park Arboretum
Pierce, Nebraska

- Spans 14 acres on the banks of Bill Cox Memorial Lake
- Features six landscaped gardens and more than 800 trees and shrubs

Lauritzen Gardens
Omaha, Nebraska

- Offers 20 themed gardens to explore, as well as art and water features
- Highlights include a tropical conservatory and the Founder's Garden

Maxwell Arboretum
Lincoln, Nebraska

- A five-acre arboretum on the campus of the University of Nebraska-Lincoln
- Also contains a one-acre prairie with grasses and wildflowers

D.A. Murphy Panhandle Arboretum
Scottsbluff, Nebraska

- A teaching and demonstration site for the University of Nebraska
- Collections include irises, ground cover, cottonwoods, and woody plants

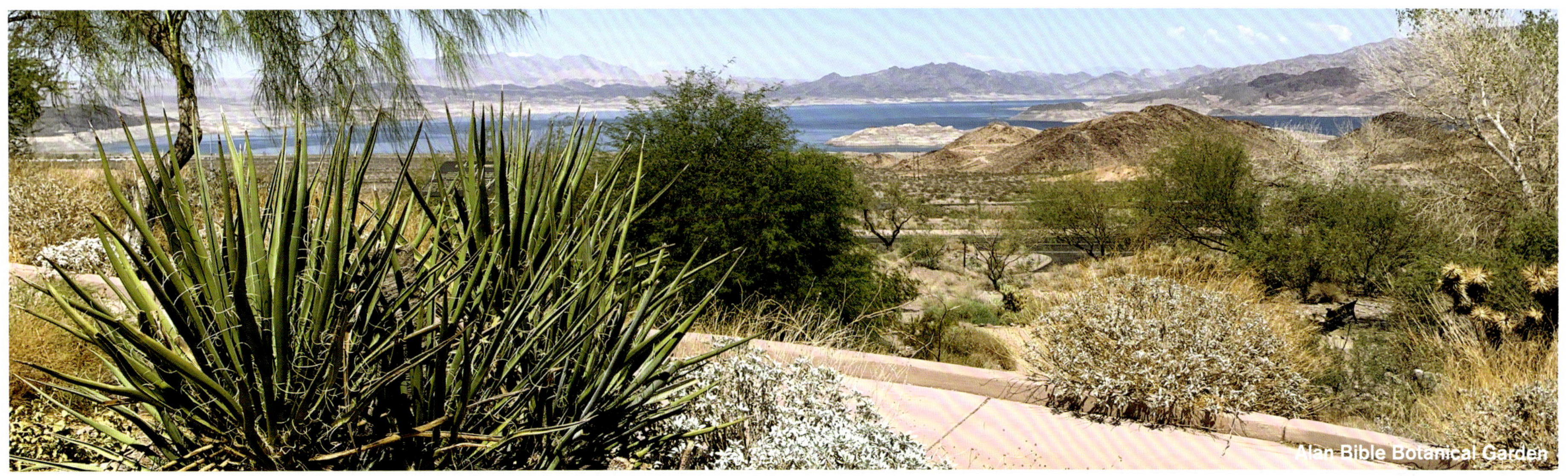
Alan Bible Botanical Garden

With Lake Mead shimmering in the background, visitors will discover not only cacti and desert trees, but a surprising amount of flower species, which will bloom spectacularly during spring rains.

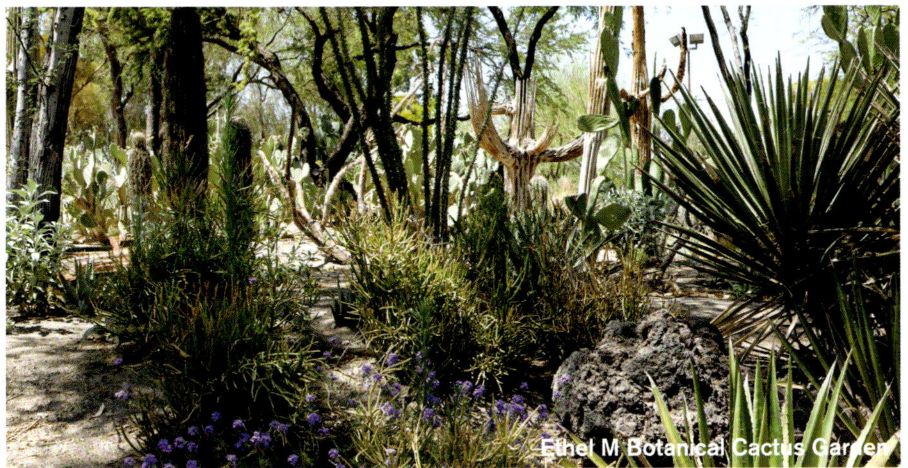
Ethel M Botanical Cactus Garden

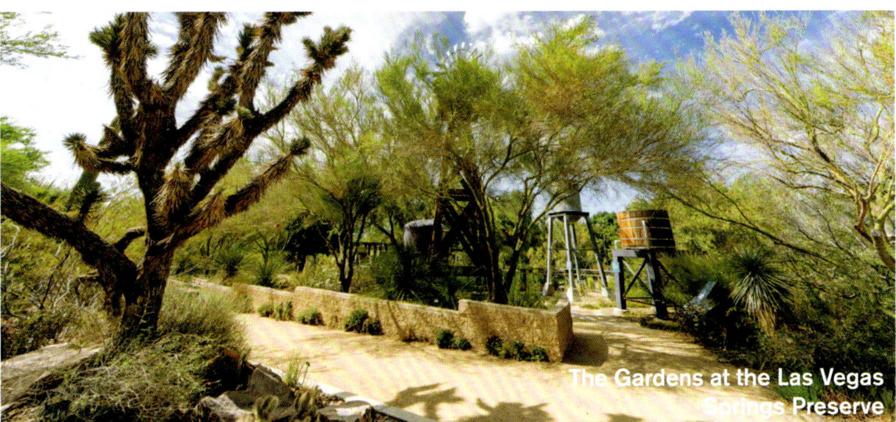
The Gardens at the Las Vegas Springs Preserve

Alan Bible Botanical Garden
Boulder City, Nevada

Alan Harvey Bible was a lawyer and politician who served as a U.S. senator from Nevada for 20 years, from 1954 to 1974. He also often worked with park service officials in the Lake Mead National Recreation Area, where this botanical garden was established in his honor. Containing mostly cactus, the property also showcases some of the trees and shrubs that grow in this dry, desert region.

Ethel M Botanical Cactus Garden
Henderson, Nevada

This unique property pairs the natural beauty of the arid desert with the tastiness of a dessert: chocolate! The Ethel M Chocolates shop and factory offers tastings and self-guided tours of its small-batch confection operation. After sampling sweet treats, guests can wander through the three-acre cactus garden, featuring more than 300 species of cacti and succulents from both the Mojave Desert and around the world.

The Gardens at the Las Vegas Springs Preserve
Las Vegas, Nevada

It should come as no surprise that this garden, located within the arid climate of Las Vegas, focuses on water conservation and water efficient in landscape design. The eight-acre property contains thousands of native and desert-adapted vegetation, and even offers classes and demonstrations on smart water usage. Highlights include the native Mojave Collection and the Deserts of the World Garden, featuring species from all five of the world's major deserts.

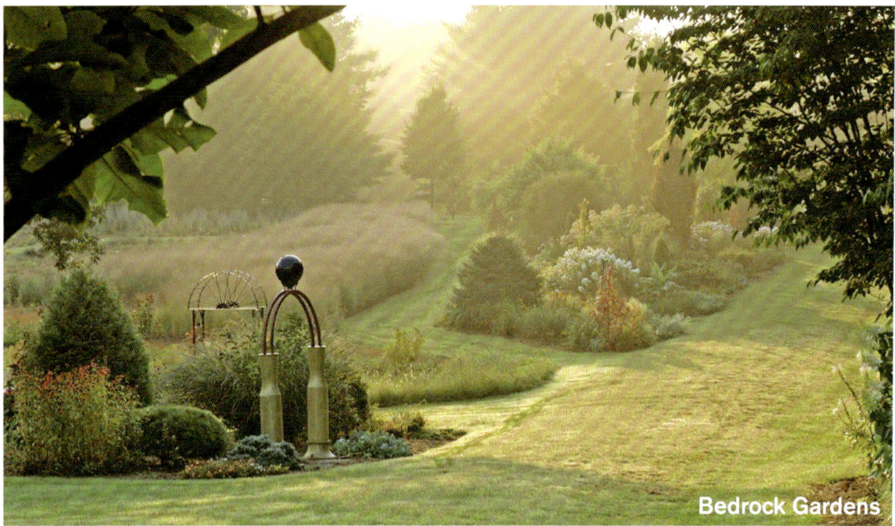
Bedrock Gardens

Bedrock Gardens
Lee, New Hampshire

In the 1700s, this property was home to a dairy farm. But today, after decades of renovation, 20 acres of the original farm has been transformed into a botanical garden focusing on landscape design, horticulture, and art. More than 1,000 plant species are found on the site, as well as water features and sculptures.

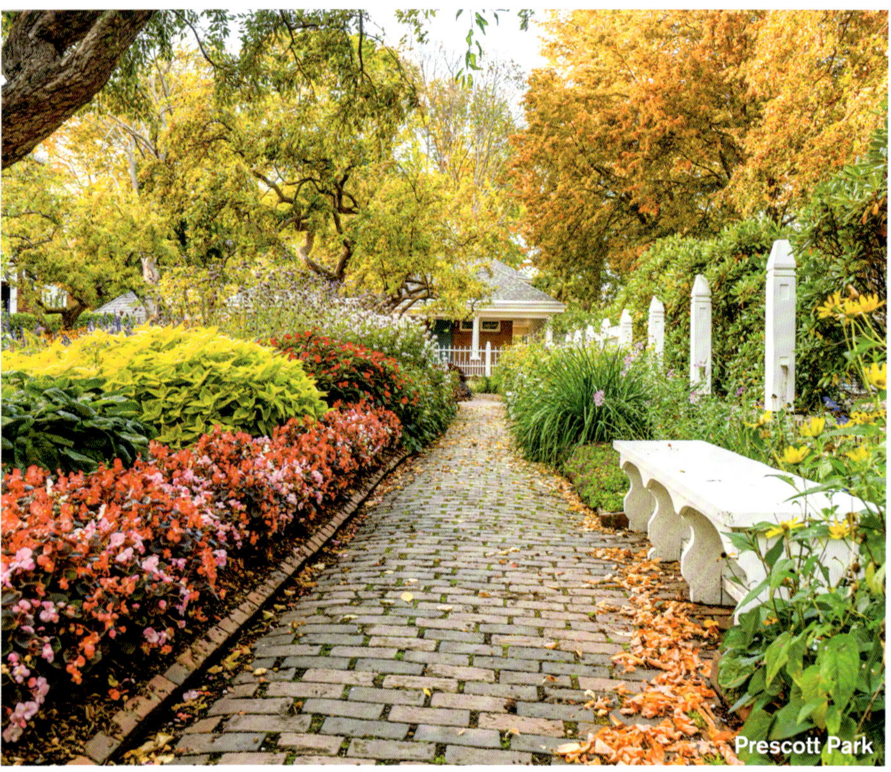
Prescott Park

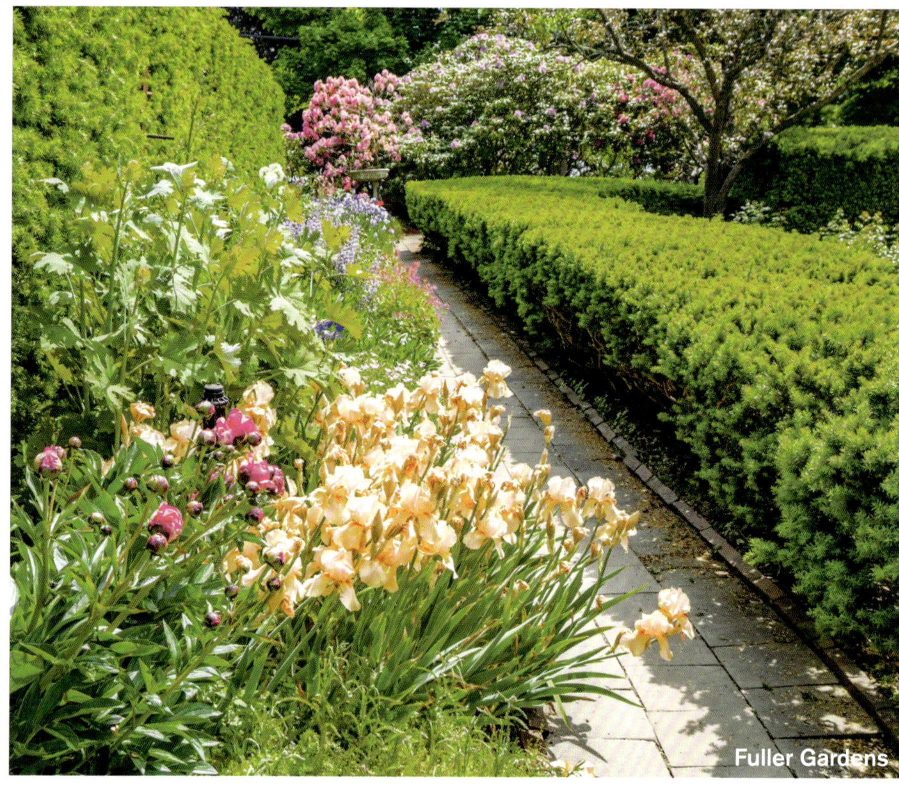
Fuller Gardens

Fuller Gardens
North Hampton, New Hampshire

This coastal New Hampshire garden was once the home of businessman and philanthropist Alvan T. Fuller. The three-acre property is best known for its formal rose gardens, containing thousands of flowers, created in the late 1920s in a Colonial Revival style. The garden also features a Japanese garden, a dahlia display, and a conservatory.

Prescott Park
Portsmouth, New Hampshire

A waterfront park in the heart of Portsmouth, this ten-acre property was willed to the city by two sisters, Josie and Mary Prescott. Today, the park is a popular summer gathering spot for locals and visitors alike, who can wander through several formal garden spaces or enjoy a Broadway show performed on the park's outdoor stage.

Rhododendron State Park
Fitzwilliam, New Hampshire

As its name suggests, this state park and nature preserve is famous for a 16-acre patch of land that contains a stand of native rhododendrons, one of the largest such collections in New England. While blueberries, cranberries, and mayflowers are also found on the property, most people come to walk the trail that encircles the rhododendron grove.

Bamboo Brook Outdoor Education Center
Far Hills, New Jersey

From 1911 to 1959, this property was the home of one of the country's first female landscape architects, Martha Brookes Hutcheson. Today, Hutcheson's gardens have been carefully restored on the 687-acre site, featuring the plants used in her original designs. Spaces include the East Lawn and Coffee Terrace, Circular Pool, and the Upper and Lower Waters at Bamboo Brook, as well as historic buildings.

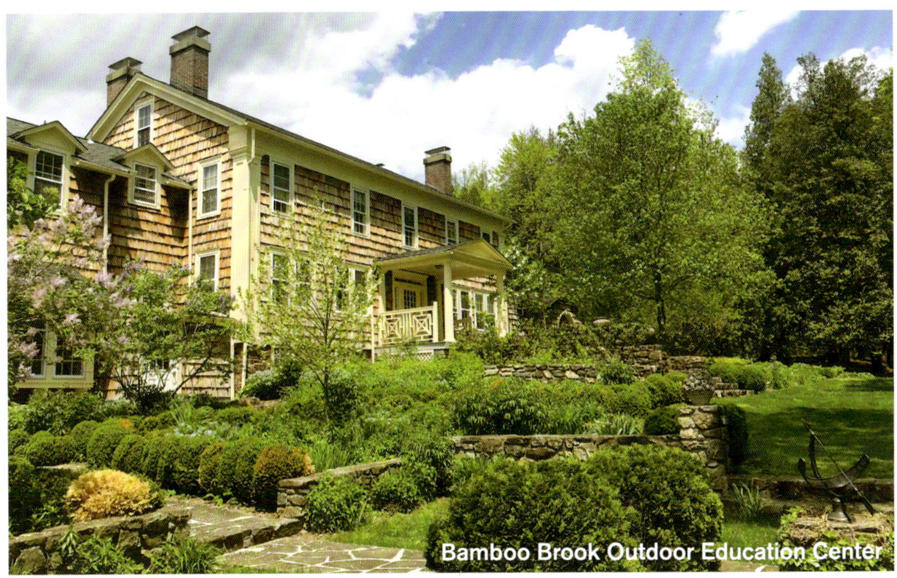

Bamboo Brook Outdoor Education Center

Hutcheson House and garden.

Sister Mary Grace Burns Arboretum
Lakewood, New Jersey

Located on the campus of Georgian Court University, this site was cultivated in the late 1800s to resemble a Georgian country house garden and established as an arboretum in 1989. The property, which was named in honor of former biology professor Sister Mary Grace Burns, contains an Italian Garden, Sunken Garden, Wellness Garden, Japanese Garden, and Formal Garden, all of which can be toured for free.

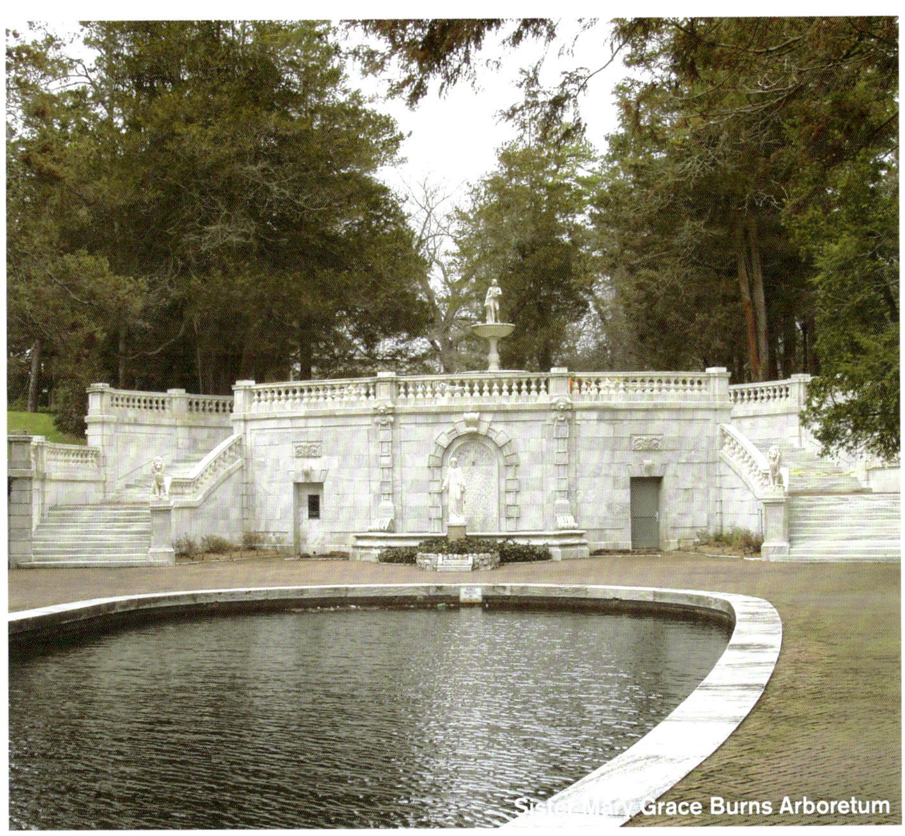

Sister Mary Grace Burns Arboretum

The Sunken Garden and Lagoon.

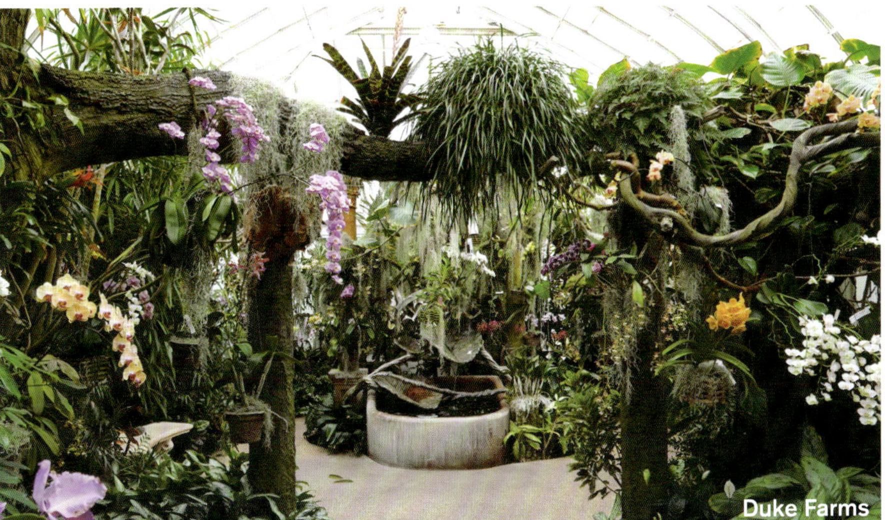

Duke Farms

The Orchid Range.

Duke Farms
Hillsborough Township, New Jersey

The 2,700-acre Duke Farms was created by American Tobacco Company founder James Buchanan Duke. His daughter, Doris Duke, designed and installed the 11 gardens that are now found on the site, including the Orchid Range–home to nearly 4,000 plants representing 1,300 varieties–and the tranquil Meditation Garden. The property also contains miles of hiking trails, almost 250 bird species, and several Champion Trees.

Worth Exploring in New Jersey

Leonard J. Buck Garden
Far Hills, New Jersey

- A 33-acre wooded property with wildflowers and native and exotic plants
- Considered one of the country's premier rock gardens

Colonial Park Arboretum and Gardens
Somerset, New Jersey

- Features flowering trees, evergreens, shade trees, and flowering shrubs
- Known for its award-winning formal rose garden and fragrant sensory garden

Herrontown Woods Arboretum
Princeton, New Jersey

- A 142-acre natural hardwood forest
- Contains 60 species of trees and shrubs, wildflowers, and wetlands with frogs and salamanders

Holmdel Arboretum
Holmdel, New Jersey

- Also known as the David C. Shaw Arboretum
- Home to almost 3,000 trees and shrubs, including a large collection of cedars and a conifer garden

Presby Memorial Iris Gardens
Montclair, New Jersey

- Features 14,000 irises that produce 100,000 blooms annually
- Blooming season is typically several weeks between May and June

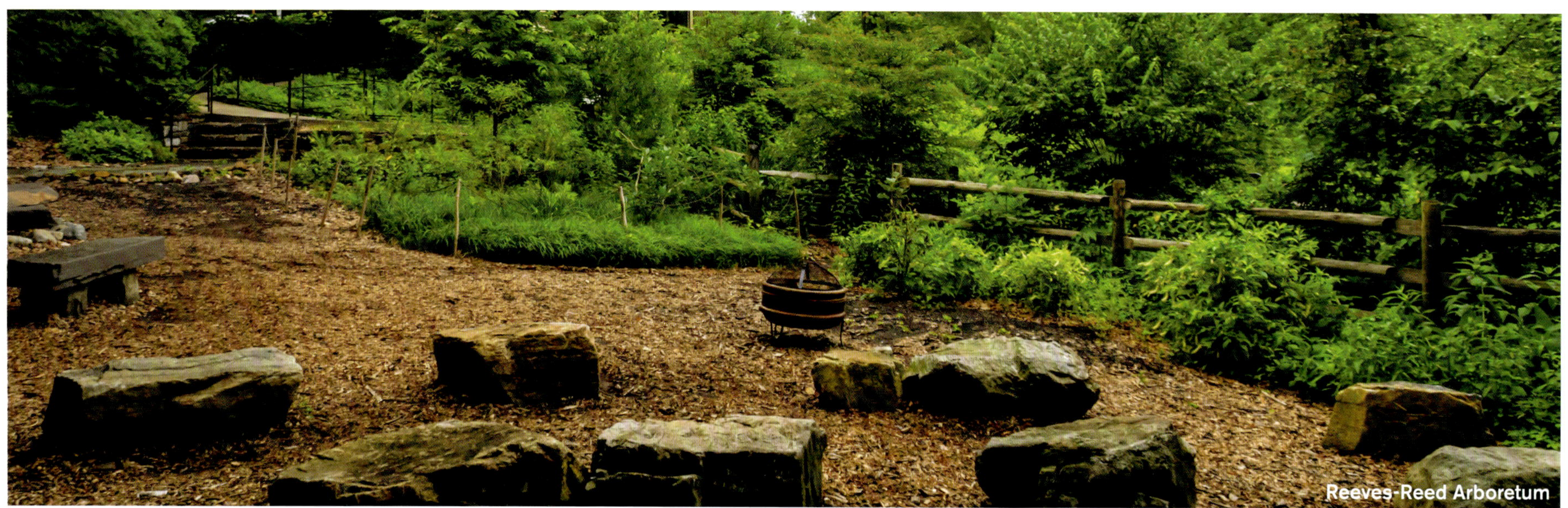
Reeves-Reed Arboretum

Reeves-Reed Arboretum
Summit, New Jersey

The Lenni Lenape Native Americans once passed through this property on their travels through what is now New Jersey, setting the foundations for what would become a site with a rich history. Now listed on the National and State Registers of Historic Places, the gardens in this arboretum were designed to reflect trends that were popular in the late nineteenth and early twentieth centuries. Highlights include the historic Rose Garden, Azalea Garden, and Rock Garden, which strive to maintain a sense of botanical nostalgia, as well as an aromatic Herb Garden, a vibrant Daffodil Bowl, and a delicate Primrose Path.

Rutgers Gardens

New Brunswick, New Jersey

As the official botanical garden of Rutgers University, this 180-acre property provides learning opportunities for students, faculty, and visitors. Campus collections include a rhododendron garden, the Pollinator Garden, a bamboo grove, and the 60-acre Helyar Woods, named after College of Agriculture professor and hiking proponent Frank G. Helyar.

Sayen Park Botanical Garden

Hamilton, New Jersey

In 1912, world traveler and avid gardener Frederick Sayen purchased this 30-acre parcel of land in order to fill it with the plants and flowers he acquired during his travels. Today, thousands of Sayen's plants, which he collected from China, Japan, and England, are still found on the property, including more than 1,000 azaleas and 500 rhododendrons.

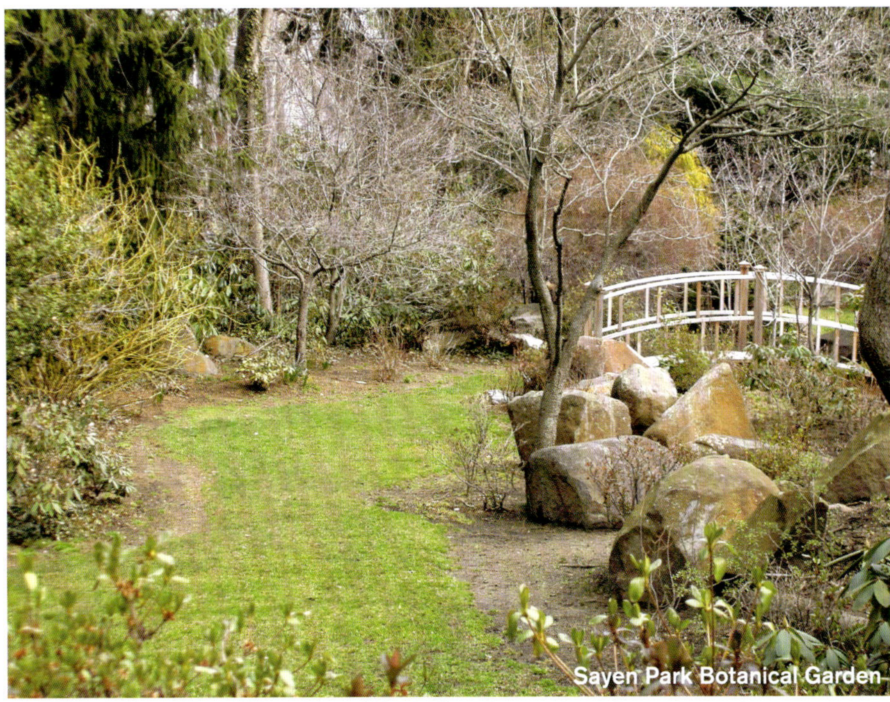

Sayen Park Botanical Garden

The loop trail through the gardens is just over a mile long.

Willowwood Arboretum

Far Hills, New Jersey

More than 2,100 plant species can be found within this garden, which was established in the early 1900s by two brothers, Robert and Henry Tubbs. The avid gardeners dubbed the property *Willowwood* due to the large stands of willow trees in the area. Today, the arboretum also contains oak, maple, lilac, pine, and a 98-foot-tall dawn redwood.

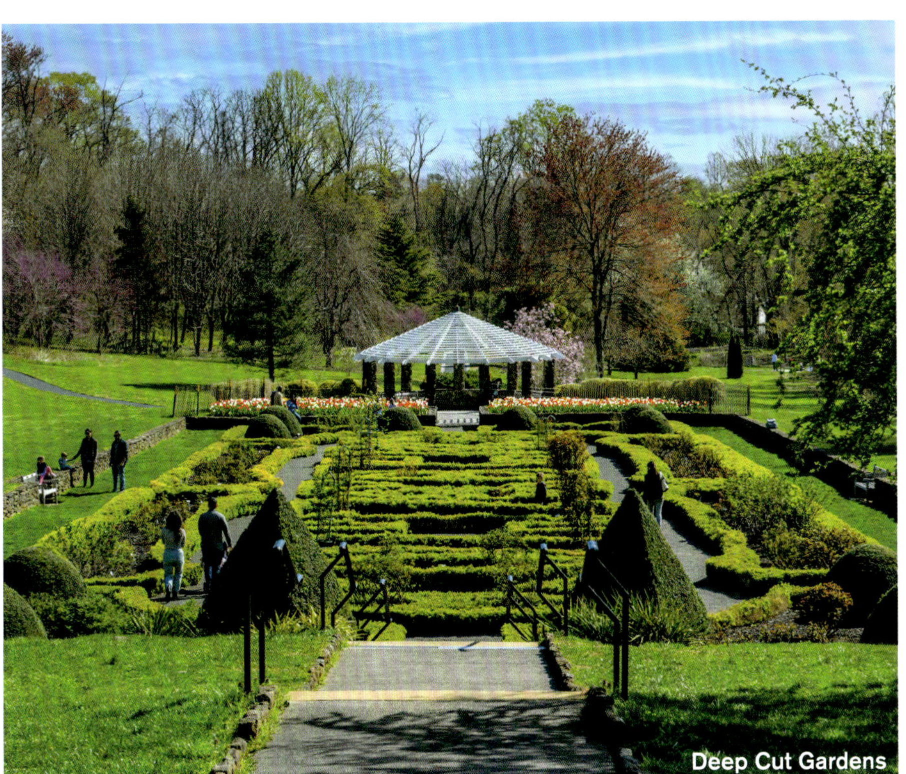

Deep Cut Gardens

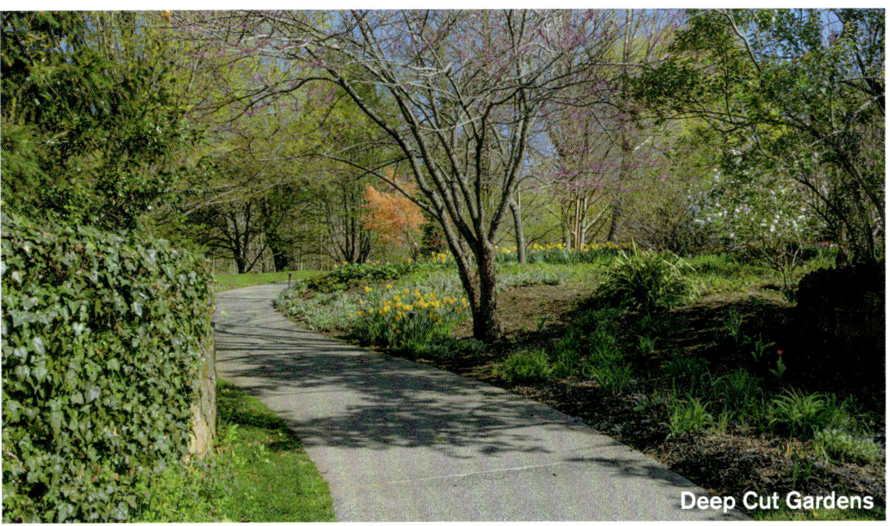

Deep Cut Gardens

Deep Cut Gardens

Middletown, New Jersey

The 54 acres of gardens and greenhouses on this property are geared towards inspiring and educating home gardeners. The property is home to a rock garden, a formal rose garden, a Japanese garden, and a display greenhouse, featuring orchids, palms, hibiscus, and a collection of succulents from around the world.

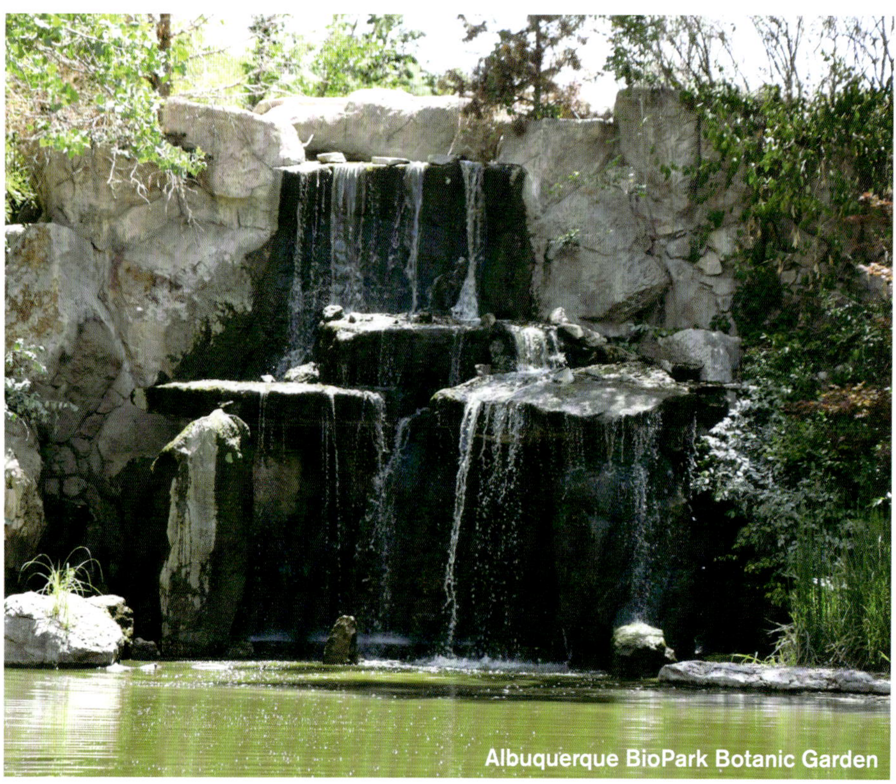
Albuquerque BioPark Botanic Garden

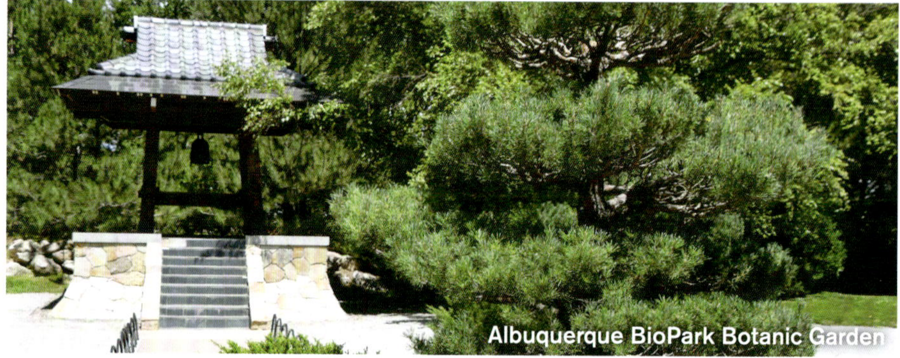
Albuquerque BioPark Botanic Garden

Albuquerque BioPark Botanic Garden
Albuquerque, New Mexico

Welcoming 1.5 million visitors a year, this unique attraction is the top tourist destination in the state of New Mexico. Established as a zoo in 1927, the park is home to more than 900 animals from around the world. In 1996, the property added 32 acres of botanic gardens and exhibits, plus the aptly named "BUGarium" housing insects and arthropods. Garden collections include the Mediterranean Conservatory, which contains plants in a simulated coastal environment, the Sasebo Japanese Garden, named in honor of Albuquerque's Japanese sister city, and the Dragonfly Sanctuary Pond, which features native dragonflies and other wildlife.

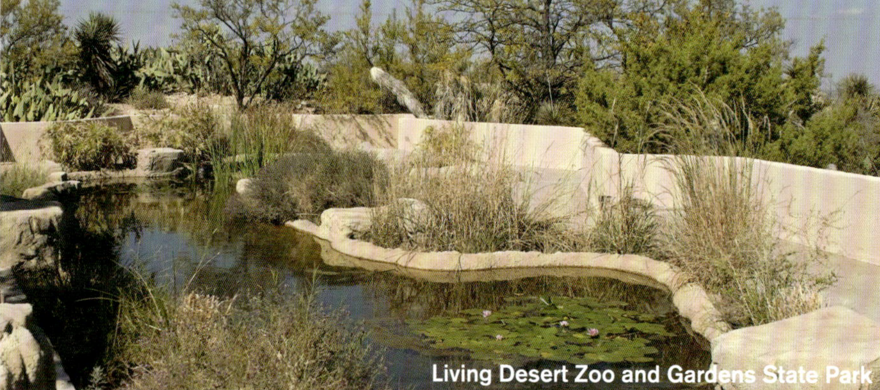
Living Desert Zoo and Gardens State Park

Living Desert Zoo and Gardens State Park
Carlsbad, New Mexico

Located at an elevation of 3,482 feet and overlooking the Pecos River, this zoo and botanical garden is home to Chihuahuan desert animals and plants in their native habitat. Forty animal species, including bobcats, mule deer, elk, cougars, and Mexican wolves, are located within the park, as well as 14 types of snakes, and a variety of eagles, hawks, and songbirds. The gardens contain cacti and succulents from around the world, and a 1.3-mile hiking trail leads visitors through a landscape full of sand dunes, pine and juniper forest, and views of the Pecos River Valley.

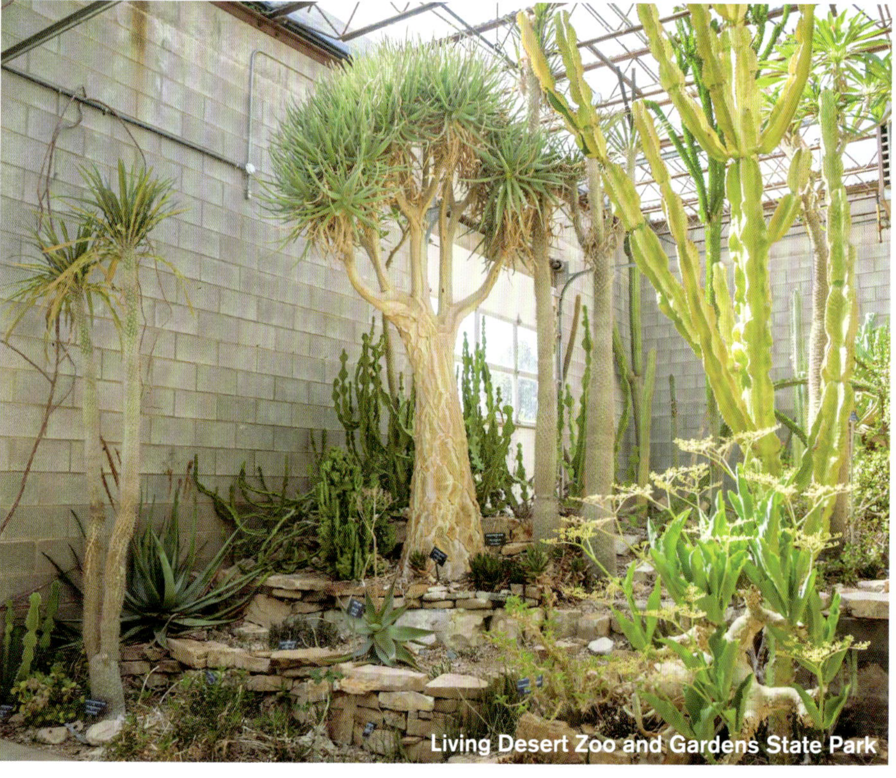
Living Desert Zoo and Gardens State Park

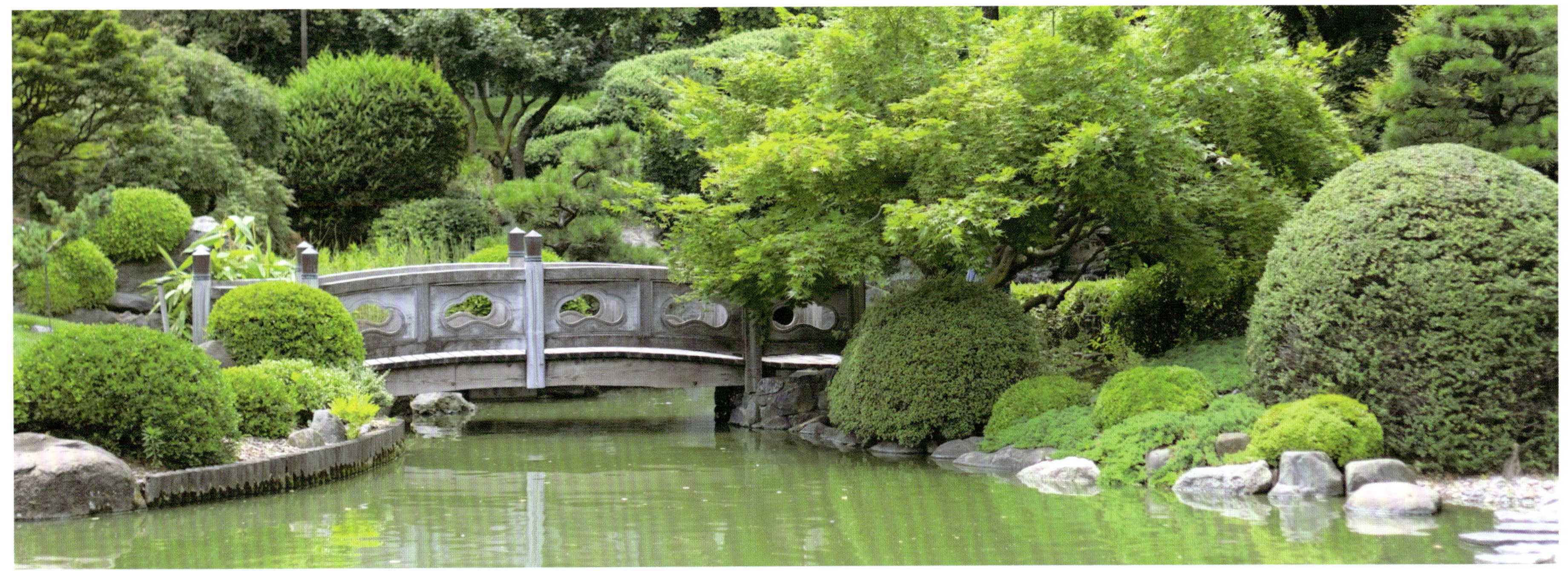

A bridge crosses a pond in the Japanese Hill-and-Pond Garden. Other architectural elements in this section include a Shinto shrine, viewing pavilion, and stone lanterns.

Brooklyn Botanic Garden
Brooklyn, New York

New York City is known for its skyscrapers, bright lights, and intensely urban atmosphere. But there are still places within the city, like this 52-acre public garden, that offer tranquil green space and natural beauty. The garden officially opened in 1911, with the goal of showcasing and preserving native plants and wildflowers, which are still featured in the park's Native Flora Garden. This three-acre area of the property is the one of the first to signal the arrival of spring in the city, bursting forth with colorful flowers and attracting bees and butterflies.

The property's popular Children's Garden and Japanese Hill-and-Pond Garden have each existed for more than 100 years and continue to delight visitors. The Children's Garden allows kids to learn about horticulture and sustainable practices by planting their own vegetables, herbs, and flowers, while the Japanese Garden is one of the oldest and most visited outside of Japan.

In addition to other specialty gardens, including the Shakespeare Garden, the Rose Garden, and the Tropical Pavilion conservatory, the park is famous for developing the first yellow magnolia, known as "Elizabeth," for which it received a patent in 1977. Today, the Brooklyn Botanic Garden is beloved by the surrounding community, where it continues to fascinate, teach, and inspire.

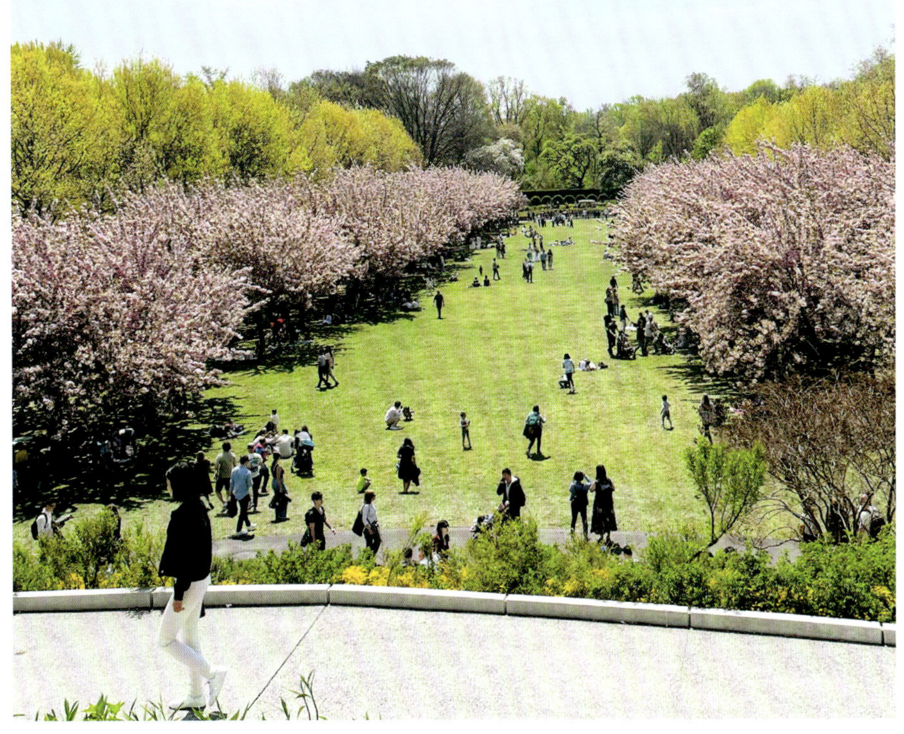

Urbanites flock to the Cherry Esplanade every spring for the bright pink blooms.

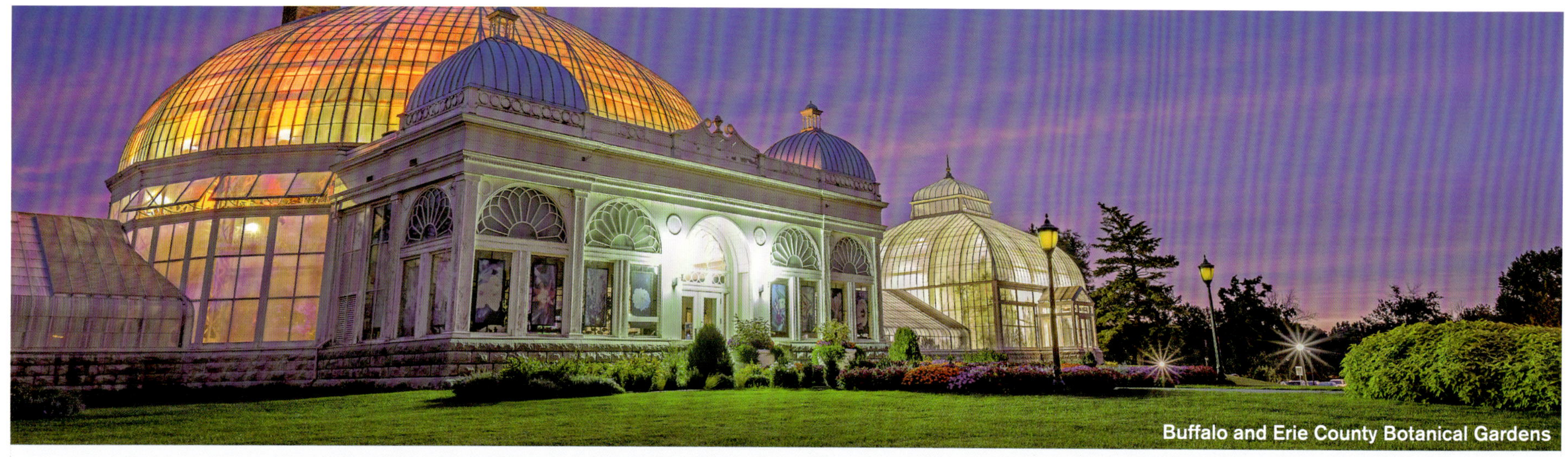

The Palm Dome houses palms, evergreens, and other plants that require a warm, moist environment.

Buffalo and Erie County Botanical Gardens
Buffalo, New York

In 1900, a trifecta of botanical talent–landscape architect Frederick Law Olmsted, glass-house architects Lord and Burnham, and botanist John F. Cowell–came together to create this 11.5-acre property. The 67-foot-high Palm Dome is the most iconic structure at the garden, but other spaces include a rose garden, native garden, and an arboretum.

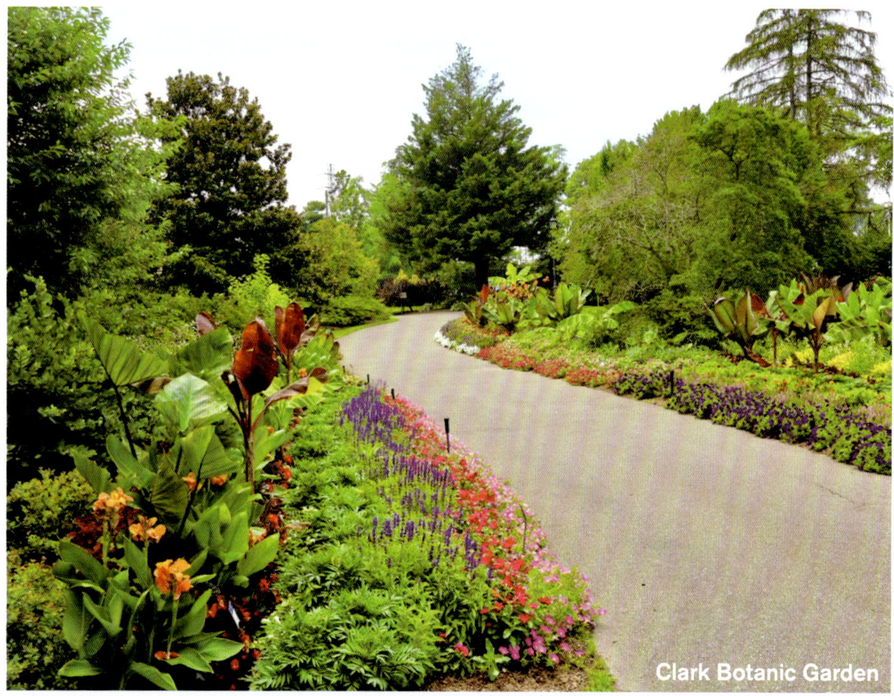

The garden's main walking trail is about a half mile long.

Mary Flagler Cary Arboretum
Millbrook, New York

Heiress to part of the Standard Oil fortune, Mary Flagler Cary was a philanthropist with a love of nature, especially the maple trees on her nearly-2,000-acre property. She willed her estate to a trust, and this arboretum, containing wildflowers, ferns, and 150 species of trees, was established in her honor in 1972.

Clark Botanic Garden
Albertson, New York

This 12-acre garden is best-known for being listed as an official Daylily Garden by the American Hemerocallis Society, one of 325 such gardens in the United States. But this serene oasis is also home to collections of wildflowers, perennials, conifers, herbs, wetland plants, and more than 100 types of roses.

Cornell Botanic Gardens
Ithaca, New York

Located adjacent to Cornell University, this site serves as an outdoor classroom for seven of the university's colleges. The property specializes in plants and trees native to the state of New York and consists of a 25-acre botanical garden and the 150-acre F.R. Newman Arboretum, as well as 3,600 acres of natural areas.

Cutler Botanic Garden
Binghamton, New York

This garden features 14 different specialized zones that teach visitors about horticulture and help to foster an appreciation of the environment. These discrete sections feature perennials, roses, ornamental grasses, native habitats, and heath and heathers, as well as areas that demonstrate the benefits of composting and usage of rain barrels.

Ellwanger Garden
Rochester, New York

Once the private garden of nineteenth-century horticulturalist George Ellwanger, this property is included in the world-famous Rochester Lilac Festival every May. The garden is mostly accessible by appointment only, but is open to the public for the Lilac Festival and for the similar "Rose and Peony Weekend" in June.

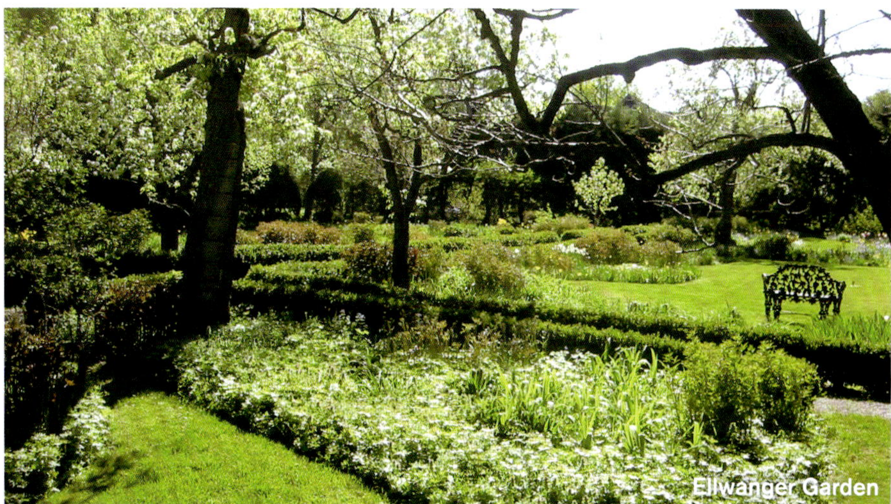

Ellwanger Garden

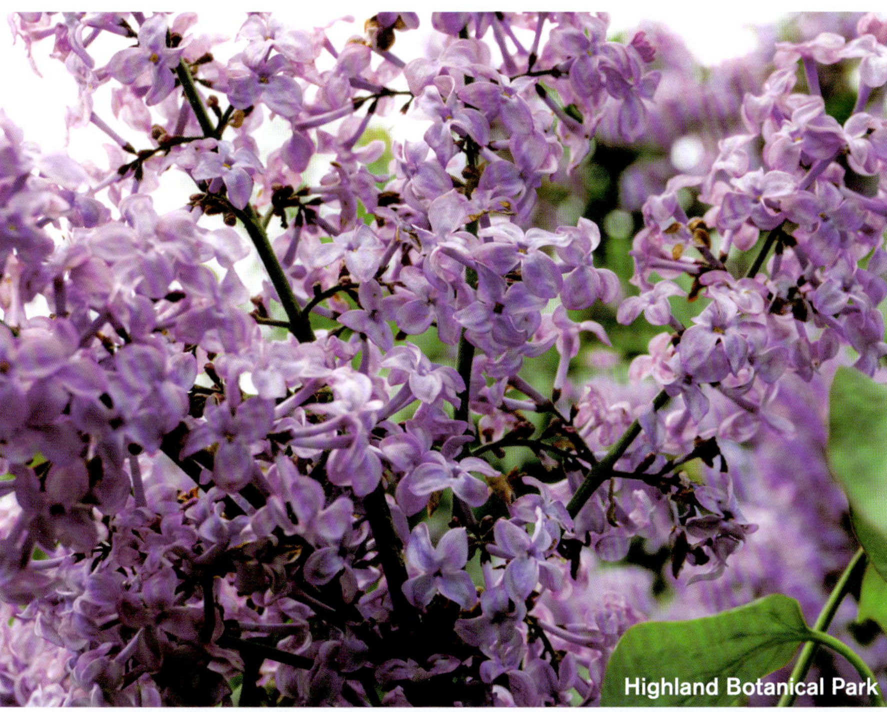

Highland Botanical Park

The park's Lilac Festival happens every May.

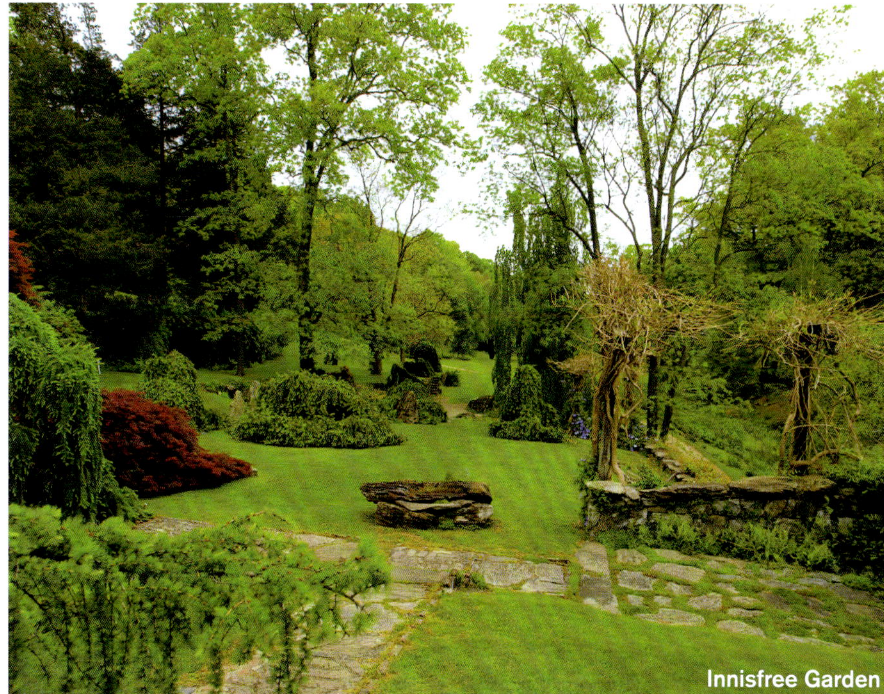

Innisfree Garden

Innisfree's picturesque vistas compel visitors to slow down and enjoy the view.

Highland Botanical Park
Rochester, New York

This park is home to more than 1,200 lilac shrubs, and the host of North America's largest festival celebrating the fragrant flowers. In addition to the Lilac Festival, the 150-acre garden features 700 varieties of rhododendrons, 10,000 pansies, and an arboretum with Japanese maples, evergreens, magnolias, and other tree species.

Innisfree Garden
Millbrook, New York

A 185-acre property that draws inspiration from Chinese and Japanese garden design, this serene sanctuary is composed of "cup gardens" or "garden rooms"–themed areas in the landscape. These include the steep and rocky Hemlock Woods, the centrally located and meandering Meadow, and the Kwan Yin walking path.

Lasdon Park and Arboretum

The one-acre Memorial Garden section consists of carefully manicured boxwood hedges, heather, flowering annuals, a synoptic garden, and a fragrance garden.

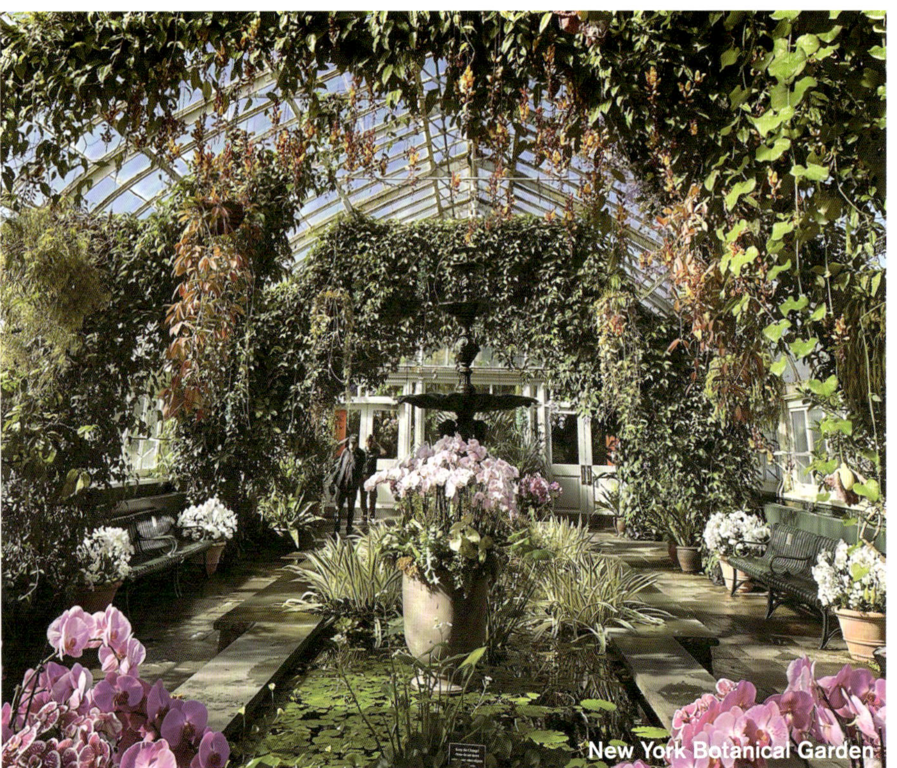

New York Botanical Garden

Lasdon Park and Arboretum
Katonah, New York

In the 1930s, this public park was the property of William and Mildred Lasdon, who imported many tree specimens to the site. Today, the 234-acre garden and arboretum not only contains an extensive collection of trees, but also features an azalea garden, flowering annuals and bulbs, and a 22-acre bird sanctuary.

New York Botanical Garden
Bronx, New York

Encompassing 250 acres in the heart of the Bronx–New York City's "greenest" borough–this garden has been delighting visitors since 1891. More than one million plants can be found in its 50 different gardens, which include a Conifer Arboretum, a Native Plant Garden, and a Children's Adventure Garden.

Planting Fields Arboretum
Oyster Bay, New York

The Camellia Greenhouse on this 400-acre property showcases the largest collection of the flowers in the northeastern United States. The site is also home to a Main Greenhouse, which features hibiscus, orchids, and succulents, and Coe Hall, a 65-room Tudor Revival mansion, as well as manicured lawns and woodland paths.

Queens Botanical Garden
Flushing, New York

Originally an exhibit for the 1939–1940 World's Fair, this garden was preserved and expanded by local residents who wanted to appreciate its beauty for years to come. Some of the 39-acre property's highlights include a popular Rose Garden, a colorful Perennial Garden, a Meadow filled with wildflowers, and a buzzworthy Bee Garden.

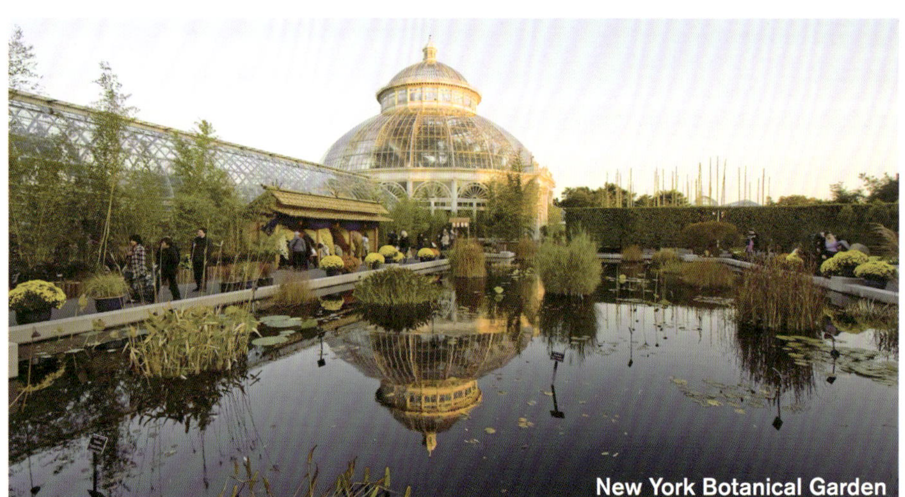

New York Botanical Garden

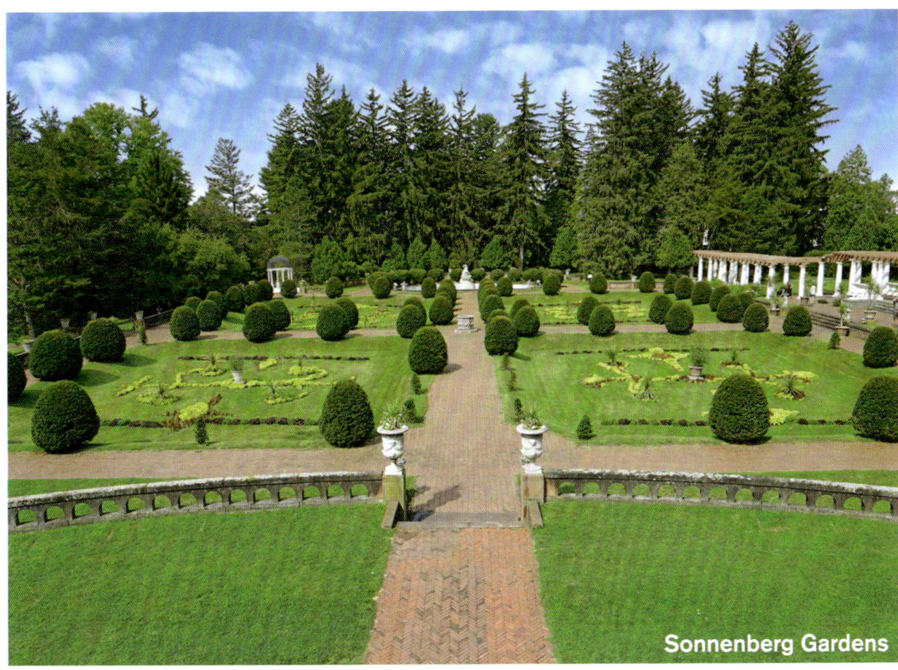

The Italian Garden.

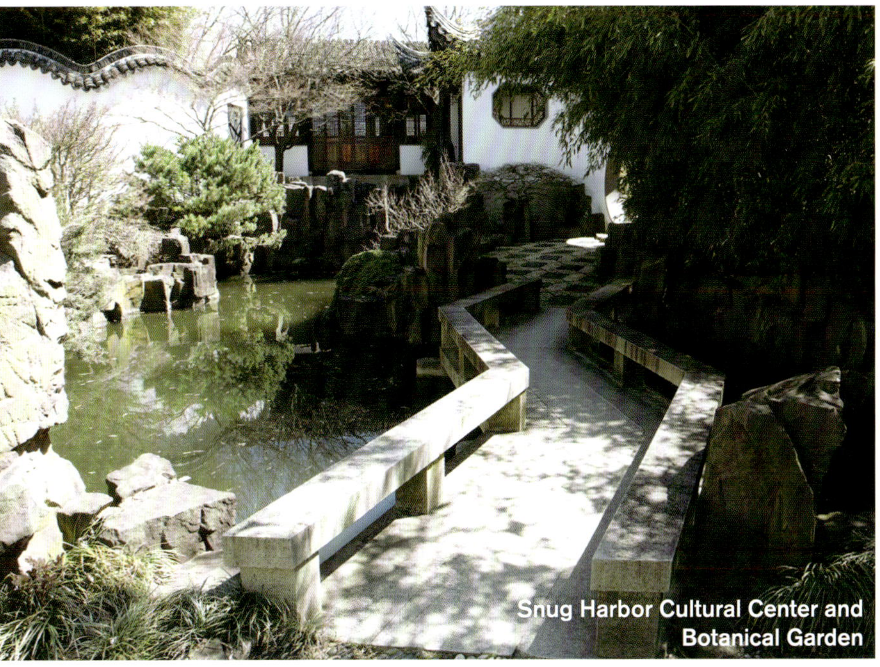

A zigzag bridge in the New York Chinese Scholar's Garden.

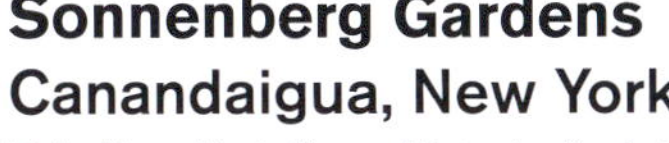

Sonnenberg Gardens
Canandaigua, New York

This New York State Historic Park is located in the Finger Lakes region, one of the state's most picturesque areas. It contains a Queen Anne Victorian-style mansion surrounded by nine formal gardens, many of which were designed by the property's original owner, Mary Clark Thompson. Visitor favorites include the Italian Garden, first created in 1903, and the 1913 Pansy Garden, showcasing Thompson's favorite flower.

Snug Harbor Cultural Center and Botanical Garden
Staten Island, New York

Informally known as Snug Harbor, this collection of historic nineteenth-century buildings is contained in an 83-acre park. Once used as a retirement community for sailors, the property is now a cultural center and botanical garden with extensively landscaped grounds. Gardens include the White Garden, the New York Chinese Scholar's Garden, and the Secret Garden, which contains a castle and a maze.

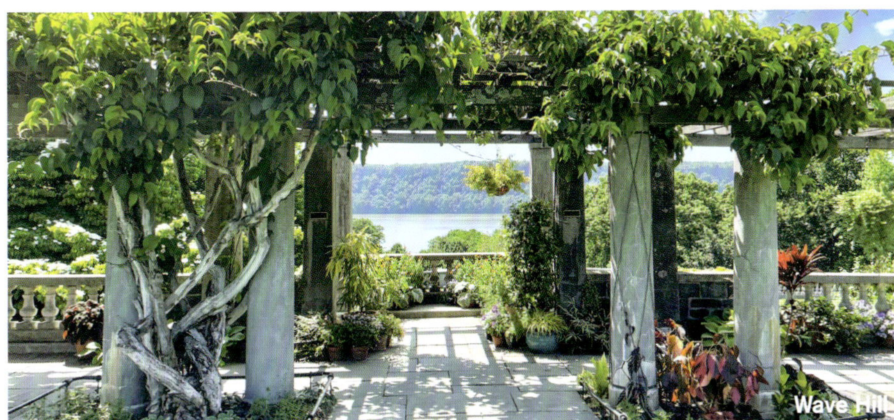

Pergola Overlook.

Wave Hill
Bronx, New York

Located above the Hudson River estuary, this 28-acre garden offers sweeping views of the Palisades, the steep cliffs along the west side of the river. The property's Pergola is the perfect location to take in the vistas, while the Flower Garden, Wild Garden, and Paisley Bed showcase colorful flora. The Marco Polo Stufano Conservatory offers botanical beauty from warmer regions of the world, on display year-round.

Airlie Gardens
Wilmington, North Carolina

The 67 acres spanning this property are full of gardens, walking trails, and historic buildings dating back to the 1800s. One of the central features is the Airlie Oak Lawn, home to an almost 500-year-old southern live oak tree. Other highlights include the Spring Gardens and the seasonal Butterfly House.

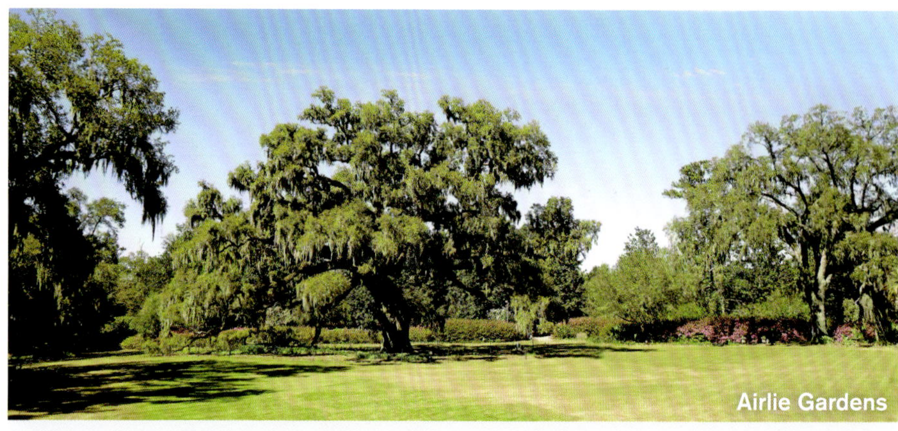
Airlie Gardens

The Airlie Oak stands about 130 feet tall.

The Bog Garden
Greensboro, North Carolina

Visitors to this unique seven-acre property can wander along an elevated boardwalk that leads through natural wetlands. Wildflowers, bamboo, ferns, individually labeled trees, and native vegetation thrive on the property, which is also a sanctuary for migratory birds. Serenity Falls, a 150-foot, man-made, recirculating waterfall lends tranquil atmosphere.

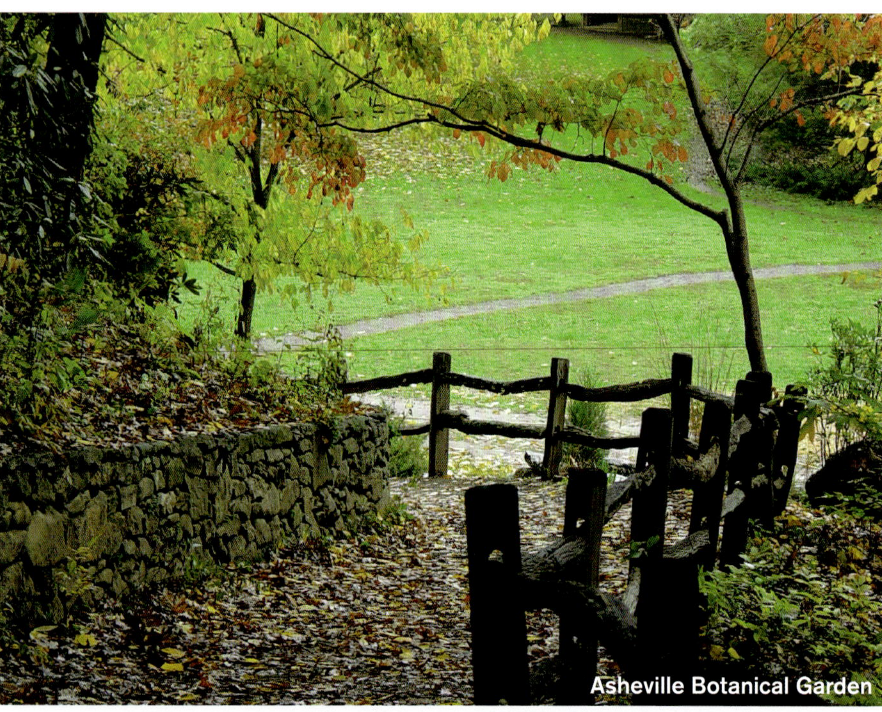
Asheville Botanical Garden

The Crayton Trail winds around the property.

Asheville Botanical Garden
Asheville, North Carolina

Located adjacent to the University of North Carolina at Asheville, this ten-acre garden is focused on cultivating the native flora of the region. A half-mile looped trail guides visitors past more than 750 species of plants found in the southern Appalachian Mountains. It also features a water garden, a botany center, and bird-viewing deck.

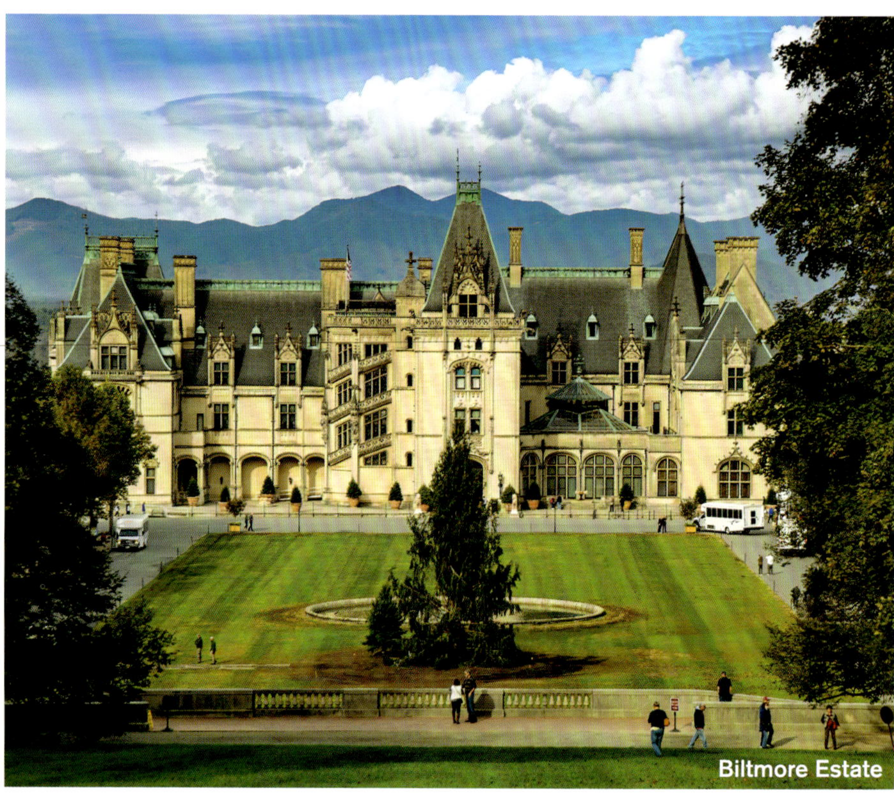
Biltmore Estate

Biltmore Estate
Asheville, North Carolina

The Châteauesque-style mansion, built for George Vanderbilt, located on this sprawling 8,000-acre property is famous for being "America's largest home." But the estate also features six formal and informal gardens, nature trails, and a conservatory. From vibrant spring flowers to winter poinsettias, something is always in bloom in the colorful gardens.

Cape Fear Botanical Garden
Fayetteville, North Carolina

The Cape Fear River runs through eastern North Carolina before flowing into the Atlantic Ocean. The unique plant species found along the river's banks are showcased at this garden, which was established in 1989 to teach horticulture students at Fayetteville Technical Community College. Today, it is a popular site for educational programs for both kids and adults.

Daniel Boone Native Gardens
Boone, North Carolina

Established in 1963, this three-acre garden features a collection of native North Carolina plants, as well as a stone gatehouse, rustic bridge, reflection pool, and the historic Squire Boone Cabin. The garden strives to not only teach the public about the diversity of flora in the region, but also about the history of Boone and his time.

Sarah P. Duke Gardens
Durham, North Carolina

The landscaped areas of this 55-acre property, located at Duke University, are comprised of four areas: The Historic Gardens, the H.L. Blomquist Garden of Native Plants, the William Louis Culberson Asiatic Arboretum, and Doris Duke Center Gardens. Five miles of trails and pathways lead through the diverse collections.

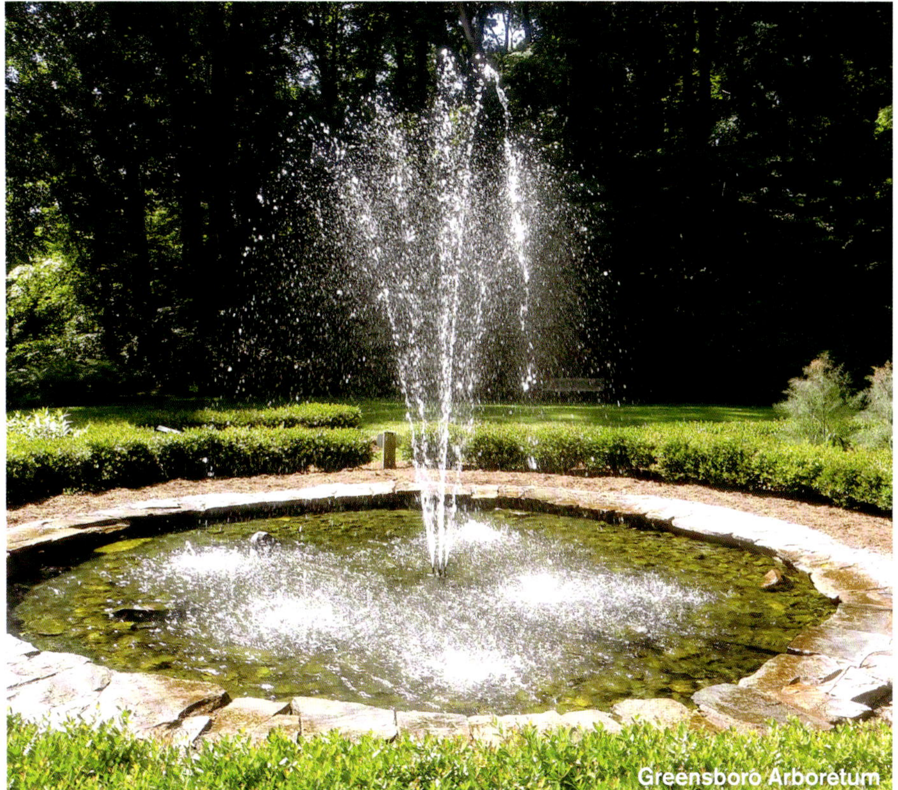
Greensboro Arboretum

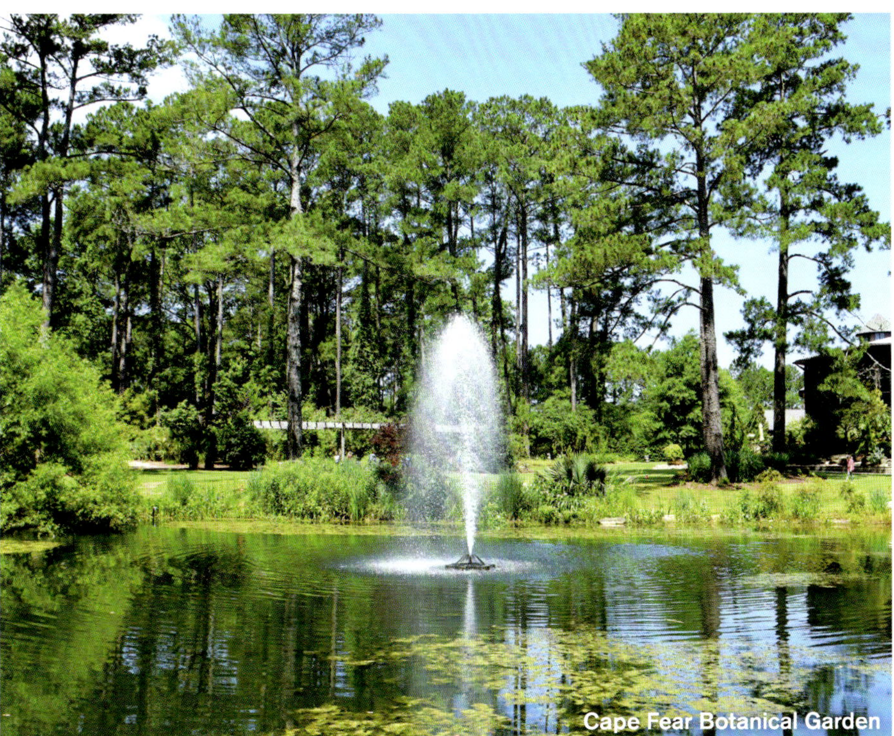
Cape Fear Botanical Garden

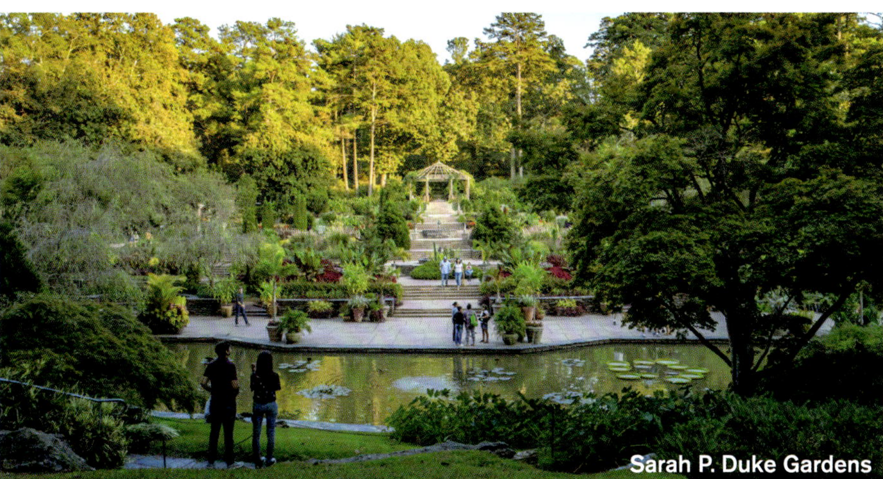
Sarah P. Duke Gardens

Greensboro Arboretum
Greensboro, North Carolina

Fourteen plant collections are located throughout this 17-acre site, which was founded in 1991. Collections include a Rose Garden, a Wildflower Trail, a Conifer Collection, and a Butterfly Garden, as well as a Rhododendron Garden with 70 varieties. A scenic gazebo on the property is a popular wedding location.

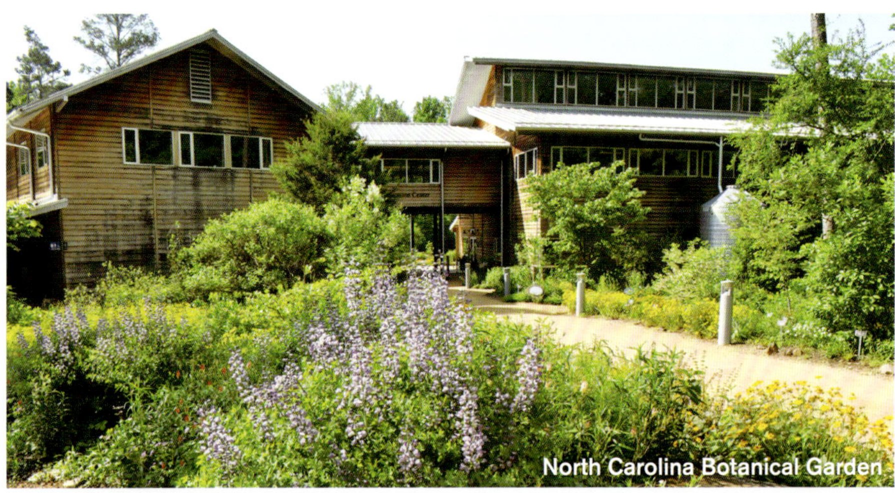

Visitors attend workshops and seminars at the James and Delight Allen Education Center.

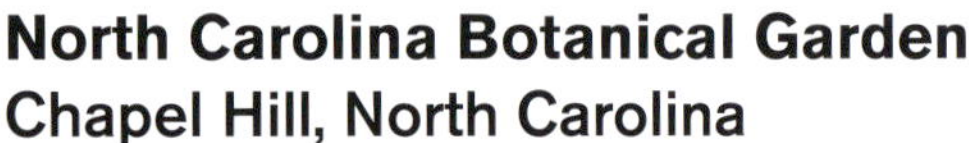

North Carolina Botanical Garden
Chapel Hill, North Carolina

This garden is operated by the University of North Carolina at Chapel Hill, whose goal is to protect and display the native flora of the state. The property contains 14 collections and display gardens containing about 2,500 different plant species. Popular spaces include the Fern Collection and the Horticulture Therapy Demonstration Garden.

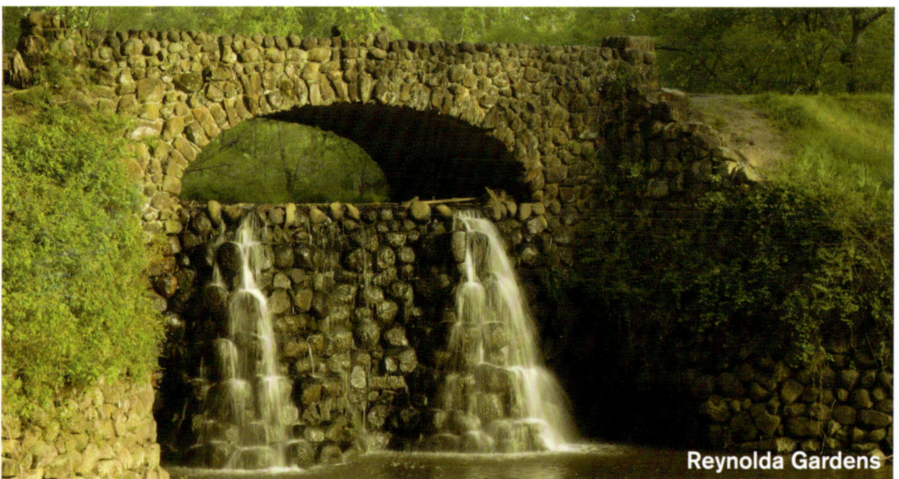

The stone bridge, with its artfully picturesque waterfall, was constructed in 1913.

Reynolda Gardens
Winston-Salem, North Carolina

Originally the estate of tobacco magnate J.R. Reynolds, this 125-acre property now maintains natural areas along with four acres of formal gardens. The formal gardens are divided between the Greenhouse Gardens, featuring roses and hedges, and the Fruit, Cut Flower, and Nicer Vegetable Garden, growing vegetables, vines, and fruit.

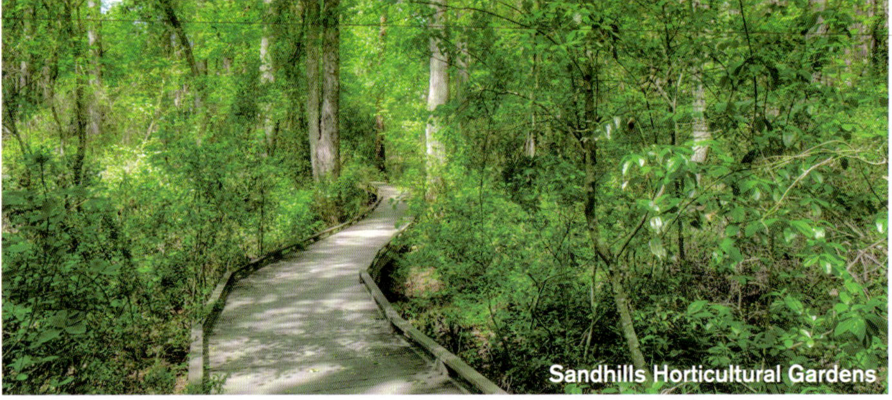

A woodland trail winds through the property for about a mile.

Sandhills Horticultural Gardens
Pinehurst, North Carolina

This garden, located on the campus of Sandhills Community College, was established in 1978 with the creation of the Ebersole Holly Garden. Today, the 32-acre property includes a Rose Garden, Conifer Garden, and a Fruit and Vegetable Garden, as well as a xeriscape area showcasing cacti and succulents.

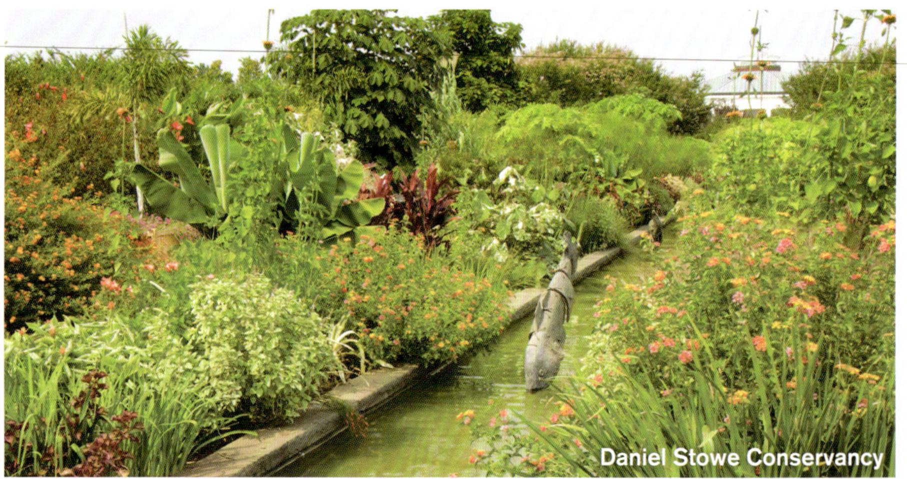

Daniel Stowe Conservancy
Belmont, North Carolina

Meadows, woodlands, and lakeshore make up the landscape of this 380-acre property, which was named after its founder. The main area of the site is known as the Gardens at Stowe, featuring the Four Seasons Garden and a children's garden. Also popular is the William H. Williamson III Conservatory, showcasing orchids and tropical plants.

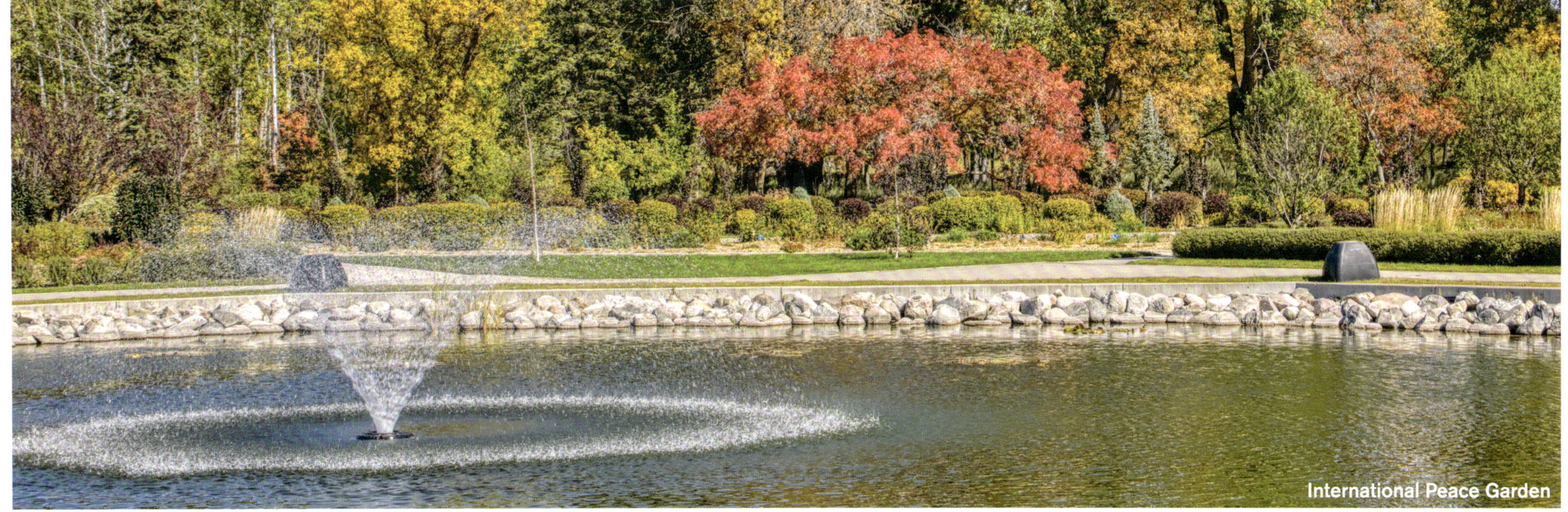

International Peace Garden

International Peace Garden
Dunseith, North Dakota

This unique property straddles the border between the United States and Canada and is located close to the geographical center of North America. The garden was the brainchild of Dr. Henry J. Moore of Islington, Ontario, Canada, who envisioned a gathering place for people to celebrate international friendship. Construction began in the 1930s and concluded in the 1940s. Both Manitoba and North Dakota donated land to the site, and the Civilian Conservation Corps performed much of the heavy labor. Today, this 3.65-square-mile park is home to more than 150,000 flowers and contains formal gardens, a sunken garden, a conservatory, and a famous 18-foot-diameter floral clock.

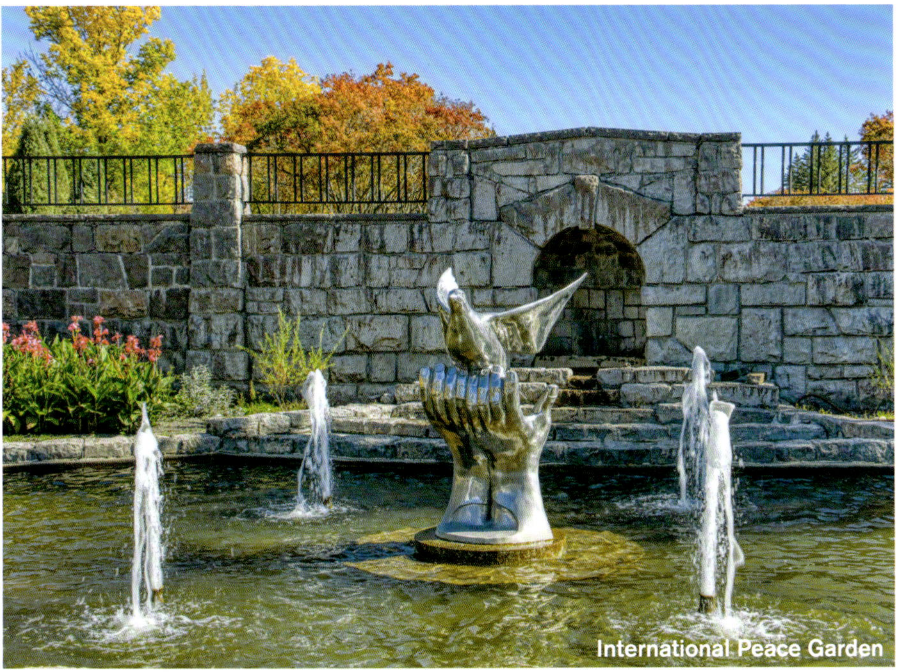

International Peace Garden

Worth Exploring in North Dakota

Fort Stevenson State Park Arboretum
Garrison, North Dakota

- Located on the shore of Lake Sakakawea
- Contains more than 50 native and non-native trees, shrubs, wildflowers, and grasses

Gunlogson State Nature Preserve
Cavalier, North Dakota

- Home to mature elm and basswood trees, along with 100 other species
- Rare plants include ladyfern, water arum, and two-seeded sedge

Myra Arboretum
Larimore, North Dakota

- A 26-acre garden with more than 500 varieties of trees and shrubs
- Trees include varieties of ash, maple, juniper, willow, and pine

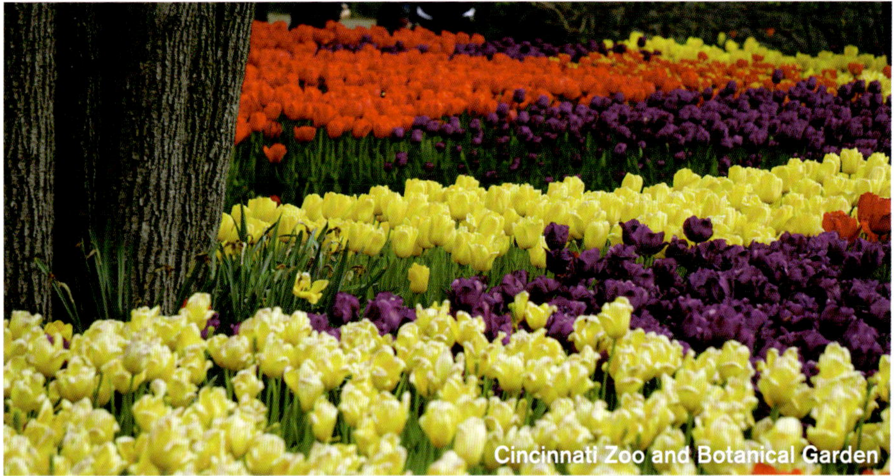

Tulips bloom every spring at the Cincinnati Zoo.

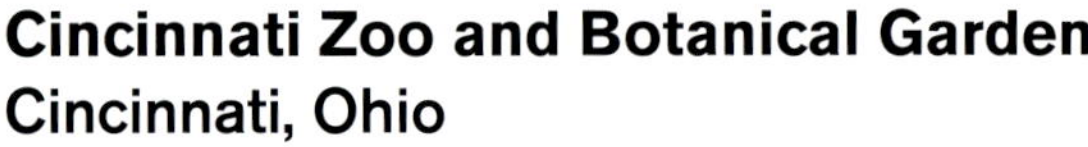

Cincinnati Zoo and Botanical Garden
Cincinnati, Ohio

The gardens at this zoo—the second oldest in the U.S.—are frequently used to trial plant species for home garden use in the Midwest. Highlights include the Native Plants Garden, the Education Rain Garden, and the Asian Waterfall Garden, as well as Bamboo Groves that serve as food for many of the zoo's animals.

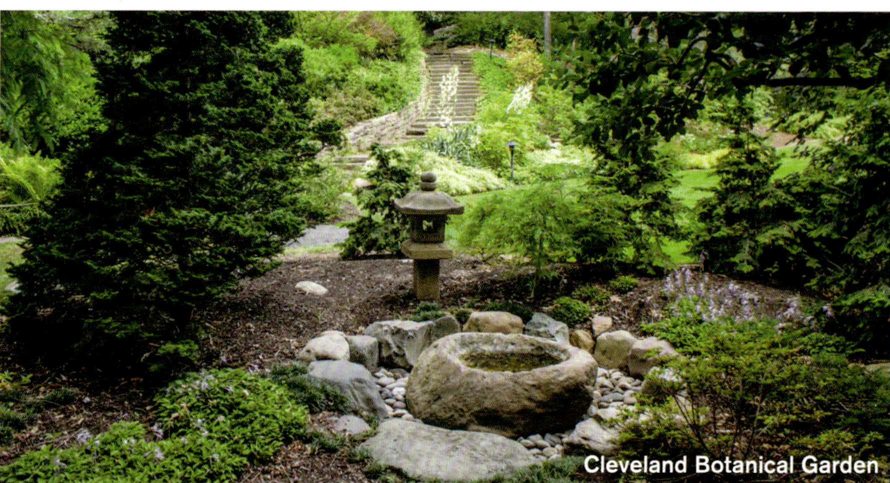

Plants and flowers of all kinds make the site a welcome oasis in urban Cleveland.

Cleveland Botanical Garden
Cleveland, Ohio

Founded in 1930 as the Garden Center of Greater Cleveland, this botanical garden is now housed on the site of the old Cleveland Zoo. The garden's pride and joy is the Eleanor Armstrong Smith Glasshouse, a 17,000-square-foot conservatory, which features both plants and animals from Madagascar and Costa Rica.

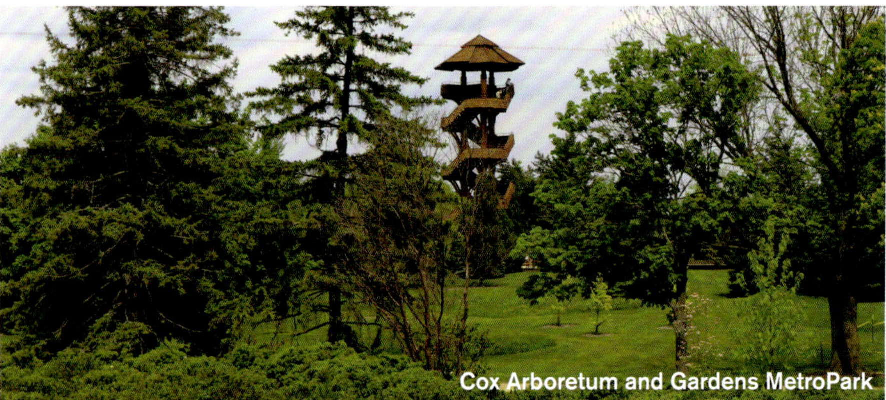

Visitors can climb the Tree Tower for views of the surrounding grounds.

Cox Arboretum and Gardens MetroPark
Dayton, Ohio

The arboretum and gardens in this park were founded in 1963 in an effort to combat Dayton's urban sprawl. The serene oasis contains more than 500 varieties of trees and shrubs, an ornamental grass collection, pollinator gardens, a children's maze, and the Barbara Cox Center for Sustainable Horticulture, which teaches visitors about sustainability.

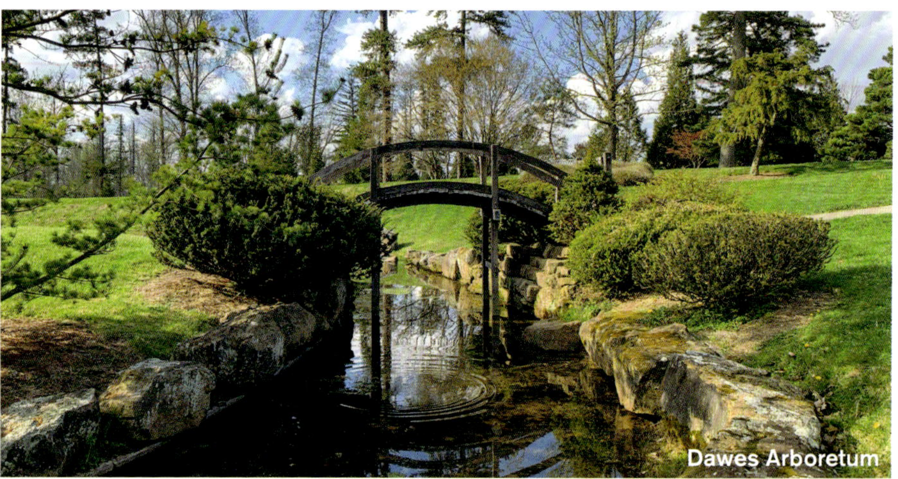

The Dawes Arboretum
Newark, Ohio

More than 2,000 acres of gardens and natural areas are found within this sprawling site, which was listed on the National Register of Historic Places in 2016. The property features 16,000 trees, flowers, and plants, including a Japanese Garden, a Dogwood Trail, and an Azalea Glen, as well as 12 miles of hiking trails.

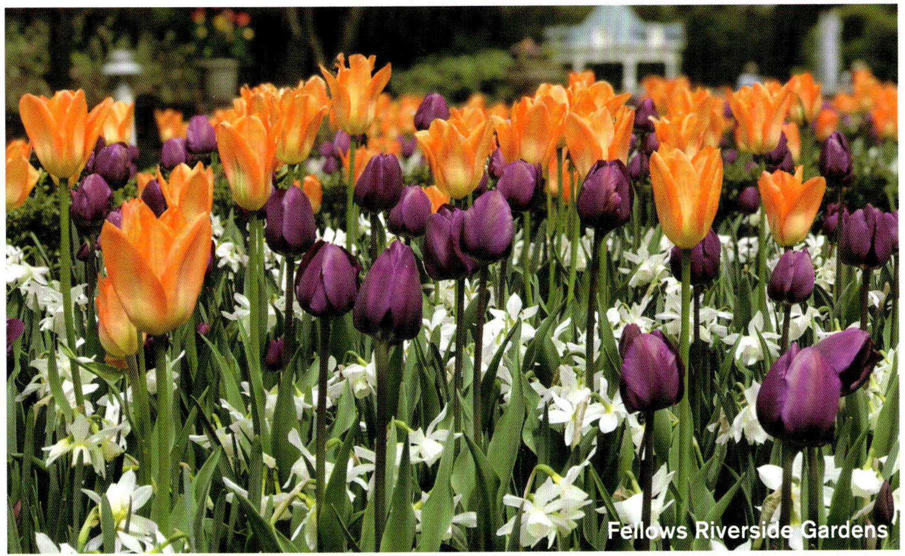
Fellows Riverside Gardens

Fellows Riverside Gardens
Youngstown, Ohio

This 12-acre garden showcases seasonal annual, perennial, and flowering bulb displays, plus a diverse collection of trees and shrubs. More than 40,000 tulips, crocus, and narcissus are on display every spring, and a formal rose garden features floribunda, grandiflora, and hybrid tea varieties. A gazebo and pavilion offer picturesque locations for special events.

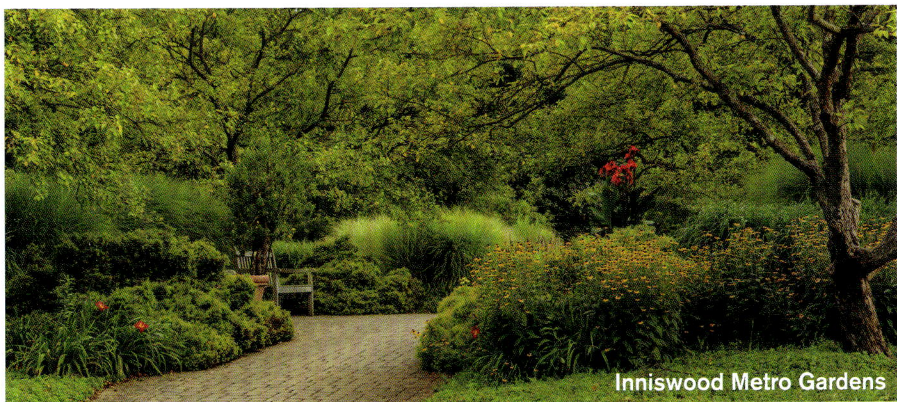
Inniswood Metro Gardens

A woodland trail winds through the property for about a mile.

Inniswood Metro Gardens
Westerville, Ohio

Part natural woodlands and part manicured gardens, this 123-acre property contains more than 2,000 species of plants and a variety of themed gardens. The natural area is filled with wildflowers, waterways, and several miles of trails. The gardens include the Rose Garden, Conifer Garden, and a 2.8-acre children's garden.

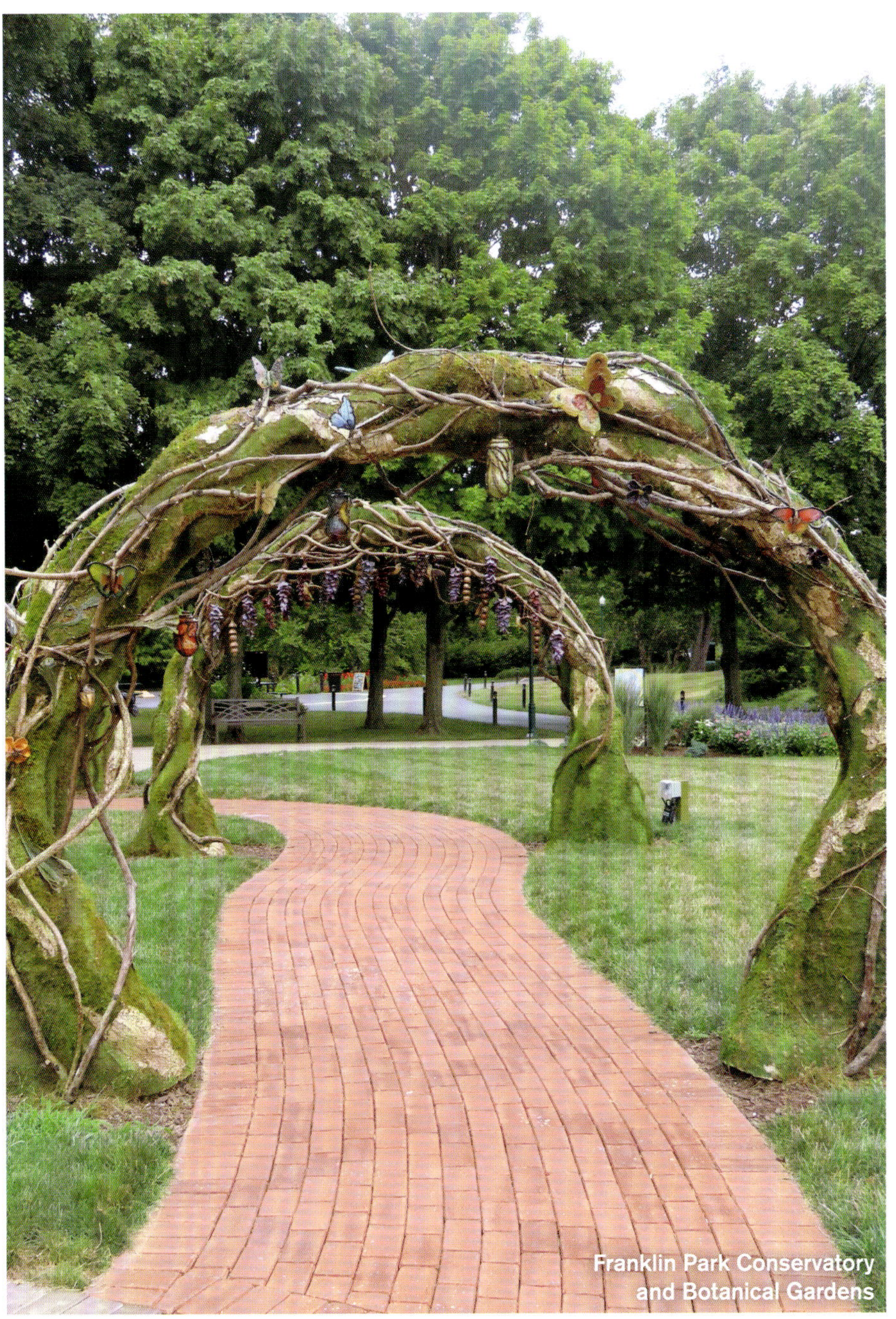
Franklin Park Conservatory and Botanical Gardens

Franklin Park Conservatory and Botanical Gardens
Columbus, Ohio

Several different global climate zones are represented within this garden's conservatory, which was built in 1895 and added to the National Register of Historic Places in 1974. Biomes include the Himalayan Mountains, Tropical Rainforest, Desert, and Pacific Islands, as well as a Palm House with more than 40 species of palm trees.

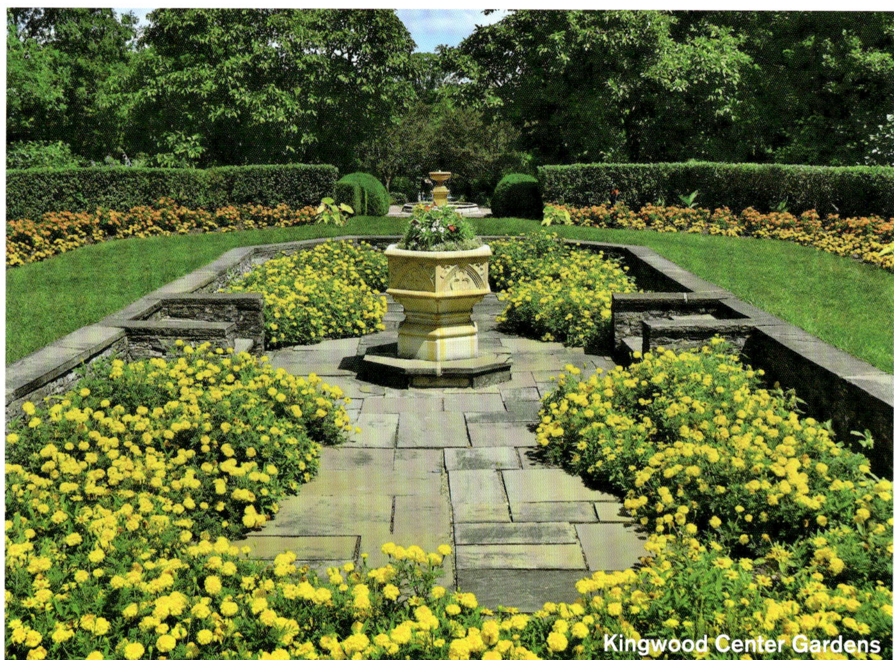

Garden sections include the Perennial Garden, Terrace Garden, Woodland Garden, Herb, Rose, and Trial Gardens, and the Formal Gardens (pictured here).

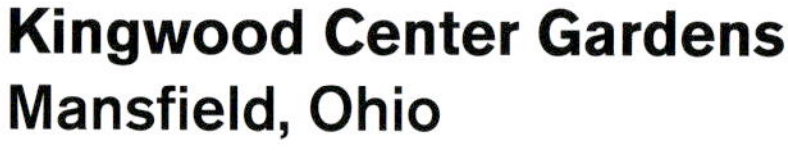

Kingwood Center Gardens
Mansfield, Ohio

This garden, which opened in 1953, was originally the home of its founder, Charles Kelley King. Today, the garden is known for its daylily and iris collections, its perennial garden featuring 300 types of plants, and its tropical house filled with specimens from around the world. Visitors can also tour King's historic mansion.

Irwin M. Krohn Conservatory
Cincinnati, Ohio

This Art Deco-style glass greenhouse is the centerpiece of Eden Park, an urban oasis that offers views of the Ohio River Valley. The conservatory contains more than 3,500 plant species, including a seasonal floral display, a citrus tree collection, a desert garden with succulents and cacti, and numerous tropical plants and palms.

Mount Airy Arboretum
Cincinnati, Ohio

Located within the Mount Airy Forest, this 30-acre arboretum features one of the best collections of dwarf conifers in the Midwest. It is also home to thousands of plants in its annual, perennial, and pollinator gardens. Gazebos, ponds, and tranquil trails offer lovely backdrops for weddings and special events.

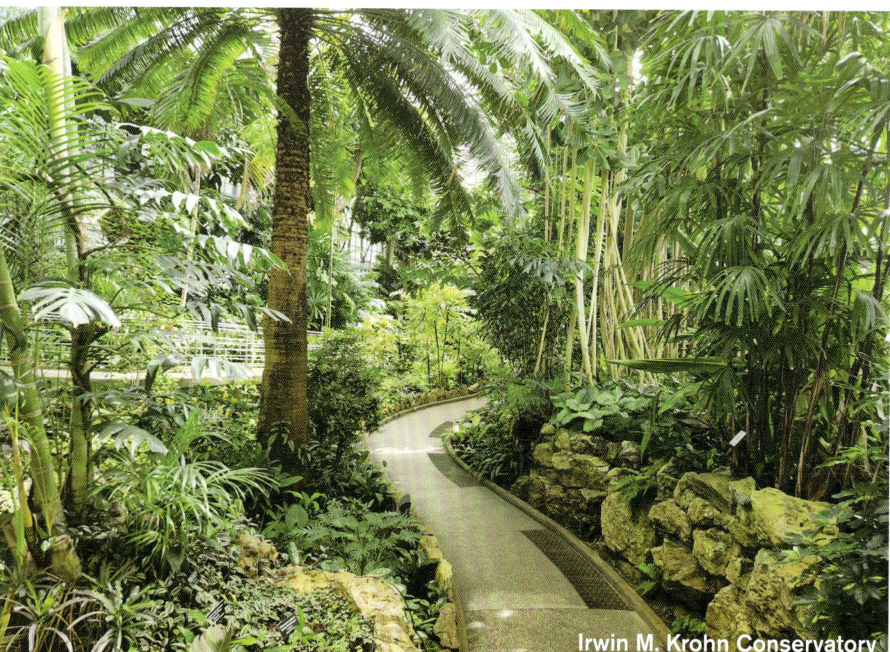

Visitors can stroll under towering palms and past orchids and ferns on the greenhouse's winding pathways.

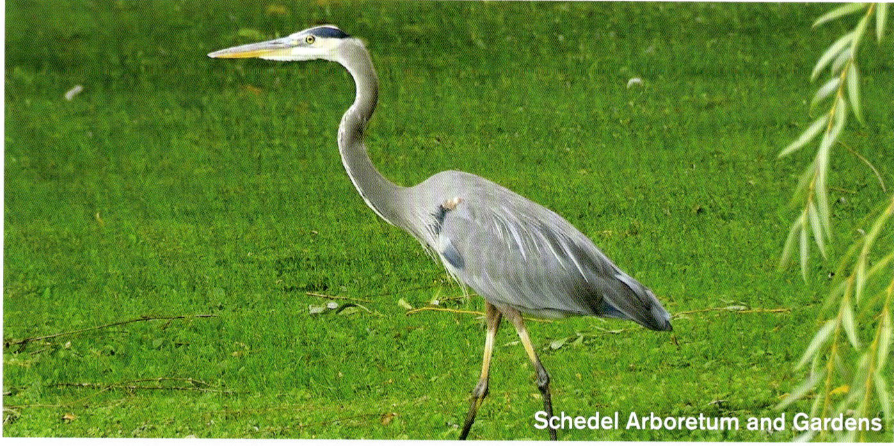

Avian visitors to the gardens include great blue herons.

Schedel Arboretum and Gardens
Elmore, Ohio

Themed gardens, more than 10,000 annual plants and flowers, and unusual and exotic species are found on this property along the Portage River. Gardens include the Japanese Garden, Rose Garden, Perennial Garden, Tropical Garden, and the Leo Pelka Bonsai Shelter, containing the largest bonsai collection in northern Ohio.

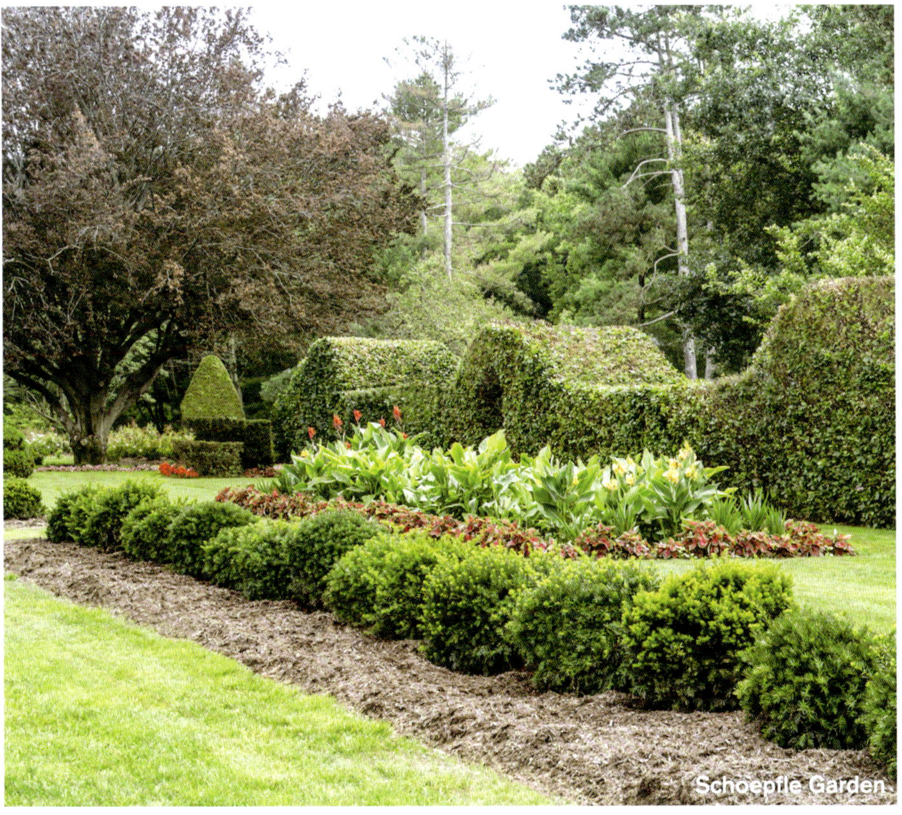

The formal gardens.

Schoepfle Garden
Birmingham, Ohio

Located along the banks of the Vermilion River, this 77-acre property is full of vibrant color year-round. From snowdrops, hollies, and witch hazel in the winter to roses, hydrangeas, and passion flowers in the summer, the garden offers a beautiful natural respite for visitors. The property is divided into several sections, including formal gardens lined with hedges and topiaries, a shade garden, and a children's garden.

Stan Hywet Hall and Gardens
Akron, Ohio

The historic home that occupies this property was built in 1915 for F.A. Seiberling, the co-founder of the Goodyear Tire and Rubber Company. He dubbed it *Stan Hywet*, an Old English phrase for "stone quarry," in honor of the site's original use. Today, the 70-acre estate contains formal gardens, including a Japanese Garden, English Garden, and Perennial Garden, as well as a conservatory, greenhouses, and five man-made ponds.

Toledo Botanical Garden
Toledo, Ohio

This 60-acre botanical garden is known not only for its focus on education and art, but also for its unique spaces, like the Doneghy Inclusive Garden. With wheelchair-accessible flowerbeds, a sensory water wall, and fragrant plantings to smell and touch, the garden is truly made for everyone. Also notable is the Secret Forest, a children's garden with multilevel discovery areas, and Artisan Village, a collection of sculptures.

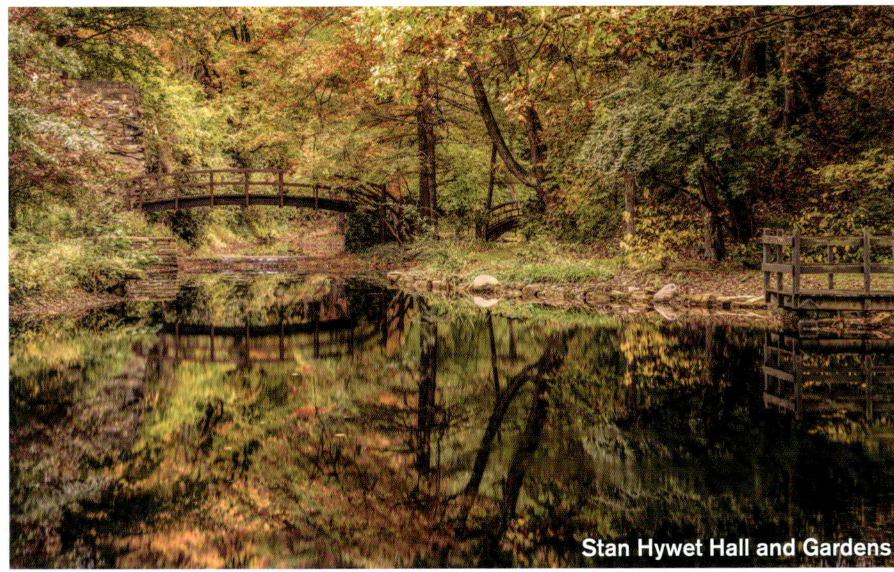

Autumn foliage frames a bridge on the pond.

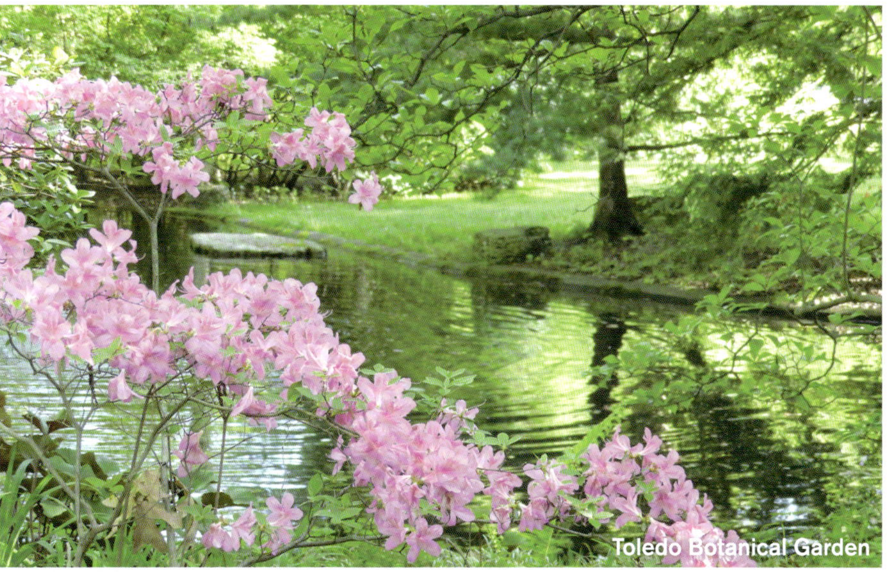

A charming, shady pond is surrounded by trees and flowering plants.

Worth Exploring in Oklahoma

Cann Memorial Botanical Gardens
Ponca City, Oklahoma

- Contains color-coordinated groupings of annuals and perennials
- Home of the annual Ponca City Herb Festival held the first Saturday of June

Puterbaugh Center
McAlester, Oklahoma

- Formerly known as the Garrard Ardeneum and the McAlester Arboretum
- Features rocky trails lined with redbud trees and azaleas, as well as historical artifacts

Hambrick Botanical Gardens
Oklahoma City, Oklahoma

- Located on the grounds of the National Cowboy and Western Heritage Museum
- Features the Norma Sutherland Garden, Atherton Garden, Western States Plaza, and Hambrick Garden

Kerr Arboretum and Botanical Area
Hodgen, Oklahoma

- Spans more than 8,000 acres in the Ouachita National Forest
- Interpretive trails wander through dwarf white oaks, yellow buckeye, Ouachita indigo, and grass seeps

Lendonwood Gardens
Grove, Oklahoma

- An eight-acre garden with shady paths, koi pond, and monarch butterfly way station
- Collections include daylilies, azaleas, peonies, hostas and Japanese maples

Morrison Arboretum
Morrison, Oklahoma

- Open daily to the public with no charge
- Trees include maples, oaks, juniper, and dawn redwood, as well as a hybrid "Nellie R. Stevens" holly

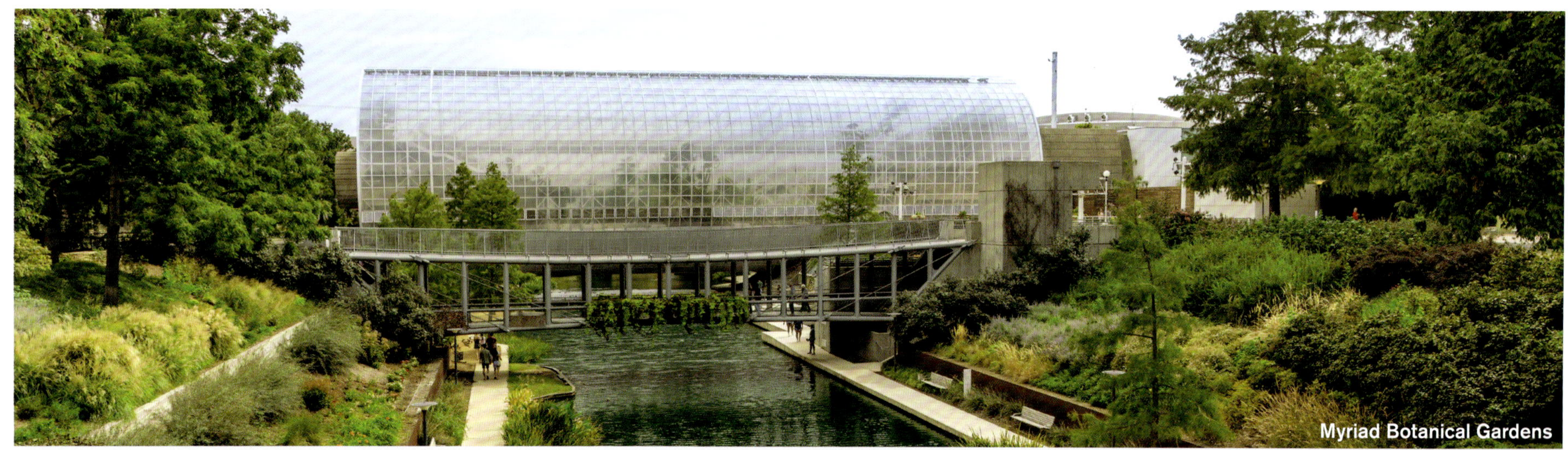
Myriad Botanical Gardens

The Crystal Bridge Conservatory.

Myriad Botanical Gardens
Oklahoma City, Oklahoma

This free public garden in the heart of downtown Oklahoma City spans 15 acres of botanical beauty. The grounds include tree and shrub collections, ornamental gardens with flowering annuals and perennials, a lake surrounded by green spaces, and a children's garden. The property also features the Inasmuch Foundation Crystal Bridge Conservatory, a 13,000-square-foot conservatory containing plants from both wet tropical and dry tropical zones.

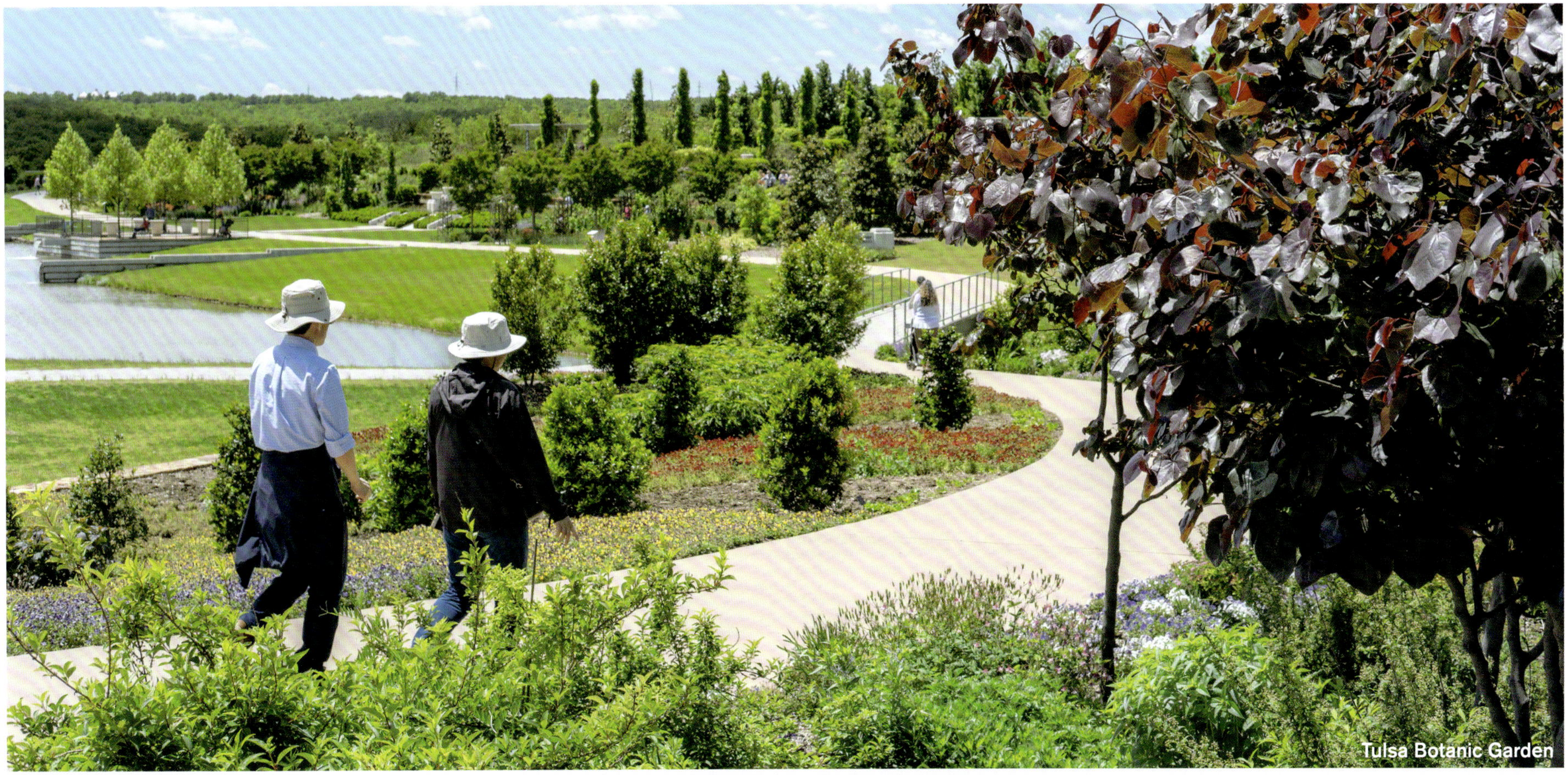

Eight miles of trails wind through the 170-acre site.

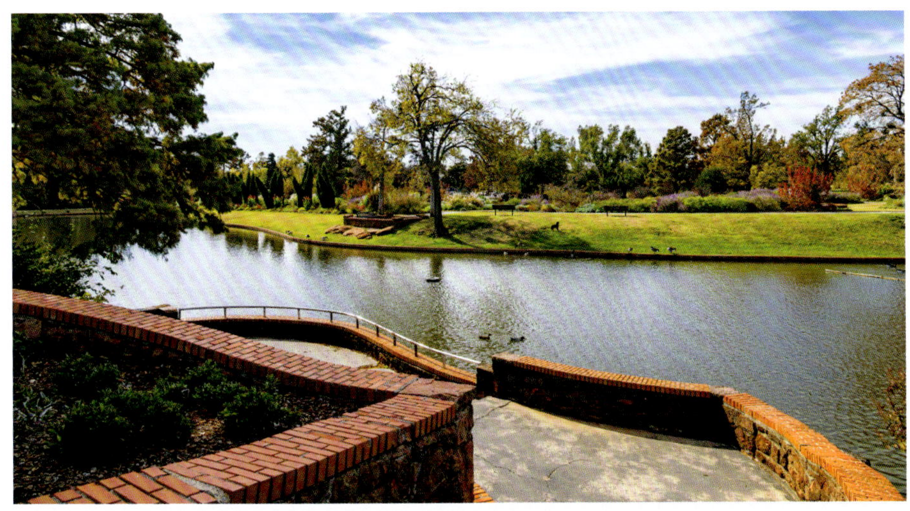

Autumn color comes to Will Rogers Gardens.

Tulsa Botanic Garden
Tulsa, Oklahoma

The Jim and Cherry Bost Arboretum is the most recent addition to this relatively new botanical garden, which opened in 2024. Other spaces include a display of floral terraces containing more than 8,000 plants, the Lakeside Promenade encircling the garden's seven-acre lake, the Children's Discovery Garden, and the one-mile looping Cross Timbers Nature Trail, which leads visitors through tallgrass prairie and deciduous forest.

Will Rogers Gardens
Oklahoma City, Oklahoma

Named for the famous actor and social commentator who was "Oklahoma's Favorite Son," this tranquil 30-acre park was developed in the 1920s and is listed on the National Register of Historic Places. The site includes an arboretum with hundreds of native and rare species, a color garden filled with roses and other vibrant blossoms, and the Ed Lycan Conservatory, a Victorian-style greenhouse named in honor of the Park Department's first employee.

Bush's Pasture Park
Salem, Oregon

Just a 10-minute walk from Oregon's capitol building, this 90.5-acre property is famous for its groves of Oregon white oaks and fields of purple-blue camas flowers. Cherry and apple orchards, a rose garden with more than 2,000 blooms, and the state's oldest conservatory can be found in the park, which is also the site of two university stadiums used for football, baseball, and track and field events.

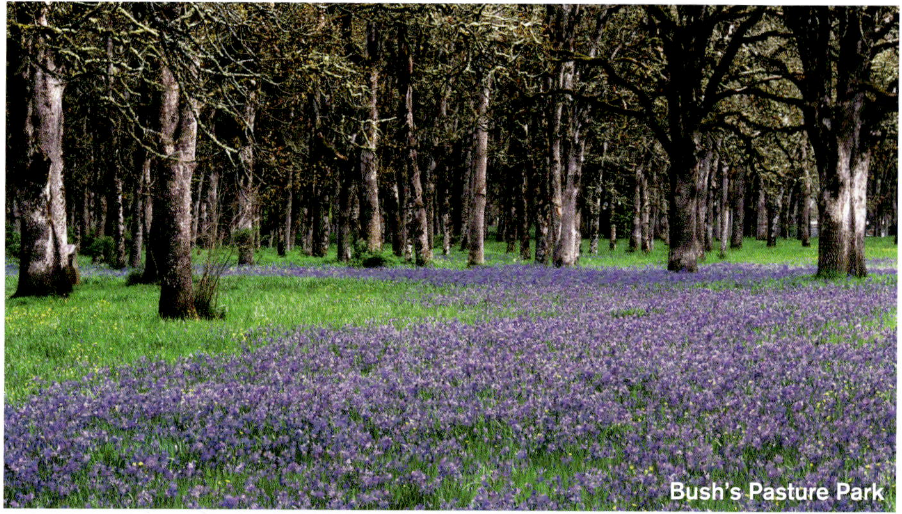

Brilliant camas burst into bloom.

Crystal Springs Rhododendron Garden
Portland, Oregon

More than just rhododendrons can be found within this 9.5-acre garden, which was founded in 1950 by the Portland Parks and Recreation Bureau and the American Rhododendron Society. Azaleas, unusual trees and shrubs, and picturesque waterfalls thrive in the tranquil oasis, which is also home to more than 90 species of birds. From April through June, the rhododendrons charm visitors with washes of vibrant color.

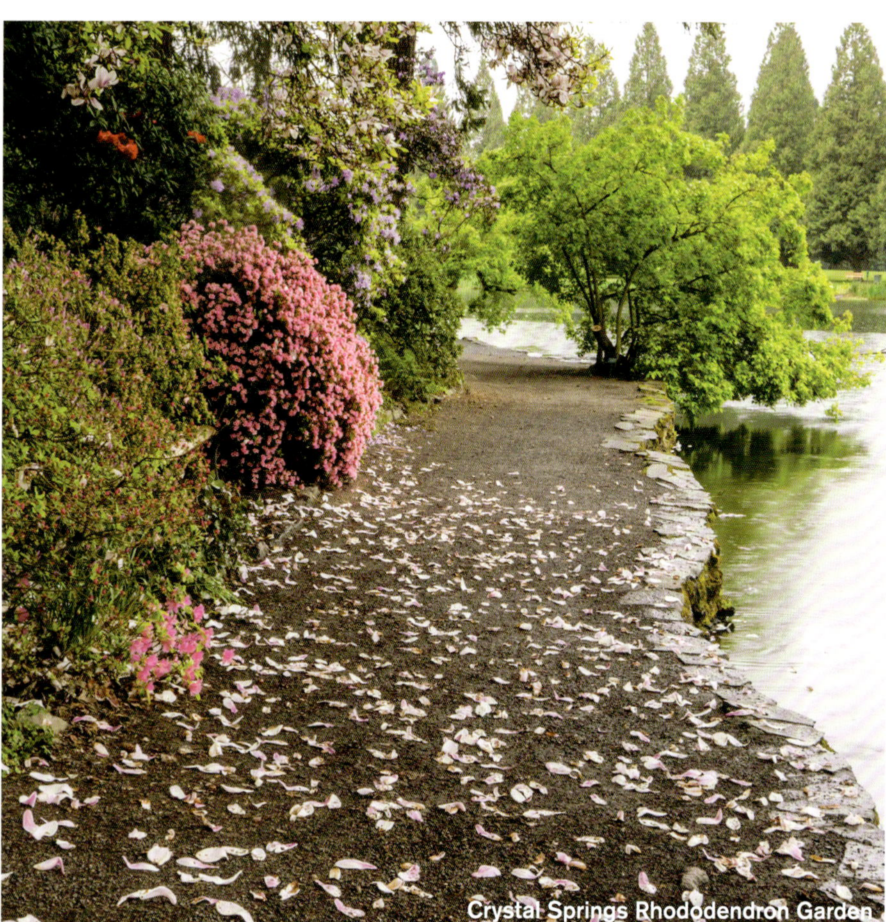

Flower petals gracing a waterside walk add to the charming scenery.

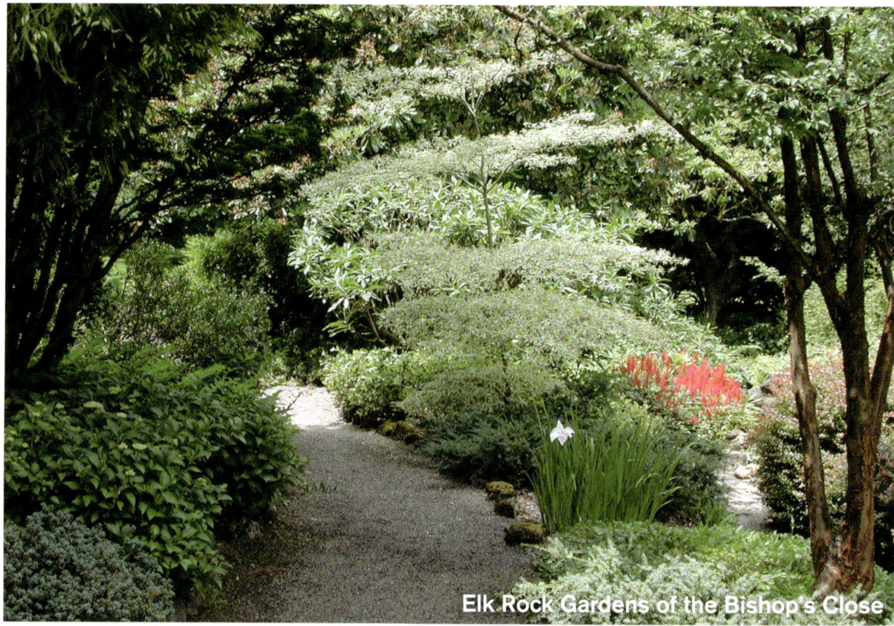

Garden sections include formal, botanical, Asian, children's, and an arboretum.

Elk Rock Gardens of the Bishop's Close
Portland, Oregon

Scottish immigrant Peter Kerr spent decades planning and planting this garden, one of the oldest and largest in Oregon. When he died at the age of 95 in 1957, the property was donated to the Episcopal Diocese of Oregon, who maintained Kerr's gardens and opened the grounds to the public. Today, the property, which overlooks the Willamette River, features expansive lawns, picturesque gardens, and Kerr's historic estate.

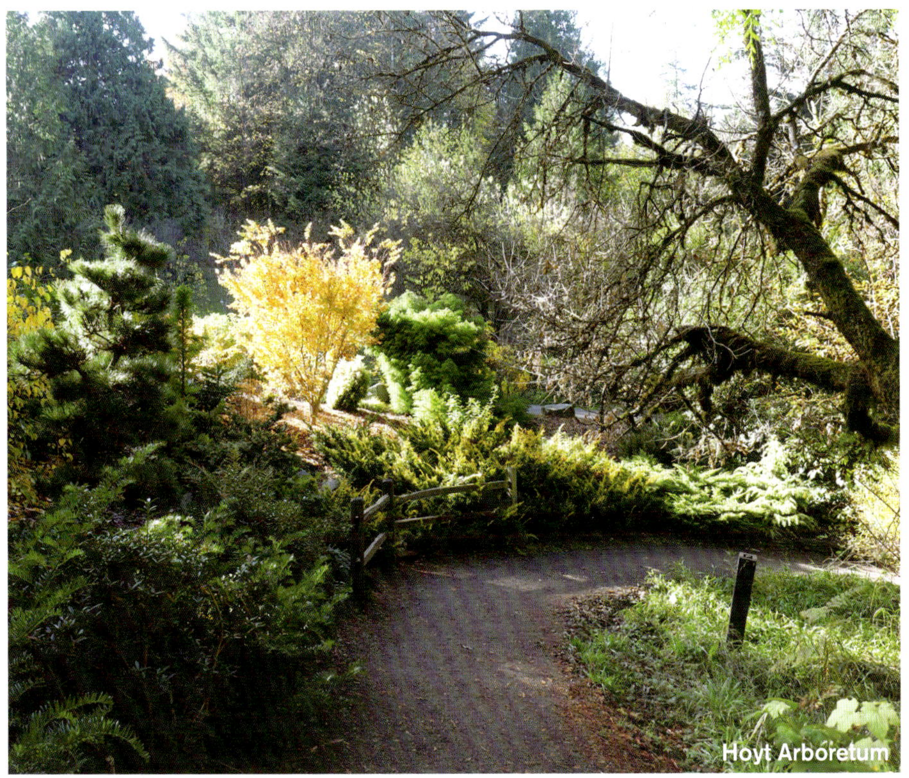
Hoyt Arboretum

Hoyt Arboretum
Portland, Oregon

Free to the public and open every day of the year, this living museum provides visitors with a place to explore, learn, and recharge. The 189-acre park contains more than 2,300 types of trees from six continents and at least 6,000 trees, plants, and shrubs in total. One of the most extensive collections of conifers is located here, including a dawn redwood, which, in 1952, became the first of its kind in the Western Hemisphere to produce pinecones in six million years! Other highlights include a nationally recognized magnolia collection, 12 miles of hiking trails, and the Bamboo Forest featuring 30 species of bamboo.

International Rose Test Garden
Portland, Oregon

As its name suggests, this property is a rose-lover's paradise, underscoring Portland's reputation as the "City of Roses." The garden is the oldest continually operating public rose test garden in the country, and it regularly evaluates new cultivars from around the world, testing them for disease resistance, color, and fragrance. While its primary purpose may be these scientific and horticultural endeavors, the garden attracts 700,000 visitors every year, who simply enjoy the colorful blooms and their distinctive heady scent. An impressive 10,000 rose bushes, representing 650 varieties, are found on the property, blooming from late May until October.

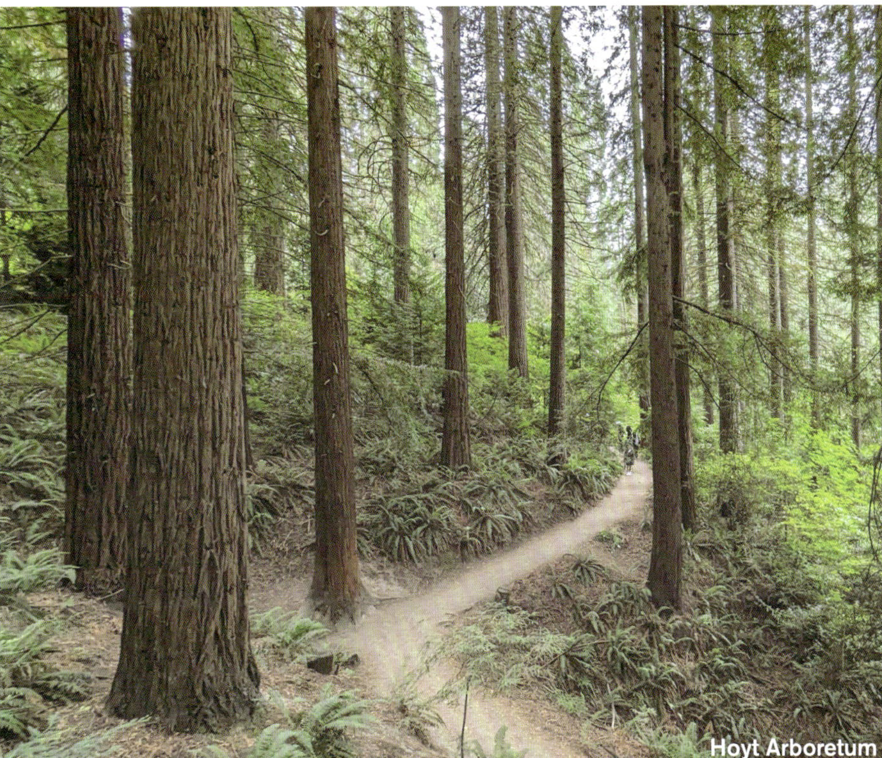
Hoyt Arboretum

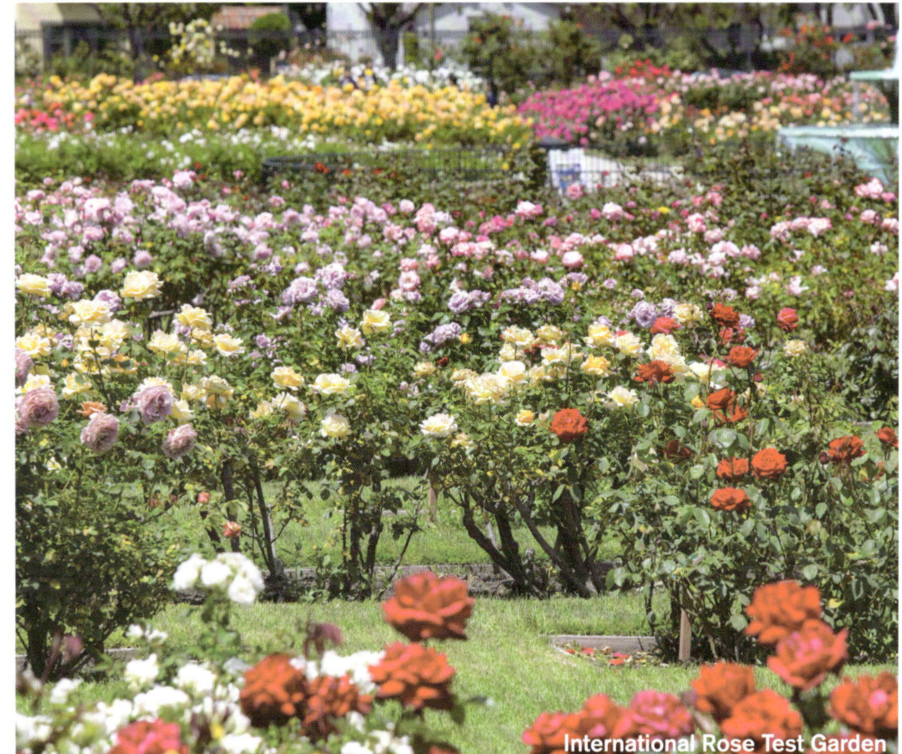
International Rose Test Garden

The garden includes the magnificent Moon Locking Pavilion and Tower of Cosmic Reflections.

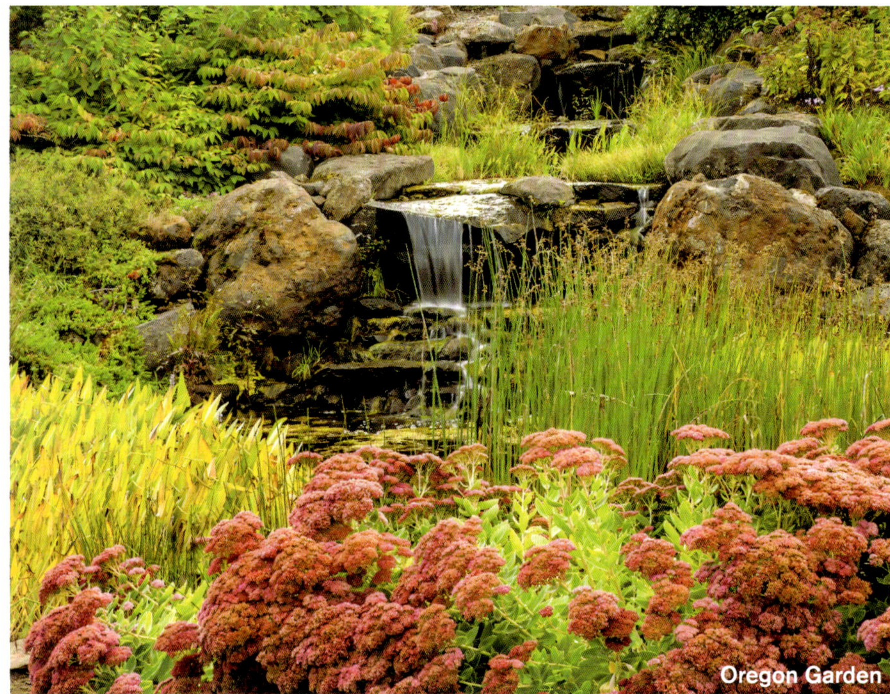

The garden uses a series of terraced wetlands to filter Silverton's wastewater.

Lan Su Chinese Garden
Portland, Oregon

Occupying an entire city block in downtown Portland, this authentic walled Chinese garden takes up about 40,000 square feet of space in the city's Chinatown neighborhood. The majority of the plants in the garden are indigenous to China, including Yulan magnolia, star jasmine, and the Chinese parasol tree.

Leach Botanical Garden
Portland, Oregon

This tranquil 17-acre garden is situated next to a burbling creek and features many plants native to the Pacific Northwest. The popular Aerial Tree Walk gives visitors a bird's eye view of towering Douglas firs, Oregon grape, ferns, and more than 2,000 other types of plants on the forest floor below.

Oregon Garden
Silverton, Oregon

More than 20 individual gardens are contained within the 80-acre Oregon Garden, which was established in 1999. The property focuses on the plants of the Willamette Valley and the Pacific Northwest, with highlights including the Conifer Garden, the Northwest Garden, a Children's Garden, and a Pet Friendly Garden.

Peavy Arboretum
Corvallis, Oregon

Established in 1926, this arboretum operated as a camp for the Civilian Conservation Corps in the 1930s and early 40s. In fact, the CCC was instrumental in creating the arboretum that exists today, planting trees and building infrastructure. The historic property contains fir, birch, pine, and juniper, as well as collections of flowering shrubs.

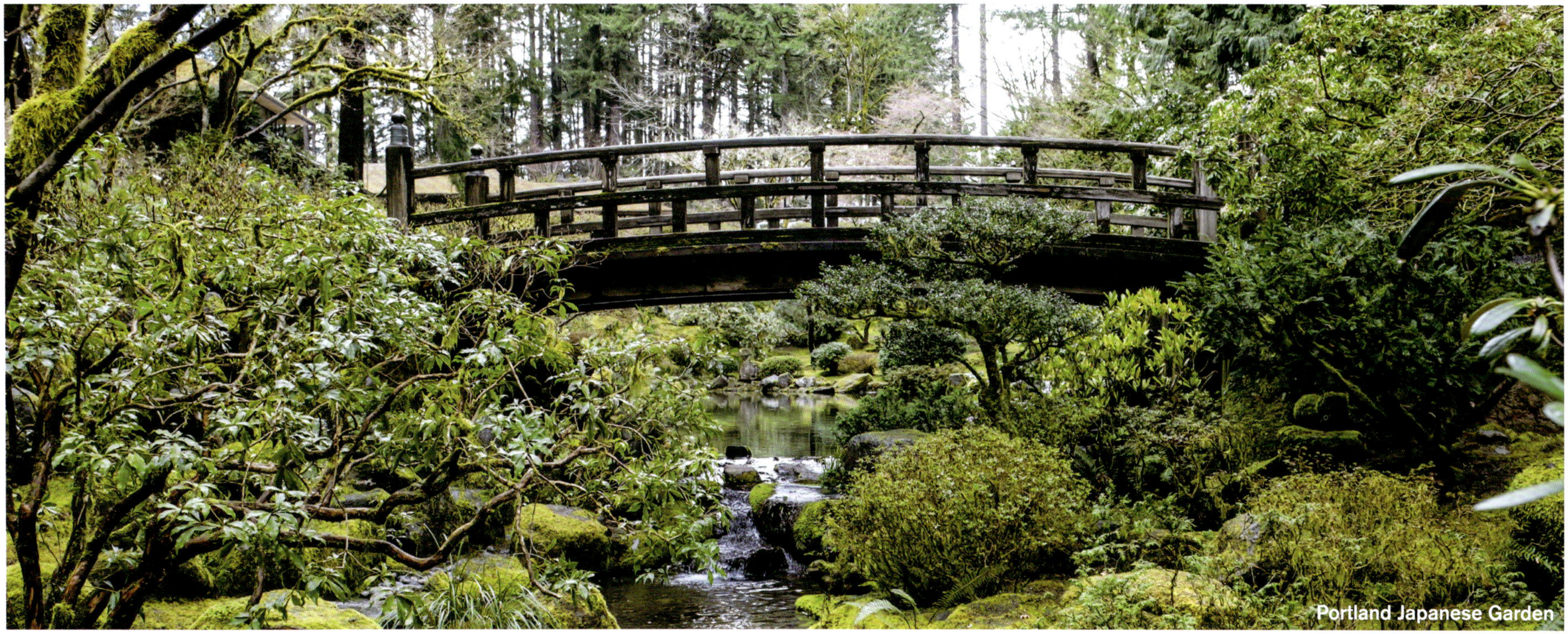

Portland Japanese Garden

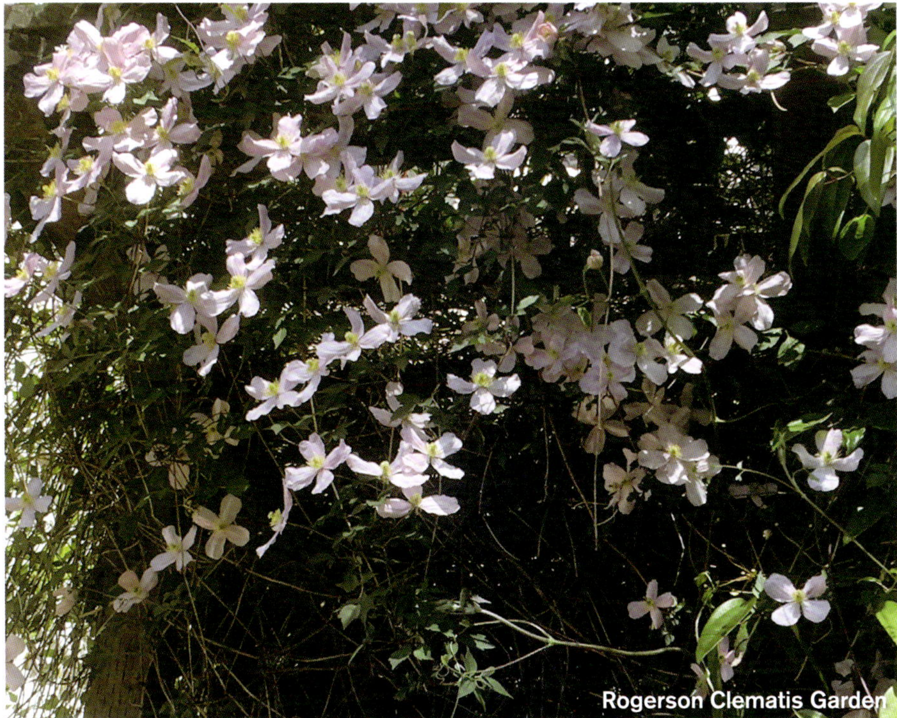

Rogerson Clematis Garden

The collection includes the "Brewster," named after the site's founder.

Portland Japanese Garden
Portland, Oregon

The former ambassador of Japan to the U.S., Nobuo Matsunaga, once called this property "the most beautiful and authentic Japanese garden in the world outside of Japan." And it's no wonder: the 12.5-acre garden features eight distinct gardens that reflect the history of Japanese garden design, as well as flowing streams, winding paths, a teahouse, and stunning views of snowcapped Mt. Hood. Historic spaces include the Sand and Stone Garden, the Strolling Pond Garden, the Tea Garden, and the Flat Garden. The site also contains the Cultural Village, which includes the Jordan Schnitzer Japanese Arts Learning Center, a library with 3,000 publications, and a Bonsai Terrace.

Rogerson Clematis Garden
West Linn, Oregon

Named after Brewster Rogerson, a former professor at Kansas State University who moved to Oregon in 1981, this small, one-acre property showcases one specific plant, the clematis. Rogerson began collecting clematis plants in 1975, and became the founding member of the International Clematis Society in 1984. What began as a small collection of 100 specimens has since grown to more than 2,000 individual clematis plants, representing almost 900 species from around the world. Fifteen individual gardens are located on the property, including the Heirloom Garden, which features clematis plants from before World War I, and the Antipodes, containing varieties from New Zealand and Australia.

Barnes Arboretum at St. Joseph's University
Merion Station, Pennsylvania

Dr. Albert Barnes and his wife, Laura, started this arboretum in 1922 as a space for horticultural education and botanical beauty. Today, the site contains more than 2,500 types of woody and herbaceous plants on a 12-acre plot of land. The lilac, peony, and fern collections, which date to the early 1900s, are particularly notable.

Bartram's Garden
Philadelphia, Pennsylvania

Founded back in 1728 by botanist and explorer John Bartram, this National Historic Landmark is considered the oldest botanical garden in North America. Bartram's stone house still stands on the property, as well as his original garden and greenhouse. Visitors can wander through flower gardens, hike on the River Trail along the Schuylkill River, or go bird-watching.

Chanticleer Garden
Wayne, Pennsylvania

Fittingly, references to roosters are found throughout this 48-acre property, which takes its name from the French word for rooster. Gardens include the traditional cottage-style Cutting Garden, the small Teacup Garden, the rustic Vegetable Garden, and Bell's Woodland, which showcases plants that are endemic to the eastern United States.

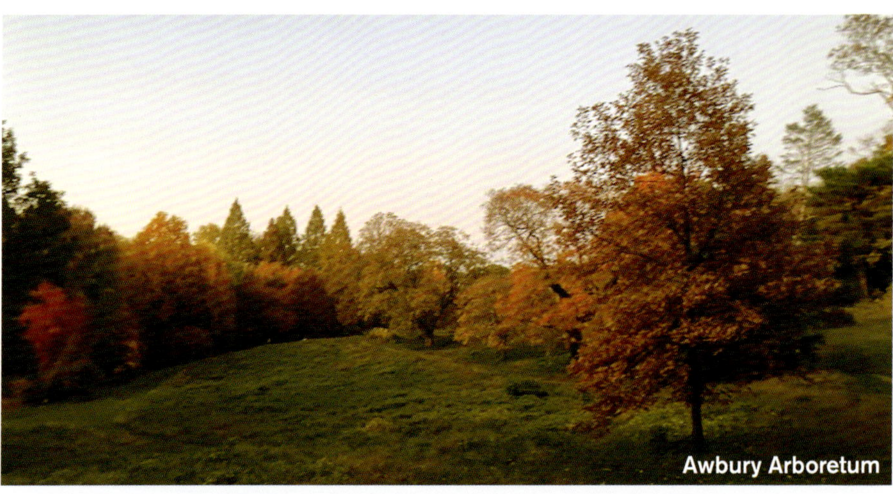

Awbury Arboretum

Autumn comes to the wildflower meadow.

Awbury Arboretum
Philadelphia, Pennsylvania

This arboretum is located within the Awbury Historic District in Philadelphia's East Germantown neighborhood, a National Historic District since 2001. The grounds feature stands of trees and shrubs, man-made ponds, and a wildflower meadow. A State Champion River Birch tree is among the noteworthy specimens on the property.

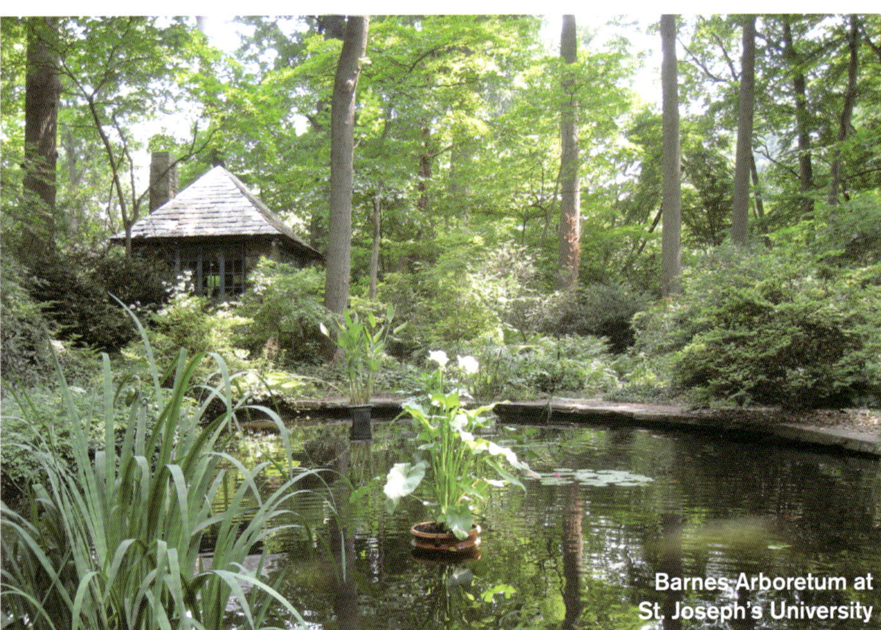

Barnes Arboretum at St. Joseph's University

A quiet, landscaped pond is nestled on the property. There is also a formal rose and perennial garden and greenhouse to explore.

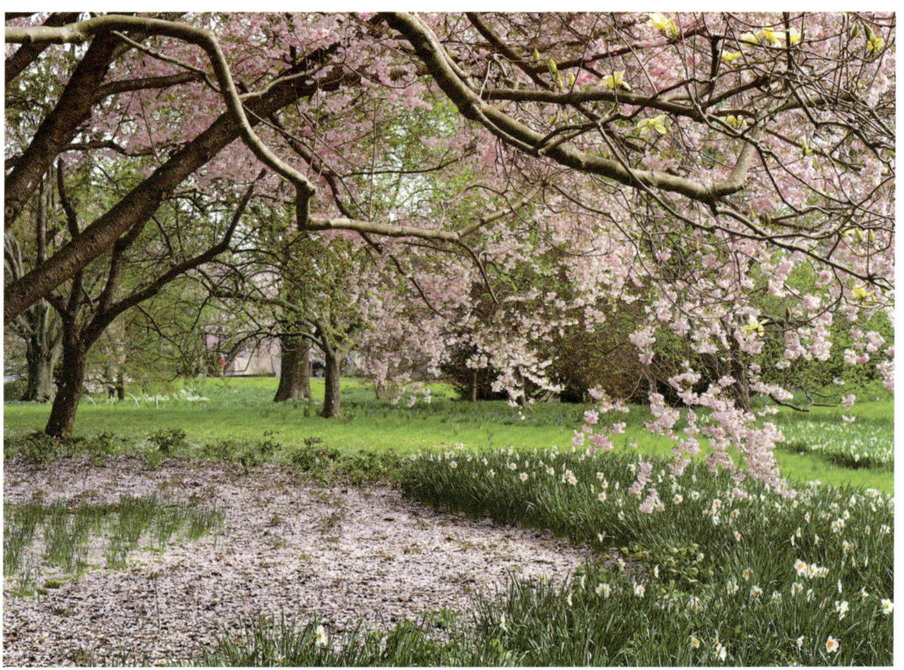

Spring brings intense blooms to Chanticleer Garden.

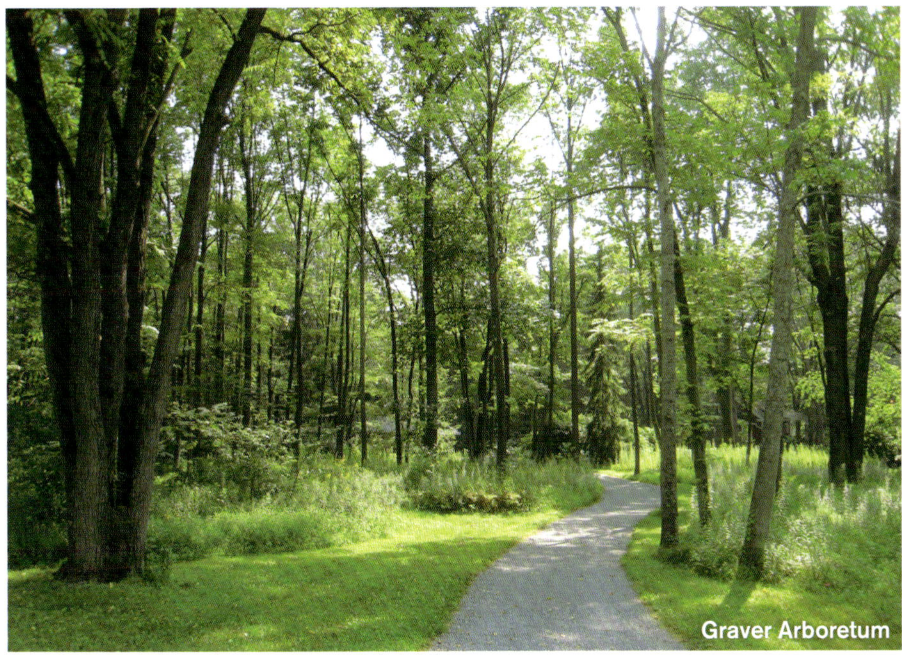

The arboretum includes many rare and uncommon trees from around the world.

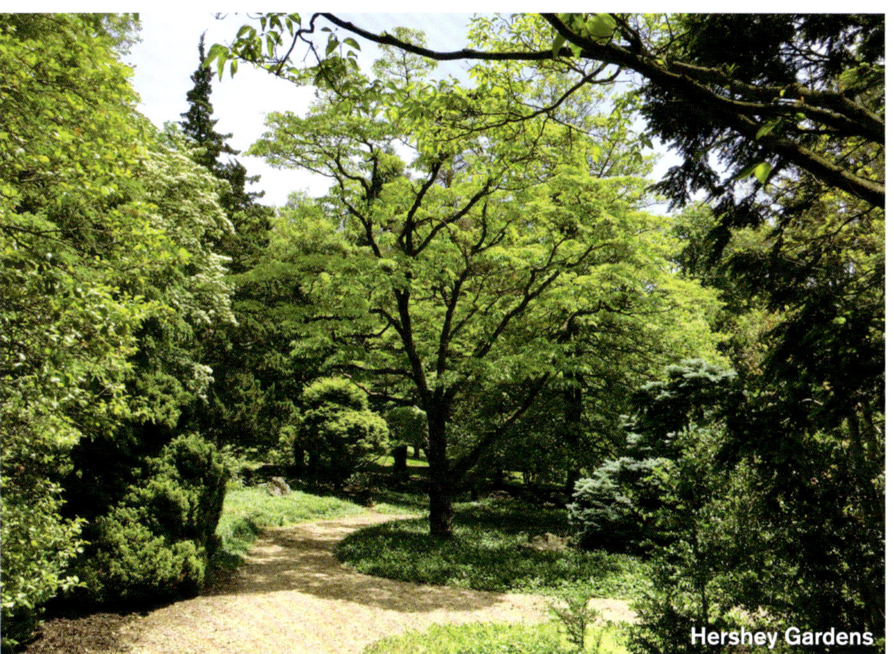

The grounds include an arboretum featuring native "signature trees."

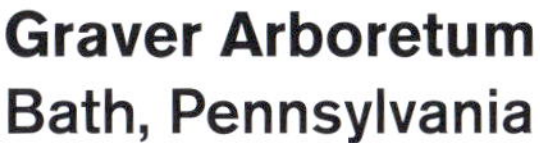

Graver Arboretum
Bath, Pennsylvania

Founded by Dr. Lee and Virginia Graver, this arboretum was donated to Muhlenberg College in 1994. The Gravers cultivated many of the plants found on the grounds, including rhododendrons, ferns, wildflowers, and more than 150 species of conifer. Today, the arboretum is divided between conifers, wetland plants, and wildflowers.

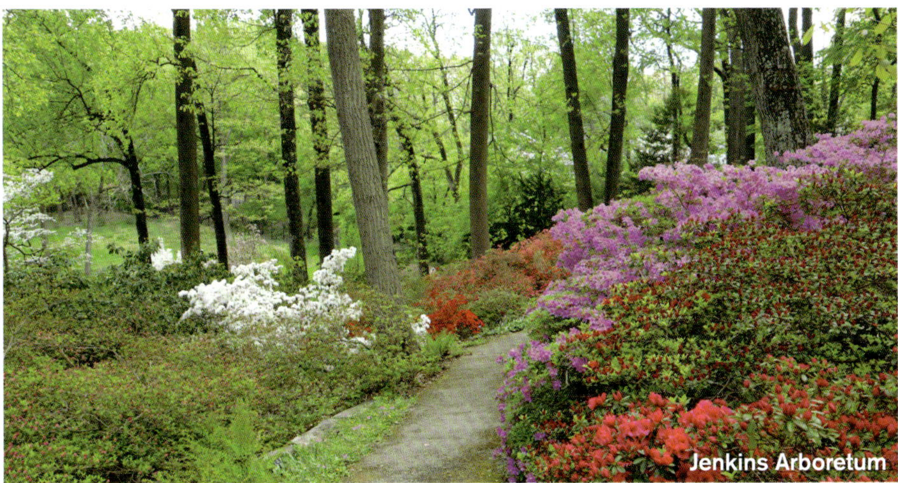

Visitors discover washes of colorful flowers set in a woodland landscape.

Hershey Gardens
Hershey, Pennsylvania

The town of Hershey may be best known for its chocolate, but this garden, overlooking the Hersheypark amusement park, is certainly worth a visit. The 23-acre garden was opened in 1937 with a display of 7,000 roses, and has grown substantially since then. The property also includes rare trees, an indoor tropical Butterfly Atrium, and a Children's Garden.

Jenkins Arboretum and Gardens
Devon, Pennsylvania

The founder of this arboretum, H. Lawrence Jenkins, established the property in 1963 as a tribute to his late wife, Elisabeth, who loved the natural environment surrounding their home. Over the years, these gardens have expanded, now encompassing 48 acres of rhododendrons, azaleas, blueberries, mountain laurels, and thousands of other plants and trees.

Lake Erie Arboretum
Erie, Pennsylvania

In 1998, the first tree was planted in this arboretum. Today, more than 1,000 trees have been planted, and six attractions have been added, including walking trails, a playground, and the Benjamin Winter Garden, which contains plantings that bloom in the winter and early spring, when most other plants are dormant.

Longwood Gardens
Kennett Square, Pennsylvania

Welcoming 1.6 million guests a year, this 1,100-acre property is one of the most visited botanical gardens in the country. More than two dozen unique horticultural spaces are found on the site, including the European-inspired Main Fountain Garden, a gallery-like Orchid House, the whimsical Topiary Garden, and an Open Air Theater and Theater Garden.

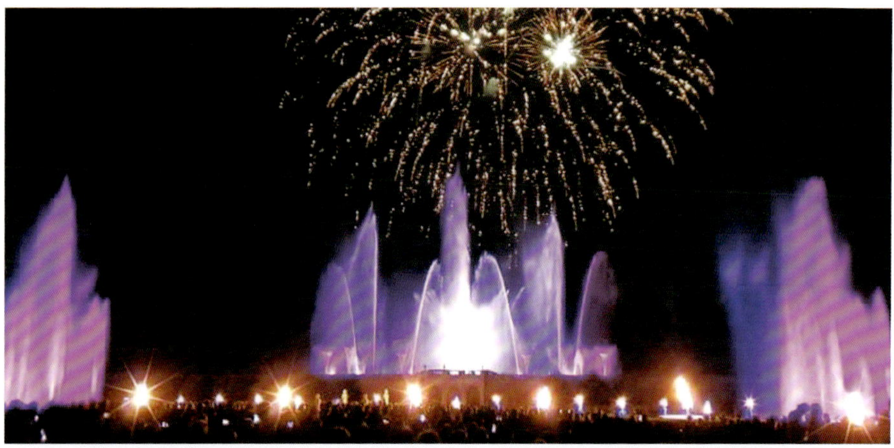

The fountains are both a daily and nightly attraction, with colorful nighttime spectacles keeping visitors enthralled after dark.

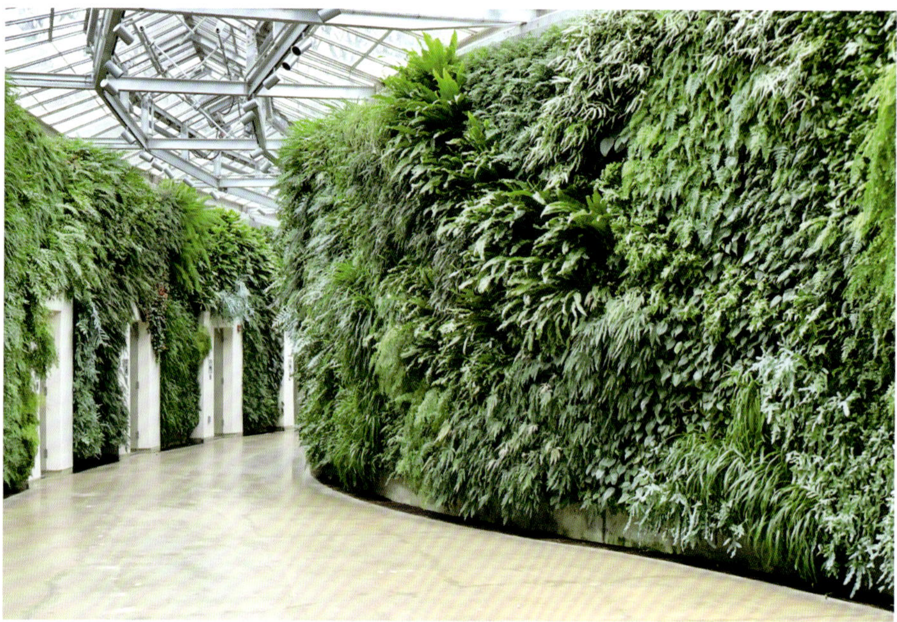

The standout Conservatory District features acres of glassed-in foliage the public may stroll through year-round. Sections include the Cascade Garden, Acacia Passage, East Conservatory, Indoor Children's Garden, Green Wall, Orchid House, Bonsai Courtyard, Silver Garden, Historic Main Conservatory, West Conservatory, and Waterlily Court.

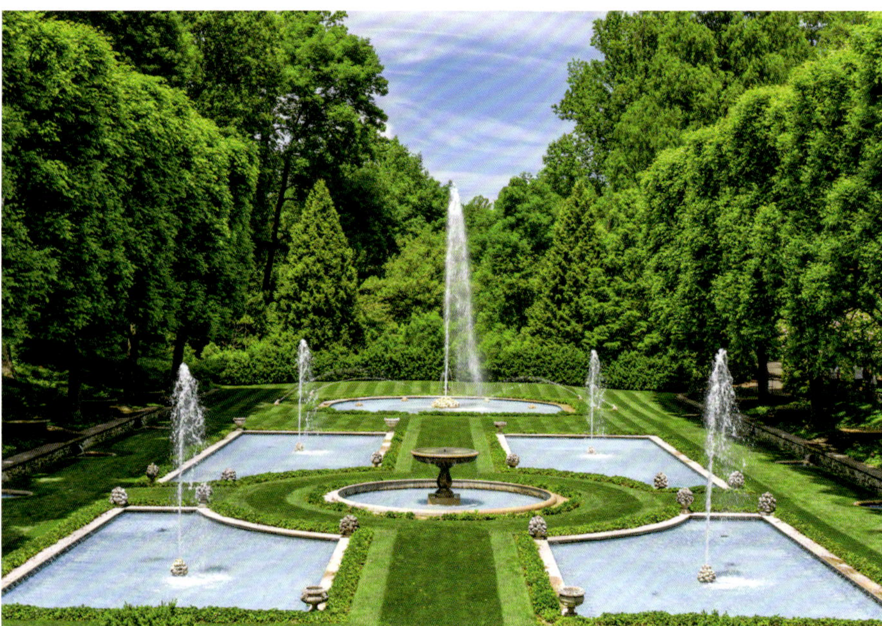

The Italian Water Garden, with its striking, blue-tiled pools and gorgeous fountains is enclosed by lindens, charming visitors with its fairytale-like ambience.

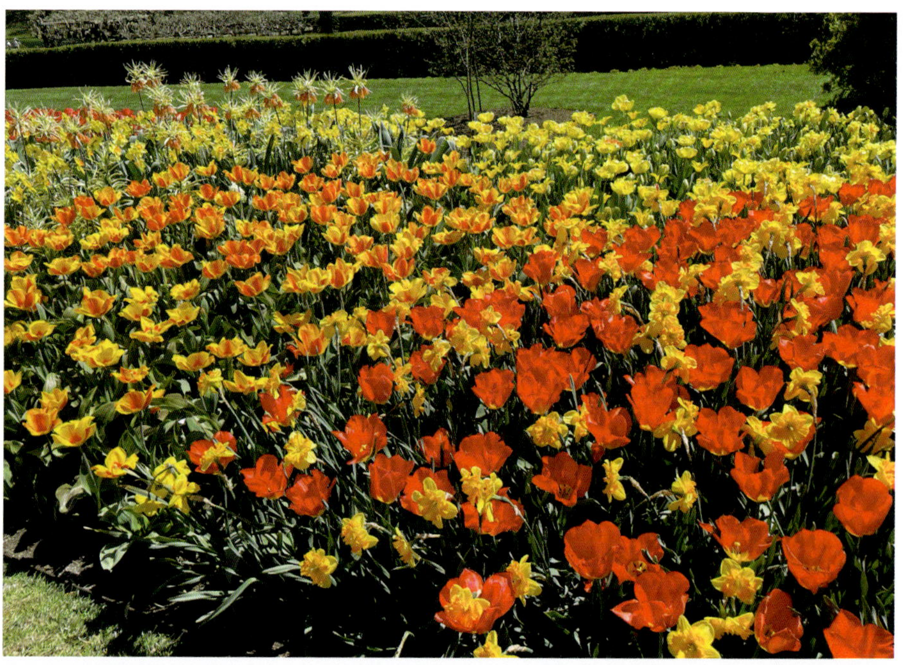

A mosaic of colorful spring tulips at the Flower Garden Walk draws gasps every spring.

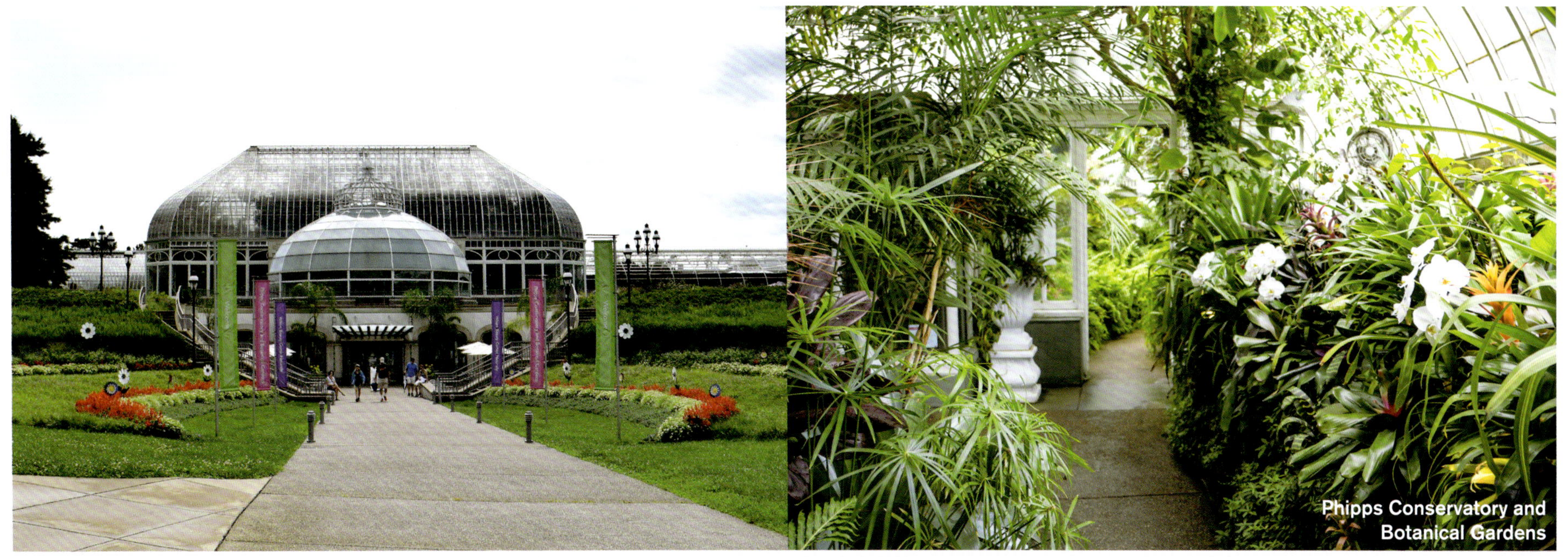

The greenhouses are incredibly spacious, allowing visitors to lose themselves in display after dazzling display.

Phipps Conservatory and Botanical Gardens
Pittsburgh, Pennsylvania

Gifted to the city of Pittsburgh by steel and real estate magnate Henry Phipps Jr. in 1893, this 15-acre site's centerpiece is a 14-room conservatory designed by famous greenhouse manufacturer Lord & Burnham. The conservatory contains tropical and desert plants, and outdoor gardens include an Aquatic Garden and an Edible Garden.

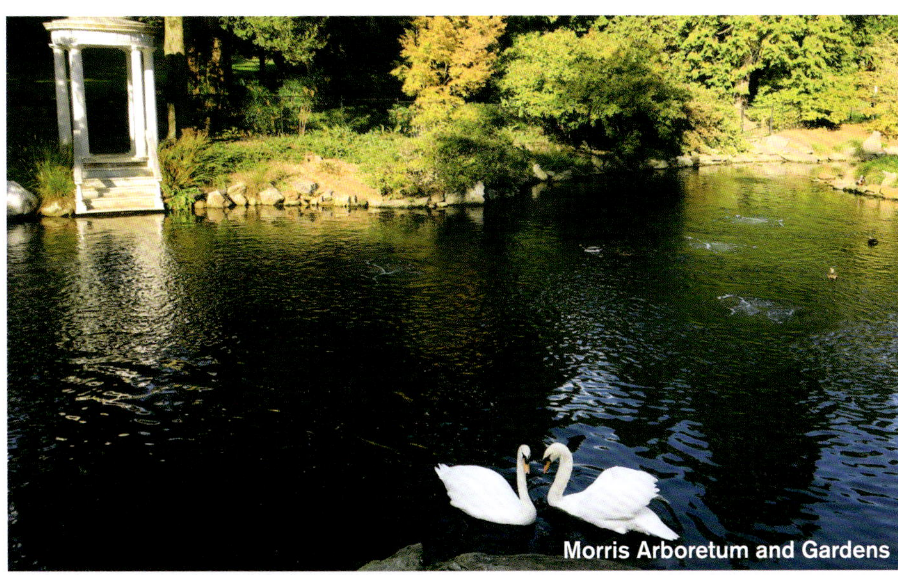

The Swan Pond was designed and built in 1905.

Morris Arboretum and Gardens
Philadelphia, Pennsylvania

This 92-acre property, designed in an English park style with Japanese influences, is the official arboretum of Pennsylvania. More than 11,000 plants flourish on the site, with signature gardens including the Rose Garden, the Rock Wall Garden, the English Garden, and the Alice and J. Liddon Pennock Flower Walk.

Pittsburgh Botanic Garden
Pittsburgh, Pennsylvania

This 460-acre property, located on a former coal mining site, is considered one of the largest botanical gardens in the country by area. Native Allegheny Plateau trees, a Japanese Garden with a lotus pond, a Pollinator Garden, and a 1700s-themed Heritage Homestead are all found within the sustainability-minded gardens.

Worth Exploring in Pennsylvania

Merion Botanical Park
Merion Station, Pennsylvania

- A 13.5-acre garden established in 1944, open daily and free of charge
- Features azaleas, magnolias, maples, rhododendrons, and dogwoods

Renziehausen Park Rose Garden and Arboretum
McKeesport, Pennsylvania

- Contains 1,200 rose bushes and 300 miniature rose bushes, which are maintained by volunteers
- The second-largest rose garden in Pennsylvania

Rodef Shalom Biblical Botanical Garden
Pittsburgh, Pennsylvania

- Contains plants once grown in ancient Israel, labeled with biblical verses
- Plants include cedars, dates, pomegranates, olives, and figs

Henry Schmieder Arboretum
Doylestown, Pennsylvania

- Spans 40 acres on the campus of Delaware Valley University
- Collections include an Herb Garden, 1920s Cottage Garden, and a Rose Garden

Scott Arboretum and Gardens
Swarthmore, Pennsylvania

- Named in honor of Arthur Hoyt Scott, the inventor of the paper towel
- Contains 4,000 ornamental plants, including 650 roses

Taylor Memorial Arboretum
Wallingford, Pennsylvania

- Contains mature dogwoods, magnolias, and hollies, with younger shadbush and viburnums
- Features a grotto once used as a quarry

Welkinweir
Pottstown, Pennsylvania

- Covers a sprawling 224 acres and features gardens, an arboretum, and an eighteenth-century mansion
- Two miles of trails wind through rare and unusual plants and trees

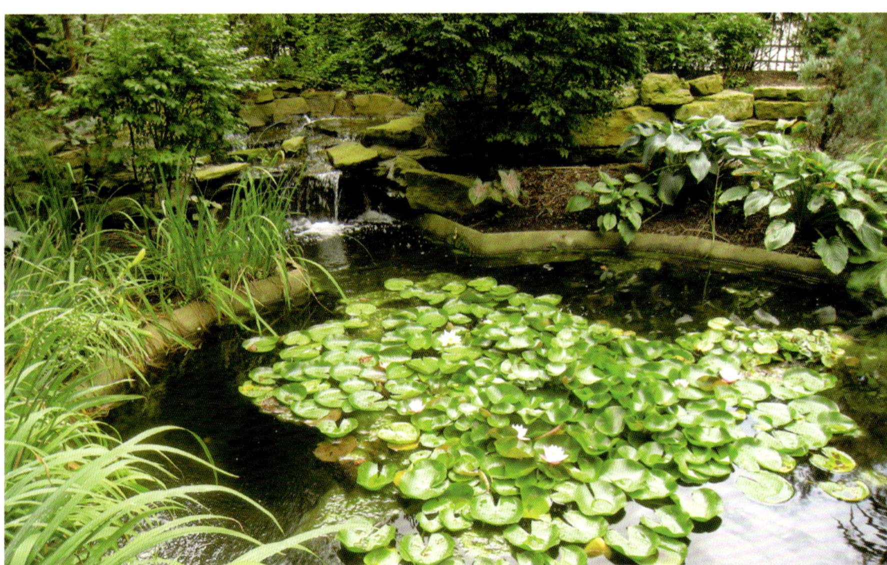

The Rodef Shalom Biblical Botanical Garden was established in 1987. The grounds feature a series of ponds and creeks meant to represent bodies of water in Israel.

University of Rhode Island Botanical Gardens
Kingston, Rhode Island

The 4.5 acres of gardens on the University of Rhode Island campus have been used for teaching horticultural science for decades. But more than just a teaching tool, the grounds are also loved by visitors who come to see the Annual Garden, the Shade Garden, the Chester Clayton Rose Garden, and the Matthew J. Horridge Conservatory.

Roger Williams Park Botanical Center
Providence, Rhode Island

With a total area of 23,000 square feet, this property is New England's largest indoor public garden. The center is comprised of several buildings, including a 12,000-square-foot glass and steel conservatory that houses large palms, succulents, 10-foot cacti, and carnivorous plants. An outdoor perennial garden and rose maze are also featured.

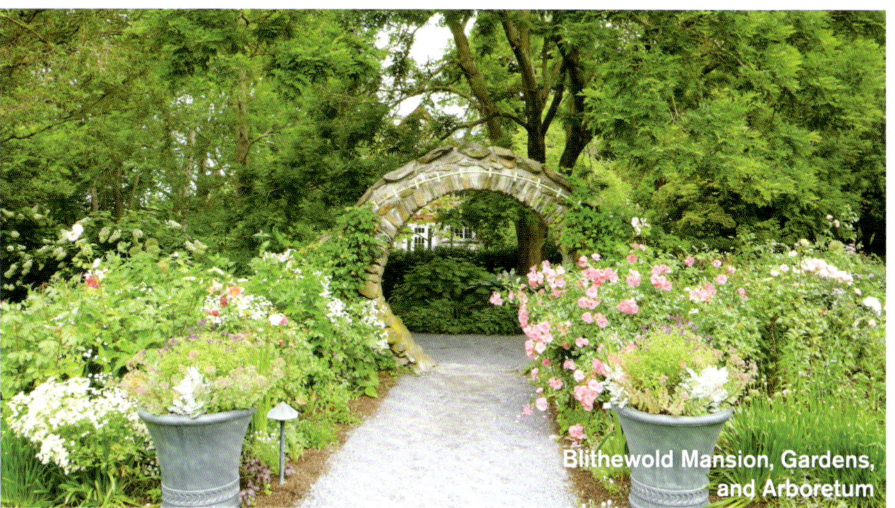

Blithewold Mansion, Gardens, and Arboretum

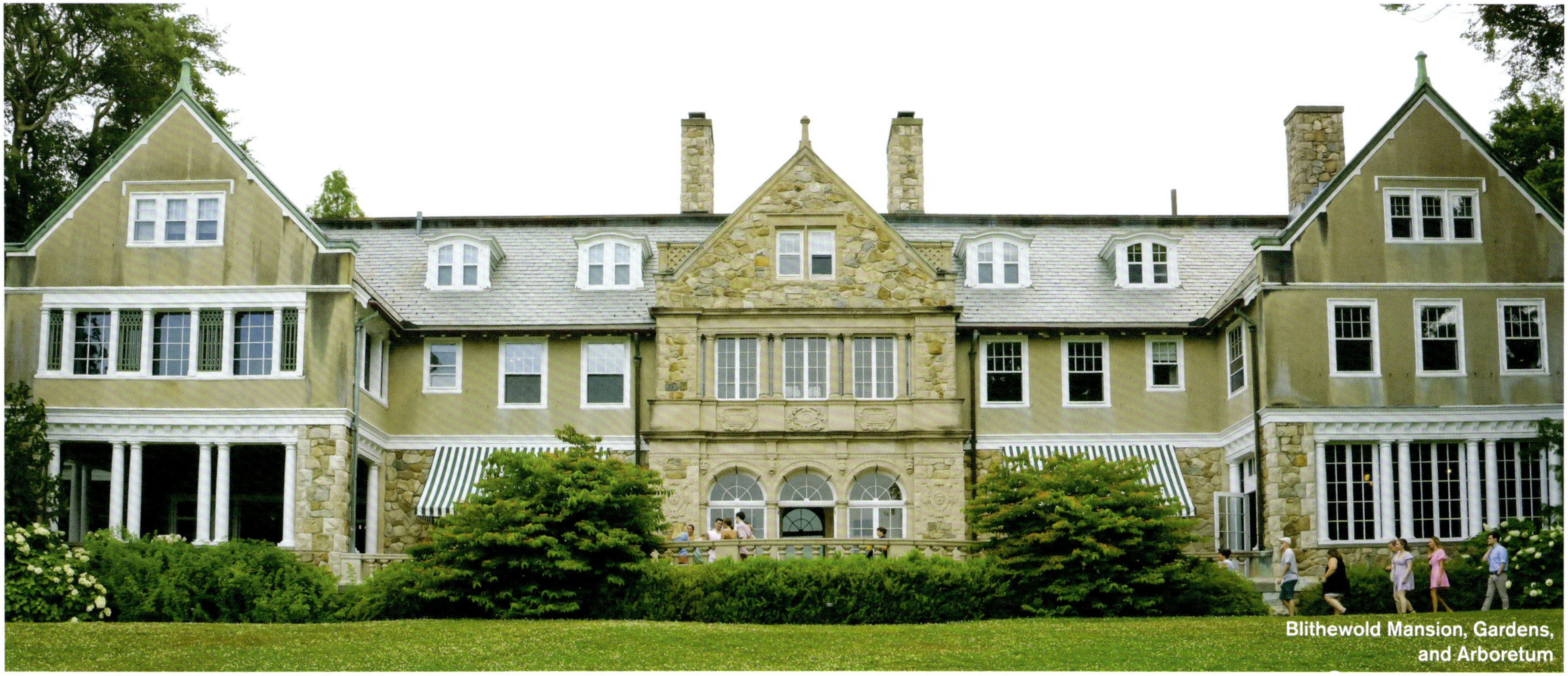

Blithewold Mansion, Gardens, and Arboretum

Blithewold Mansion, Gardens, and Arboretum
Bristol, Rhode Island

Located on the shores of Narragansett Bay, this 33-acre property was originally the summer home of several wealthy New England families. The grounds feature Blithewold Estate, an excellent example of the "Country Place Era"–a period which lasted from 1890 to 1930 and was marked by the use of European-style landscape design in American gardens. The gardens, situated around a 45-room mansion filled with family heirlooms, include a 10-acre Great Lawn, an Orchard, Vegetable Garden, Rose Garden, and Rock Garden in both historic and contemporary styles. The site is also home to an extensive arboretum, filled with 2,000 trees and shrubs.

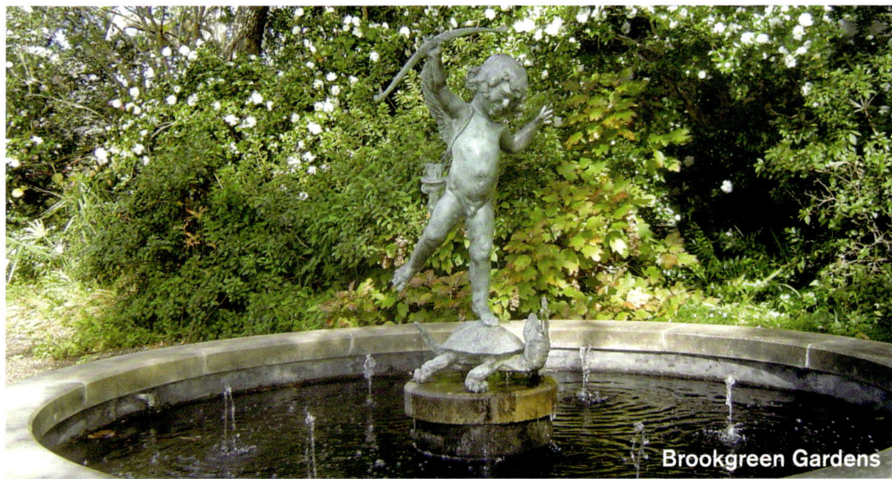

Sculpture lovers will discover beautiful creations in every nook and corner.

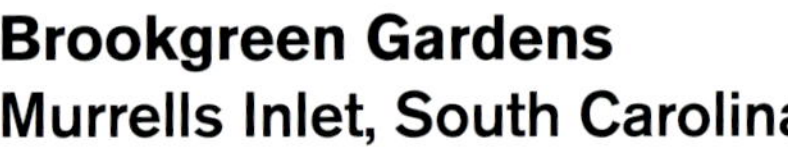

Brookgreen Gardens
Murrells Inlet, South Carolina

In the 1930s, sculptures, plants, and animals were all collected to create this outdoor museum, the first public sculpture garden in the country. Today, the property contains more than 2,000 sculptures, displayed throughout the expansive 9,127 acres of themed gardens. The Lowcountry Zoo is home to native animals and a butterfly house.

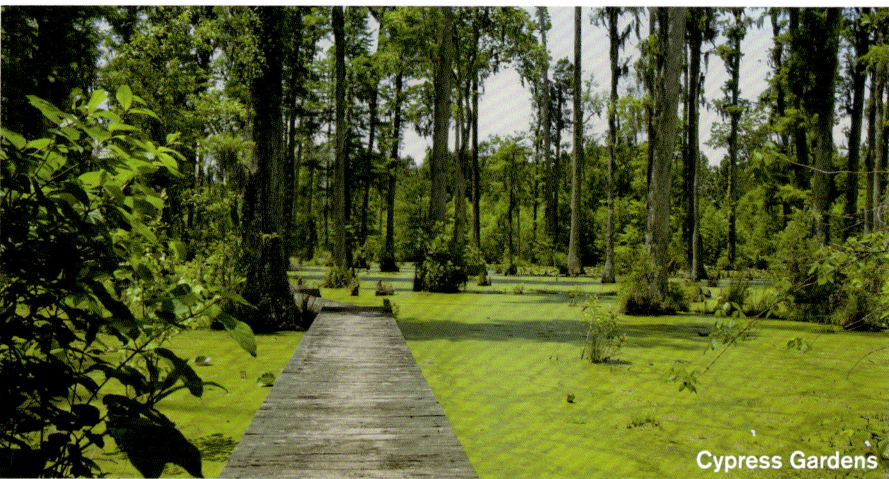

The gardens may be viewed along walkways or via flat-bottom boat.

Cypress Gardens
Moncks Corner, South Carolina

This unusual 170-acre preserve centers around 80 acres of blackwater bald cypress/tupelo swamp. Azaleas, daffodils, blueberries, and a rose garden grow on the property, which also contains a daylily island and a rice field. Other features include a butterfly house, aviary, and the "Swamparium," housing fish, reptiles, and amphibians.

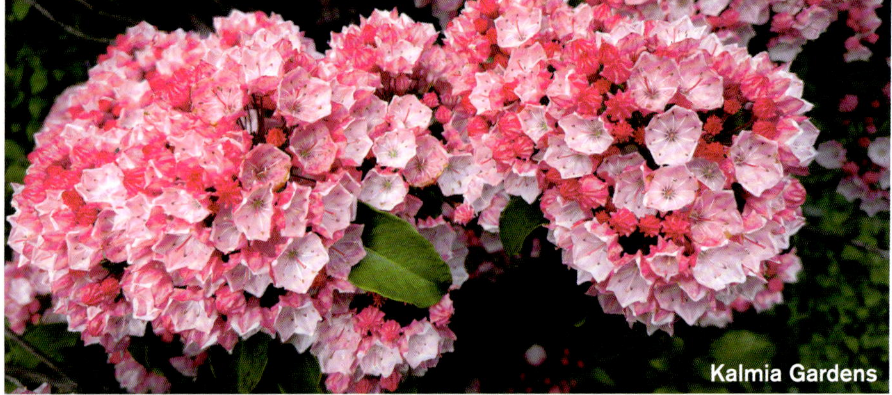

May is the best month to catch the mountain laurels blooming in abundance.

Kalmia Gardens
Hartsville, South Carolina

Once a rundown nineteenth-century plantation and neglected dump, this 38-acre site was transformed into a garden in the 1930s. It is named for the abundance of *Kalmia latifolia*, or mountain laurel, found on the property, a result of its geology and location. Restored historic buildings and year-round blooming plants lend their charm to the grounds.

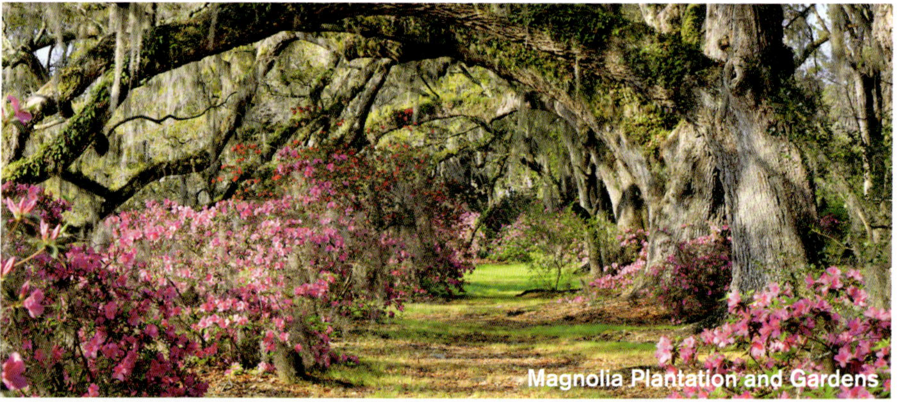

Azaleas bloom in the spring under live oak trees draped with Spanish moss.

Magnolia Plantation and Gardens
Charleston, South Carolina

This 464-acre property is one of the oldest plantations in the south, dating to 1679, and is listed on the National Register of Historic Places. In addition to gardens like a Camellia Collection, the indoor Barbados Tropical Garden, and a Biblical Garden, visitors can learn about the African-American history of the plantation.

South Carolina Botanical Garden
Clemson, South Carolina

Located on the campus of Clemson University, this 230-acre garden is also home to the Bob Campbell Geology Museum–featuring 10,000 rocks, minerals, and fossils–and the Fran Hanson Visitor's Center and Art Gallery. In addition to its numerous plants and trees, the garden contains sculptures created with natural materials and living plants.

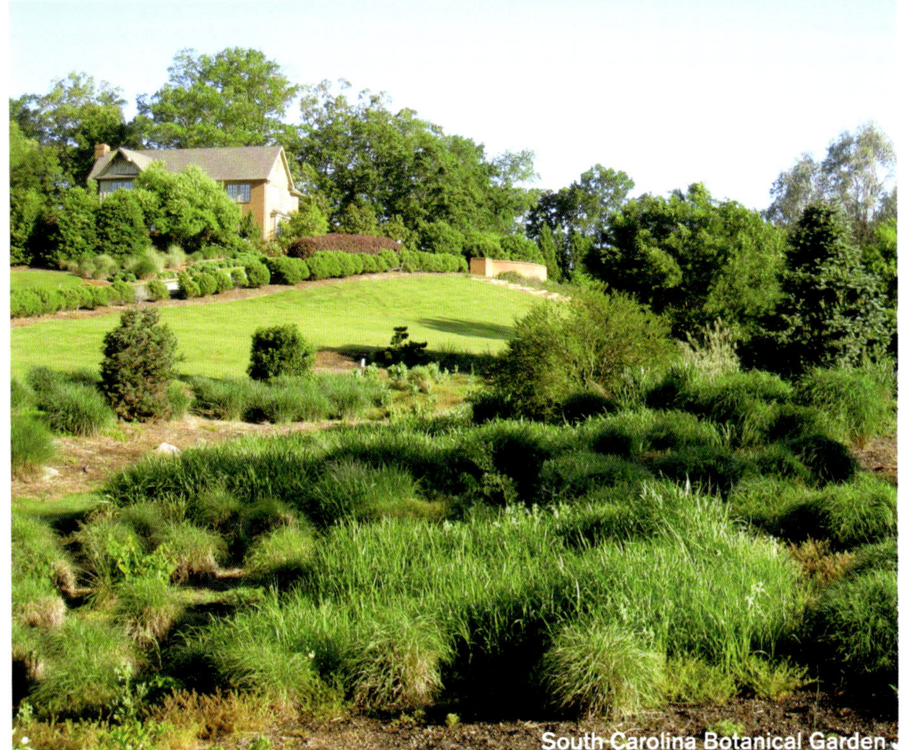
South Carolina Botanical Garden

Summerville Azalea Park
Summerville, South Carolina

During the Great Depression, this azalea-filled park was created as a way to boost the local economy. Since then, the 16-acre property has added pine trees, tranquil ponds, and sculpture installations. Gazebos, tennis courts, ornamental gardens, and walking trails are found throughout the park, making this property about so much more than just azaleas!

Wells Japanese Garden
Newberry, South Carolina

Added to the National Register of Historic Places in 1980, this Japanese garden was originally created in 1930. Today, the grounds are home to ponds, Japanese-style bridges, a teahouse, and a *torii*–a traditional Japanese gate. The gardens feature both indigenous and exotic species, including lotus, water lilies, dogwood, and crepe myrtle.

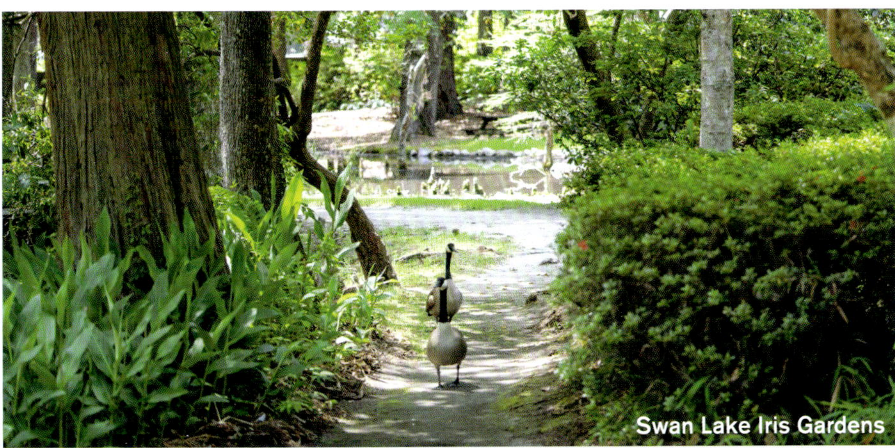
Swan Lake Iris Gardens

Geese find the gardens bird-friendly too!

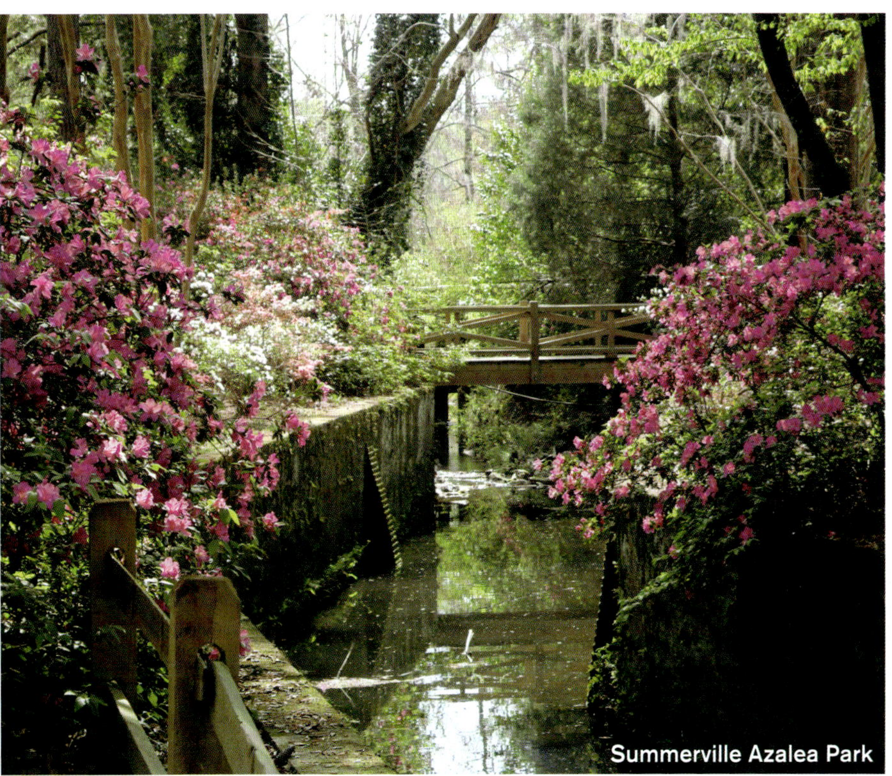
Summerville Azalea Park

Swan Lake Iris Gardens
Sumter, South Carolina

As the only public park in the country to feature all eight swan species, this aptly named garden is one of the most unique in South Carolina. The 150-acre property is also known for its extensive collection of Japanese iris plants, azaleas, daylilies, and camellias, as well as a Rose Garden and Butterfly Garden.

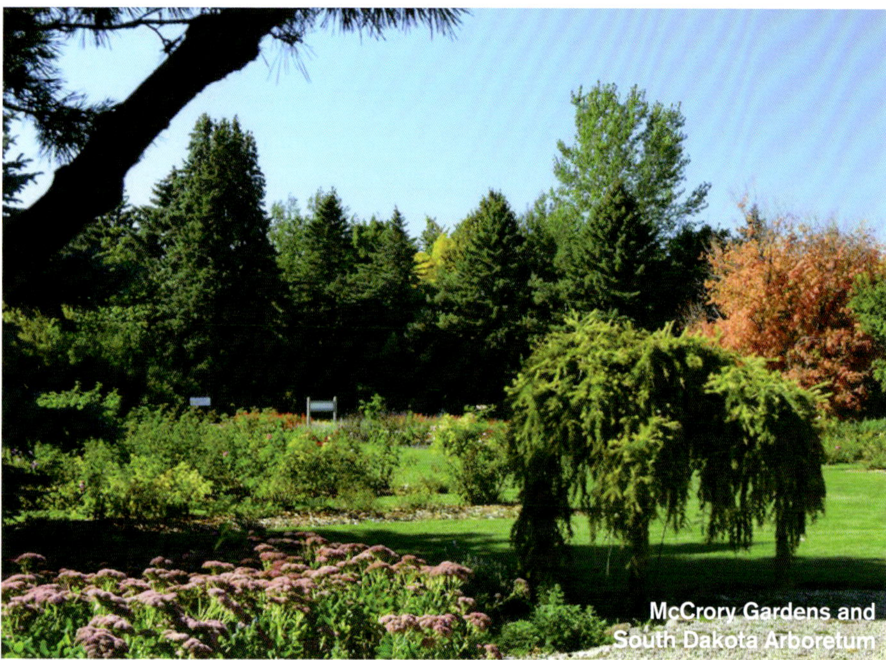

The arboretum features over 240 species of trees and shrubs.

McCrory Gardens and South Dakota Arboretum
Brookings, South Dakota

Nearly 25 acres of formal display gardens and a 45-acre arboretum make up this property, which is operated by the University of South Dakota. Development of the garden began in the 1960s, and was named in honor of Professor S.A. McCrory, who headed the department of horticulture at the university until his death in 1964. The site still follows McCrory's vision of an educational space and research garden, with plants chosen for their ability to thrive in South Dakota's sometimes harsh climate. Highlights include two All-America Display gardens featuring All-America Display winners, an Azalea and Rhododendron Collection, a Hummingbird Garden, a Children's Maze, and a Lilac Collection.

Mary Jo Wegner Arboretum
Sioux Falls, South Dakota

Mary Jo Wegner was an environmental advocate and supporter of the arts who fell in love with the city of Sioux Falls when she moved there in 1962. After she succumbed to cancer in 2003, this scenic arboretum, where Mary Jo had found moments of quiet respite during her illness, was named in her honor. Today, visitors who wander the 155-acre property can explore the history, beauty, and tranquility that Mary Jo found so enthralling. Gardens, wetlands, ponds, and native plants are found throughout the arboretum, which also features several walking trails of varying difficulty. Hikers should keep an eye out for deer, turkey, bald eagles, and other wildlife.

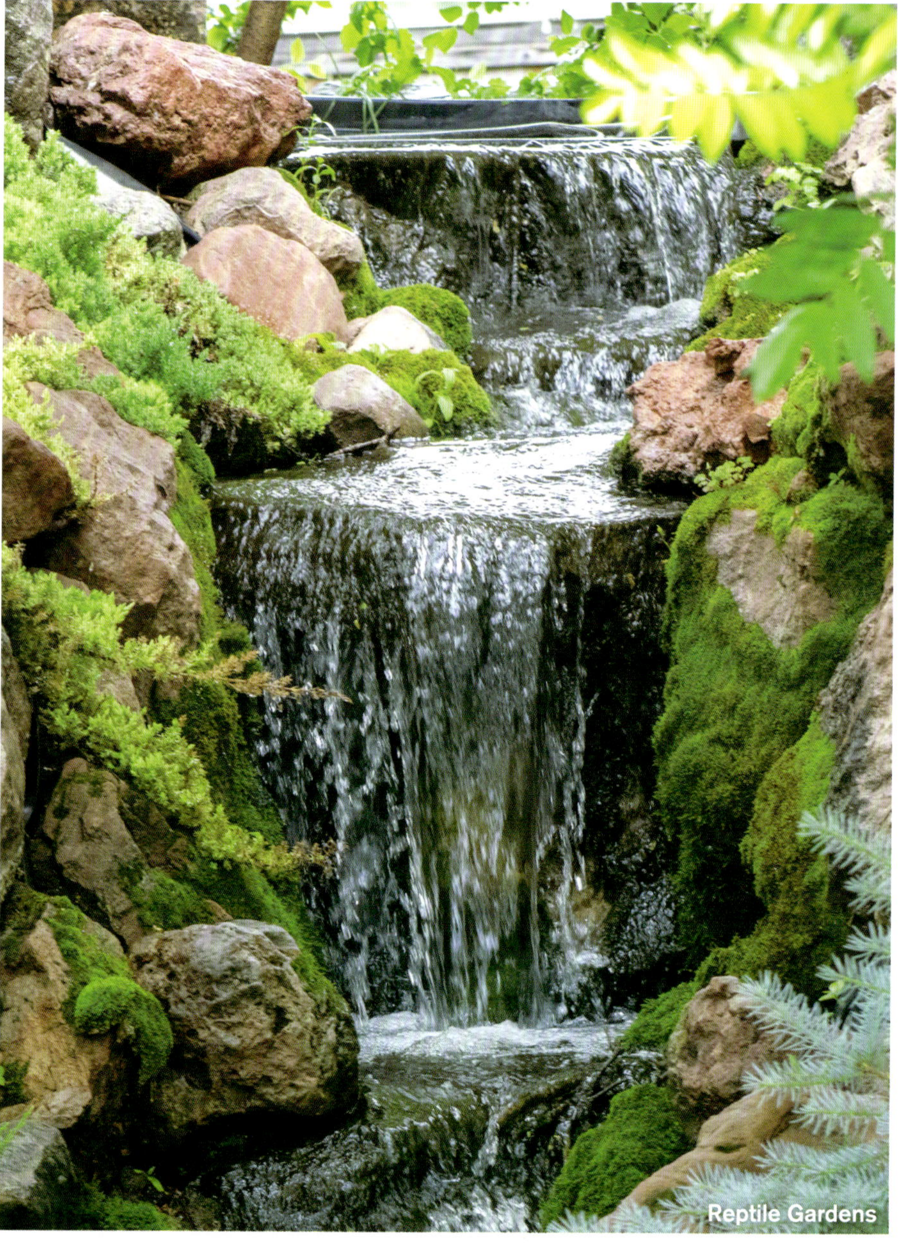

Tortuga Falls.

Reptile Gardens
Rapid City, South Dakota

In addition to its amazing collection of wildlife, Rapid City's Reptile Gardens features a surprising botanical garden filled with tropical plants and lush greenery. One of the newest attractions is Tortuga Falls, a cascading waterfall that leads to a fish and turtle pond. The massive Sky Dome features an indoor jungle.

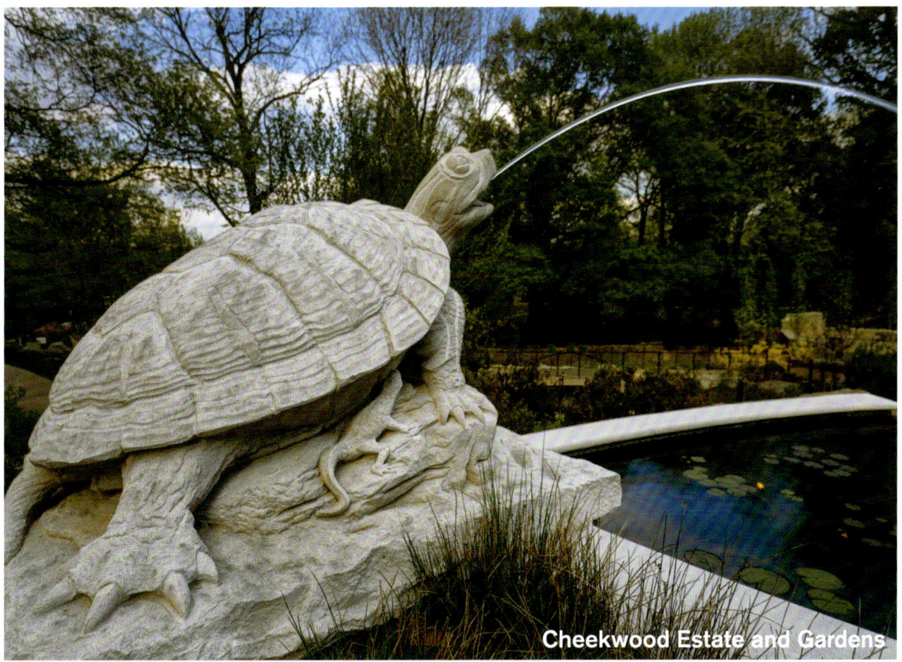

Playful sculptures and artworks await discovery, like this turtle fountain at the turtle pond in the Children's Garden.

Cheekwood Estate and Gardens
Nashville, Tennessee

This historic 55-acre property and its 30,000-square-foot Georgian-style mansion was constructed in 1929 as the home of Leslie and Mabel Cheek. One of the finest examples of an American Country Place Era estate, the property was converted into a museum and botanical garden in 1960, which today attracts more than 400,000 visitors a year, making it one of Nashville's top cultural sites. More than a dozen themed gardens are located here, including the Rose Study Garden, the Wills Perennial Garden, and the Blevins Japanese Garden. In the spring, more than 250,000 bulbs bloom on the property, filling the gardens with vibrant pops of color.

Deerwood Arboretum and Nature Center
Brentwood, Tennessee

Established on the site of what was once a wastewater treatment plant, this arboretum now features wildflower meadows and more than 65 species of native trees. Walking paths wind through the property, and visitors are encouraged to use the Tree Identification Trail Guide as they explore, which provides information about each tree specimen.

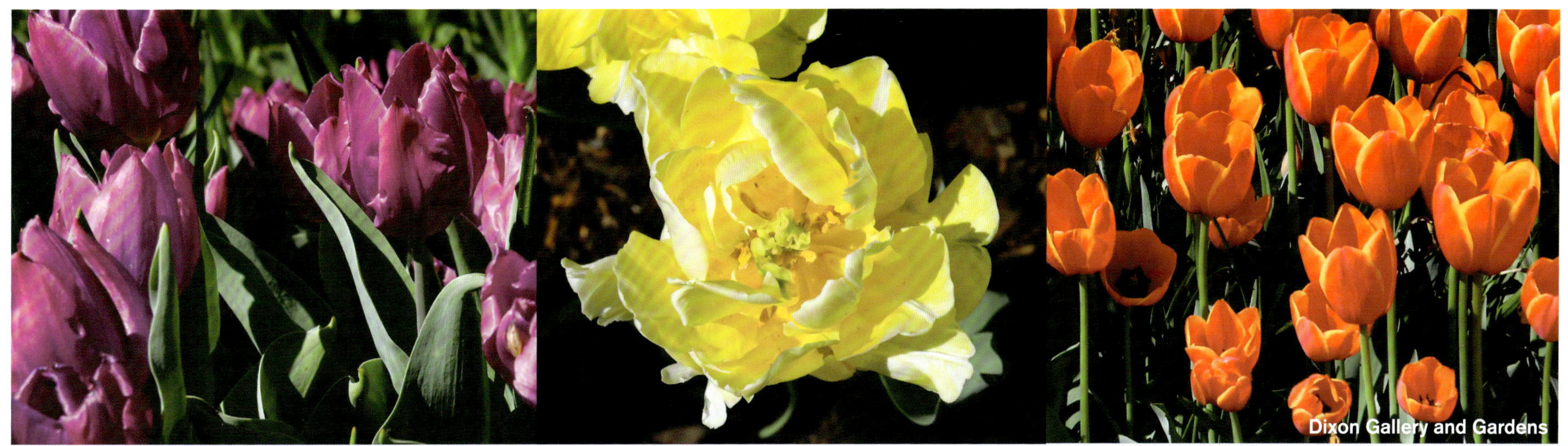

Flower lovers will discover hundreds of unique plants packed onto a handful of acres along with an amazing array of colorful blooms.

Dixon Gallery and Gardens
Memphis, Tennessee

The art museum located on the grounds of this 17-acre property showcases French and American impressionism and features works by Monet, Degas, and Cassatt, to name just a few artists. The vibrant gardens are just as enthralling as the art, and include the Memphis Garden Club Cutting Garden–a working flower farm.

Hermitage Arboretum
Nashville, Tennessee

Located on the grounds of The Hermitage, once the cotton plantation of President Andrew Jackson, this arboretum lines the 1.5-mile trail between the property's visitor center and Jackson's mansion. More than 100 native trees are showcased, along with a flower garden adjacent to the mansion that was originally installed in honor of Jackson's wife, Rachel.

Knoxville Botanical Garden and Arboretum
Knoxville, Tennessee

This 44-acre garden sits just outside of downtown Knoxville, offering a peaceful oasis for weary city dwellers. The gardens, which are free to the public, include a Bamboo Forest, the Native Medicinal Garden, and the Family Garden, which is available to members of the community who wish to start their own garden.

Louise Pearson Memorial Arboretum
Jackson, Tennessee

Established by the Bells Garden Club in 2001, this arboretum was named in honor of former club member, the late Louise Pearson. The site features 200 different species of trees, including several that have been donated as memorials, each labeled with their common and scientific names.

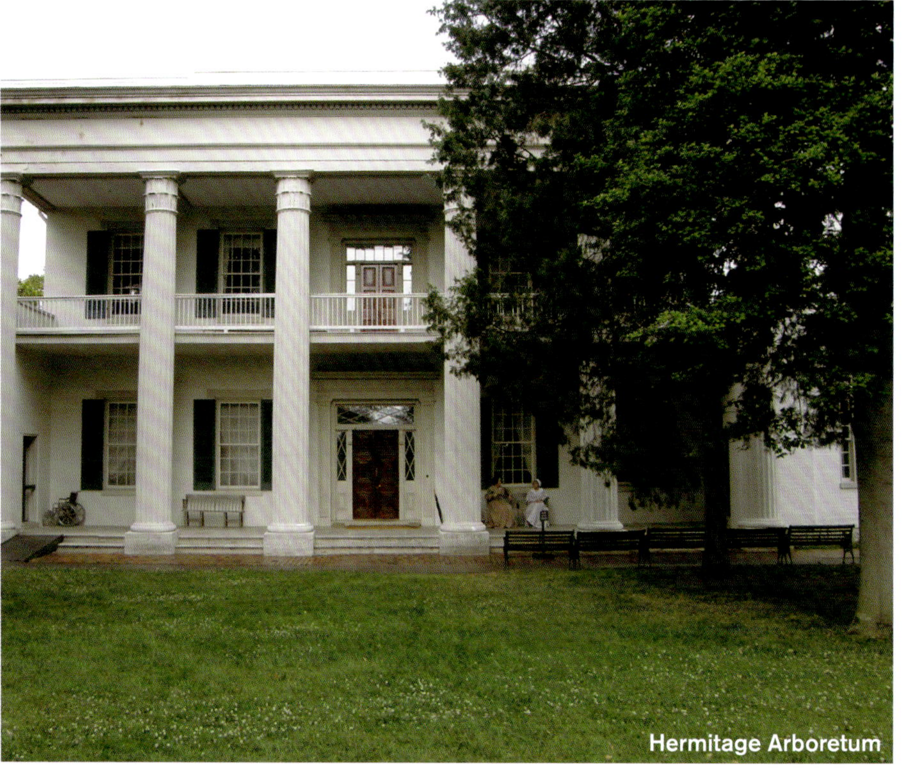
Hermitage Arboretum

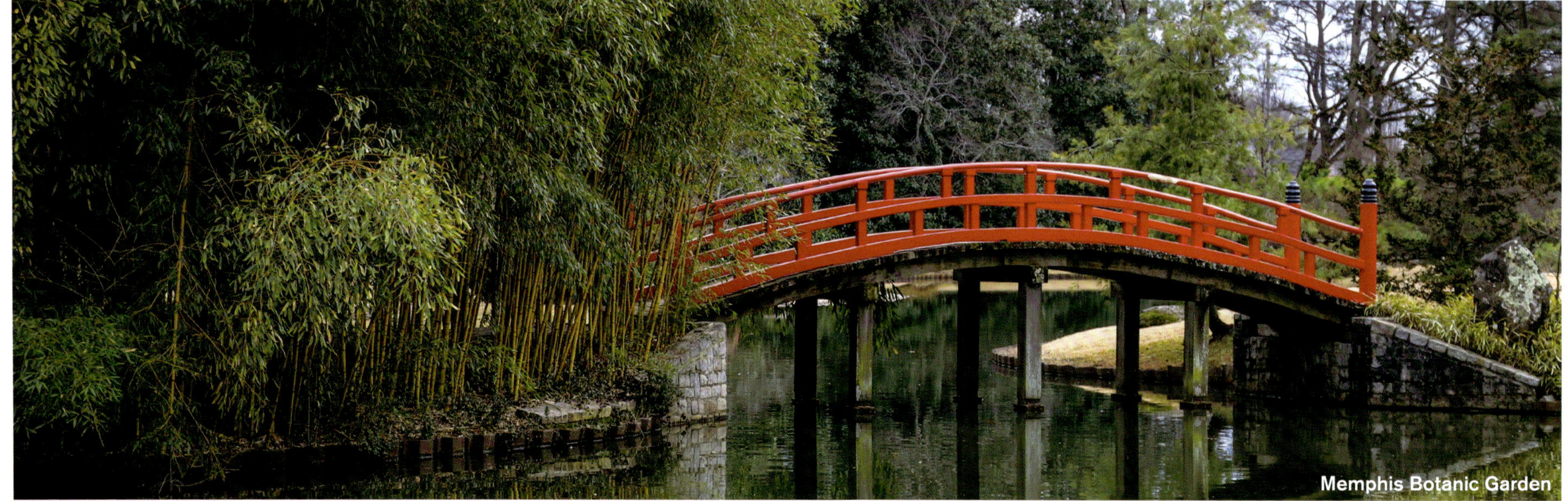
Memphis Botanic Garden

Memphis Botanic Garden
Memphis, Tennessee

Thirty specialty gardens are located on this 96-acre property, which prioritizes education and welcomes 40,000 schoolchildren annually. Gardens include the Urban Home Garden, the Japanese Garden, and, the whimsically named My Big Backyard–a family garden with multiple educational spaces to teach children about gardening, rain, birds, and more.

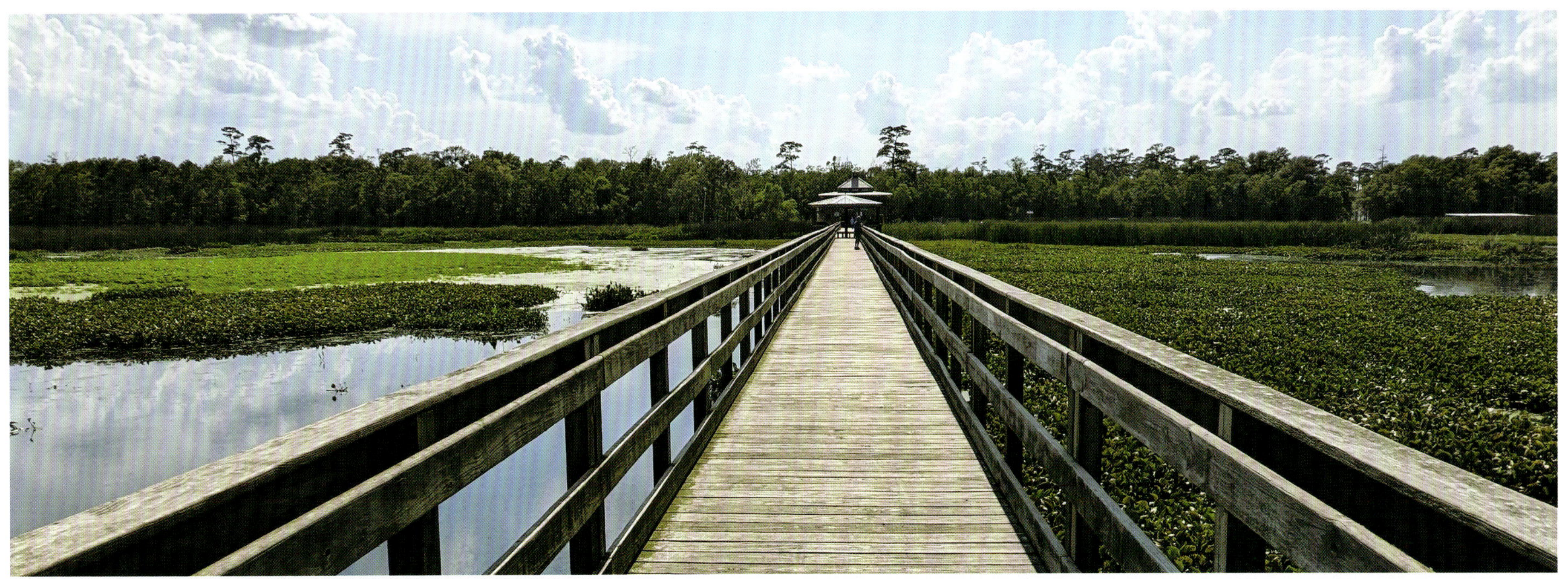

Adjacent to Beaumont Botanical Gardens is the 900-acre Cattail Marsh Nature Area, where visitors may walk along a 520-foot boardwalk and observe the surrounding marsh from viewing platforms.

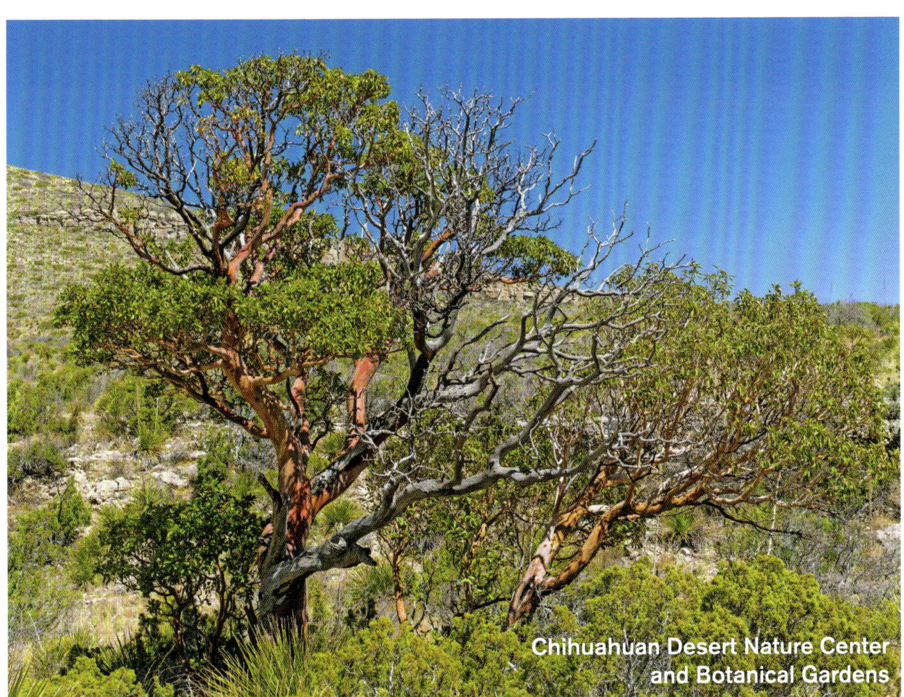

The stout and hardy madrone trees that grow in the region grow on mountainsides, in canyons, and on rocky plains.

Beaumont Botanical Gardens
Beaumont, Texas

Also known as the Tyrrell Park Botanical Gardens, this property occupies 23.5 acres of the 500-acre municipal park. An accessible, paved walkway, known as the "Friendship Walk," connects the themed gardens and landscaped spaces, which include an Antique Rose Garden, Camellia Garden, Native Plant Garden, and Azalea Trail. The site's Garden Center building, with picture-perfect views of the garden and conservatory, is a popular wedding and event venue.

Chihuahuan Desert Nature Center and Botanical Gardens
Fort Davis, Texas

Although it is dry and arid, the Chihuahuan Desert contains a diverse collection of hardy plant species. This botanical garden, located in the middle of the Texas desert, showcases many of these unique specimens. Historic artifacts and ore displays speak to the 507-acre property's past as a mining area, while an exhibit at the visitor's center–located at an elevation of 5,040 feet–explains the region's geological history. Almost five miles of hiking trails wind through the property, leading to some of the largest madrone trees in Texas and to ferns growing in canyon walls. A demonstration greenhouse on the grounds grows 200 species of cacti and succulents.

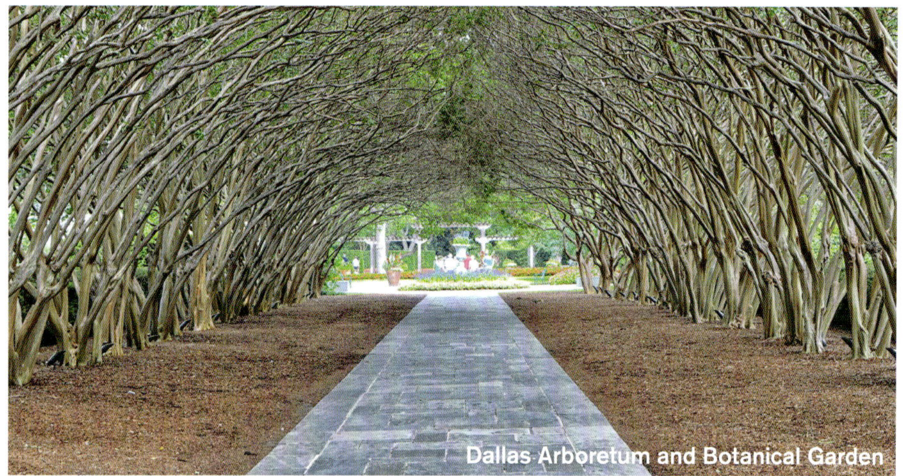
Dallas Arboretum and Botanical Garden

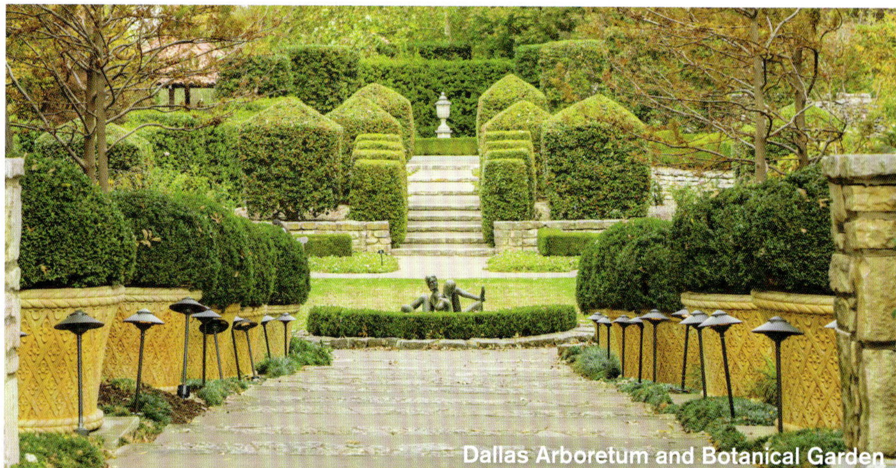
Dallas Arboretum and Botanical Garden

Dallas Arboretum and Botanical Garden
Dallas, Texas

Considered by many to be the crown jewel of Dallas, this botanical garden has been repeatedly named among the best in Texas, the country, and even the world. The property spans 66 acres and contains nearly two dozen individual gardens, including a rose garden, pecan grove, and camellia garden. Signature spaces include A Tasteful Place, a 3.5-acre garden and kitchen that offers cooking demonstrations with freshly grown produce.

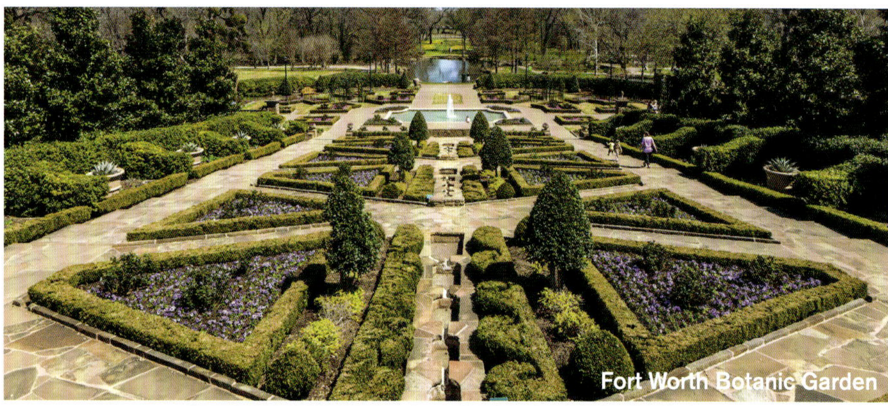
Fort Worth Botanic Garden

A ramp terrace leads down to the Lower Rose Garden.

Fort Worth Botanic Garden
Fort Worth, Texas

Established in 1934 to boost jobs during the Great Depression, this is the oldest major botanical garden in Texas. The 120-acre site contains 23 specialty gardens showcasing more than 2,500 plants. The first garden to be completed on the original site, the Rose Garden, is now on the National Register of Historic Places, and remains one of the most popular areas in the garden.

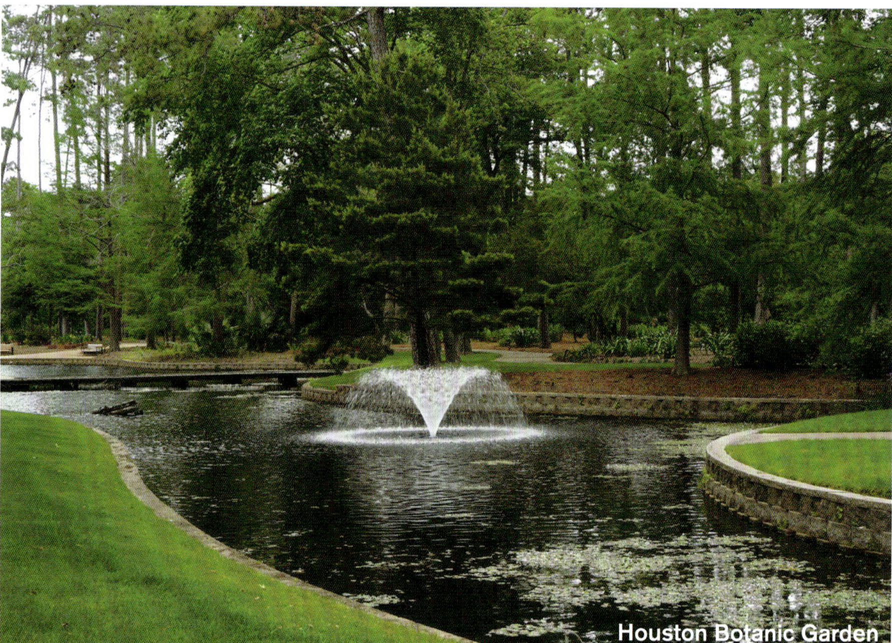
Houston Botanic Garden

Several miles of walking trails run past water features, woodlands, and a nature play area for children.

Houston Botanic Garden
Houston, Texas

This property spans 132 acres on what used to be a municipal golf course. It was converted into a botanical garden in 2020, and now provides visitors with nature-themed art exhibits, educational workshops, and plenty of green space within the city. Highlights include the shady Woodland Glade, a Culinary Garden with edible and medicinal plants, and the Global Collection Garden, featuring tropical and subtropical plants from around the world.

Lady Bird Johnson Wildflower Center
Austin, Texas

As First Lady of the United States from 1963 to 1969, Lady Bird Johnson was known for her passion for the environment, famously leading the charge to pass the Highway Beautification Act. During her time in the White House, Johnson found ways to incorporate her love of flowers into her duties as First Lady, holding dinners in the Rose Garden and choosing a china pattern with a wildflower border.

After she left the White House, Johnson made it her priority to establish a National Wildflower Research Center, which she accomplished in 1982 with the help of actress Helen Hayes. Johnson and Hayes founded the center in Austin, close to the site of the LBJ Presidential Library. In 1997, the center was renamed in honor of the First Lady, who continued raising funds for the facility and advocating for the beautification of natural spaces until her death in 2007.

Today, the Lady Bird Johnson Wildflower Center stands as a tribute to the First Lady and the flowers she loved so much. The Central Gardens are the focal point of the center, containing 650 species of native plants, including the ubiquitous Texas bluebonnet. An arboretum features a variety of Texas oaks, and a family garden provides interactive and educational experiences.

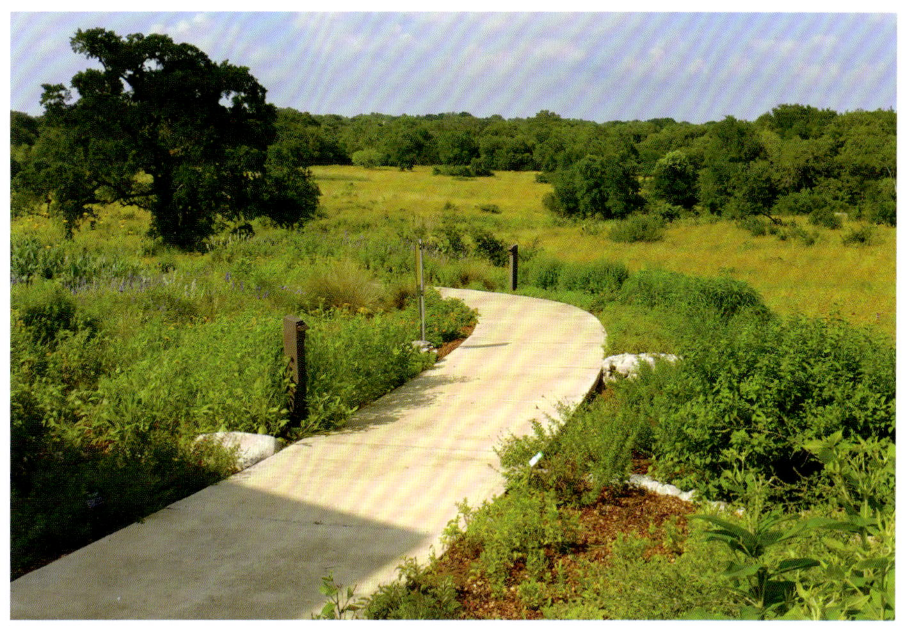

Several miles of trails wind through the Center, including the Arboretum Trail, Roadrunner Trail, Simmons Research Trail, Keli Howell Wagner Woodland Trail, Savanna Meadow Trail, and John Barr Trail.

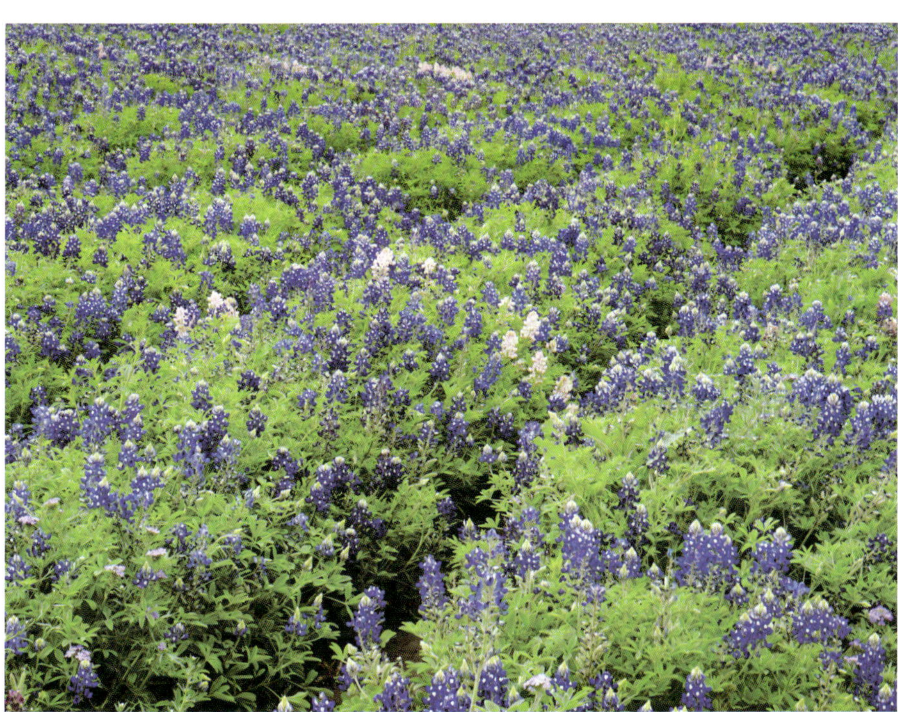

For those who love bluebonnets, the Center delivers plenty!

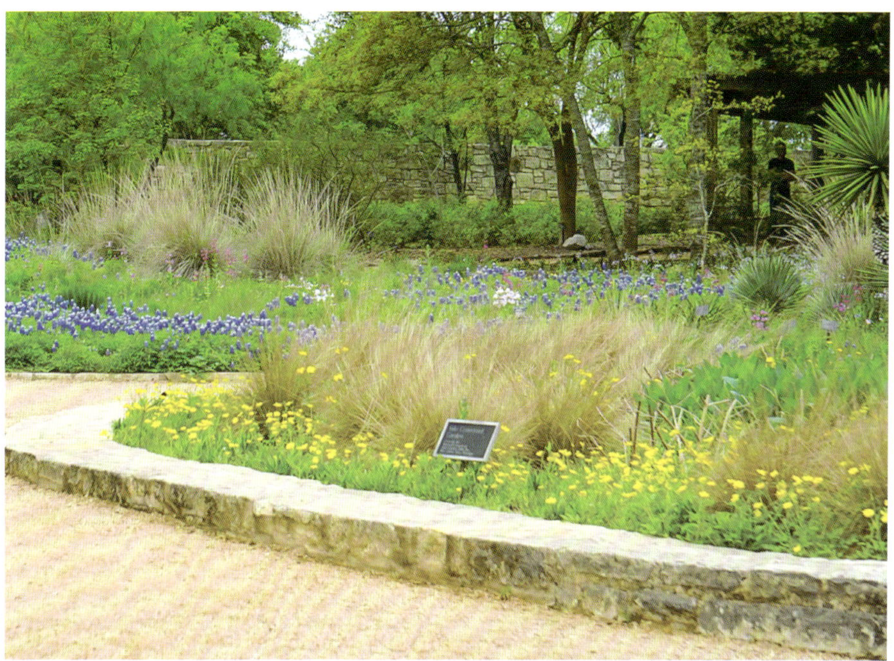

The Center has created the most comprehensive native plant database in the country, and showcases plants and wildflowers especially from the state of Texas.

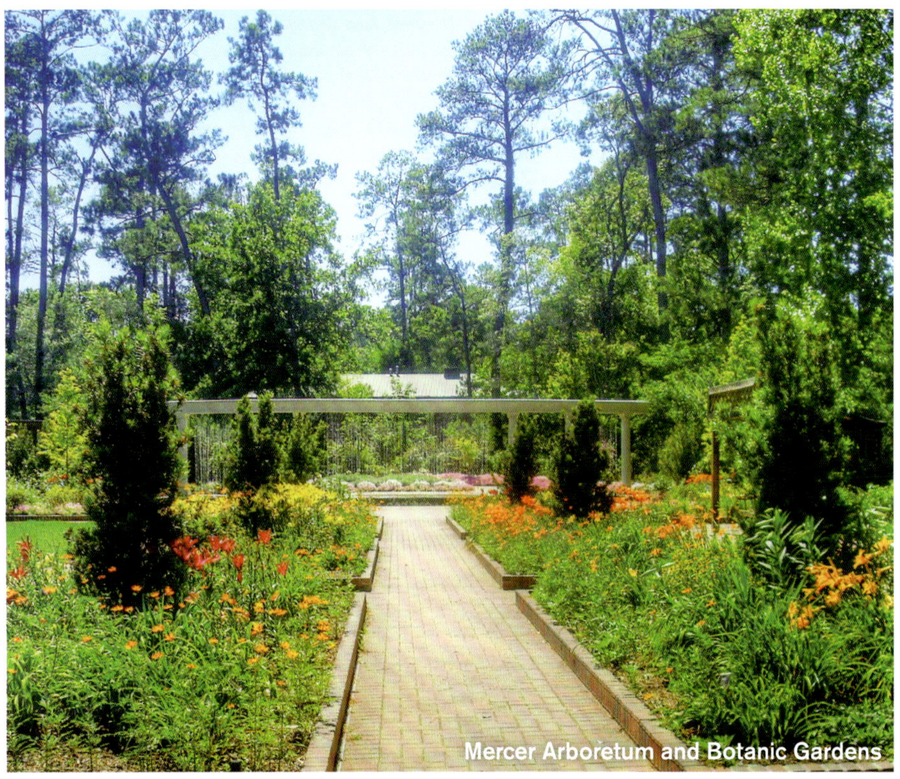
Mercer Arboretum and Botanic Gardens

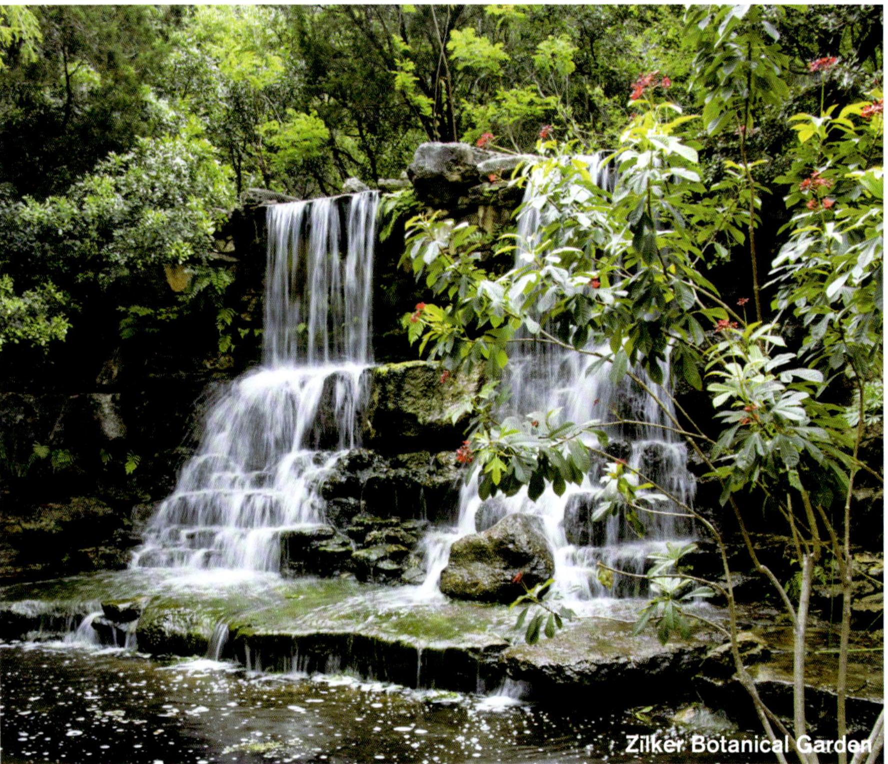
Zilker Botanical Garden

Mercer Arboretum and Botanic Gardens
Humble, Texas

This 250-acre property was once the home of Thelma and Charles Mercer, who sold their land to Harris County for use as a botanical garden. The site now contains the largest collection of native and cultivated plants in the region, including dogwood trees, camellias, orchids, and rare camphor daisies.

San Antonio Botanical Garden
San Antonio, Texas

Established in 1980, this 39-acre garden is considered one of the best in the state, showcasing collections of native Texas plants as well as more than 100 rare and endangered species. Spaces include an authentic Japanese garden, formal and display gardens, and the world-renowned, 90,000-square-foot Lucile Halsell Conservatory.

Shangri La Botanical Gardens and Nature Center
Orange, Texas

A mixture of deciduous forest, wetlands, cypress tupelo swamp, and a lake make up this 252-acre garden, which features more than 300 plant species. Several gardens are arranged according to plant color, shape, or texture, while others are arranged around artistic sculptures. The property is also known for its excellent bird-watching.

South Texas Botanical Gardens and Nature Center
Corpus Christi, Texas

What began in 1987 as a one-acre cottage garden and nature trail is now a 182-acre nature center complete with floral gardens, wetland habitats, and even an exotic parrot collection! Some of the highlights include the Samuel Jones Orchid Conservatory, the Anderson Bromeliad Conservatory, the Rose Garden and Pavilion, and the Plumeria Garden. The grounds also feature a butterfly house, hummingbird garden, and reptile room, where visitors can see iguanas and African spurred tortoises. A mesquite nature trail winds through 30 acres of trees and brush, leading hikers past at least 35 species of woody trees, shrubs, cacti, herbs and grasses.

Zilker Botanical Garden
Austin, Texas

A 28-acre garden that overlooks downtown Austin, this peaceful oasis, set on the banks of the Colorado River, offers a break from the busyness of urban life. The property was established in 1955 on the grounds of the 350-acre Zilker Metropolitan Park, and consists of several unique and independently maintained gardens, including the Cactus and Succulent Garden, the Herb and Fragrance Garden, and the City of Austin's Green Garden. Of particular note is the Isamu Taniguchi Japanese Garden, which was created in 1969. Taniguchi, a retired farmer, worked without a salary to build the garden as a symbol of peace and as a gift to the city of Austin.

Brigham Young University Arboretum
Provo, Utah

Also known as the Bertrand F. Harrison Arboretum in honor of a retired BYU botany professor, this university arboretum contains native plants from the eastern and western regions of the country. Around 14,000 trees, representing 900 species, are found throughout the grounds, including American elm, dawn redwood, and saucer magnolia.

International Peace Gardens
Salt Lake City, Utah

Ironically, World War II interrupted the construction of this garden dedicated to peace, which was founded in 1939 but not opened until 1952. Almost 30 countries, from the Americas, Europe, Africa, and Asia, are represented in the garden, which is divided into sections that are individually designed and maintained.

Conservation Garden Park
West Jordan, Utah

With an emphasis on eco-friendly techniques and conservation practices, this six-acre garden makes the most of its location in the high mountain desert. The park shows visitors a variety of plantings and garden designs that are possible in Utah's arid climate, giving residents of the country's second-driest state plenty of inspiration.

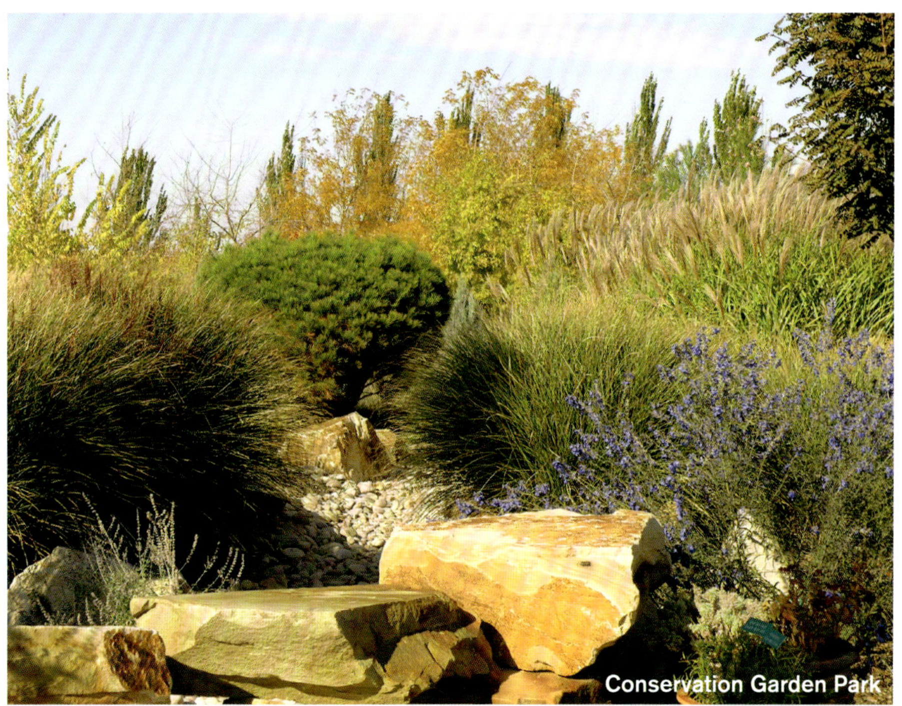

Conservation Garden Park

Careful layering results in a lush-appearing landscape in an otherwise dry environment.

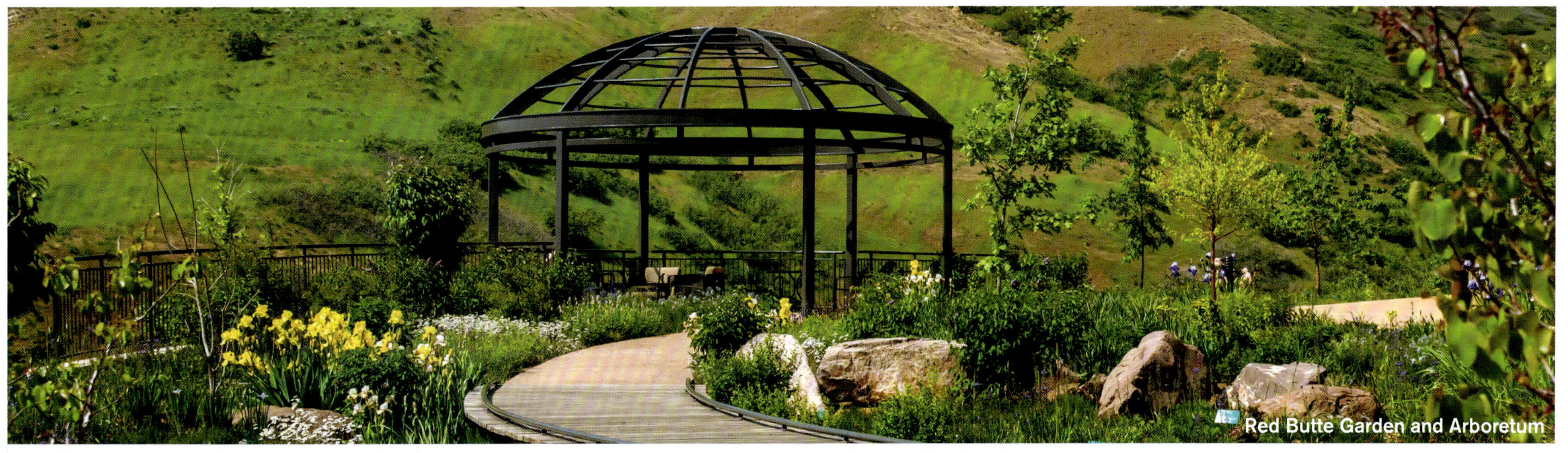

Red Butte Garden and Arboretum

The site is framed by the foothills of the Wasatch Range.

Red Butte Garden and Arboretum
Salt Lake City, Utah

This 100-acre garden is one of the largest in the region, showcasing 2,000 trees and a stunning 590,000 blooming bulbs every spring. Themed gardens include the Four Seasons Garden, with ornamental grasses, conifers, daffodils, and crabapples, and the Burton Fragrance Garden, featuring hyacinth, lavender, roses, and chrysanthemums.

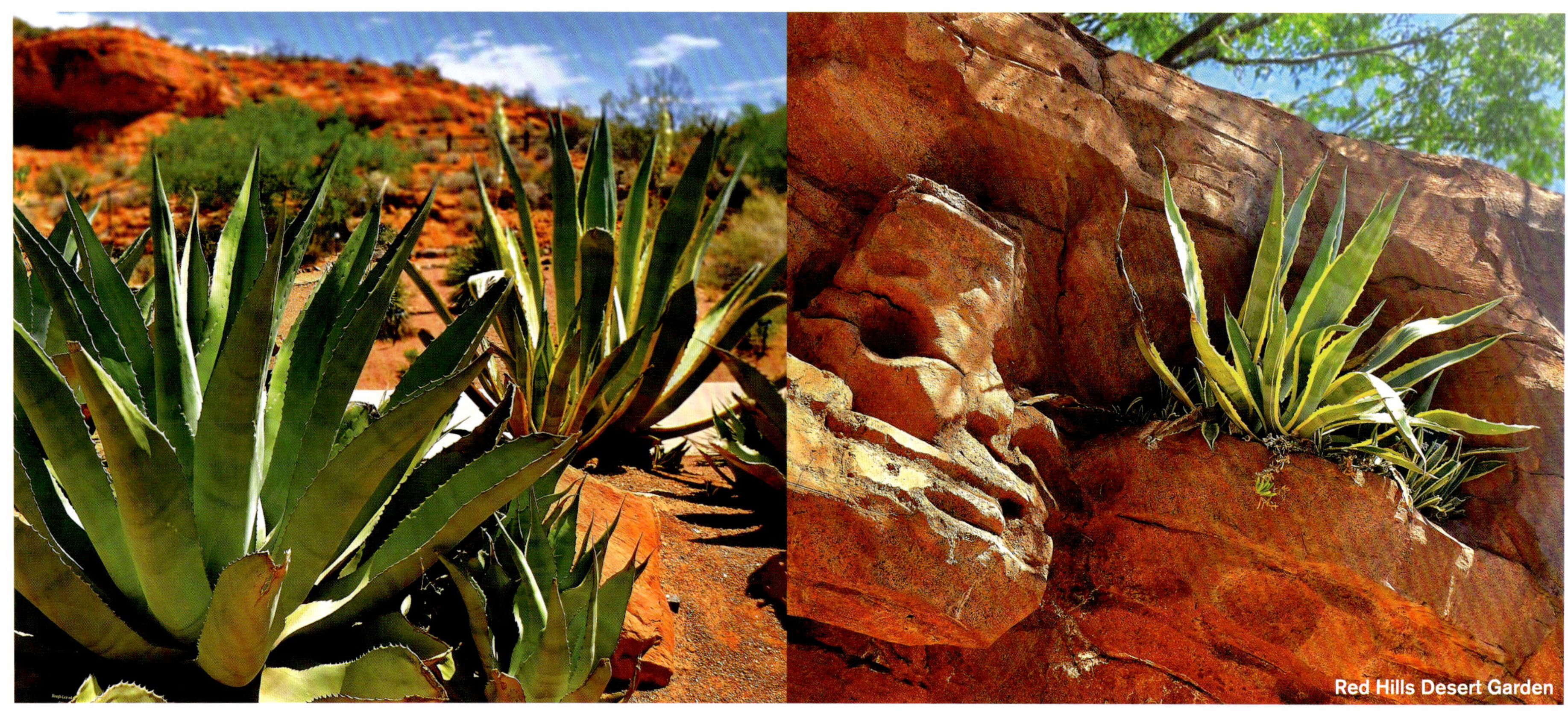

Amazing and resilient, the desert plants cultivated here seem to be able to survive the harshest conditions.

Red Hills Desert Garden
St. George, Utah

Spanning five acres of arid terrain, this property is Utah's first desert conservation garden, demonstrating the hardiness of desert plants. The garden is curated by the Washington County Water Conservancy District, which aims to teach visitors about the importance of smart water usage. More than 5,000 plants are found on the site, from succulents and cacti to trees and flowering shrubs, all of which thrive in the harsh conditions of the desert climate. The grounds are also home to a stream stocked with native and endangered fish species, as well as sets of dinosaur tracks that date back 200 million years.

Robert L. Shepherd Desert Arboretum
Santa Clara, Utah

This arboretum, also known as the Santa Clara City Arboretum, is named after the local artist who established it in the early 1980s. The property consists of desert park, wetlands, a wildlife sanctuary, and ancient lava rocks, with a continually changing topography due to floods, fires, and other natural events. Some of these setbacks have yet to be overcome, and the arboretum continues to undergo restoration.

Utah Botanical Center
Kaysville, Utah

Offering classes and informative programs for both children and adults, this property on the campus of Utah State University prioritizes education and research. Highlights at the center include an arboretum with more than 300 trees and shrubs, plus an Edible Demonstration Garden, a Pollinator Garden, and several more specialty gardens.

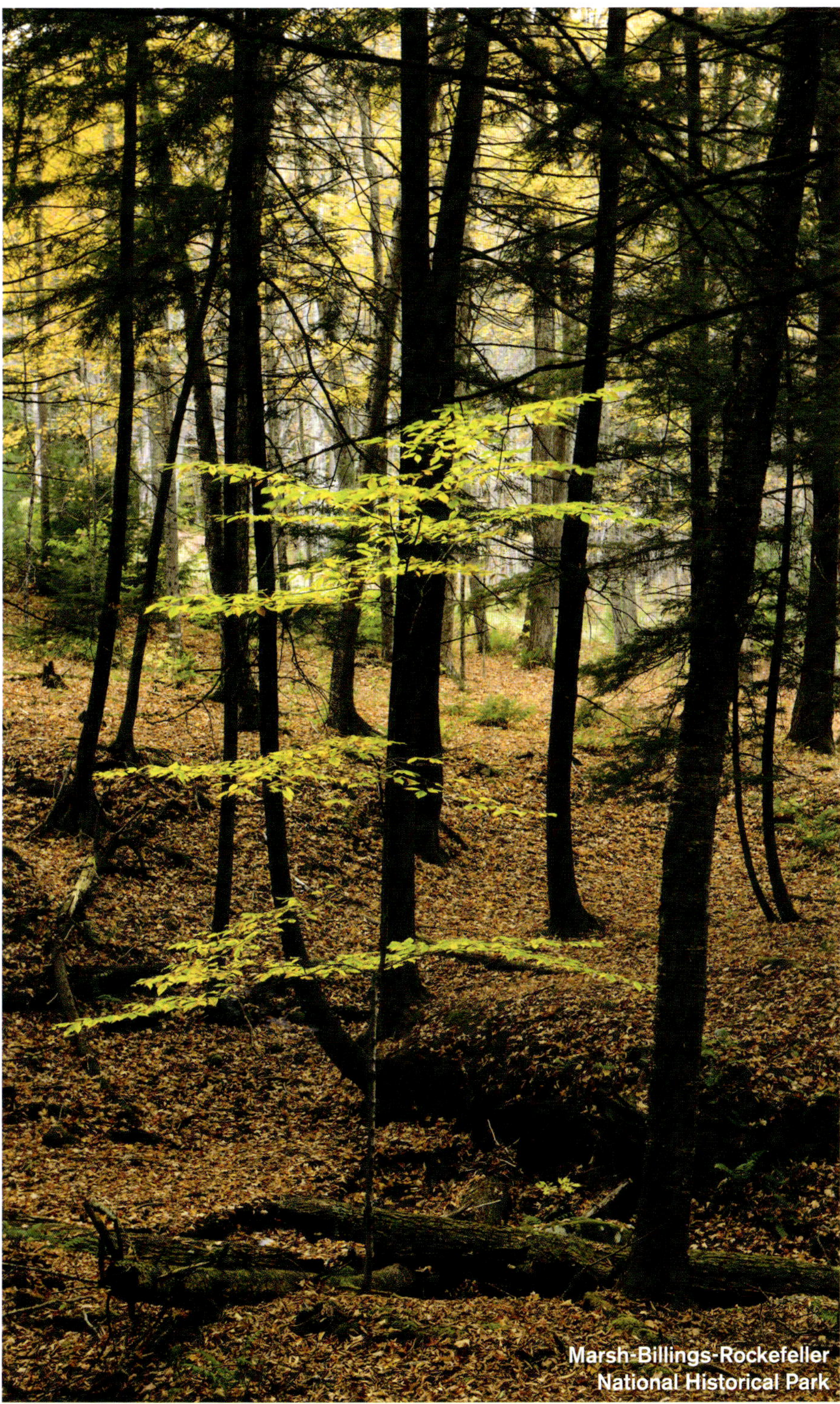

The site includes peaceful Vermont woods and over 20 miles of trails.

Marsh-Billings-Rockefeller National Historical Park
Woodstock, Vermont

George Perkins Marsh, who was appointed by Abraham Lincoln to be the first U.S. ambassador to Italy, is considered by some to also be America's first environmentalist. The diplomat recognized the impact humans can have on the natural world long before "eco-friendly" became an everyday term. So, it is fitting that his boyhood home, built in 1805, is now the centerpiece of this National Historical Park. The 550-acre estate, which was later occupied by Frederick Billings and then his granddaughter Mary French Rockefeller, was given to the people of the United States by the Rockefellers in 1992. Today, the property protects the woodlands and natural landscapes surrounding the home, including a large collection of ferns and an apple orchard.

Cady's Falls Botanical Garden
Morrisville, Vermont

For decades, this property was a nursery that cultivated trees, shrubs, and perennials for home gardeners. But in 2021, the site's owners pivoted to a botanical garden, showcasing their lush collection of plants to the public. More than 1,400 species are grown here, including unique specimens like trilliums, pitcher plants, and dwarf conifers.

Vermont Experimental Cold Hardy Cactus Garden
Middlebury, Vermont

When we think of cacti, we usually associate them with arid deserts and hot temperatures. But this small, unique garden, which is found at a private home and is only 100 square feet in size, demonstrates how hardy cold-weather cacti and succulents can be. While the public is welcome, visitors must call ahead to view the garden.

Worth Exploring in Virginia

Boxerwood Gardens
Lexington, Virginia

- Established in 1952, and listed on the National Register of Historic Places in 2015
- Features 1,300 varieties of trees and shrubs on 15 acres

Joseph Bryan Park Azalea Garden
Richmond, Virginia

- Occupies 17 acres within the 262-acre city park
- Contains more than 450,000 azalea plants, which bloom between April and May

Green Spring Gardens
Alexandria, Virginia

- Home to more than 20 themed demonstration gardens
- Also contains a greenhouse, horticultural reference library, and historic house

Hahn Horticulture Garden
Blacksburg, Virginia

- Spans seven acres on the campus of Virginia Tech
- Highlights include the Trident Maple Allee and the Conifer Display

River Farm
Alexandria, Virginia

- The headquarters of the American Horticultural Society
- A 25-acre site containing a manor house, formal and informal gardens, and woodlands

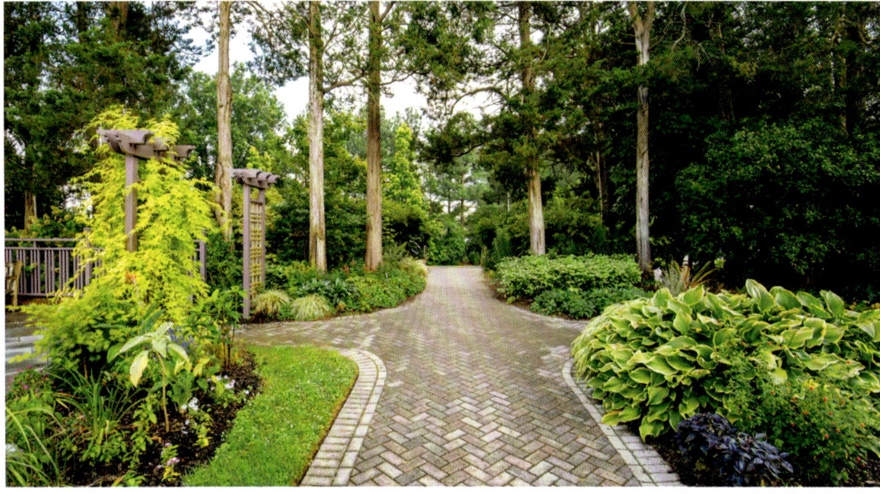

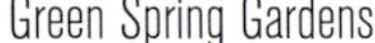
Green Spring Gardens.

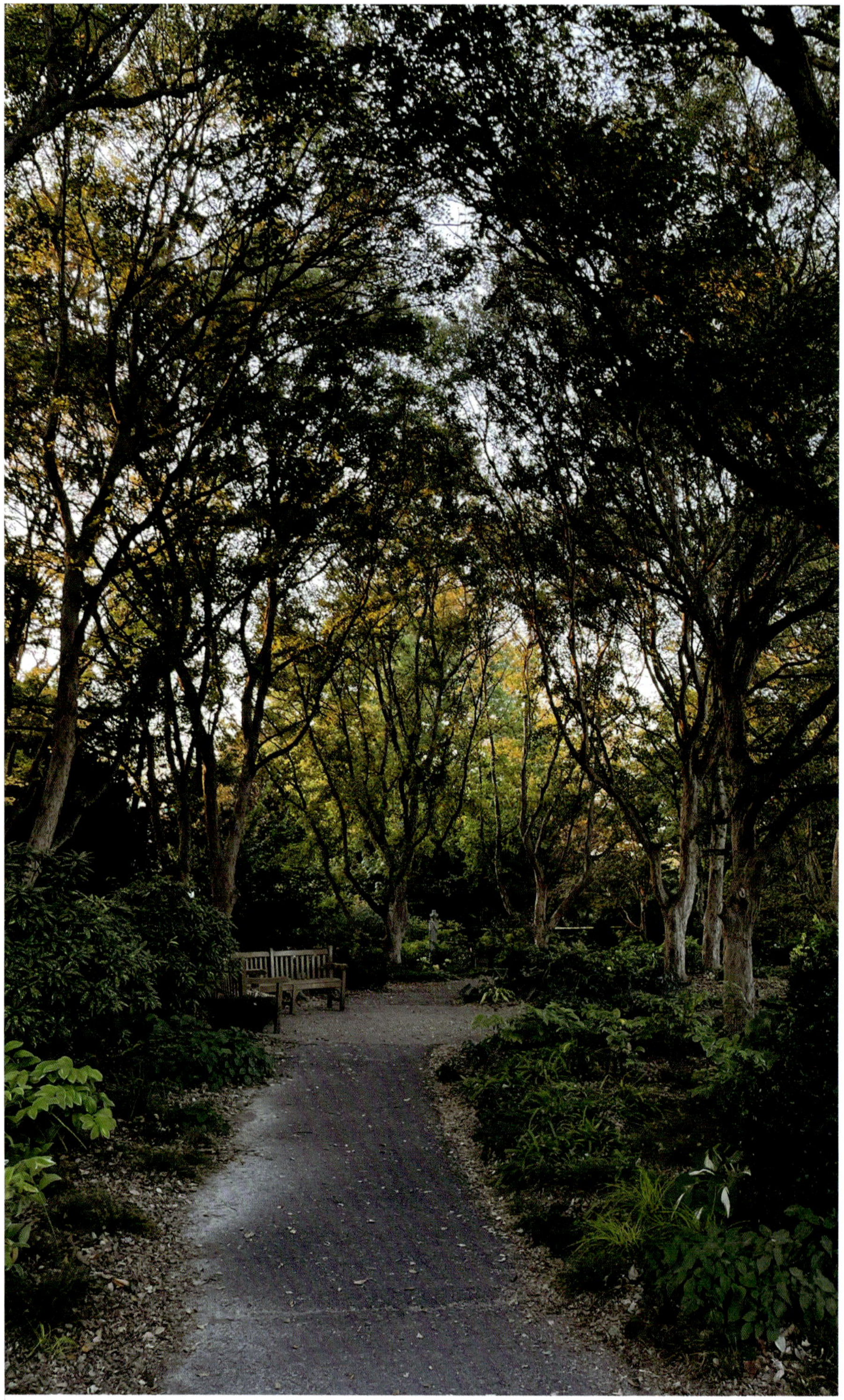

Hahn Horticulture Garden.

Lewis Ginter Botanical Garden
Richmond, Virginia

This 50-acre botanical garden has repeatedly earned high accolades from the public, the Travel Channel, and publications including *USA Today, Condé Nast Traveler,* and *Better Homes and Gardens*, often being named among the top ten botanical gardens in the country. The land it now occupies was once owned by Virginia Governor Patrick Henry–of "Give me liberty or give me death!" fame–and later purchased by its namesake, businessman and real estate developer Lewis Ginter.

The property was passed along to Ginter's niece, Grace Arents, who willed the land to the city of Richmond with the stipulation that it be transformed into a botanical garden. After decades of planning, the Lewis Ginter Botanical Garden officially opened in 1984. Today, the grounds are home to more than a dozen themed gardens, plus a classical domed conservatory, the only one of its kind in the mid-Atlantic region.

Popular gardens include the Cherry Tree Walk, which bursts with pink blossoms every spring, and the Grace Arents Garden, a Victorian-style garden which was originally tended by Grace herself and has been restored to its original early 1900s glory. The garden is also famous for its yearly GardenFest of Lights–a visitor-favorite holiday event.

Millions of lights twinkle after dark during GardenFest of Lights.

The Klaus Family Tree House in the Children's Garden offers kids opportunities for adventurous play and exploration.

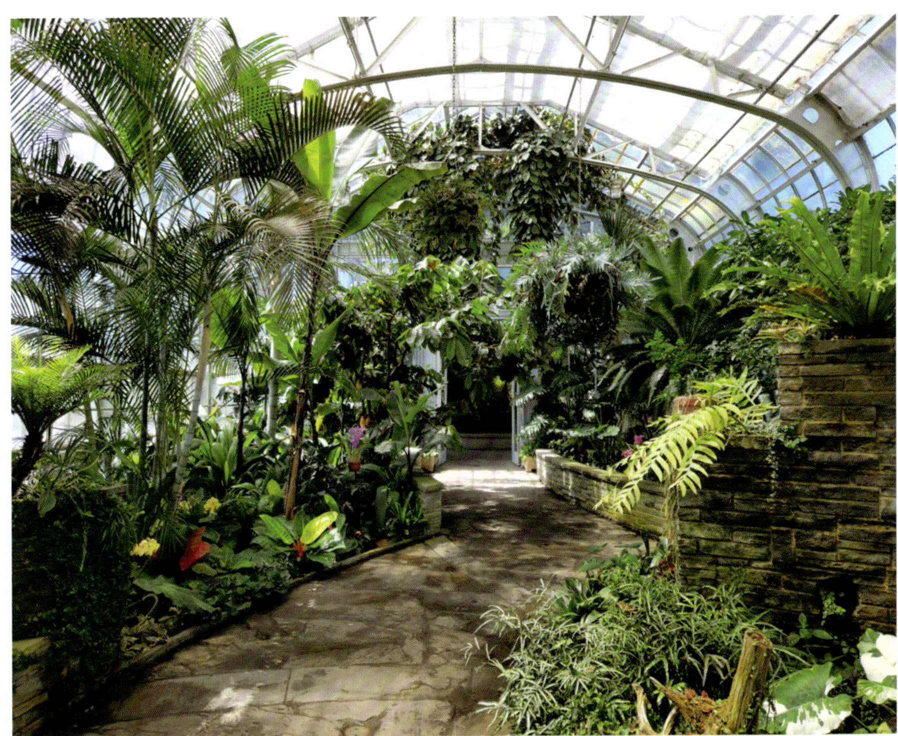

The 11,000-square-foot Conservatory includes exotic plants from around the world.

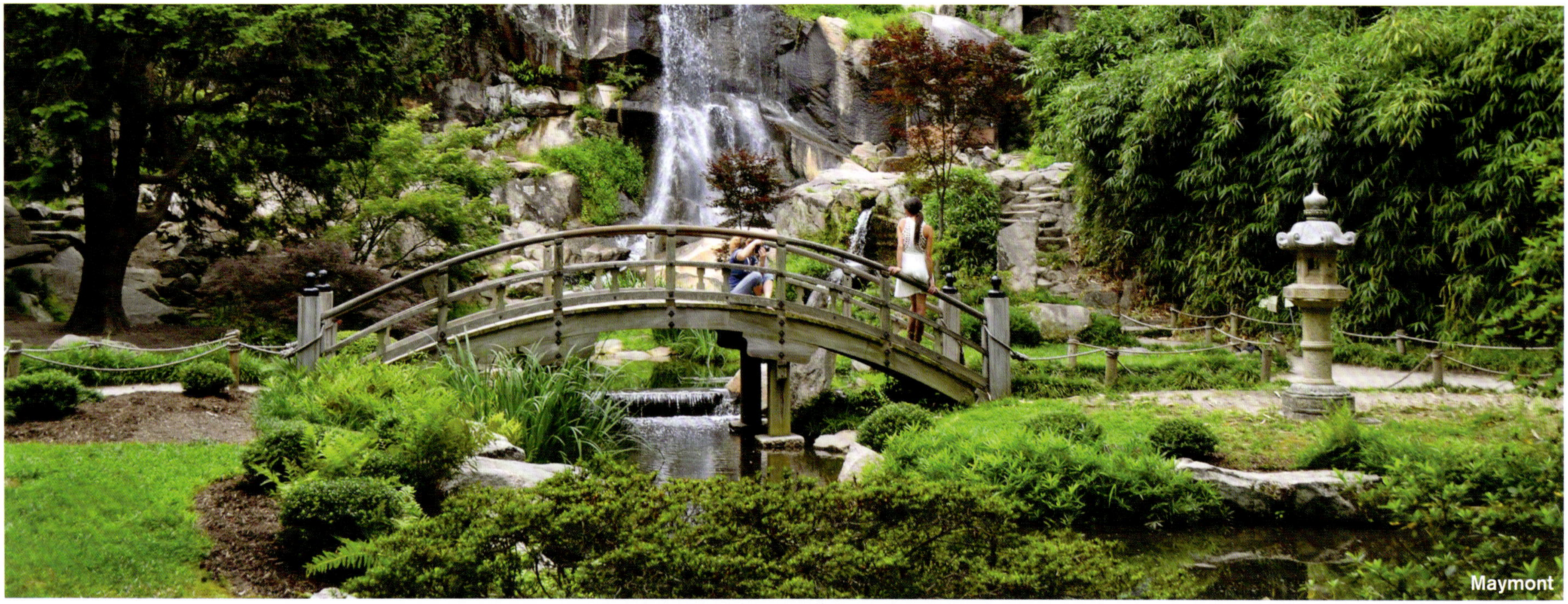

Maymont

The Japanese garden features a koi pond and large waterfall.

Maymont
Richmond, Virginia

A striking Gilded Age mansion serves as the focal point of this 100-acre property, which also contains gardens, a nature center, and an animal habitat. The house was opened as a museum in 1925, and some of its manicured gardens date back more than 100 years. These include both the artful Italian Garden and the naturalistic Japanese garden–the oldest on the East Coast–which were established in 1911.

National Botanic Garden
Chantilly, Virginia

A dragon's spine made of stone, a medieval-style castle, and a tiny village called Hobbit Town are just a few of the whimsical details found on the grounds of this unique site. The garden is the largest constructed garden in the world, its materials equaling the Hoover Dam in volume, much of it reclaimed wood, concrete, and bricks. The property is the work of Peter and Beata Knop, who had sustainability, water conservation and eco-friendly practices in mind when they created the space. The site contains America's largest bamboo garden, numerous artificial lakes, and the east coast's largest xeric garden, as well as a bald cypress arboretum and flowering plant collections.

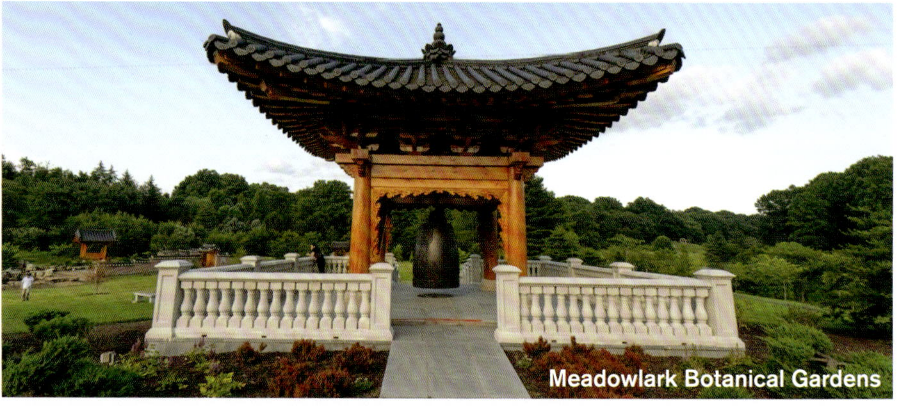

The Korean Bell Garden features a massive Bell of Peace and Harmony.

Meadowlark Botanical Gardens
Vienna, Virginia

This 95-acre botanical garden contains more than 20 varieties of cherry trees, an herb garden, a butterfly garden, a Korean Bell Garden, and collections of ferns, azaleas, hostas, and perennials. But it is perhaps best known for protecting and preserving native Virginia plants and trees. The grounds feature a Potomac Valley Collection of plants, the Virginia Native Tree Trail, and the Virginia Native Wetland collection.

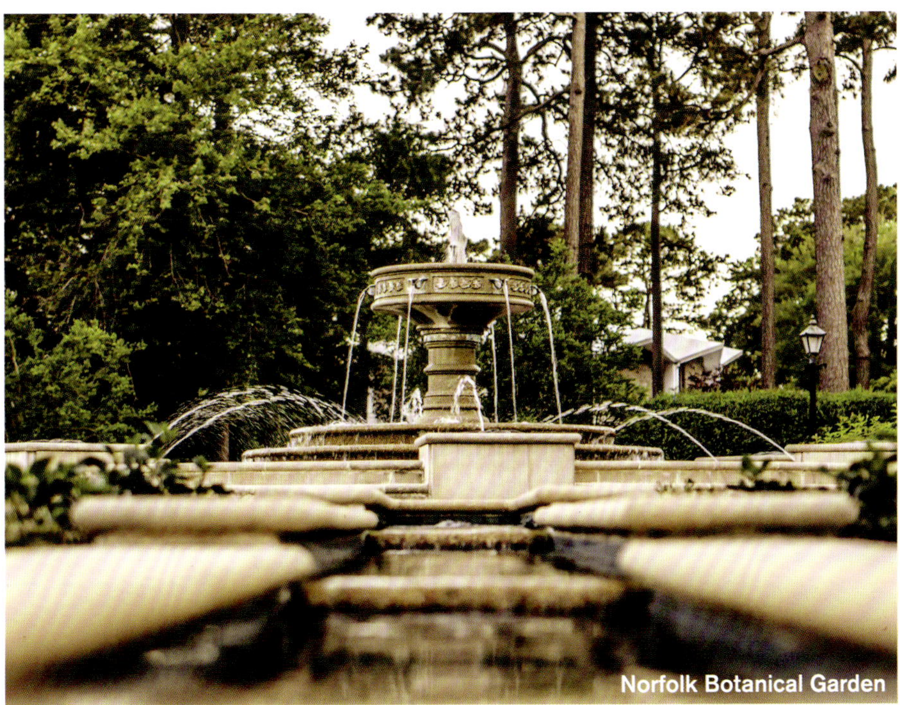

A fountain, sculpture, and terraced canals are the main attraction of the Perennial Garden.

Norfolk Botanical Garden

Norfolk, Virginia

Spanning 158 acres, this property is Virginia's largest botanical garden, containing more than 60 unique spaces for visitors to explore. Gardens are arranged by season, including everything from a springtime Rhododendron Garden to a winter Holly Garden, offering nature lovers a year-round botanical experience. The site also includes the World of Wonders (or WOW) Children's Garden, with enriching educational activities appealing to all ages.

Williamsburg Botanical Garden

Williamsburg, Virginia

This relatively young botanical garden, established in 2006, is located in the quintessentially historical town of Williamsburg, where well-preserved architecture, colonial buildings, and museums speak to our nation's past. In keeping with this theme, this two-acre garden features plants and flowers that are native to the Virginia Coastal Plain, which were no doubt thriving in the region even as America was founded.

Williamsburg Botanical Garden

The garden has plenty of local plants to attract local pollinators, like this male fiery skipper.

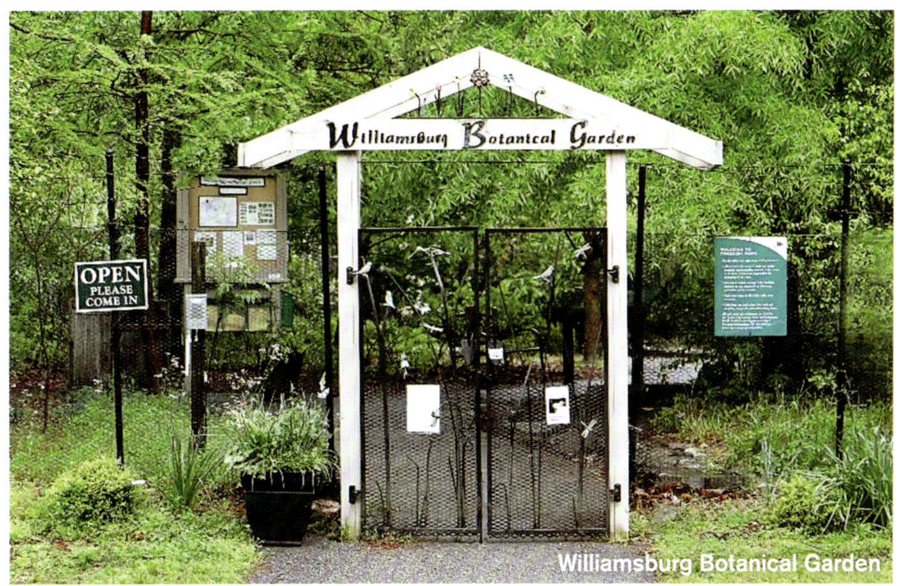

Eighteen different habitats are represented on the grounds, including native grasses, pine woodlands, and wetlands. Highlights include a Shade Garden with Virginia bluebells and summer snowflakes, and the Fall and Winter Border Garden featuring colorful bluebeard and sweet coneflower.

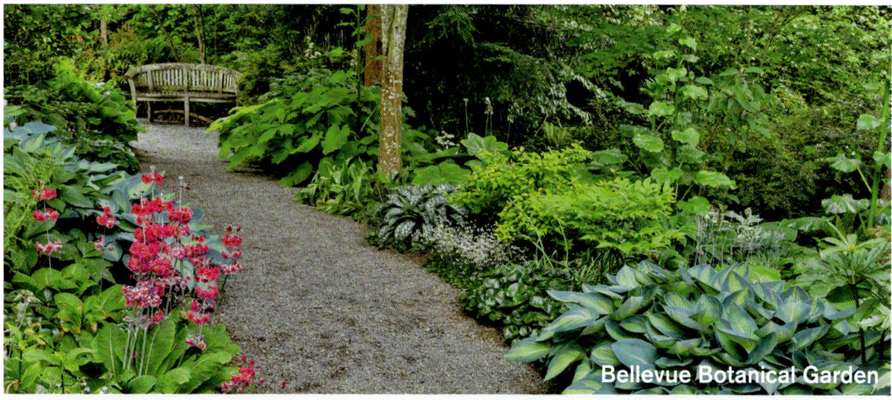

Visitors may discover garden sections via several miles of artfully winding trails, or take docent-led tours.

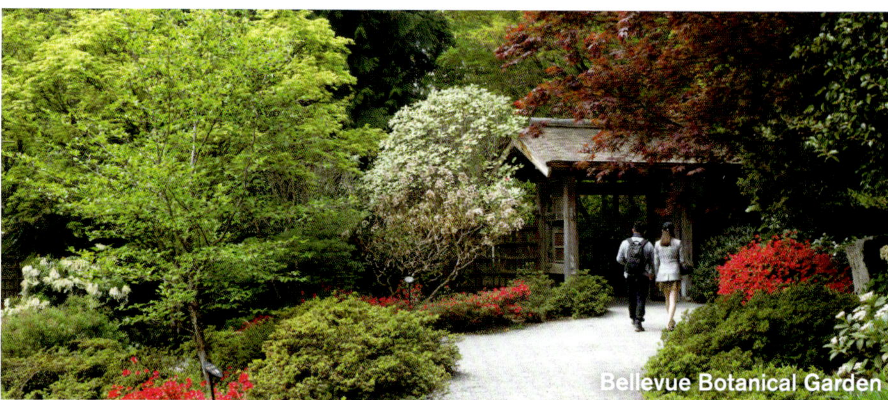

Bellevue's Yao Garden is filled with plants from Japan and the Pacific Rim, along with species from the Pacific Northwest.

Bellevue Botanical Garden
Bellevue, Washington

What began as a modest 7.5-acre plot of land donated to the city of Bellevue in 1981 has since grown to a popular 53-acre botanical garden that attracts 450,000 visitors a year. The land was originally purchased by Cal and Harriet Shorts in 1946, who, when bequeathing their land to the city, requested that it one day be used as a public space. Today, the Shorts' house has been converted to the garden's Visitor Center, and the gardens that they once maintained have been meticulously restored and expanded. Popular spaces include the Perennial Border–the largest public perennial garden in the country–and the Native Discovery Garden, showcasing native Pacific Northwest plants.

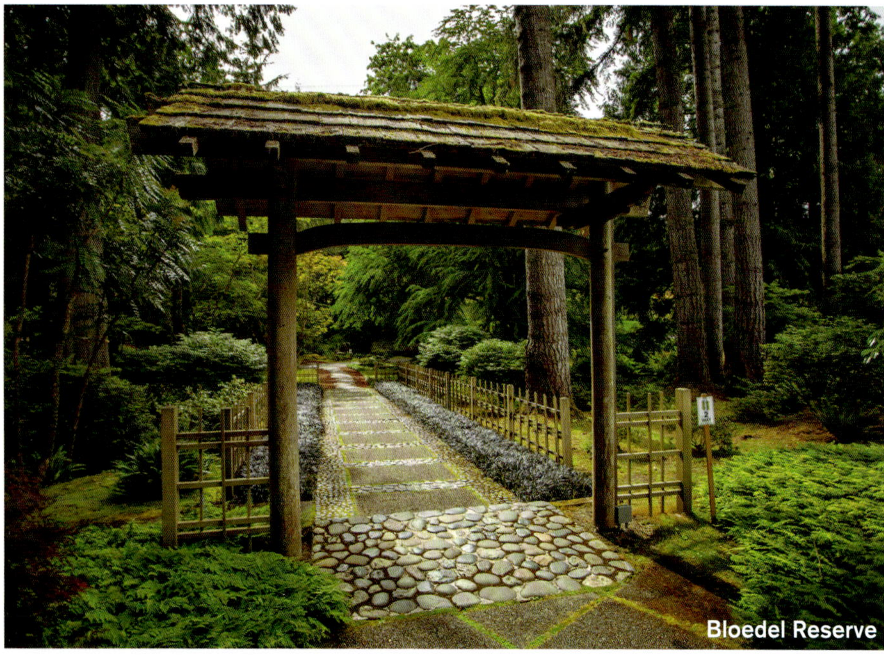

The gate at the entrance to the Japanese Gardens is known as a *mon*, and is typical of such gardens.

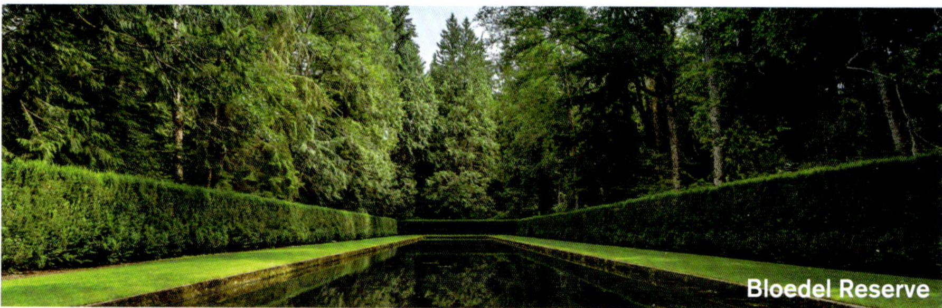

The site features a pleasing array of both organic design and artful symmetry.

Bloedel Reserve
Bainbridge Island, Washington

For more than 30 years, the land on which this garden sits was the home of Virginia and Prentice Bloedel, a couple who were passionate about nature and the environment. Today, this 140-acre garden and forest preserve stands as a tribute to the Bloedels' love of the natural world. The property contains immersive, connected gardens that allow visitors to seamlessly wander from one space to another. A Trestle Bridge and Boardwalk carves a graceful, curving path through forests and bogs, a Japanese Garden is perfect for peaceful reflection, and the visitor-favorite Rhododendron Glen is alive with blooms in the spring and summer.

Bonhoeffer Botanical Gardens
Stanwood, Washington

Part of the Pilchuck Learning Center, which strives to preserve the beauty of the Pacific Northwest, this garden is the only one in the region that exclusively showcases native plants. Almost a mile of accessible paths wind through the property, where visitors can see Oregon oak trees, conifers, Indian plum, and hundreds of other species.

Carl S. English Jr. Botanical Garden
Seattle, Washington

In 1931, U.S. Army Corps of Engineers botanist Carl S. English Jr. transformed this seven-acre plot of land–left barren after the construction of the Ballard Locks–into a lush botanical garden. Today, more than 1,500 varieties of plants from around the world thrive here, including displays of roses, lilies, and fuchsias.

John A. Finch Arboretum
Spokane, Washington

This arboretum, which spans more than 56 acres, was established in 1949 along the scenic Garden Springs Creek. The property contains at least 2,000 trees and shrubs, including collections of lilacs, rhododendrons, and conifers, and is home to the Touch and See Trail, which features braille signs for the visually impaired.

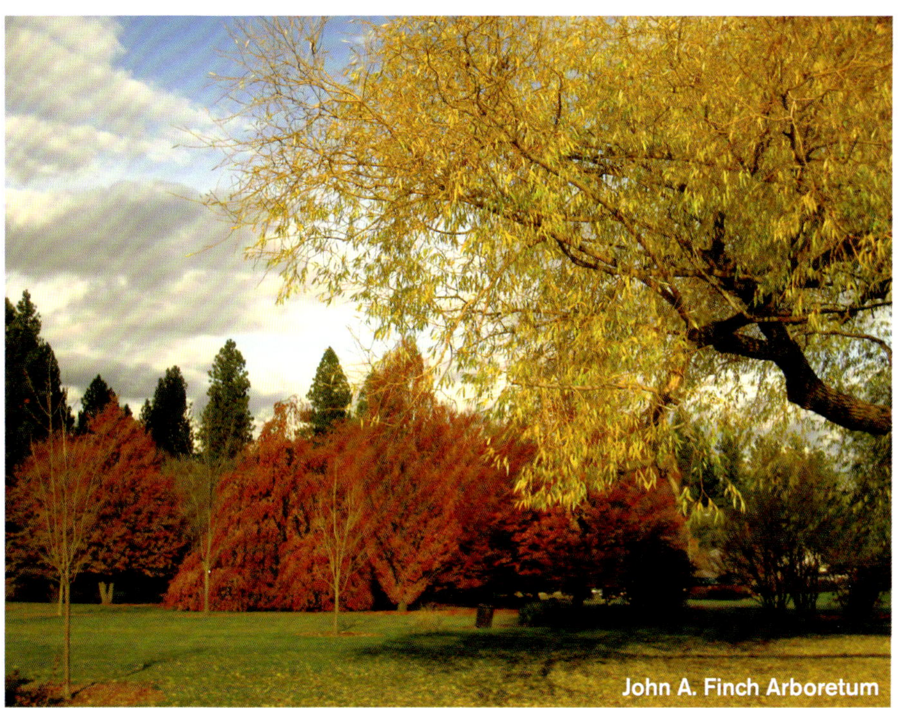

John A. Finch Arboretum

Autumn splendor at the arboretum.

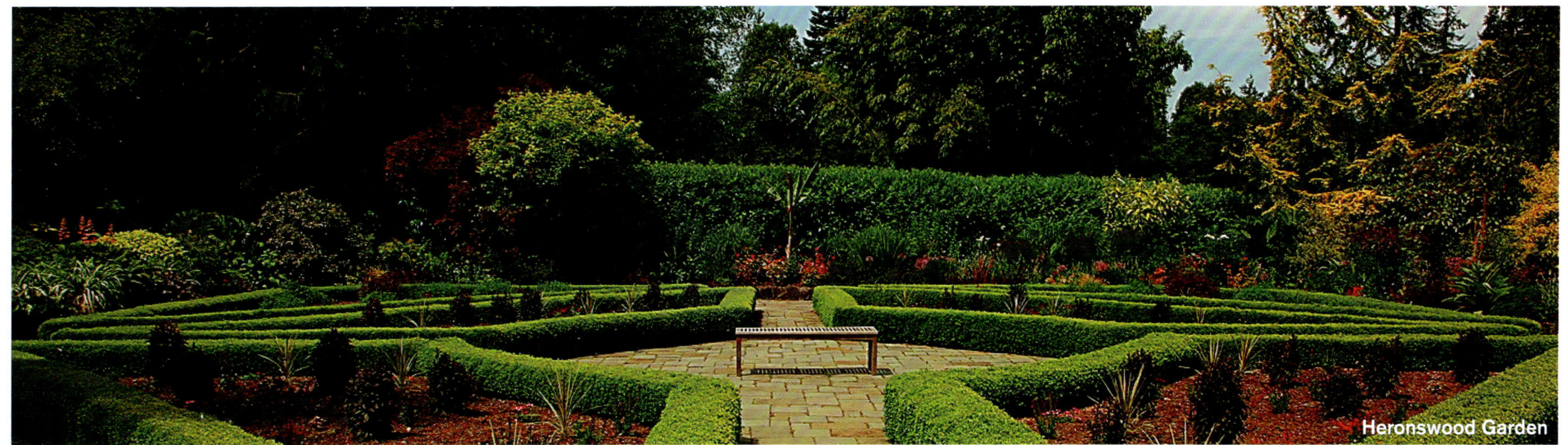

Heronswood Garden

The Formal Gardens were one of the first sections to be established at Heronswood. Other sections include the Renaissance Garden, Rock Garden, Traveler's Garden, and Woodland Garden.

Heronswood Garden
Kingston, Washington

Established in 1987, this 15-acre garden was purchased by the Port Gamble S'Klallam Tribe–descendants of the Salish people–in 2012. The garden features 8,000 varieties of plants, including significant collections of conifers, buttercups, hydrangeas, and ferns, and also seeks to showcase tribal culture with the S'Klallam Connections Garden.

Highline SeaTac Botanical Garden

The Paradise Garden section features a stream flowing into a 7,000-gallon pond.

Manito Park and Botanical Gardens

The three-acre Duncan Garden follows the rules of a classical European Renaissance garden.

Highline SeaTac Botanical Garden
SeaTac, Washington

The expansion of the Seattle-Tacoma International Airport led to the creation of this garden, which began as two private gardens: The Elda Behm Paradise Garden and the Seike Family Japanese Garden. The two gardens were relocated and combined, and now cover a total of 10.5 acres and display more than a million plants, flowers, and shrubs.

Hulda Klager Lilac Gardens
Woodland, Washington

As its name makes clear, this seven-acre garden specializes in fragrant lilacs. It was named after its founder, Hulda Klager, who began hybridizing lilacs in 1905 and displaying them for the public in 1920. The popular "Lilac Days," a celebration of the blooming flowers, occurs every spring.

Kruckeberg Botanic Garden
Shoreline, Washington

This four-acre property was established in 1958 by University of Washington botany professor Arthur Rice Kruckeberg, who grew nearly every plant in the garden from a seed or cutting. The garden now contains native species as well as exotic varieties from China and Japan, and features four State Champion trees.

Manito Park and Botanical Gardens
Spokane, Washington

Containing 78 acres of native and cultivated landscape plus 20 acres of botanical gardens, this park is one of Spokane's crown jewels. Six themed gardens are located on the site, including the Renaissance-style Duncan Garden, Rose Hill, and the Lilac Garden. The grounds are also home to the Gaiser Conservatory, featuring tropical and desert plants.

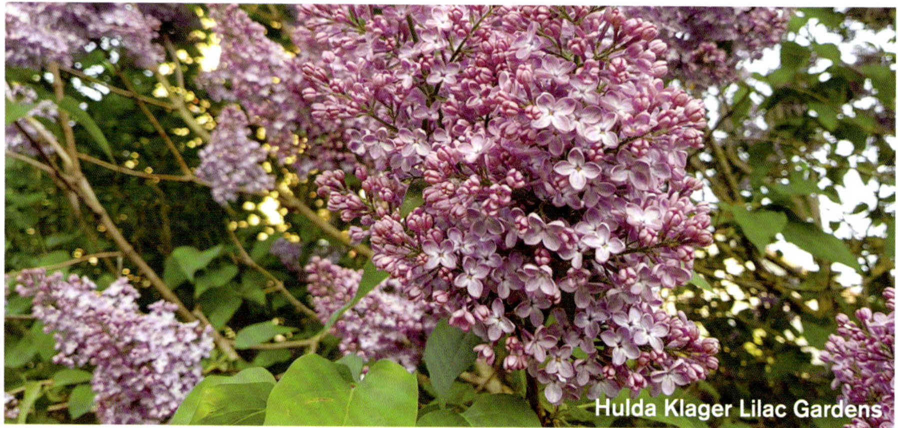

More than 90 varieties of lilacs are grown on the site.

Meerkerk Rhododendron Gardens
Greenbank, Washington

Offering much more than just rhododendrons, this property consists of ten acres of display gardens and 43 acres of woodlands. Two miles of trails allow visitors to wander the grounds, which contain azaleas, Mount Fuji cherry trees, tulip magnolias, and a giant sequoia tree in addition to the vibrant rhododendrons.

Rhododendron Species Foundation and Botanical Garden
Federal Way, Washington

It comes as no surprise that this garden, founded by the Rhododendron Species Foundation in 1974, contains the largest collection of rhododendron species in the world, including more than 300 tropical varieties known as vireyas. But the site is also home to Himalayan blue poppies, camellias, magnolias, and rare plants.

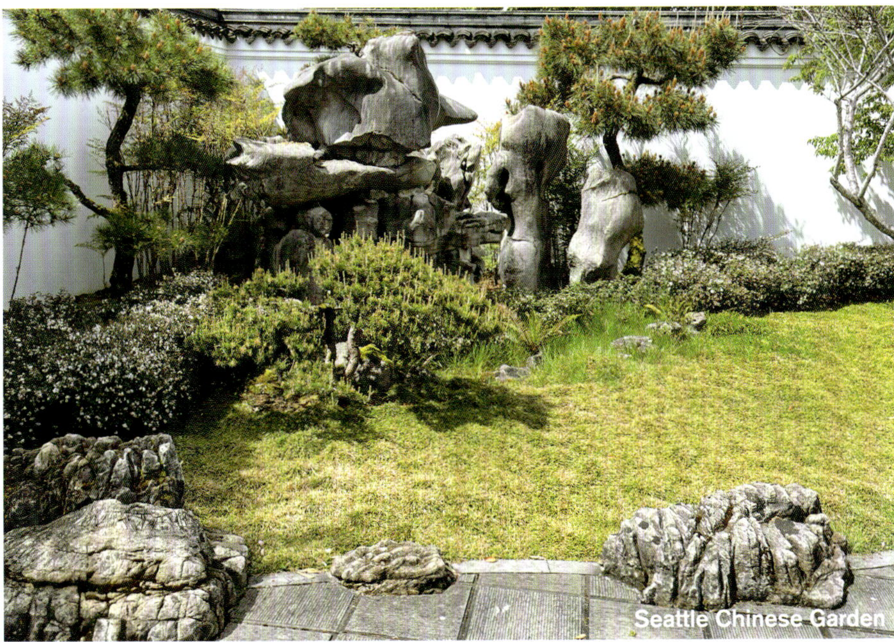

Seattle Chinese Garden

The rock formations are inspired by the Yangtze River gorges.

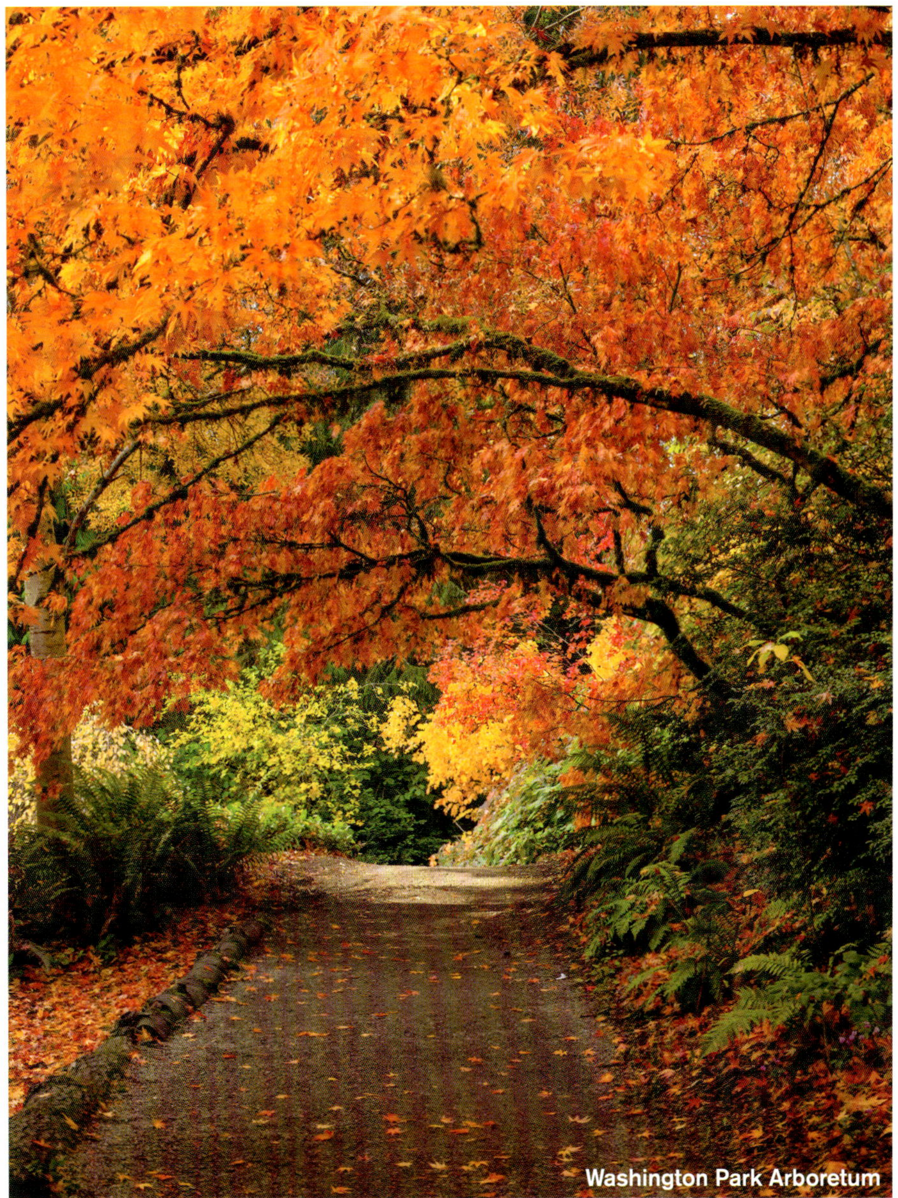

Washington Park Arboretum

The arboretum offers tree-lined paths for urbanites looking for a quick, peaceful escape.

Seattle Chinese Garden
Seattle, Washington

Occupying a site that offers views of downtown Seattle and Mount Rainier, this garden has no shortage of both natural and man-made beauty to share with visitors. The Sichuan-style garden was created as a symbol of friendship between Seattle and its sister city in China, Chongqing. Classical Chinese architecture, water features, and bamboo groves lend authentic Chinese atmosphere.

Washington Park Arboretum
Seattle, Washington

This 230-acre property is located on the shores of Lake Washington, where it is home to a world-class collection of plants. Highlights include the Pacific Connections Garden, which contains specimens from Australia, China, Chile, and New Zealand, and Marsh and Foster Islands, home to both native and exotic trees, including some of the oldest plantings in the arboretum.

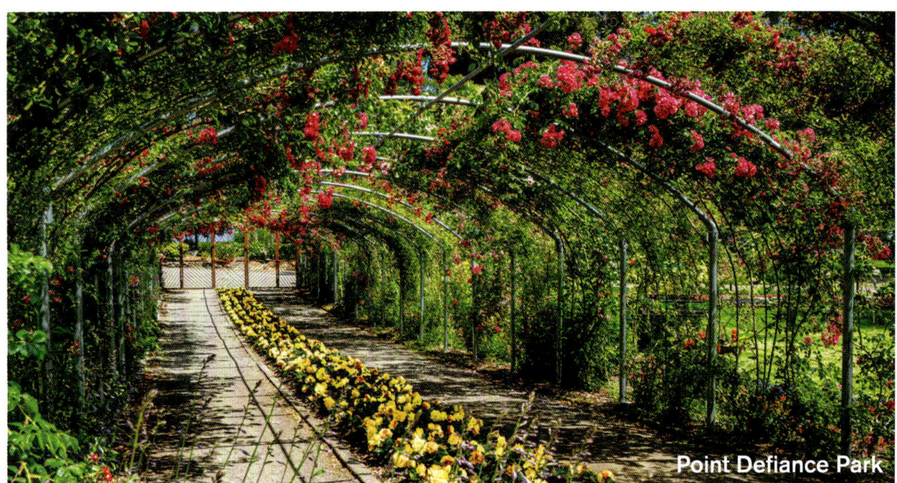

Sculpture lovers will discover beautiful creations in every nook and corner.

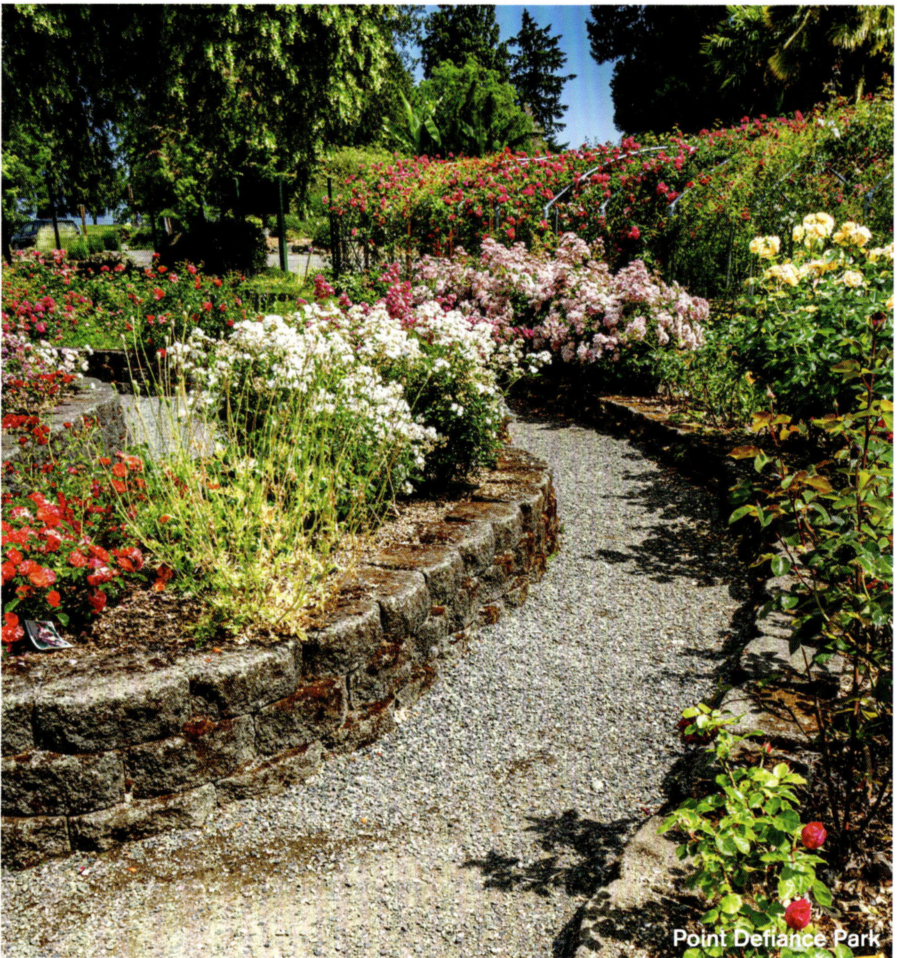

Point Defiance Park
Tacoma, Washington

This popular 760-acre urban park welcomes more than three million visitors a year, who flock to the tranquil peninsula just north of Tacoma to enjoy the gardens, forests, and wildlife of the region. The 400-acrea northern area of the park is made up of old-growth forest, and is home to bald eagles, mule deer, foxes, and pileated woodpeckers. The park's gardens occupy a bluff overlooking a waterfront, and contain historic structures including the old superintendent's home, built in 1898, and the Japanese Garden Pagoda, constructed in 1914. Other spaces include a Rose Garden, Native Plant Garden, and collections of dahlias, fuchsias, and irises.

Wright Park Arboretum
Tacoma, Washington

As president of the Northern Pacific Railroad in 1874, financier Charles Barstow Wright participated in the founding of the city. He also donated the land on which this 27-acre park, named in his honor, now sits. The arboretum contains more than 700 trees from North America, South America, Asia, and Europe–many of which are more than century old–and boasts 18 Washington State Champion Trees. The property is also home to the Victorian-style W.W. Seymour Conservatory, built in 1907 and containing 3,500 glass panes. The conservatory houses more than 550 plant species, including orchids, palms, ferns, figs, and cacti.

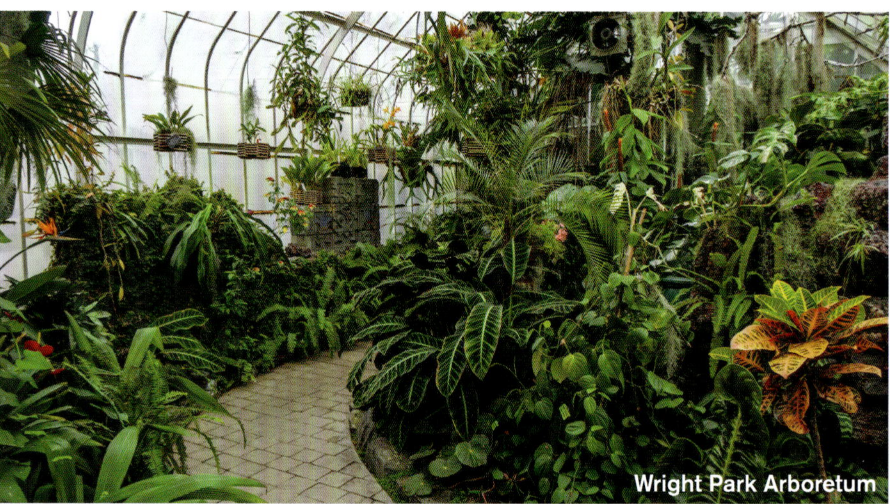

The W. W. Seymour Conservatory features exotic plants and a rotating display of flowers.

Worth Exploring in West Virginia

Brooks Memorial Arboretum
Marlinton, West Virginia

- Located in the 10,100-acre Watoga State Park
- Contains a 4.4-mile loop trail that winds past wildflowers and labeled trees

Earl L. Core Arboretum
Morgantown, West Virginia

- Named for University of West Virginia biology professor Earl L. Core
- Features old-growth forest and miles of walking trails

Mary Price Ratrie Arboretum
Charleston, West Virginia

- Features tailored trails with excellent views overlooking the city
- Grounds include Champion Trees, pollinator gardens, and dedicated native habitats

Sunshine Farm and Gardens
Renick, West Virginia

- An arboretum, botanic garden, garden center, and wholesale and retail nursery located at 3,650 feet in the West Virginia mountains
- Contains more than 10,000 perennials, bulbs, trees, and shrubs, with several acres focusing on woodland wildflowers

West Virginia Botanic Garden
Morgantown, West Virginia

- The only botanical garden in the state of West Virginia
- Themed gardens include the Secret Garden, the Rhododendron Garden, and the Butterfly Garden

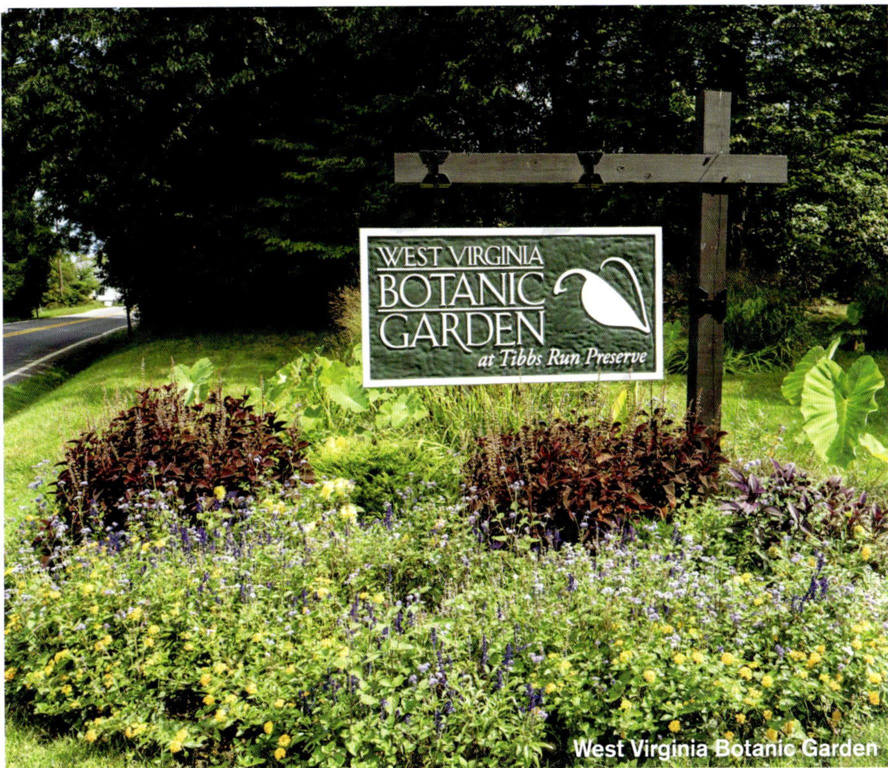

West Virginia Botanic Garden

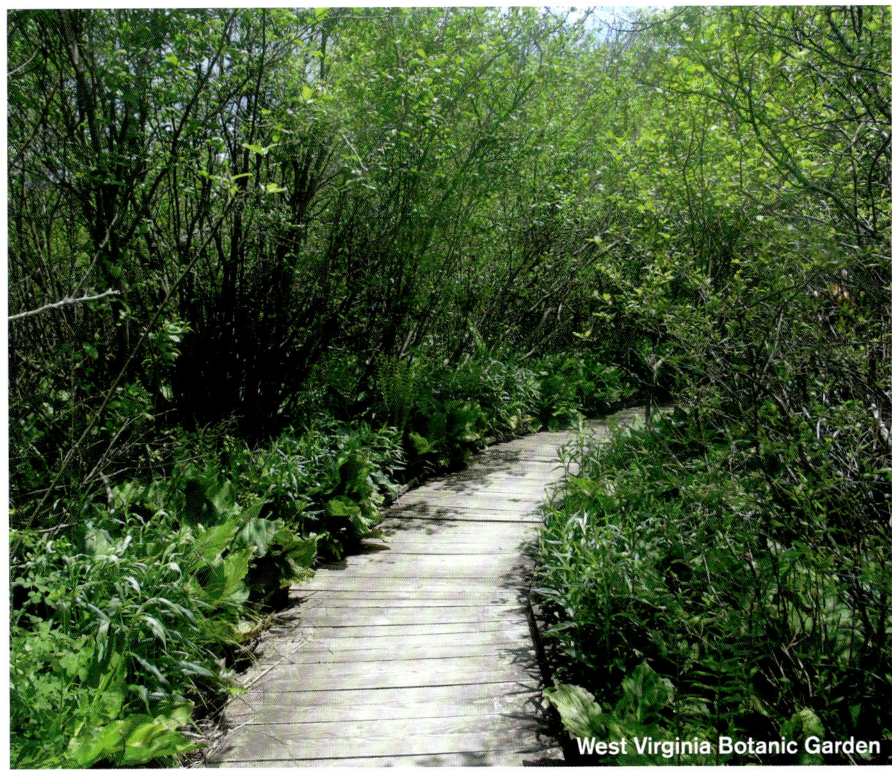
West Virginia Botanic Garden

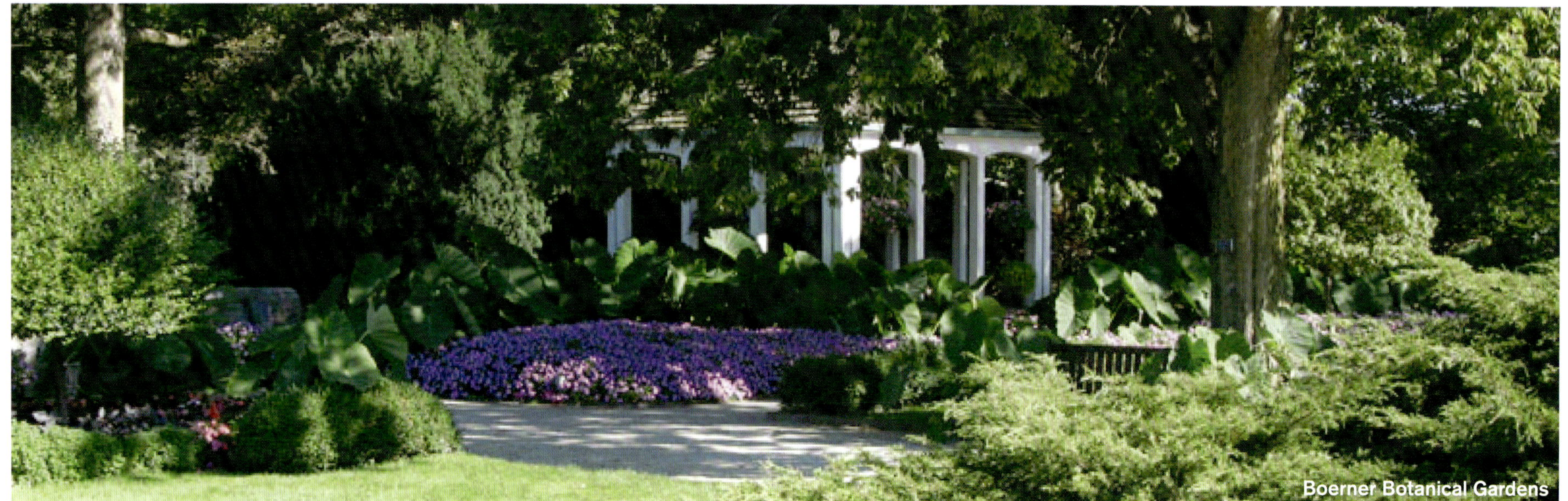
Boerner Botanical Gardens

Boerner Botanical Gardens
Hales Corners, Wisconsin

The original five formal gardens on this property were designed by its namesake, Alfred Boerner, in the 1930s. Today, the garden's manicured spaces are maintained by professional horticulturalists and include a Rose Garden, Peony Garden, and Rock Garden, as well as collections of lilies, herbs, shrubs, and hostas.

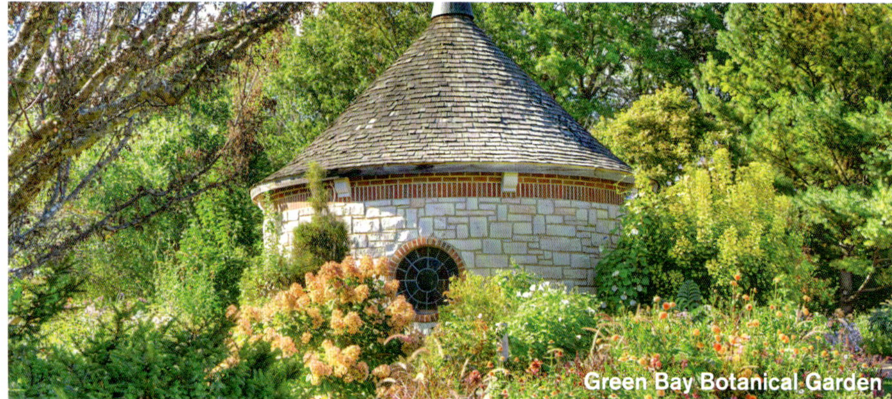
Green Bay Botanical Garden

The Meredith B. Rose Cottage peeks out from the Vanderperren English Cottage Garden.

Green Bay Botanical Garden
Green Bay, Wisconsin

The 47 acres of gardens and natural areas on this property feature a variety of diverse plants that thrive in the upper Midwest climate of Wisconsin. More than 120,000 plants and flowers are found on the site, which offers everything from a xeriscaped Vietnam Veterans Garden to the visitor-favorite Vanderperren English Cottage Garden.

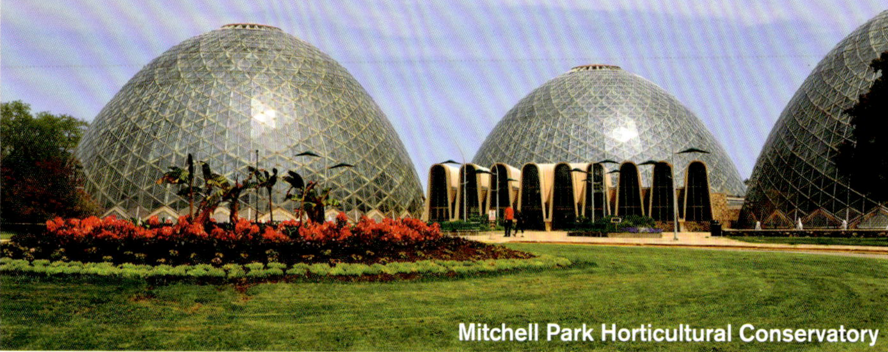
Mitchell Park Horticultural Conservatory

Nearly 2,000 plants in total are housed in the Conservatory. In total, the domes cover 45,000 square feet.

Mitchell Park Horticultural Conservatory
Milwaukee, Wisconsin

Located just minutes from downtown Milwaukee, this property is known locally as "The Domes," due to its three distinctive dome-shaped conservatories. Each dome contains a different climate type: The Floral Show dome hosts several seasonal floral shows every year; the Desert Dome contains cacti and succulents; and the Tropical Dome showcases 1,200 rainforest plants.

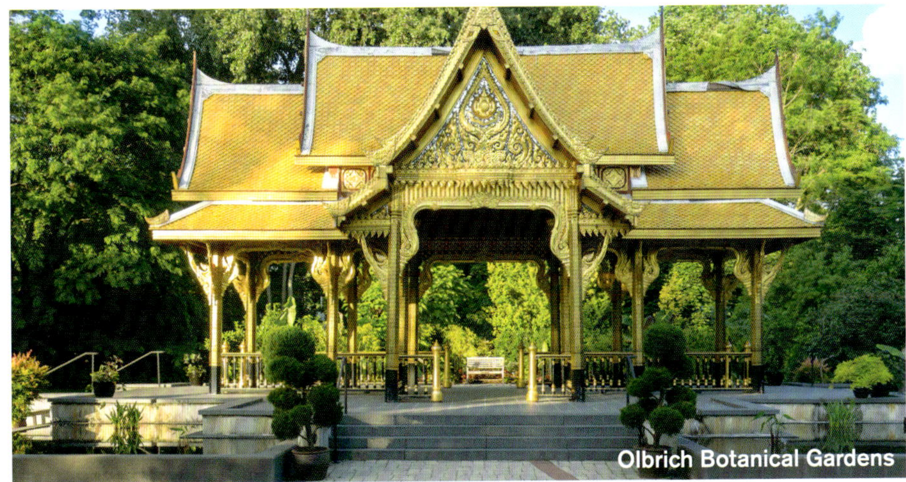

The Thai Garden *sala*.

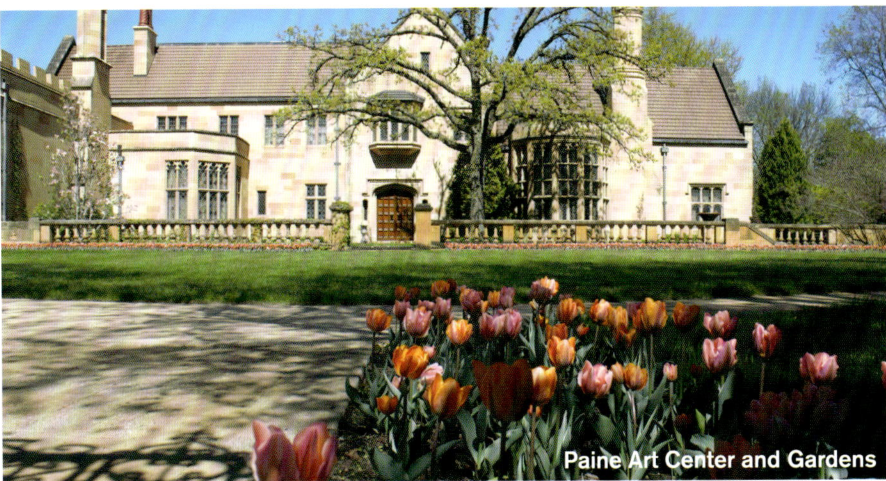

The historic house museum is surrounded by its gardens.

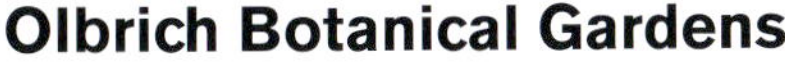

Olbrich Botanical Gardens
Madison, Wisconsin

Placing environmental advocacy, stewardship, and accessibility among its highest principles, this 16-acre garden strives to be a welcoming place for all. The property, which was named for its founder, Michael Olbrich, is notable for its sunken, traditional English garden and its Thai Garden and *sala*—one of only six such pavilions outside of Thailand. The site also contains the Bolz Conservatory, home to more than 650 tropical plants.

Paine Art Center and Gardens
Oshkosh, Wisconsin

The Tudor Revival-style estate on the grounds of this property was commissioned by Nathan and Jessie Paine in 1925, with the ultimate goal of sharing the house and surrounding gardens with the public. Their dream was finally realized in 1948, when the estate was opened as a museum and art gallery. The gardens are divided into 20 individual themes, including a Contemporary Garden, a Rose Garden, and a Children's Garden.

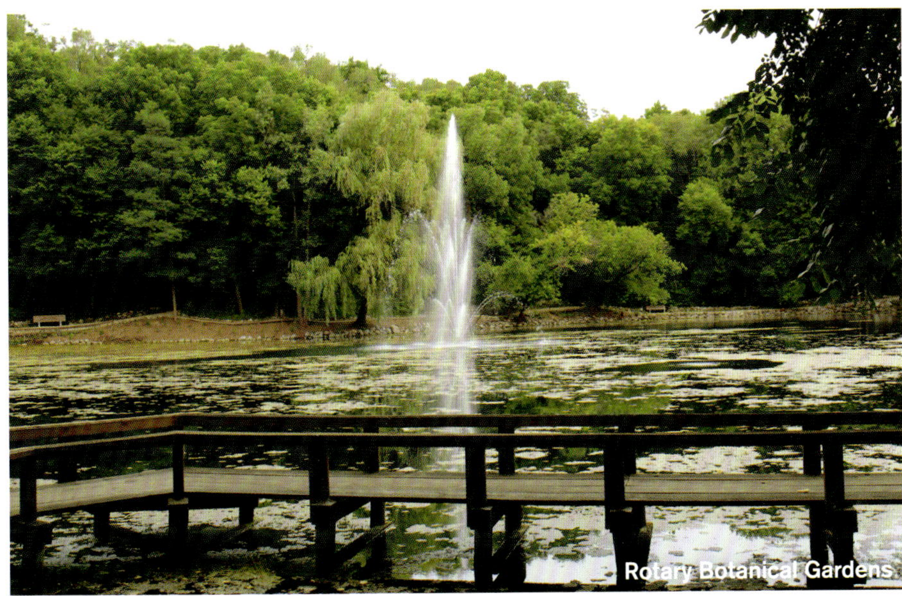

Water features at the park include a "Fleur de Lis" fountain that shoots water nearly 40 feet high.

Rotary Botanical Gardens
Janesville, Wisconsin

This 20-acre garden contains 4,000 varieties of plants spanning 26 different garden styles. The property features several internationally themed gardens, including the Japanese Garden, one of the first gardens established on the grounds; the French Formal Rose Garden, a popular spot for weddings; and the lush English Cottage Garden. Other spaces include the Cherry Blossom Walk, the Sunflower Collection, and the tropical-themed Terrace Garden.

Scheig Center Gardens
Appleton, Wisconsin

Formerly known as Gardens of the Fox Cities, this property features a variety of themed gardens showcasing mostly native Wisconsin plants and flowers. The Native Rose Garden, Butterfly Garden, and other vibrant spaces surround the Frank Lloyd Wright-inspired Scheig Learning Center, a popular venue for weddings and events.

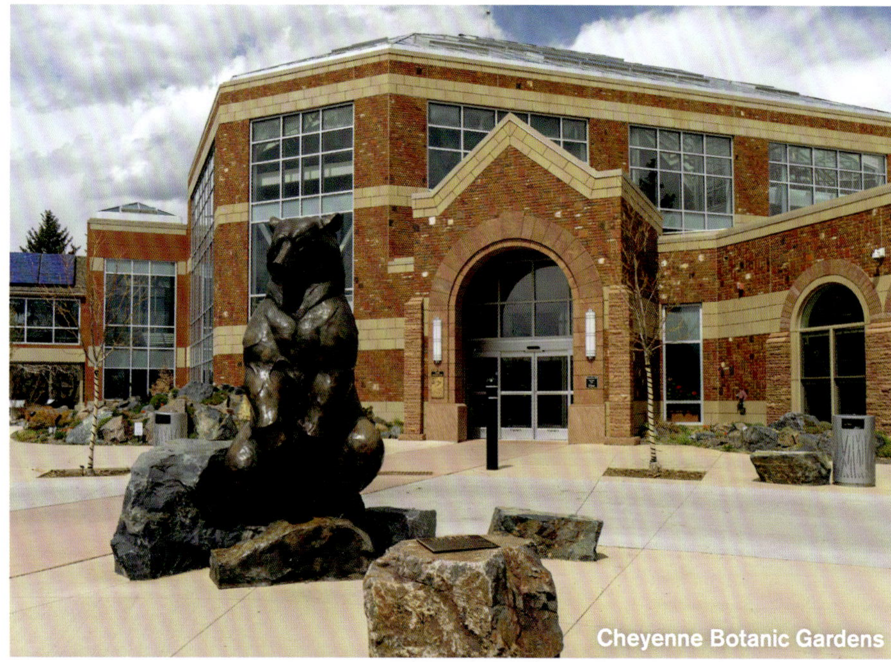

The Conservatory provides a year-round tropical environment for visitors.

Cheyenne Botanic Gardens
Cheyenne, Wyoming

The city of Cheyenne, sitting at around 6,000 feet above sea level, has one of the harshest climates in the lower 48 states. Frequent hailstorms, high winds, and cool evenings presented challenges to the creation of this nine-acre botanical garden, which is now considered one of the most innovative public gardens in the country. The site's centerpiece is its 6,800-square-foot conservatory, made up of three 100-percent-solar-heated greenhouses that contain tropical plants, cacti, vegetables, bedding plants, and flowers. Outside, the grounds feature a Sensory Garden and Gazebo, a Rose Garden, a Rock and Conifer Garden, and the award-winning Paul Smith Children's Village.

Williams Conservatory
Laramie, Wyoming

This conservatory sits on the campus of the University of Wyoming, where it provides a space for important research within the university's Department of Botany. Established in 1994, the greenhouse is named in honor of botanist Louis Williams and his wife, Terua, who provided many of the funds needed for its construction. The conservatory, which is free to the public, houses hundreds of tropical and subtropical plants from at least 76 different families. Specimens include an unusual black bat flower from southeastern Asia, showy red and yellow hanging lobster claws (native to Central and South America), and the foul-smelling but fan-favorite corpse flower, native to Indonesia.

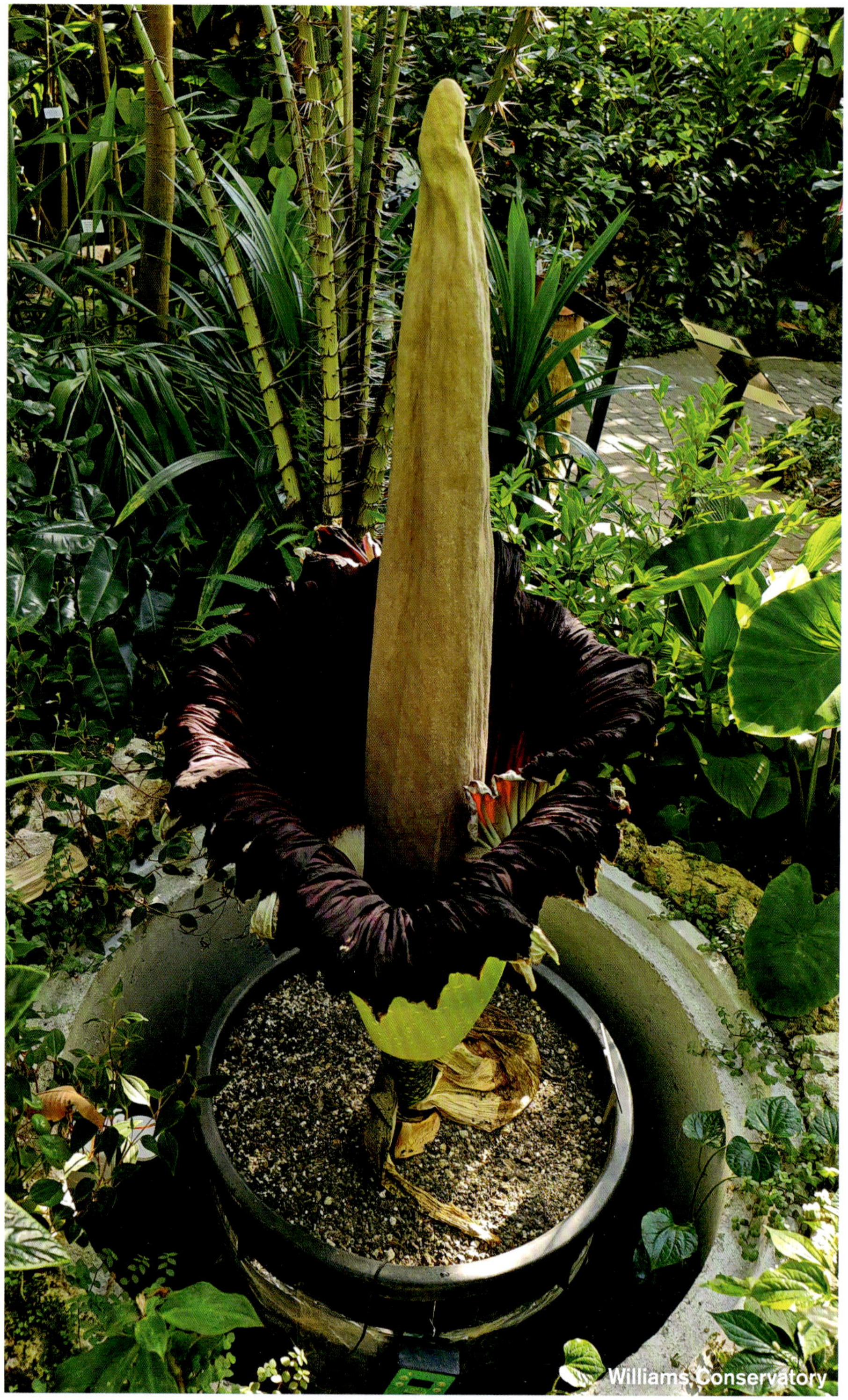

Williams Conservatory

The irresistibly stinky corpse flower attracts visitors on the rare occasions when it blooms.

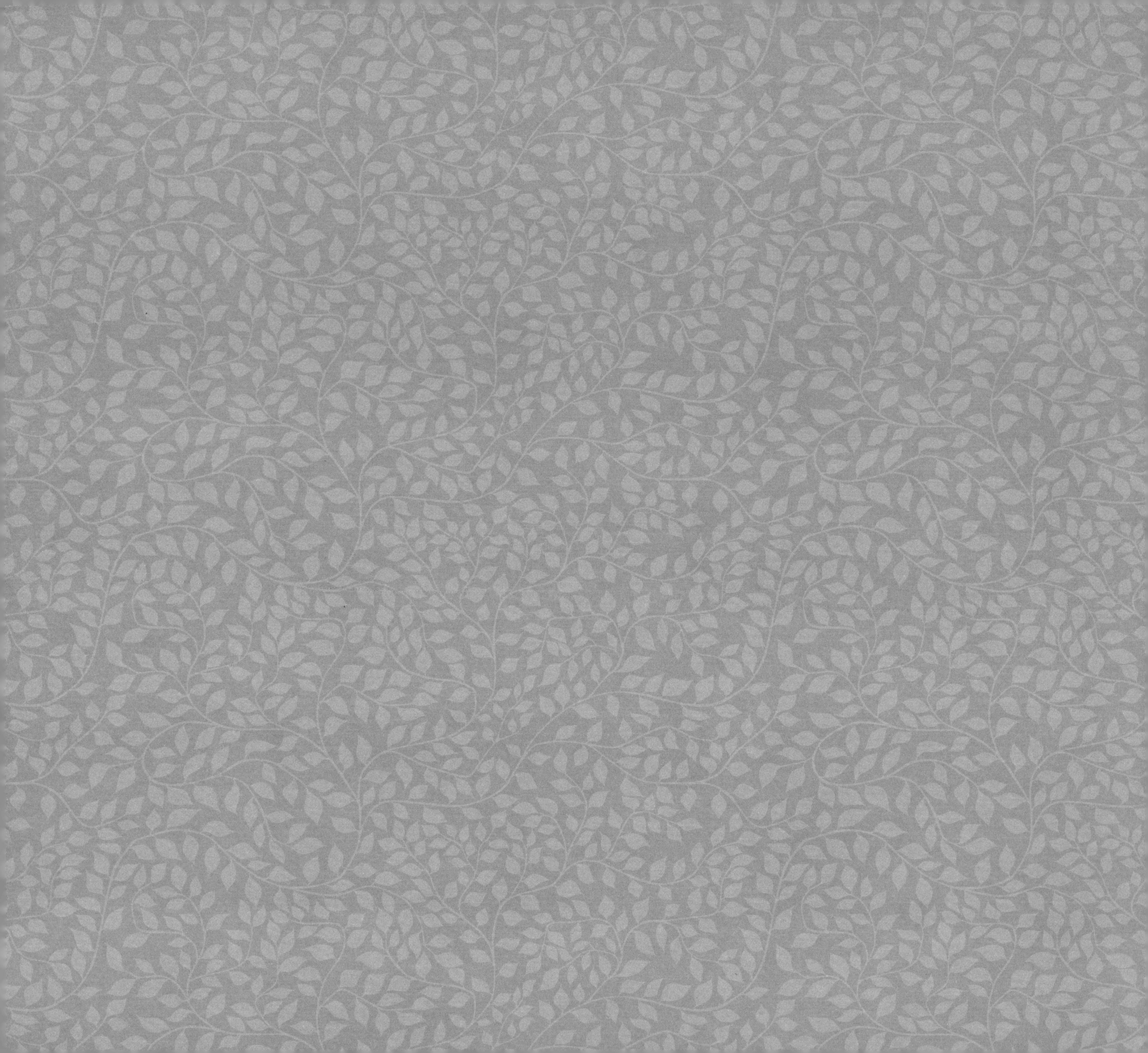